D1296872

The War that Changed the World

The Forgotten War that Set the Stage for the Global Conflicts of the 20th Century and Beyond

John-Allen Price

Legacy Books Press

Published by Legacy Books Press
RPO Princess, Box 21031
445 Princess Street
Kingston, Ontario, K7L 5P5
Canada

www.legacybookspress.com

© 2009 John-Allen Price, all rights reserved.
The moral rights of the author under the Berne Convention have been asserted.

The scanning, uploading, and/or distribution of this book via the Internet or any other means without the permission of the publisher is illegal and punishable by law.

First published in 2009 by Legacy Books Press
3   2   1

Price, John-Allen
    The War that Changed the World: The Forgotten War that Set the Stage for the
    Global Conflicts of the 20th Century and Beyond
    Includes bibliographical references and index
    ISBN-13: 978-0-9784652-1-6
    1. History : Europe - Franco-Prussian War 2. History : Military - General 3. History
    : Europe - France 4. History : Europe - Germany

All illustrations, citations and quotations are used under fair dealings and fair use. If you are a copyright holder of one of the works cited and feel your copyright has been infringed, please contact Legacy Books Press.

Illustrations from "The Great War of 1870 Between France and Germany, Comprising a History of its Origin and Causes, the Biographies of the King of Prussia, the Ex-Emperor of France, and the Statesmen and Generals of the Two Countries, the Financial, Social and Military" by L.P. Brockett. c1871.

Printed and bound in the United States of America and the United Kingdom.

This book is typeset in a Times New Roman 11-point font.

This book categorically denies any involvement in accidentally issuing Prussian needle guns to doctors as medical equipment.

To my father, John Lee Price (1929-1978),
who, above all things, taught me to love history.

Table of Contents

The Weapon of the Future

Acknowledgments

NO WORK OF this scope can be done by its author alone. To all those who offered support, my heartfelt thanks. To all those who told me writing a book about a forgotten war was a stupid waste of time, you can shove it.

And in particular, among those who helped, I wish to thank:

Joy Moreau, whose library of French history and culture proved so invaluable. And who's willingness to research obscure words was always enthusiastic.

Dr. David Stephenson, whose library of British history and 19th Century science proved insightful.

Lawrence Watt-Evans, a SF/Fantasy/Horror writer who nonetheless knows the value of a cover-less, broken-spine book about a long-forgotten war when he found it.

Dave Jeffrey, who filled in information from the InterNet when the books occasionally failed.

Col. Derwin Mak, whose support was of great comfort, not to mention his access to the Royal Canadian Military Institute.

Mike Stackpole, whose support has been constant and honest.

J.R. (Jeff) Dunn, SF novelist and military historian, whose career path I may be following.

Jon Gallo, who gave me access to a book no one else could.

Edward F. O'Farrell, my oldest friend and, as an artilleryman in Patton's Third Army, told me what it was like to fight in the forests of the Argonne and the Ardennes.

Don Shears, whose continuing service in Canada Armed Forces took him to France. And his photographs of Paris, the military museums and battlefield memorials he visited helped me picture the landscape.

Kjeld Hald Galster of the Royal Danish Defence College, who informed me of aspects of European history often unknown to Americans.

To all my other friends, one-time acquaintances and relatives who gave me book and magazines they considered surplus to their needs, or useless. They have no idea what eclectic research can make use of.

To my parents, who gave my brother and I the greatest start in life by giving us anything we wanted, just so long as it was a book...

And most of all to my editor, Robert Marks, who had the courage to give me a carte blanche contract to write any book I wanted, just so long as it was history.

Introduction: The Forgotten Wars, and Why We Should Remember Them

"Only the dead have seen an end to war."
-Plato (c.428 - 348 B.C.)

IN AMERICAN POP culture and popular consciousness there appears to be room for only three historical wars: World War II, the Vietnam War and the American Civil War. Of the thousands of lesser-known wars only occasionally does one temporarily rise above the obscurity they are consigned to.

The Korean War surfaces every so often, as does World War I, an ancient Greek or Roman conflict and then there are numerous British civil wars. This can be gauged by the movies and mini-series, documentaries and TV shows that appear every year. We are, remember, talking about pop culture.

In this arena, by far and away World War II is the most popular conflict with literally thousands of movies set in its time period. Vietnam and the American Civil War have far fewer, but still respectable, numbers and then there are all the others.

Of these, World War I does have an amazing amount, but only if you include the one- and two-reelers from the silent era. Without that vast assemblage, the Great War sinks to the obscurity level of most other conflicts. But at least it does better than the Franco-Prussian War.

If you were to include *all* the movies from the silent era to the present age, including the ones produced by the highly nationalistic German cinema, then there are less than a dozen movies about the Franco-Prussian

War. One of the last, excepting Kenneth MacMillan's *1871*, which is really about the Paris Commune and not the war, was released more than 30 years ago.

1975's *Royal Flash* had seemingly everything going for it, but not its history. It was produced by Alexander Salkind, who a year earlier had scored a major financial and critical success with *The Three Musketeers*. It was directed by Richard Lester, who had previously directed both *The Three* and *Four Musketeers*. Its screenplay was by the novelist George MacDonald Fraser, who not only adapted one of his own *Flashman* novels for the script, he was also responsible for the adaptation of the Dumas novels *The Three Musketeers* and *Revenge of Milady*.

And then there was its cast. A then-young Malcolm McDowell played the lead, Britt Ekland his romantic interest and a supporting cast which included Alan Bates, Oliver Reed, Lionel Jeffries, the great Alastair Sim in one of his last film roles, Michael Hordern, Joss Ackland and an also-then-young Bob Hoskins.

Royal Flash's plot, and that of the original novel, borrowed heavily from the oft-filmed old chestnut of a novel by Anthony J. Hope: *The Prisoner of Zenda*. And yet it also slyly referenced the final precipitating incident to the Franco-Prussian War, the Hohenzollern Candidature. Filmed and acted in the same serio-comic style as Salkind's *Musketeer* films, and generally well-received by the critics who saw it, *Royal Flash* was a production that should not have missed.

But it did. *Royal Flash* was never theatrically released in the United States. It was never released on cable, barely released on videotape and only recently released on DVD. It remains a "lost film," lost just like the war it's set in.

More recently, two movies of varying success were released which should have dealt directly with the Franco-Prussian War, but did not at all. In December, 2003, *The Last Samurai* was released and supposedly told the "true" story of how the Meiji Emperor's army was modernized by the U.S. Army and the defeat of the Samurai Rebellion of 1877: the last major vestige of feudalism in Japan.

Approximately a year later *The Phantom of the Opera* was released and this was the much-anticipated movie version of the Andrew Lloyd Webber musical. Like most of the previous versions, at least eight, its Gothic story is set in a Paris opera house in the late-19th Century. But instead of an 1880s or turn-of-the-century time period, this *Phantom* is set between the summer of 1870 and the early spring of 1871. The very period of the Franco-Prussian War, yet the conflict is never depicted or even mentioned.

To say these movies are historically inaccurate is an understatement.

They are historical abominations in every sense of the word. It's hard to say which is worse. *Phantom of the Opera* is so bad it's almost funny while *The Last Samurai* is so bad it's insulting. *Phantom* actually shows Emperor Louis Napoleon III and the Empress Eugénie attending a New Year's Eve performance at the Paris Civic Opera House. One wonders how they managed it. By this time in real, as opposed to cinema, history Napoleon was in prison and Eugénie was in exile. I guess it was those good-conduct passes from Helmuth von Moltke.

Though more tangentially related to the Franco-Prussian War, *The Last Samurai* is worse because, unlike the world's first Alternate History Musical, it's taken a little more seriously. Far too many people think it's a reasonably accurate portrayal of America's first disastrous foray into Asian policy. Its first "Vietnam."

If this should be anyone's "Vietnam," and in no way can it be, then it's Germany's. By the late-1870s the then-new German Army was the most powerful and respected army in the world. But *The Last Samurai* insists on showing the wrong army, the American Army, training and modernizing the Meiji's Army. Wrong even down to the uniforms the Japanese soldiers wore, which is particularly sad since the one thing a Hollywood costume drama could always be counted on getting right is the costumes.

Apart from proving the moral "you should not learn history from the movies," let alone TV shows, novels or stage plays, these films also prove just how far into obscurity the Franco-Prussian War has sunk. And this should not be. Not just for those who have an interest in forgotten 19th century wars but for anyone who wants to understand the great global conflicts of the 20th Century and even into this age.

Why? Because wars are not set-piece events, occurring independently and bearing no relationship to each other. But this is exactly the way they are taught, especially in the American public schools I've attended, not to mention the battles that compose any war. At least most people understand the relationship between last century's global wars; it probably helps that they were eventually numbered.

Unfortunately most other conflicts are not understood in this way. If they are understood at all it's as sudden, violent seismic events about as predictable as earthquakes. And yet, in the last few decades science has shown earthquakes do bear a complex relationship to one another, and can possibly even be predicted.

Historians have long known this about wars and other human events, but unfortunately the really important ones are not always the best known. It isn't always the bloodiest and most destructive wars which are the truly important ones. The wars that create as well as destroy are the most important and this leads us to the Franco-Prussian War.

It destroyed forever monarchial rule in France, destroyed its last imperial empire, destroyed the dreams of Bonapartists and Bourbons alike; but the war also played mid-wife to the longest-serving republic in French history, and then there is Germany. It forged a nation out of what had once been, at the beginning of the 19th century, a vast collection of hundreds of countries and city-states. It created Europe's last imperial empire, a new hereditary enemy for France and a new competitor and threat to Britain.

The Franco-Prussian War was the first modern war in history. The first to see universal use of breech-loading, cartridge rifles: the Chassepot and the Dreyse. The first to see large-scale use, on one side, of cast-steel breech-loading artillery. The first to see large-scale use, on the other side, of rapid-fire weapons. The first to see universal use of railroads and telegraphs to transport, command and supply armies in the field, though only one side did it well. And it was the first conflict to see the evolution of tactics and strategic doctrine into what would later be called Maneuver Warfare.

In the Preface to one of the principal sources used for this book its author, L.P. Brockett, states: "The writer feels that no apology is necessary for the attempt here made to portray the progress of a war which, in its rapid movement, in its terrible destructiveness, and its stupendous results, is without parallel in history." These sentiments, if not these exact words, have been used to begin countless histories of the Second World War. And the Blitzkrieg tactics of that conflict owe more to the Franco-Prussian War than the First World War. The latter conflict gave Blitzkrieg the tools needed to fully exploit its concepts: wireless communications, airpower and armored vehicles. But not the knowledge how to use them.

In its day the Franco-Prussian War was the most studied and written about war in history. But most of that writing was in French and German, not in what would become the dominant language of the military: English. In literature and entertainment it would take 20 years for Emile Zola to write the one great novel set in the Franco-Prussian War. And soon after that its day would end in the cataclysm which would start in a Serbian town in the summer of 1914.

Since then the war has been little visited, has had little attention paid to it. In the last 40 years the number of authoritative texts published on it can be counted on one hand. Few monuments remain to its victories or its fallen. Even its participating nations have apparently forgotten about it, and since neither of these nations speak English it has truly become forgotten in popular consciousness and pop culture.

Until some action-figure movie star does a successful movie about the

Franco-Prussian War then it will be lost to pop culture, but it should still be remembered. Not only for itself, but for what it grew out of, what it ended, what it created and what it lead to. The echoes and consequences of this war can still be heard to this day, if you listen carefully enough. It is indeed "the war that changed the world," as this book will outline.

Prelude: Bratislava, December 26, 1805 – The End of What Was Neither Holy, Nor Roman, Nor an Empire...

> *"You write to me that it's impossible; the word is not French."*
>
> -Napoleon Bonaparte (1769 - 1821)

IF EVER A military historian were to write a book entitled *The Ten Greatest Victories of All Time* then the battle the Peace of Bratislava (also called Pressburg) codifies would surely be among them. Taken on its own the Battle of Austerlitz qualifies as Napoleon Bonaparte's greatest victory. But *when* it happened raises it an order of magnitude higher.

Austerlitz, fought on the morning and afternoon of December 2nd, 1805, came just six weeks after Admiral Horatio Nelson's crushing victory over the combined Spanish and French fleets off Cape Trafalgar on the southwestern coast of Spain. This victory did not just eclipse Napoleon's capture, a day earlier, of an Austrian army at Ulm; it was thought at the time to have ended the threat of invasion to Britain and presaged the eventual defeat of Bonaparte by the allied coalition arrayed against him.

Austerlitz reversed it all. In around eight hours of heavy fighting Bonaparte used his outnumbered and outgunned army to defeat the two armies advancing against him. By late afternoon both Czar Alexander I of Russia and Kaiser Francis II of Austria were in retreat, along with what remained of their forces. They left behind some 26,000 dead while the French Army lost 9,000.

As news of the victory spread, it stunned the world. It shook the confidence and resolve of the Allied coalition, and it began to unravel. In

Britain, the victory Nelson gave his life for suddenly meant nothing. Bonaparte's great enemy in its Parliament, William Pitt "the Younger" fell into a depression and would be dead by early in the new year. Sweden and Naples, the lesser partners in the coalition, wavered. Austria and Russia started arguing, and would negotiate with Napoleon separately.

And then there was that other major German power: Prussia. Nominally neutral in this latest round of wars with France, it had been edging toward joining the coalition and had even sent its Foreign Minister Count von Haugwitz to Vienna with an ultimatum for Napoleon. Prudently he withheld it and Prussia, for the moment, remained neutral.

In the meantime Kaiser Francis II and Czar Alexander I negotiated with Napoleon, and Francis was the first off the mark. Two days after Austerlitz he requested an audience with Bonaparte and Alexander was reduced to refusing an alliance with Austria and France against England, and promising to vacate Austrian territory after the signing of the peace treaty.

By December 26, the treaty, hammered out by Foreign Ministers Talleyrand and Stadion, was ready. The Peace of Pressburg, as Bratislava was then called, gave Napoleon everything he should have expected and should have wanted. It forced Austria to cede all of Venetia, except the port of Trieste, and the Lombardy region of northern Italy to the Kingdom of Italy and it recognized Bonaparte as its king. Austria was also forced to surrender the Tyrol region and the Vorarlberg to Napoleon's main ally of the moment, Bavaria. Smaller lands were ceded to the Kingdoms of Baden and Würtemberg; in all around three million people found themselves with new nationalities.

More importantly, the Peace of Pressburg made Napoleon Bonaparte the master of mainland Europe. For over a thousand years, since the crowning of Charlemagne by Pope Leo III on Christmas Day in the year 800, rulers had sought to recreate the empire the King of the Franks had forged: the Holy Roman Empire.

Entire lines of monarchs fought with each other to achieve the goal. The Bourbons of France and Spain aspired to it, the Hapsburgs of Central Europe and Spain owned the franchise, though the success of the Protestant Reformation in the 16th Century and the Thirty Years' War of the 17th Century doomed it.

And now, on the day *after* Christmas, a thousand and five years after Charlemagne's coronation had created it, the Holy Roman Empire ceased to exist in all but name with the rise to dominance of Europe's second Charlemagne: Napoleon Bonaparte I.

His coronation had already taken place with great pageantry the year before. As for the Holy Roman Empire, its final death knell would be sounded about eight months later when, on August 6th, Kaiser Francis II would abdicate his throne and title. He would become Emperor Francis I of Austria. And the title of Kaiser would not be officially used again for 65 years.

In this age the long-dreamed of goal of German unification by German statesmen, philosophers and warrior-kings seemed as remote a notion as it had ever been. Napoleon controlled almost as much German territory and German subjects as French. Already his civil code was changing the German states under his rule in ways many German philosophers and leaders at the time believed would make them even less likely to unite, though Goethe didn't seem to mind. And, as events unfolded in the new year, the dream seemed to be consumed by the reality of what was then the new world order: Napoleonic Europe.

On July 19th, 1806, he would ratify the Treat of Saint Cloud, which he used to create the "Confederation of the Rhine." By his fiat what had formerly been a realm of some 360 separate Kingdoms, Duchies, Grand Duchies, Principalities and Imperial Free Cities was reduced by almost an order of magnitude to roughly 40 states.

With the stroke of his pen, Napoleon swept aside most of the medieval power structure of the German lands. Hundreds of German princes, barons, counts, dukes and knights of the soon-to-be-defunct Holy Roman Empire lost their independence, though not their lands. Borrowing the recently restored structure of Switzerland, at this time a wholly-owned puppet state of France, the new confederation Napoleon set up was something he hoped to use to administer his new territories and subjects. But not all were willing to accept.

Within a month of the Holy Roman Empire's disappearance, Saxony and Prussia were reversing their earlier policies of appeasement and mobilizing their armies. Czar Alexander I had not yet given up on his dream of destroying the French Revolution and its Corsican leader. In what he hoped was great secrecy he concluded an alliance with the two German states as well as Sweden.

However, through his spies, Napoleon knew of the correspondence between Berlin, Dresden, Stockholm and St. Petersburg. And he not only mobilized first, he already had his army in Bavaria, where it was picking up more forces, by the time the Prussian/Saxon ultimatum reached him on October 7th, 1806.

And that army would easily be the finest he would ever command. Even the Bavarian troops were mostly veterans of Austerlitz, and the French troops were veterans not only of it but many of the earlier successful campaigns Napoleon had led, excepting of course his disastrous

Egyptian Expedition.

The coming war would also be the only time where most of his best commanders would take the field with him. The marshal called "the bravest of the brave," Michael Ney was Bonaparte's most loyal corps commander, and joining his staff was his apprentice, a former brigade commander in the Swiss Army: Antoine Henri de Jomini, the modern era's most famous military strategist. Louis Davout and Jean Baptiste Bernadotte were his other corps commanders and his brilliant logistics chief, Louis Alexandre Berthier, saw to it the supply depots were well-stocked for his gathering troops.

By comparison, the Prussian Army had decayed to a shadow of its former abilities and prowess under the greatest of Prussia's warrior-kings: Friedrich Wilhelm II/Frederick the Great. Those glories belonged to the previous generation as the results of the battlefield quickly showed.

On October 10th, three days after receiving the ultimatum, Napoleon's Grand Army made initial contact with the Prussians at Saalfeld. It destroyed the better part of a division led by Prince Ludwig Ferdinand and killed the prince, who had been one of the major supporters in the Hohenzollern family for war with France.

On October 14th, only a week after receiving the ultimatum, Napoleon met the Prussian main army at Jena, a town on the Saale River southwest of Berlin. While the Battle of Jena, or more accurately the Battle of Jena/Auerstädt, does not rank as high as Austerlitz it belongs in the same league as again Europe was stunned by it.

Before the battle there were many, among them the British, Russians and the Prussians themselves, who ranked the Prussian Army as one of the most formidable on the continent. But that estimation was based on fond, respectful, memories by the outsiders of the Silesian Wars and the Seven Years' War, and by self-delusion among the Prussians.

The twin battles – they occurred about 12 miles apart – all but destroyed the Prussian Army and sent the remnants into flight. Its officer corps was especially hard hit as those who were not killed in the battles were captured. Among them was one of Prussia's most respected generals, Gebhard Leberecht von Blücher, and another was a young staff officer named Karl von Clausewitz, destined to be Jomini's rival as a strategist.

As news of the defeats spread throughout the North German States, the temper of the populations changed from martial aggression to shock and docility. Saxony disassociated itself from the alliance and recalled its troops. When the Grand Army entered Berlin, on October 25th, the population was meekly subservient. Except for a few skirmishes, the army would not engage in major combat again until early December.

What followed, from December 1806 until June 1807, was one of Napoleon's less-destructive winter wars. He laid waste to most of Prussia's eastern provinces and Russia's western territories, much of what is present-day Poland, but it nearly destroyed his army. Had he suffered a single major defeat anywhere approaching the scale of Austerlitz or Jena/Auerstädt it would have meant the end of his empire.

Instead, what took place was a series of bloody, inconclusive battles which, combined with the inhospitable terrain, the bitter weather and a supply mess not even Berthier could resolve, almost ground down the Grand Army. Not even the coming of warmer weather improved the situation for what had been rock-hard frozen earth became an endless quagmire crossed by few good roads. It bogged down men, horses, wagons and artillery. But it did afflict both sides.

Not until June 14th did a Russian attack give Napoleon the opportunity to inflict a decisive defeat, near Friedland in East Prussia. The victory was not quite as stunning as the earlier thunderclaps, it didn't destroy either army, but it gave each ruler a chance to get much of what he wanted.

In the most remarkable and bizarre event in the entire series of Napoleonic Wars, Bonaparte and Czar Alexander I met alone on a raft moored in the middle of the Niemen River, near the town of Tilsit. For three hours they talked without benefit of Foreign Ministers, General Staffs, interpreters or even aides-de-camp. In three hours of flattery and hard negotiations they decided the fate of Europe.

For the Czar it meant ending one very destructive war to concentrate on a smaller one with Turkey, which Bonaparte had encouraged. It meant he got back his Polish territories and would not have a French army sitting anywhere on his borders. He was to mediate a peace between Britain and France, or join France in an alliance against it if negotiations failed.

For the Emperor it meant ending a war that threatened to unravel his entire domain. He had a free hand to humble Prussia, the only Germanic power which could destroy his Confederation of the Rhine, and render it impotent. He got other threats, and flashpoints for war, removed from his borders: namely the Russian troops in Dalmatia and the Ionian Islands. And if he could not get Russia itself to join him as an ally, at least she would remain neutral.

The Tilsit Treaties, three of them signed between July 7th and 9th, codified all this and more. They made France and Russia allies, after a fashion, and the dominant powers of Europe. For Prussia, the other power at the talks but not allowed to negotiate, it appeared to be the end of its role as a power of any size or significance.

It would lose nearly half its population and territory to other German states, such as Saxony, who had been more subservient to Napoleon. Its army was also to be cut in half and many of its officers, such as Blücher, who had fought against the French would not be allowed to rejoin it. Prussia was not allowed to join the Confederation of the Rhine, not allowed to negotiate and sign any treaties with other foreign powers, and finally was not allowed to join any alliance other than one commanded by France.

In all but name, and much like Switzerland, Prussia had become a puppet state. And with her humiliation the dream of a united and independent Germany appeared to retreat even farther from reality. It retreated into the idling dreams of philosopher-poets, into the realm of legend, where it would reside with Friedrich Barbarossa, in his centuries-long sleep somewhere under the Austrian Alps, awaiting the call to awaken him and defend his Reich in its greatest hour of peril.

But now, between Austerlitz and the Peace of Pressburg, and Friedland and the Treaties of Tilsit, the reality of German unification would be under the auspices of the Confederation of the Rhine. And the sovereignty of Emperor Napoleon Bonaparte I: the new Charlemagne of Europe.

Part I – The Paths to the War

"War, war is still the cry,
war even to the knife!"

-Lord George Gordon Byron (1788 - 1824)

Chapter I: Europe After Napoleon

*"Tyrants never perish from tyranny, but always from
folly – when their fantasies have built up a
palace for which the earth has no foundation."*
-Walter Savage Landor (1775 - 1864)

Europe: From July 9, 1807, to July 15, 1815

CHARLEMAGNE'S MASSIVE EMPIRE managed to last some 44 years
after his coronation in 800. It even managed to outlast his death in 814 by
some 30 years, but Napoleon's would only last, depending on which
starting date you use, approximately 15 years.

In the end it was not so much Wellington and his coalition army, or
Blücher and his Prussians, or even Czar Alexander and his armies that
defeated Napoleon but Napoleon himself. His imperial greed, grandiose
schemes, imperious and irrational behavior, misuse and alienation of allies
on both the personal and national level had cast the die by the time he sent
his last Grand Army into Russia in June of 1812.

By then his army was composed more of allied forces than French and
their quality, particularly the French, would not be equal to the men of
previous Napoleonic armies. There were fewer veterans, the attrition rates
of earlier campaigns had been heavy, and there were fewer of his greatest
weapon: his loyal, brilliant and combat-experienced marshals.

When the Grand Army crossed the Niemen River, Napoleon still had
marshals like Michael Ney, Davout and Berthier with him. But Joachim
Murat, who was also his brother-in-law, was now the King of Naples and

Bernadotte had taken up a similar offer from the Swedish royal family to be their crown prince.

Antoine de Jomini served reluctantly in the Grand Army, as he was also a general in Czar Alexander's army, and so did the Austrian marshal, Karl von Schwarzenberg. Blücher refused to come out of retirement and fight in a Prussian Army under Napoleon's control. And Clausewitz did them all one better by deserting the Prussian Army and joining Alexander's.

Nine months later he was joined by his nation, the first major power to break with Napoleon, and by the fall of 1813 Emperor Francis I and the Austrian Army had also switched sides. Sweden joined the reformed Allied Coalition by sending Bernadotte to the continent with a corps of 30,000. And finally the aged Gebhard von Blücher, 71 at the time, came out of retirement.

To many in the Prussian Army his return was treated like Barbarossa himself had at long last awakened from his sleep to defend ancestral Germany. Initially given command of all Prussian field forces, by early October he would lead the coalition forces at the pivotal Battle of Leipzig.

Also called the Battle of Nations, Leipzig was fought over a momentous six days, between October 14th and 19th. Much like the pivotal battle of the American Civil War, the Seven Days' Battles, it was a protracted series of indecisive engagements with heavy loses – until the afternoon of the 18th when Bernadotte arrived with his Swedish corps, plus an additional Prussian corps and 70,000 Russian reinforcements. And with the tide of battle swinging against the battered Grand Army something completely unexpected happened: the Saxon Army turned its guns on the French lines.

By the afternoon of the 19th Napoleon was in headlong retreat and from this point on he would know little except defeat. All around him there appeared nothing but disaster. His Confederation of the Rhine was coming apart at the seams as country after country responded to Prussia's call for German unity. To the north Holland was rebelling against French rule and throwing out its officials. To the south Murat had allied his Kingdom of Naples with the Austrians in order to save his illegitimate throne.

Also in the south Sir Arthur Wellesley, the Viscount of Wellington, was capping a six-year campaign on the Iberian Peninsula by entering southern France and taking the city of Toulouse. And finally to the west, what had been Napoleon's greatest foreign policy triumph: his maneuvering of the United States into declaring war on Britain at about the same time he invaded Russia, was being easily contained by existing British forces in the Canadian colonies and the Royal Navy.

It was only Allied hesitancy and squabbling that gave Napoleon roughly another six months on the throne, from early November, 1813 until April 13th, 1814 when he at last signed the Act of Abdication. From here he should have passed into history and exile on the Mediterranean island of Elba, while the Congress of Vienna convened to clean up the mess he had made of Europe.

But, of course, this is where it did not end. Napoleon's exile lasted ten months, until history's consummate opportunist detected opportunity in the near-breakup of the Congress. By the beginning of 1815 it had become so deadlocked and antagonistic that Prussia and Russia had signed a secret defensive alliance while France, Austria, Britain and many smaller German states were negotiating one of their own.

It was onto this quarrelsome chessboard that Napoleon stepped when he landed at night in the Gulf of Juan in southern France on March 1st, setting off seismic shockwaves which reverberated across Europe, and initiating the legendary One Hundred Days.

The hindsight and judgment of history is that this event was brazen, foolish and could not possibly have succeeded. And yet, at the time the impossible repeatedly happened in Napoleon's favor and it looked, however briefly, as if he might regain power.

He persuaded unit after unit of French troops he encountered to join him until it became a triumphal procession on the road to Paris. At Châlons he met Michael Ney, commanding the French Army and following a promise he made to Louis XVIII, the restored Bourbon king, that he would bring the renegade emperor back "in an iron cage." But the impossible happened, the marshal who was the "bravest of the brave" returned to his original loyalty, and brought the rest of the army into Napoleon's camp.

This shockwave drove Louis XVIII out of Paris, under the personal protection of Marshal Berthier, and stunned the Congress of Vienna back to reality. A week before its participants had considered Napoleon's return to indeed be folly. Now, on March 13th, the four Allied Powers declared war on Napoleon, not France, and two weeks later they plus France signed a new formal alliance.

But by then Napoleon was back in Paris and most of the French army and public was with him. However, Louis Berthier was not; he had retired to his estate in Bavaria after seeing to the king's safety. For over a year Antoine de Jomini had been a personal adviser to Czar Alexander. And then there were Napoleon's most successful enemies: Wellington was in Belgium raising a British-Dutch-Hanoverian army and Blücher was mobilizing the Prussian Army.

Against all the odds Napoleon organized a new army and on June 16th gained another impossibility; he attacks both Blücher's and Wellington's armies and prevents them from linking up. Alas, two days later the three armies meet again at Waterloo where the folly ends with 25,000 French casualties.

Four days later, on June 22nd, Napoleon abdicates for the last time after returning to the Elysee Palace in Paris. He did it not so much because of the defeat and disintegration of his last army. Or because Blücher was hot on his heels and promising to shoot him like a common outlaw. He did it due to the actions of another French hero, the Marquis de Lafayette.

The hero of both the American and French revolutions, he had stayed out of Napoleon's wars until he became convinced that Bonaparte was going to turn France into a dictatorship. Finally accepting a political position, as a leading Senator in the Chamber of Peers, he got the members of both it and the Chamber of Representatives to carry a resolution agreeing with the alliance signed in Vienna on March 25th.

The resolution declared France was in danger, that both Chambers would remain in session for as long as the danger existed, a not-too-subtle recognition of Napoleon being the problem, that the danger would end when the Bourbon monarchy was restored and anyone attempting to dissolve the Chambers would be guilty of high treason.

Faced with being shot like an outlaw by the Prussians, or being guillotined as a traitor by the French, Napoleon signed the Order of Abdication, again, and retired to the château at Malmaison. A poignant choice as the château's former owner, Empress Josephine, had died but a few months earlier, some say of the heart he broke when he divorced her for Princess Marie Louise of Austria.

Three weeks later, with the Allies in Paris and Louis XVIII back on the throne, Napoleon left Europe forever on the Royal Navy frigate HMS *Bellerophon*. On August 7th he was transferred to a larger ship, HMS *Northumberland*, and after ten weeks at sea he reached St. Helena. Having passed out of history, he would now spend the remaining years of his life crafting his legend.

After Napoleon: The Winners and Losers

Many historians, also novelists, poets and playwrights, talk about a great peace/calm/silence settling over Europe after Napoleon departed its shores. Unless they are speaking metaphorically this is not true; not even the fighting died away completely after he left. There was the fate of the artificial kingdoms and thrones he had created. Problems that the Congress of Vienna wrestled with even as the armies converged on each other in southern Belgium.

With other monarchs and generals in the field, it was left to the ministers, chief counsels and foreign secretaries to decide the future of Europe. Count Aleksei Arakcheyev represented Russia whenever Czar Alexander was not in court. Maurice de Talleyrand represented what was now a French government-in-exile and hoped to prevent its dismemberment as advocated by Arakcheyev and the Prussian delegation, lead by Chancellor Karl von Hardenberg and Foreign Minister Wilhelm von Humboldt. Viscount Robert Castlereagh was Britain's Foreign Secretary and Prince Klemens von Metternich represented Austria and was the chief architect of the conference's decisions.

On June 9th, 1815, a week before Napoleon's heart-stopping initial victory over Wellington's and Blücher's forces, they issued their imposing Final Act. They jointly declared it would change the structure of Europe forever, provided the resurgent Napoleonic threat was first defeated. In reality what they decided upon would only remain intact for 15 years, and in less than 50 years would be in tatters. But for now it would apportion out the lands, reward the winners and punish the losers.

Russia: The recreated Kingdom of Poland would be its puppet state, under the rule of Czar Alexander, as would the Grand Duchy of Finland, which it grabbed from Sweden in 1809. Plus, it would get an equal portion of the reparations France would now be forced to pay out.

Austria: Would also receive reparations and the Kingdom of Lombardy-Venetia in Italy, to add to its empire of Hungarians, Czechs, Germans Slavs, Serbs and dozens of other races. It would emerge from the Wars as the leading military power in mainland Europe – a position it would retain until 1859.

Prussia: Did not get any vassal states but had all the territory it lost after Jena restored to it and then some. It gained territory from Saxony and on both sides of the Rhine; in all it doubled in size. It returned to its preeminent position among the Germanies, only Austria would rival it.

Britain: Got its share of reparations and some overseas territories, but its greatest reward from the Napoleonic Wars was something far more valuable than land or money: mastery of the seas. After Trafalgar, no other nation would seriously threaten its naval supremacy during the 19th Century, though that didn't mean someone would not occasionally try.

Other states to gain were the Kingdom of Holland, which got its independence back plus all the Belgian territories, and Switzerland – it also regained its fabled independence. The Papal States were also restored, to the Pope, and the Kingdoms of Sardinia and Naples were restored to their original ruling families. And finally Sweden, which had gained a crown prince from the Wars, had Norway ceded to it by Denmark.

France: In the first Treaty of Paris, signed on April 12th, 1814, France lost the empire Napoleon had created and was reduced to its borders of 1792. However, in return for Bonaparte's abdication, it did not have to pay reparations and would not have occupation troops in its territories.

Now, its borders were reduced to those of 1790. It lost Nice and the Savoy region to the Kingdom of Sardinia and its Rhineland territories to Prussia and other German states. It was saddled with a billion francs in reparations and would have British and Prussian occupation troops garrisoned on its lands until they were paid. A few of its overseas territories were ceded to Britain, but France lost something far more important – its *ennemi héréditaire*.

Never again would she be able to compete with her centuries-old, traditional hereditary enemy to be the world's dominant power. In fact, the two would now cooperate, even become allies if the threat or the local, meaning colonial, situation made this advantageous to them. If France wanted a new *ennemi héréditaire* it would have to create one.

Bavaria: The largest German state south of the Main River, and among the Germanies one of Napoleon's earliest allies, lost most of the territory it had gained through that alliance. It also lost some of its independence – it was forced to sign a new alliance with Prussia – but the Wittelsbach family, the oldest ruling family in the Germanies, got to stay on the throne.

Saxony: Despite its dramatic change of sides at the pivotal Battle of Leipzig, this North German state was dealt with a little more harshly than Napoleon's other Germanic allies. It lost most of its Grand Duchy of Warsaw to Prussia and Russia, as well as other lands, but its king, the former elector of Saxony, was allowed to keep his throne.

Poland: Invaded by Sweden and dismembered by Prussia, Austria and Russia a generation earlier, this nation had been toyed with by Napoleon throughout his reign. Alternately encouraged and suppressed by him, the dream of Polish independence had been all but ignored by the Congress of Vienna. Paid lip service by the creation of the Kingdom of Poland, under the Czar's dominion, it would remained unfulfilled until after the end of World War I.

Italy: Similarly encouraged and suppressed on Napoleonic whims, the dream of Italian unity and independence was also ignored by the Congress, as it split the lands between Austria, Sardinia and Naples, and restored the Papal States to the Pope. However, this dream would not have to wait quite as long as Poland's to be fulfilled.

Denmark: Having first lost its fleet to Britain in September of 1807 – what was not sunk ended up taken as war prizes – Denmark now lost

Norway to Sweden. It was given the Duchy of Lauenburg, but this would not be enough. Denmark would bide its time and turn its attention to the principalities on its southern border, Schleswig and Holstein.

Portugal: Britain's oldest European ally had suffered terribly during the Peninsula War phase of Napoleon's conflicts. While it got some of the reparations, it lost power and prestige, and in eight years would lose the crown jewel of its overseas empire. Already, there were independence movements forming in Brazil.

And the title of the biggest loser in the Napoleonic Wars goes to:

Spain: At differing times France's most powerful ally and her bitterest enemy, Spain easily suffered more casualties in this long era of conflict than any other nation except for France and Russia. Material damage was even greater as there was scarcely a city or town which had not been turned into a battlefield during a six year-long campaign marked not just by major battles and sieges but by a new form of operations the Spanish called "Little War": Guerrilla Warfare.

Whether in the countryside or the cities, the following term was first used in Saragossa, *Guerra y cuchillo*: "War to the Knife." It was a nightmare, memorably chronicled by the painter Francisco José de Goya, in which no quarter was given and atrocities were frequent.

It destroyed Spain. First as a major power and then as a stable country with a cohesive, nominally functioning society. While its slide as a major power started before Napoleon came to power, its imbecilic royal family truly did not help the situation; it was accelerated by Britain's partial destruction of its fleet at Trafalgar, by the interdiction of its overseas trade and virtually completed by Napoleon's ludicrous attempt at seizing the Spanish throne for his family.

It turned the craven idiot, Ferdinand VII of the Bourbon-Parma House, into a national hero and sparked a national uprising which, quite unlike the French Revolution of a decade earlier, had no group of leaders, no desire to change its existing government but wanted simply to destroy the French. The uprising soon found common cause with the Portuguese rebels and within a year, Wellington had arrived on the Iberian Peninsula with a small but disciplined force of British troops.

As bad as the war was for Spain itself, it had far graver consequences for the Spanish colonial empire in the Americas. In hindsight it's not too ironic that the empire's decline was initiated by Napoleon, before he even started his attempt to take the Spanish throne.

Fifteen years earlier, in the then-secret Treaty of San Ildefonso of 1800, he engineered one of the greatest real estate swap/swindles in history. In exchange for the tiny, and fated to be short-lived, Kingdom of Etruria in Italy, part of present-day Tuscany, Spain returned the Louisiana Territory to France. Napoleon had wanted it to establish his empire in North America, but in three years the world situation had changed and he began negotiations with the American minister/ambassador to his court for the Re-sale of the Century.

In the astonishingly short time of two weeks the deal was worked out. France got 80 million francs, roughly 15 million dollars, it needed for the imminent resumption of its war with Britain, America was doubled in size and Spain got left holding the bag.

From this point on Spain's decline in the new world was inexorable. Given the ignorant, high-handed and autocratic treatment of the colonies by the royal family and its court officials this was perhaps inevitable, but world events accelerated what Napoleonic scheming had started.

Two years after the purchase was concluded, revolutionaries in Venezuela unsuccessfully declared their independence in 1806. Spanish forces crushed them but the turmoil spread to New Granada, present-day Columbia, in the west, to Argentina in the south and the Central American colonies in the north. By 1810 a popular uprising lead by local priests was underway in Mexico.

A year later the Venezuelans tried unsuccessfully again, this time under the command of the Great Liberator himself: Simon Bolivar. Though betrayed and defeated, the Spanish colonies in South America had found a leader they eventually united around. And in the following year they took heart from the successful declaration of independence by Mexico's wealthy landowners.

It would not be until after the Napoleonic Wars had ended that another Spanish colony in the Americas would succeed in its bid for independence. When it did, Argentina in 1816, its leader was a veteran of the Peninsular War: General José de San Martin. He followed it up with victorious campaigns to liberate Chile and Peru while Bolivar finally lived up to his reputation by freeing his native Venezuela and later New Granada.

Wars of liberation continued in Spanish America into the 1840s – the Dominican Republic gained its freedom in 1844 – but its last colonies would not be lost until the United States took them at the end of the 19th Century. By then, while it still retained some overseas territories, Spain had shrunk to a shadow of its former imperial greatness. Thanks largely to the strife inflicted on it by its imbecilic royal family and Napoleon's schemes.

And the biggest future winners to emerge from the Napoleonic Wars will be:

"By this increase in territory, the power of the United States of America will be consolidated forever, and I have just given England a seafaring rival which, sooner or later, will humble her pride." Napoleon Bonaparte said this soon after concluding the Louisiana Purchase in December 1803 with the U.S. negotiators, Minister Robert Livingston and future President James Monroe.

At the time of Purchase, America was a relatively narrow strip of 17 states from the New Brunswick/Quebec border in the north to Florida, then a Spanish colony, in the south. Ohio had just been admitted to the union and the overall population was approximately six million.

The phrase "Manifest Destiny," and all that went with it, would not be heard in America for another 42 years. But it had its beginnings here, with the Purchase, the subsequent Lewis and Clark Expedition and the opening of the Santa Fe Trail by 1821.

By then Florida had been purchased from Spain, one of the more peaceful losses of Spanish Territory, and Missouri had been admitted as the 24th state. And then-President Monroe was formulating what would become the Monroe Doctrine, which he formally presented to Congress in December, 1823.

In an ironic inversion of what Napoleon had hoped for, the two seafaring rivals now cooperated, with the United States providing the policy that the Americas were "henceforth not to be considered as subjects for further colonization by any European power" and Britain supplying the might to back it up with the most powerful military force on the planet: the Royal Navy.

Though it would take another two wars of imperial conquest, something Napoleon would understand, and two global conflicts, the intensity and scale of which would astound even him, America was on the path to becoming the dominant world power.

"Judge for yourself if we have anything to fear from a nation as sensible, as reasonable, as dispassionate, as tolerant as the Germans. A nation so far removed from any form of excess that not one of our men has been murdered in Germany during a war." Napoleon wrote this to Marshal Louis Davout some eight years later in 1812, while he was heavily engaged in the Peninsular War and preparing for the invasion of Russia.

The Germanies had been at peace since the Tilsit Treaties, some four years earlier, with most of their populations either resigned to French rule, or actually enjoying it. But not in Prussia, where her shattering defeats at Jena and Auerstädt and subsequent humiliation at Tilsit sparked something remarkable.

Then Foreign Minister, later Chancellor, Karl von Hardenberg warned the Prussian royal court it must either face the new realities brought about by the French Revolution, or be doomed like the Bourbon Kings. So Friedrich Wilhelm III initiated reform, actually a quiet revolution, from the top down rather than try to suppress a far more violent one from the bottom up.

For civil and governmental reform he turned to Hardenberg and a man he had once dismissed as an "obstinate and disobedient official"– Baron Heinrich von Stein. Together, these men lifted Prussia out of the Medieval Age and recast it as a modern monarchy.

They worked quickly and efficiently and, approximately three months after Prussia's humiliation at Tilsit and a year after the defeats of Jena and Auerstädt, the King issued the era-ending Edict of Emancipation. At the stroke of his pen he ended serfdom, most of the feudal privileges of the nobles, restrictions on the sale of lands and almost all caste distinctions.

No longer was a noble restricted to living off the toil of the peasants who worked his land. He could now engage in any trade or industry he wished and sell his land to whoever he wanted, not just to other nobles. Further land reform worked out by von Stein allocated two-thirds of former noble lands to the serfs, who were now called Freeholders, and one-third to the nobles.

The growing merchant class could buy any of these lands, hold commissions in the army and engage in almost any business with the nobles. Jews, until then under a host of racist restrictions, were given the civil rights of any other Prussian citizen. Almost overnight these reforms were instituted, with few protests, and made Prussia one of the most progressive states in Europe.

To reform his army, Friedrich Wilhelm III turned to two of his best surviving generals: Barons Gerhard von Scharnhorst and August von Gneisenau. They took an army shattered by its defeats and cut in strength by Bonaparte's dictates to 42,000 active-duty personnel and transformed it in much the same way Stein and Hardenberg transformed the country.

With manpower levels now critical, incompetent officers were removed, promotion was based on merit and not birth, recruiting mercenaries was ended, skill took precedence over blind discipline and innovative tactics were encouraged. The cadre system was instituted, which allowed most units to be staffed with a skeleton force of active-duty personnel and filled out at regular intervals with either recruits for initial training or reservists for refresher courses.

In just over four years, just as the magnitude of Napoleon's disaster in Russia had become apparent, it was this army that Prussia fully mobilized and unleashed on its battered conqueror. Its success on the battlefield helped it achieve alliances with Austria and Russia and, more importantly, rallied the other Germanies to the cause of national unity.

For a short, tantalizing period in the momentous days of 1813 to early 1814, it seemed as though the dreams of philosopher-poets and warrior-kings could be realized: a united Germany. However, as soon as the threat which brought them together had left the stage, Napoleon and his first abdication, the hot desire for unity cooled.

Alas, it was not so much a want for hegemony under Prussian control that fueled the fires but a hatred of French rule. Some who favored unity wanted Austria to be included, but others feared the size of its empire and its ethnic composition – most of its population was distinctly non-German. And the Austrians themselves showed little interest in unification.

With Napoleon gone the older resentments and fear of Prussian rule reasserted themselves. So much so that by early 1814, on the eve of Bonaparte's return from Elba, many of the smaller German states were negotiating the not-so-secret alliance with Britain, France and Austria against Prussia and Russia.

Even though this crisis had largely been neutralized by the time he landed, most of the Germanies still did not rally to Prussia's new call to arms and unity. Mostly it was fear which paralyzed them. Fear that Napoleon would yet again pull off the impossible and the principle battleground of the new war would be their lands. Fear that even if this did not happen, Prussia would use the emergency to scheme for an enforced unity under its dominion.

Even her very military prowess, the speed at which she re-mobilized and fielded her armies as compared to the slow pace of Russia and Austria, now worked against Prussia. The one other German state to field any kind of force during the Hundred Days, the Hanoverian Cities, chose to ally itself with the coalition army Wellington was assembling instead of Blücher's.

In the end, Prussia had to settle for being the most powerful state in the new version of the Napoleonic Confederation of the Rhine. This time it was called the German Confederation, it was composed of mostly the same 38 states as the previous one, and its legislative body, the Federal Diet, would meet in one of the last remaining Imperial Free Cities: Frankfurt au Main, Frankfurt on the Main River, the traditional dividing line between the north German states and the southern ones.

For that brief, tantalizing period the dream of German unity flared brighter than it had in centuries and seemed so close to fruition. Now it had gone dormant again, back asleep like its legendary hero. Even the man who had been cast as the modern-day Friedrich Barbarossa, Marshal Gebhard von Blücher, soon retired from the scene. He had no desire to lead a national unity movement or to govern. His love was the command of armies in the field, but at 73 even he realized his days were at an end and he retired to his farm for the last time.

This is what it seemed like at the time, but in reality Barbarossa had not gone back to sleep – he had been reborn. On April 1st, 1815, at the same time Blücher and Wellington were organizing their respective armies, a centuries-old Junkers family welcomed its newest addition at its Schönhausen estate, near the Elbe River in Brandenburg. He was a strapping, robust son and was given a robust name: Otto Edward Leopold von Bismarck. The new Barbarossa had been born.

Chapter II: France Under the Bourbons

"They have learned nothing, and forgotten nothing."
-Charles Maurice de Talleyrand-Perigord (1754 - 1838)

Europe at Peace

HAD IT ALL *really* happened? In the Great Silence which finally settled in after such a prolonged conflict – more than 20 years – people began to ask, did it really take place? The Jacobins and Reign of Terror. Robespierre, Danton and Hebert. The Thermidor Coup against the Jacobins, the Rise of Napoleon and the endless wars, both internal and external, which wove around them.

For many people, and not just those on the other side of an ocean or a continent away, it didn't happen at all. Readers of English Literature from the period of the early 19th Century will, sooner or later, be struck by the dichotomy between many of the contemporary novels written in the period and the historic fiction written about the period from a later age.

In the novels of Patrick O'Brian and Cecil Scott (C.S.) Forester, Britain is under siege and the continued threat of invasion from Bonaparte. Jack Aubrey and Horatio Hornblower, and the fully-detailed iron men and wooden ships they commanded, are its only line of defence against, what another character says, is "an entire continent arrayed against us." Britain under threat/siege is also an underlying theme in more literary books like *A Tale of Two Cities*, by Charles Dickens, and *The Scarlet Pimpernel*, by

Baroness Emmuska Orczy. And in Bernard Cornwell's series *Sharpe's Rifles*, all of England seems to be involved in the grueling Peninsular War.

And yet, if you were to read any of Jane Austen's novels, written both of the period and in the period, you would swear they were taking place in another era, or an Alternate History universe. In her tales of provincial life among what seems a near-to-impoverished English middle class the name Napoleon is only occasionally mentioned. Nor is Horatio Nelson, Wellington, Egypt, Trafalgar, Austerlitz, Jena or any of the other personalities or events of the French Revolution and the Napoleonic Wars.

Historians, Literary Critics and readers with a love of history have wondered which version of this period is true? The reality is both are, for the Hornblowers, Aubreys and other military men, and even Sydney Carton and Lucie Manette of *A Tale of Two Cities*, belonged to a different world than the winsome and often self-sacrificing heroines of *Sense and Sensibility* and *Pride and Prejudice*.

They were different aspects of the same era, and the key words are "cities" and "provincial." For Austen's novels are of life in rural english manor homes, very isolated and all-but-independent of the cities – make that port cities – where most of the military stayed when they were not at sea or on a battlefield. News arrived, if it arrived at all, with the latest friend, relative or traveler to stop by. Newspapers existed, but rarely circulated beyond the major cities and, while there were a few stagecoach lines, travel beyond the cities was largely up to the individual.

In Europe the impact of the whole era of political turmoil, revolution and war largely depended on whether you lived a rural or urban life, and how close your home was to a battlefield. In Spain or Portugal this meant nearly everyone. In some of the more remote Germanies their only contact with the era was dealing with French officials and the ruinously high taxes they imposed.

The French Revolution and Napoleonic Wars were the last major conflict to occur before the first age of Mass Communications, before the first age of Mass Transport, and before the Industrial Revolution, which was already nascent by the end of the 18th Century and nipping at the heels of the passing era.

If the continent and the British Isles had been strung with a network of telegraph lines, if daily newspapers, much less weekly and monthly magazines, had national circulations, if there had been a greater presence of canals and Macadamized roads, not to mention the existence of railroads, then the impact of the passing era would have been more apparent. However, just because it was not obvious didn't mean it did not happen, or have a profound effect.

People discovered they had a voice. Ethnic groups began to have aspirations to their own national identities. This was particularly true among the Poles, the Italians, the Hungarians and even the Belgians. People discovered they had rights, and not just to the land they toiled. And this was particularly true of the French.

France and Louis XVIII

Shortly after returning to Paris for the second time, after having made sure the coast was clear by allowing the victorious allies to enter it the day before, Louis XVIII convened a meeting with members of the provisional government at Tuileries Palace. He reiterated his support for the Constitutional Charter he had "granted" France approximately a year before, on June 14th, 1814.

And for everyone there, as well as those who could not, a wild and daring gamble had paid off. First and foremost, Louis' return to France and the throne meant the country would not be dismembered, something Prussia and Russia strongly advocated. And second, by restating his support for the Charter, he averted a civil war between the Ultra-royalists and the Liberals.

But it did not end the conflict between them. As so often happens, an even-handed approach pleased neither side. By the provisions of the Charter, the Royalists got a Chamber of Peers, the Senate, whose members were appointed by the King. It also reserved the right to initiate legislative action to the crown and made the Catholic Church the official state religion.

While the Liberals objected to the language Louis used in "granting" the Charter to the French people, and the rights he reserved for the crown, the Royalists objected to there being a Constitutional Charter at all. They, and especially the Ultra-royalists lead by the comte d'Artois, objected to the retention of the Napoleonic Civil Code, most officials from his regime, the lower Chamber of Deputies and the confirmation of the sale of state-held property to new owners.

Thousands of Royalists abandoned lands, homes and other properties in their flight from the French Revolution and the Reign of Terror. When they returned, they had hoped most of it would be ceded back to them. Now Louis XVIII, one of their own, had ordained that all the sales had been legal and were final. Many would never forgive him for it.

However, Louis had bigger problems to resolve. He had foreign troops garrisoned in France and a billion francs in reparations to pay. Many thought the troops, who would stay until the vast sum of money had been paid, would be on occupation duty for the better part of a decade. But France had an overlooked resource it could tap.

Unlike Portugal and Spain, who were losing their overseas empires through revolution and blazingly stupid autocratic rule, France emerged with most of its empire intact. Its worst loss was its Haitian colony on the island of Hispaniola just as Napoleon was rising to power.

Before revolution swept the colony, it produced half the world's coffee crop and half the sugar Europe annually consumed. Now the colony was not only lost to France, the plantations that produced those crops were still in ruins and Haiti's economy has been a basket case ever since.

But there were still other French island colonies in the Caribbean, and then there was French Guiana on the northeast coast of South America. Almost from the moment Haiti was lost, the army Napoleon sent to retake it lost 25,000 to yellow fever and barely 2,000 to combat; plantations on the other islands and in Guiana were expanded to replace it. And this was at a time when France had a monopoly on world coffee production. Not until much later in the 19th Century would Brazil and later Columbia eclipse it in coffee and sugar output.

The result was, instead of taking five to ten years to pay off its indemnities, France had them paid off in less than three. By the end of 1818, with the artworks Napoleon had looted from across Europe returned to their rightful owners and the debt paid, the last of the occupation troops left French soil. In an ironic twist of history the last to go were Prussian troops, they would not be back for 52 years.

With these acts Louis XVIII, along with statesmen like Talleyrand and Francois de Chateaubriand, had managed to return France to the community of nations in Europe. By 1818 she was allowed to join the Quadruple Alliance of major powers (Russia, Austria, Prussia and Britain), making it the Quintuple Alliance.

By then she had also become a member of the Holy Alliance – not so much a true coalition of nations as a manifesto amongst the crowned heads of Europe. It held them to treat their subjects according to Christian principals. But more importantly it swore them to come to each other's aid if their rule was threatened. As such it was less a pact of collective security among sovereign nations as it was a promise among sovereigns for collective security against their people.

This suited most of the French aristocracy, and especially the Ultra-royalists, quite well. And yet they were still not happy. Louis was content to rule France under the constraints of the detested Constitutional Charter and France had not yet returned to its rightful place as the dominant power of mainland Europe. That title was still held by Austria, for by now the post-Napoleonic Era had acquired its own rightful name: the Age of Metternich.

Europe and the Age of Metternich

Prince Klemens Wenzel Lothar Metternich began his diplomatic career as Austria's minister/ambassador to the court of Napoleon Bonaparte. He handled the emperor's outbursts, threats and tirades better than most other court diplomats. By 1810 he had succeeded Count Philip Stadion as Austria's Foreign Minister and represented his emperor and country at some of the most important diplomatic gatherings/meetings in the 19th Century.

He negotiated the marriage between Napoleon and Emperor Francis' daughter, Marie Louise. He mediated the Prague Conference of June, 1813 between the Prussians and Russians on one side and France on the other. He hosted the momentous Congress of Vienna from mid-1814 to late-1815, and thereafter held periodic congresses of the Quintuple Alliance members.

At Vienna, Verona, Troppau and a dozen other locations they decided not so much the fate of nations but how to keep what they thought was the rightful ruler on the throne. Sometimes they helped prevent a usurpation, such as when the first great Congress was ending Napoleon's brother-in-law, Joachim Murat, tried to take back the Kingdom of Naples. They quickly supported the Bourbon claim and Murat, after he was captured, was quickly executed.

But mostly they worked to suppress revolutions and independence movements, even at the expense of keeping a despot on the throne. By 1820 the reactionary and brutal regime of Ferdinand VII finally ignited in Spain the kind of uprising it had long since sparked in its New World colonies. Barely a year later another Bourbon Ferdinand, Ferdinand I of the Two Sicilies, also created a revolution with his cruelty.

Prince Metternich, by now not just Austria's Foreign Minister but its newly-appointed State Chancellor, responded by urging the Holy Alliance to send military aid to the despotic Ferdinands. Austria, along with the King of Sardinia, sent troops and ships to Sicily while France responded to the Spanish Crisis.

Even if he had wanted to, Louis XVIII could not have refused the call for aid. He had over-stacked the Chamber of Peers with Ultra-royalist Senators who clamored to send aid to a monarch that, some 14 years earlier, France had removed from power. But that had been the France of Emperor Napoleon Bonaparte I and this was the France of the restored

Bourbon kings mobilizing to save another Bourbon king.

In the end, and in rapidly failing health, Louis XVIII could not resist Metternich, his Senators or his family, especially not his brother and sons. Their zeal to go to war in Spain reached such a fever pitch they refused to allow a Russian army the right to march through France; Czar Alexander had to content himself with aiding the Greeks in their war of independence with the Ottoman Empire.

They even refused British help and the Duke of Wellington, England's envoy to the Alliance Congress in Verona, promptly withdrew the offer. If Britain wanted combat in Europe, it was already having trouble along the Indian-Burmese border, then it would have to seek it with Russia in assisting Greek independence. And if France wanted war on the Iberian Peninsula to itself then it was welcome to it.

France and Charles X

"One hundred thousand Frenchmen, commanded by a Prince of my family, whom I fondly call my son, are ready to march with a prayer to the God of Saint Louis that they may preserve the throne of Spain to the grandson of Henry IV."

Louis XVIII used this statement to open a joint session of Chambers in January, 1823. France's ambassador to Spain had already been recalled from Madrid, then the seat of the revolutionary Constitutional Ministry, and most Senators and Deputies enthusiastically cheered the mobilizing of the army.

But it would not be until the middle of March that the Duke of Angoulême and his command staff left Paris. And it was not until April 7th when his vanguard crossed the frontier south of the port city of Bayonne and entered Irun on Spain's northeastern coast. A ponderous pace, especially compared to the movement of armies in the Napoleonic Era, though it did match the overall pace of Louis XVIII's reign.

Portly to the point of being morbidly obese, hobbled by gout, polite and tactful to a fault, Louis XVIII had proven to be more tolerant, respectful and enlightened than most of the other current European monarchs. He had tried to be all things to all people, and ended up getting respect from very few. Most had applauded him when he quickly paid off France's war reparations, but that ended five years earlier and now, seemingly everything went wrong with the Spanish Expedition.

Even when it went right, the war provided nothing but trouble for France and Louis. By mid-September the French force, with fanatical

Spanish royalists, had surrounded Cadiz, where the Constitutional Ministry held Ferdinand VII captive. In exchange for his release, he accepted the French position not to take any reprisals against the revolutionaries.

However, less than a day after his release Ferdinand reversed all his pledges and declared null and void the amnesty he had signed. Within a week he initiated a reign of terror the likes of which Europe had not seen since the Jacobins. He banned for life from Madrid and its environs anyone who had been part of the Constitutional Ministry. Then came the death warrants and lastly, the revival of the Inquisition.

Perhaps the one good thing to emerge from Napoleon's invasion of Spain, namely the suppression of the centuries-old bureaucracy of state terror called The Spanish Inquisition, came back in full force. By the end of the year several leaders of the revolt had been hanged, and they were followed to the gallows by men and even women for the crime of merely possessing a picture of one of the leaders.

Metternich was shocked by it, and soon decided the Alliance should leave Spain to her own devices. Louis XVIII was saddened by it, got blamed for it, and quickly agreed with the Duke of Angoulême to withdraw the expeditionary force. Even the Ultra-royalists were shocked and renounced what Ferdinand was doing.

Except, there was one – he was the Ultra-royalists' Ultra-royalist, the comte d'Artois and Louis XVIII's younger brother: the future Charles X. He openly approved, and less than a year after the French withdrawal, and approximately four months after his older brother's death in September of 1824, he was crowned king at the Cathedral of Reims in January, 1825.

Immediately he proved to be a different monarch than his brother. The tact, the tolerance, the respectful politeness which had marked Louis XVIII's reign vanished as Charles X set about making use of the gains the Ultra-royalists and the Clerical Party had made in both Chambers in the previous year's elections, about the time of his brother's death.

Louis' final appointments gave the Ultra-royalists an absolute majority in the Chamber of Peers, while the sympathy vote and government manipulation saw only 19 Liberals returned to the Chamber of Deputies. The political climate became so unhealthy for Liberals that Talleyrand thought of going into exile and the Marquis de Lafayette virtually did; he accepted a long-offered invitation to visit America as a hero of its revolution. And stayed until 1827.

Charles X got legislation passed to appropriate one million francs for the Royalists whose land and property had been seized and sold during the French Revolution. He also outlawed sacrilege, very broadly defined, and passed laws enforcing an old aristocratic favorite, *primogeniture*: the exclusive right of inheritance belonging to the first-born son.

By these acts and others in the following years he attempted to restore power to the Bourbon Throne, the aristocracy who supported it and the Catholic Church. In effect, he was attempting a counter-revolution to the revolution of some 40 years earlier. And what he could not get through legislation he would take by imperial decree.

In April, 1827 Charles disbanded the National Guard units of Paris after they protested to him about the re-establishment of Jesuit schools. This brought Lafayette back to defend the organization he helped create some 38 years earlier, and began an anti-clerical reaction which culminated a year later in the electoral defeat of Charles' ministry.

One would have thought a reversal like this would chasten a king. Instead it launched him, so unlike his brother and very much like the despised Napoleon, on even grander flights of fancy. In the most dangerous, Charles sought to capitalize on the Alliance victory in the naval battle of Navarino over the Turkish fleet to redraw the Ottoman Empire and the map of Christian Europe.

It only served to raise alarm in Holland and the German Confederation, and reporting on it caused more attempts at press restrictions at home. To distract an increasingly restive public he tried more meddlings in the European status quo and other foreign adventures. By the middle of 1829 he was mobilizing an expedition to Algeria, but by then it was too late.

The July Revolution and the Fall of the Bourbons

"My brother will not die in that bed."

Louis XVIII said this when, in his final days, he saw what would be his death bed. Rarely has a king spoken more prophetic words about his successor; Charles X would die in exile, as would the monarchs who came after him. Louis would have the last laugh on them all: he was the last French ruler to die in-state and in France.

For his brother the final slide began, ironically enough, with his greatest military success. The Algerian Expedition finally got underway at the beginning of June, 1830, after the Dey/Governor of the city of Algiers was foolish enough to insult the local French consul and provide the pretext for invasion.

Landings began on the North African coast by mid-June and from the start, the war was an outstanding success. Nearly 50 million francs in war booty, then a hefty sum, were seized in the opening weeks and Britain grew nervous enough about the conquest to formally ask the French government not to retain any territory once its honor had been satisfied.

But Charles would have none of it. Emboldened by the victories, he was in no mood to listen to foreign governments or even his own. Responding to an earlier vote of no-confidence by the Chamber of Deputies he issued the fateful July Ordinances on July 25th. They dissolved both Chambers, renounced the Constitution his brother had signed and returned France to an absolute monarchy. To Charles X, his Ministers and supporters their counter-revolution was complete.

And it lasted all of three days. The news was scarcely out when the streets of Paris were filled with protesters, then with barricades and by nightfall over 600 had been erected and the city was all but impassable. Charles declared a state of siege and called out the National Guard, who arrived on the streets wearing the banned tricolor cockades on their hats and even waving some lovingly preserved tricolor flags.

News rapidly spread throughout France, turning an uprising into a revolution. And then it spread beyond the borders, turning revolution into a call-to-arms across Europe. Back in Paris, Lafayette moved to take command of the National Guard and prevented it from becoming a disorganized, vengeful rabble, while Talleyrand and Chateaubriand prepared to counter any reactions by Charles X.

They feared he would call upon his fellow monarchs in the Holy Alliance to come to his aid, and foreign troops would be marching into France. In reality they need not have worried, the last Bourbon king played whist as artillery and musket fire rattled the windows of his palace. When informed that two regiments of regular troops had gone over to the revolution and the Louvre had been taken, Charles X replied, "They exaggerate the danger."

Only when Tuileries Palace was stormed and sacked, when tricolors flew from clock towers and other high points in Paris, did he rescind the fateful Ordinances and dismissed his Ministry, along with the hated Chief Minister Prince Polignac. By then it was far too late. The provisional government installed at the Hotel de Ville declared Charles X deposed and neither Metternich nor any member state of the Holy Alliance or Quintuple Alliance were willing to reverse it. Bourbon rule of France had passed into history.

France After the Bourbons

It all moved so rapidly afterward. Charles X tried to retain the throne for his family by abdicating to the Dauphin, the former Duke of Angoulême.

Lafayette was offered the role of President if he would make France a constitutional republic, something urged by firebrand new politicians like Louis Adolphe Thiers and Francois Guillaume Guizot.

But France's hero demurred. He feared the rest of Europe would attack if a new republic was declared, and more importantly he feared France itself was not ready to be a republic. Instead he gave his support to a constitutional monarch, to what he called, "a popular throne, surrounded by republican institutions."

Lafayette turned to Louis Philippe, the Duke of Orléans and the eldest son of Philippe Égalité, one of the few untainted heroes of the French Revolution. At a stroke it calmed Europe's fears of another major conflict and it gave the French people a popular ruler to support.

In spite of his initial reluctance, on August 9th, at the formal request of the Chamber of Peers and Chamber of Deputies, Louis Philippe accepted the French crown with a solemn oath to uphold its constitution. By then the Dauphin had resigned all rights to the throne and, on August 16th, sailed into exile from Cherbourg with Charles X, their families and an entourage of attendants large enough to fill two ships.

Called the "Citizen King" and his reign the "July Monarchy," Louis Philippe immediately began cooperating with new politicians like Thiers and Guizot, even helping to advance their careers. But it was in diplomacy that he really moved swiftly, employing old hands like Talleyrand and Chateaubriand to soothe European apprehensions at this new French Revolution, and something more important.

Without having meant to, and completely unlike the leaders from 40 years earlier, those who lead the July Revolution provided the spark and inspiration to insurrections across Europe. Long-simmering ethnic tensions and new-found class hatreds exploded into clashes and open revolts in Holland, the German Confederation, Sardinia, Naples, the Papal States, the Italian provinces of the Austrian Empire, its Hungarian region and finally Russia's Polish Kingdom.

And everywhere crowned heads and government officials blamed France for it all. Except in Spain, where the re-institution of the Inquisition ignited still another revolt to Ferdinand VII's rule and his mad quest to stamp out "the disastrous mania for thinking."

Fairly or unfairly, and in spite of the success in the following year that Talleyrand and Chateaubriand would have, European governments and even certain civil populations began to hold France more and more responsible for the waves of anxiety, anarchy and conflict which would periodically sweep the continent.

Chapter III: The Germanies – The Slow Road to Unity

"What is the German Fatherland? Wherever the German tongue is heard."
-Ernst Moritz Arndt (1769 - 1860)

The German Confederation: The Early Years

THE FIRES OF German unity cooled almost as soon as the Prussian and Hanoverian armies had returned from the field in 1815. Friedrich Barbarossa seemingly went back to sleep when Blücher retired to his farm, and especially when he died there in September of 1819.

In reality he was under the loving tutelage of his mother, the former Wilhelmina Mencken and would soon be sent to the Plamann Boarding School in Berlin. But his story is for a later phase, when he fully plunges his hand into the time stream, for now the story is the somnolent state of German nationalism.

It was still present. Still there in the daily lives of citizens of 38 different states. It had probably been too much to ask the peoples of 360 separate entities to unite into one state, but shrinking that number by nearly an order of magnitude had, in the end, been accepted with few difficulties.

For now the vague boundaries of German nationalism were defined by language, folk traditions and ethnic origins. It was a casual nationality, it had yet to be defined by such things as physical boundaries, unifying state institutions and documents like a national charter or constitution.

It *did* have a national legislature, a federal diet which met at regular intervals in Frankfurt au Main. But it was a weak institution, certainly not as strong as Chambers in France or Parliament in Britain. It could not even be considered as strong as Congress, as it then existed, in the United States.

The Federal Diet, from its very inception, was bedeviled by two major problems in its assembly, Austria and Prussia. Both were major world powers, charter members of the Quintuple Alliance and the Holy Alliance, and Austria was the dominant military power in Europe.

However, it was Prussia that other historians have defined as "less a state with an army but an army with a state." Smaller, but better organized and disciplined, it was Prussia where the military reforms of Scharnhorst and Gneisenau, and the social reforms of Hardenberg and Stein, had been initiated and by now institutionalized.

Austria, by comparison, was weak for its size, not nearly as efficient and had something which made most Germans apprehensive in giving it dominance in German affairs: most of its population was not German. In fact its German-speaking peoples of Bohemia, Moravia and Austria proper were a distinct minority compared to the Hungarians, Serbs, Italians, Slavs, Poles, Czechs and literally dozens of other nationalities that composed the empire.

One could call this racism but, conversely, most of the other peoples of the Austrian Empire were equally wary of what they saw as a solid German hegemony deciding their futures. Already, some were agitating for a legislature of their own, like the German Confederation, to settle their own issues. And then there were other nationalities who wanted to take it a step further – they wanted independence.

As for the Confederation itself, it often fell to the middle powers of Saxony, Baden, Bavaria and Würtemberg to decide matters before the assembly. And increasingly, despite the commanding presence of Metternich, decisions started going more and more in Prussia's favor. For it was Prussia that was seen as the state of the future while Austria appeared intent on living in the past.

The State of German Unity

Here is a topic whose complexity and history makes it worthy of a book all to its own, though it would make for some mighty dense reading. To distill it down to the essentials: the concepts of nation-state and nationality developed rather differently in Western Europe than in Central Europe.

In countries like France, Spain, Portugal, Holland, even Denmark and most especially Great Britain, these two concepts evolved together in an almost symbiotic and mutually nurturing union. In Central and Eastern

Europe the concept of nationality/national-identity greatly preceded the concept of nation-states and helped mold them into a rather different idea.

In the Germanies, what kings and warriors could not forge the philosophers and poets would ponder and exalt. And right from the start the German philosophers proved to be rather different than their British, French and New World counterparts. Intellectually they were less interested in human rights and the rights of the individual than in the freedom of the human spirit. With the nation-state concept lagging behind nationality, they idealized what the eventual united German would look like into the "Rechtsstaat": the Right State or, more loosely, the Idealized State.

From roughly 1800 to 1871, "Rechtsstaat" was the most popular word in the vocabulary of German philosophers and Liberals. This was especially true of the Bureaucratic Liberals, in the Stein and Hardenberg mold, and the Moderate Liberals, where most of the philosophers resided. Only the Radical Liberals like Heinrich Heine, Ludwig Börne and the most energetic and insulting of Friedrich Hegel's students, Karl Marx, rejected the dogma that freedom of the human spirit was more important than human rights.

But most of the Radicals were isolated literati more interested in being poets and if they did any collaborating then they were like Heine, who collaborated with Franz Schubert, Robert Schumann and Felix Mendelssohn in putting his poems to music. And there was an even more important way they were like Heinrich Heine: most lived abroad in exile. This made the Radical Liberals the smallest of the liberal movements in the Germanies and, when the time came, the weakest.

This left the field to the Bureaucratic and Moderate Liberals like Marx's mentor Georg Wilhelm Friedrich Hegel, Johann von Herder, the brothers August and Friedrich von Schlegel, Adam Müller, Johann Christoph Schiller, Johann Wolfgang von Goethe and the philosopher who really started it all: Immanuel Kant.

Of the giants of German philosophy and literature, it was Kant who most successfully fused the two meanings of "freedom" (of the human spirit and of the individual) together. He blended this with his dual beliefs in the equality and dignity of Man, the supremacy of Law and what he saw as the practical necessity of an authoritarian government. Kant is responsible for bringing the traditional German association of liberty and the absolute state, meaning the Idealized Germanic State, into the 19th Century.

It was shortly after Kant's death, in February of 1804, that German liberalism fractured into its three distinct movements. It was his friend Goethe, founder of the "Sturm und Drang" (Storm and Stress) literary movement of the previous century, who saw to it that Kant's beliefs were spread to the other German philosophers. And, since he was widely admired as the "last universal author of European literature" they gained in their day great credence.

Goethe and Kant were even admired in the great competing philosophical movement in the Germanies: Romantic Conservatism. Less well known now, mostly because it has far fewer "celebrity" philosophers whose work has survived the test of time, it was in its day quite powerful as it had the support of the Prussian Government, churches of all denominations and aristocratic orders from across the lands.

Romantic Conservatism borrowed its main philosophy from a foreigner, the British statesman and political philosopher Edmund Burke. They especially borrowed from his masterpiece book "Reflections on the Revolution in France" published in 1790. He advanced that the "social contract" theory of French philosophers actually extended through time. Between the living, the dead and the unborn, and it was a contract which could not be broken by the fancy of the living generation.

To this foreign acquisition the Romantic Conservatives added the concepts of natural law and organic theory from one of the leading Liberal philosophers of his day: Johann Gottfried von Herder. A contemporary of Kant, they would end up dying within a few months of each other, and a member of Goethe's "Sturm und Drang" movement; he was also a court chaplain at Weimar who thought states and societies were living organisms in their own right. He believed they had their own unique character and created a word for it: "Volksgeist."

"Christ died not only for men, but also for states," was written by one of the lesser lights of the Liberal Movement, Adam Müller, but it perfectly describes one of the main pillars of the Romantic Conservative Movement: the "Ständestaat." While "Rechtsstaat" was the idealized German state, the "Ständestaat" was the idealized natural state. It was an outgrowth of the revered Martin Luther's belief that God created the state to maintain order in a sinful world, and its societal groups were ordained by God.

Whether it was "Rechtsstaat" or "Ständestaat," these idealized nation-states needed absolute power, of course justly wielded, by either its sovereign or governing body, in order to work. And on the concept of absolute power both the Liberals, of whatever stripe, and the Romantic Conservatives were in agreement – they were ambivalent about it.

To the Romantic Conservatives absolute power, and by extension the Absolute State that wielded it, was the enemy of the feudal system they admired. But in the modern world, which had grown so sinful, most of them understood they needed absolute power in some form for their "Ständestaat" to maintain order.

To the Liberals, except maybe the Radicals, absolute power was the necessary means for an authoritarian government to achieve their desired "Rechtsstaat." They believed through the proper exercise of state power that the state would replace the Church as the repository of moral values and moral authority among the Germans.

The problem for both movements is they were dealing with concepts, theories and idealized states. Real nation-states had borders, unifying institutions and founding documents. They also had something else, something most of these philosophers studiously ignored: unforeseen seismic events which would compel their creation.

So while the German philosophers and poets, who did not even pretend to be spokesmen for the middle-class from which they mostly came, defined and exalted their imaginary states in their treatise papers, articles and poems, a real nation-state was being forged in the "Sturm und Drang" of the 19th Century. And on January 18th, 1871, in the Hall of Mirrors of Versailles Palace, it would be proclaimed Germany.

The Germanies and the July Revolution

To the casual observer of history, the July Revolution of 1830 was a three-day summer storm mostly confined to the Paris environs. A brief lashing of musket fire, the rumble of cannons and Bourbon rule in France finally ended in a whimper.

In reality the July Revolution set off uprisings and civil wars across Europe, and they would last for two years until the middle of 1832. They would be the first post-Napoleonic storm the German Confederation would weather, though it had been preceded, as anyone who studies meteorology would know, by a pre-frontal squall line.

Between October of 1827, around the time of the Quintuple Alliance victory over the Turkish fleet at Navarino Island, and the middle of 1829, when the whole chimerical project finally collapsed, a tremor pulsed through the Germanies. And it was caused entirely by forces outside the Confederation wishing to redraw the map of Europe.

Russian operations during the war over Greek independence from the Ottoman Empire were making Austria nervous. In addition to naval operations, Russian troops had captured the Romanian provinces of Wallachia and Moldavia; Austria officially asked for the troops to be withdrawn, Russia encouraged France to seize the Rhineland territories if Austria attacks, and soon the ill-kept secret was common knowledge throughout Europe.

Charles X only exacerbated the crisis by proposing a partitioning of the Ottoman Empire, along with a radical rearrangement of Europe. Russia was to get the Bosnian and Serbian provinces from Austria. Saxony and the Dutch regions of Holland were to be ceded to Prussia, while France was to get back the Rhineland territories and the French/Flemish-speaking provinces of Holland. Finally, the king of Holland would become the Sultan's governor of Constantinople. In all a ludicrous plan whose only result was the partial mobilizing of the German armies to prevent it from being implemented.

Approximately a year later the armies, and particularly the Prussian Army, were being fully mobilized. For there was war and revolution all along the borders of the German Confederation. The July Revolution had come, and it was hardly a passing summer storm.

In France there was revolution and its monarch deposed. In Poland the general uprising this sparked grew rapidly into a full-scale civil war, while in Holland those Flemish and French-speaking provinces so desired by Charles X united to form Belgium. Even in the south, French aid to rebel groups in Austria's Italian provinces lead to uprisings in Modena and Parma.

To be sure the July Revolution also sparked uprisings in the Germanies, but the revolts in Brunswick, Hesse and the Bavarian Palatinate were easily suppressed by the beginning of 1831. Their principal result was the reaction of the Federal Diet, repressing liberal publications, societies and college professors. In the end all the revolts caused was a new exodus of German Liberals to Switzerland, France and America.

And still the wars and revolutions continued at the borders of the Germanies. While France had quickly been settled, the civil war in Russia's Polish kingdom escalated into bitter fighting. French and Dutch troops were marching into Belgium, where the great fortress in the Grand Duchy of Luxembourg, a major eastern anchor to German defences, was threatened. The uprisings in northern Italy had by now spread to the Papal States, and there was unrest in Hungary.

Eventually the work of Metternich, Talleyrand, Humboldt, Chateaubriand and a host of other diplomats settled most of the troubles. Belgium became an independent state and chose Prince Leopold of Saxe-Coburg as its king. The German Confederation retained the fortress in Luxembourg while the grand duchy was annexed to Belgium. France ended aid to the Italian rebel forces when Austria received backing from Russia and Prussia. And Metternich added the Machiavellian touch by informing the newly-crowned Louis Philippe of the latest volunteer to join the Carbonari political movement in Italy. A name he knew would stoke the fears of any French monarch – the son of a one-time king of Holland: Charles Louis Napoleon Bonaparte.

Metternich also worked hard on his German brothers. From Prussia he secured an alliance with his country to aid Russia under the protocols of the Holy Alliance to subdue the Polish revolt. From the Federal Diet he got even more repressive measures passed: forbidding all political meetings and associations, new press censorship rules and declaring the refusal by any legislature to pay taxes to be an act of rebellion.

By the middle of 1832, nearly two years after the official ending of the July Revolution, it finally did end with the successful suppression of another Paris uprising. By then Belgium, with Luxembourg, were independent of Holland, Poland was once again part of the Russian Empire, the status quo had been restored in Italy and the German Confederation found itself rather uncomfortably more like the Austrian Empire: a police state.

The Zollverein: Unity Through Free Trade

A year and a half later, on January 1st of 1834, a far-reaching step toward German unification was achieved through legislative agreement on a new German Customs Union: the Zollverein. This was to be the Prussian Foreign Minister's, Baron Wilhelm von Humboldt, last and greatest gift to a unified Germany. Nothing he achieved at the Congress of Vienna, or the frantic rounds of negotiations following the July Revolution, would quite equal the establishment of a Pan-Germanic free trade union.

Under the Zollverein, 36 of the 38 states in the Confederation abolished all inter-state tariffs and taxes. Economically, 30 million Germans became one nation and another unifying institution would be created: the Zollparlament. This was an interstate parliament created by the Federal Diet to deal with administering the customs union.

And it could not have come at a more opportune time for the most pervasive and sweeping revolution of the 19th Century was finally making its presence felt on the European continent. The one that would erase the feudal system so loved by the Romantic Conservatives, and reinforce the class-ridden social structure so hated by most Liberals: the Industrial Revolution.

In its early days it had largely been confined to the British Isles by the Napoleonic Wars and especially Napoleon's Continental System of anti-British embargoes. After the wars Europe was too devastated to think about building factories or exploiting new technologies. And many countries, such as Austria and most notoriously Spain, actively fought to hold back the future.

But the Industrial Revolution was not a tide which could be stopped, only delayed. It arrived piecemeal in France, Holland and the Germanies. And brought with it the First Age of Mass Production, the First Age of Mass Communications and the First Age of Mass (Mechanized) Transport. It was the Germanies, much more so than anywhere else in Europe, where the importation of the Industrial Revolution went from imitation of all things British to original invention.

In the year preceding the Zollverein's creation, the German mathematician and astronomer Johann Karl Friedrich Gauss displayed the first practical results of his experiments in magnetism. Four years before either Charles Wheatstone in Britain or Samuel Morse in the United States, the celebrated discoverer of non-Euclidean Geometry demonstrated the world's first electromagnetic telegraph at the university town of Gottingen. And among the people who saw this demonstration was an impressionable college student, the future Barbarossa himself, Otto von Bismarck.

Already the first public railroads were in operation, and doing a booming business, in Great Britain. Modern steamships, at this point almost entirely paddlewheel-types, were plying the Atlantic, Mediterranean and moving into inland waterways. The future was arriving, and the German Confederation had just created the bureaucracy to manage it.

Strasbourg, and a Future Emperor Makes His Appearance

1836 had not been a good year for Louis Philippe. In January his Ministry was defeated over budgetary issues and forced to resign. Francois Guizot formed a new Ministry, however, by the end of February it too had unraveled. Louis Thiers formed a third Ministry in as many months and for a time conditions looked better.

Alas, it did not last part mid-year with military reverses in Algeria, they lead to Marshal Clauzel being relieved of command, and the worsening situation in Spain. The endemic revolts there had grown to a level of frequency and intensity that they acquired a name of their own: the Carlist Wars.

Even though Britain refused Philippe's offer for a joint intervention, they were already involved in enough wars, Thiers persisted in mounting one until his Ministry had to resign over this issue in early-September. And then, at the end of the month, when things seemingly could not get worse, events turned amusing.

Entering France at the border city of Strasbourg, Louis Napoleon Bonaparte met up with his few allies and appealed to the city's garrison to support him the same way the French Army had supported his uncle when he returned from exile on Elba. Amazingly enough, they did, but at the very next garrison Louis Napoleon was quickly arrested, along with most of his supporters. What he meant to be his entrance onto the world stage had turned into a pratfall.

Apart from a brief flare-up of tensions with Prussia, Louis Philippe had initially accused them of being behind this brazen fiasco, the King treated it as comic relief and was lenient. He gave the Bonaparte prince a less-than-princely sum of 15,000 francs per year provided he went into exile in America like his more common-sense uncle, Joseph.

Louis Napoleon did in fact sail to America. But he did not stay there long, and when he returned to France for another coup attempt it would be under even less opportune conditions and the penalty for his foolishness would be far more severe.

1840: The Egyptian Crisis and the Germanies

At first glance these two subjects should have nothing in common and many Germans of the period wished they did not, but great power machinations made it so. In particular, and yet again, it was France who took what should have been a diplomatic quarrel and turned it into a major war crisis.

One of the results of Napoleon's Egyptian Campaign at the beginning of the century was the separation of Egypt from the Ottoman Empire. Though it was restored, in a vicious war between 1805 and 1811, the man who did it was Mehemet Ali, an ambitious officer who admired Napoleon and molded his career after him.

Made Pasha of Cairo in 1805, he slaughtered the Mameluke ethnic minority, expanded Ottoman rule into the Sudan and started a massive westernization of the lands he controlled. He raised an Egyptian Army, the first since the days of the Pharaohs, and set his family up as the heredity rulers of a virtually independent Egypt.

By 1840 Mehemet Ali controlled Palestine and Syria as well as Egypt and Sudan, and had the backing of France, the principal customer of her cotton crop. But other members of the Quintuple Alliance supported at least a partly reconstructed Ottoman Empire and excluded France from the negotiations.

Louis Philippe responded to this affront by expanding his army and navy budgets, initiating the construction of new Paris fortifications, the first since the days of the legendary French engineer-general Sébastien de Vauban, and incited a call to recover the Rhine provinces. In this he hoped to capitalize on the recent death of Friedrich Wilhelm III and the ascension to the throne of his son, Friedrich Wilhelm IV.

All Philippe ended up doing was rallying the German Confederation to Prussia's side and mobilizing most of the German armies. Austria mobilized its army and a joint British/Austrian fleet rapidly took control of the Mediterranean, assisting in Turkish operations to retake Syria, and eventually making a show of force off Alexandria which compelled Mehemet Ali to come to terms. And in the midst of all this, on August 6th to be exact, events once again turned amusing.

Reprising his role as Bonnie Prince Charlie, Louis Napoleon Bonaparte returned to France to claim the throne. This time he crossed the English Channel with a corps of around 50 true believers, and a pet eagle, to land at Vimereux near Boulogne. An apocryphal tale from this incident claims the eagle flew away the first chance it got. If this is true then it acted with some common sense as Louis and his "army" were quickly arrested as conspirators.

This time Louis Philippe took a dim view of the farce by giving him a life sentence and sending him to the prison/fortress at Ham in northeastern France. Bonaparte arrived at his new home at about the same time the coalition fleet bombarded the port city of Beirut and landed part of the Ottoman force which recaptured Syria within a month.

The crisis ended in early November with Mehemet Ali accepting Allied terms and the downfall of the most recent Thiers Ministry. However, the budget increases to the French Army and Navy remained and the fortress construction continued. This caused tensions between France and the Germanies to lessen only very gradually, which in turn served the cause of German unity by strengthening alliances between Prussia and the smaller German states.

The year ended on a grandly ironic note with Philippe welcoming another Bonaparte back to France – the original one. On November 30th a French ship docked in Cherbourg carrying the body of Napoleon Bonaparte. His journey from the remote island of St. Helena in the South Atlantic was almost over.

A few days later, on a cold and somber December morning, a magnificent funeral carriage drawn by a team of 16 horses returned Napoleon to Paris. Built to commemorate his victories, but not finished until long after his death, the procession took Napoleon for the first and last time under the completed Arc de Triomphe.

As it did so, the sun broke through the grey mists. While it gave little warmth it was brilliant, it illuminated everything. Just like the sun at Austerlitz, exactly 35 years earlier, on the day of his greatest victory. The cries of "Vive l'Empereur!" filled the streets and carried the procession to the Hôtel des Invalides, where a new tomb had been built under the dome of its chapel for Napoleon.

There he was laid to rest, back in the city he so loved, but if Louis Philippe thought he was burying Bonapartism along with the first Bonaparte he was sadly mistaken. Not even the embarrassing fiasco of Louis Napoleon's second coup attempt could blunt the growing cult of personality around the late-emperor.

Whether it was the poetry of Alphonse de Lamartine, whose political actions a decade later would be so important to the next Napoleonic empire, or the songs about the "Little Corporal" by Pierre Jean de Béranger, or the early works of Victor Hugo, the history of Europe's then most-notorious dictator was being transmuted into the romanticized legend of a Republican hero.

Even the long-suppressed paintings of Napoleon's court painter Jacques Louis David were again on public display. Especially his iconographic masterpiece *Le Premier Consul Franchissant le Mont Saint-Bernard*, loosely translated as *Napoleon at Saint-Bernard's Pass*, was accepted as accurate when in reality Bonaparte climbed the pass on a mule and not a white charger with flowing mane and tail.

In the Germanies this burnishing of the Napoleonic legend was treated with rather less apprehension than the sustained, post-crisis, increases in France's military budgets and the continued construction of new Paris defences. They did more than give the Prussian Military Intelligence Service something to investigate. They served as a continual impetus to greater and greater military cooperation inside the German Confederation.

Already, three times since the end of Napoleon's Wars, French revolutions and political crises had threatened the Confederation's states with insurrection and war. Nor would they be the last, for the most dangerous was to come.

And yet, through it all the German philosophers and poets continued to idealize the future united German state without giving much thought of the mechanisms that would form or forge it. However, one of the lesser lights did at least provide a symbolic contribution to a united Germany, and he would live to see it put into action.

August Heinrich Hoffmann von Fallersleben was, by 1841, a professor of German language and literature at the University of Breslau in Prussia. In this year he would publish a book, *Unpolitische Gedichte*, that was critical of the Prussian government and would lead to his removal. But on September 1ˢᵗ the martyr would publish a poem meant as a paean to the mythical united Germany. It's title: "Deutschland, Deutschland, über alles"..."Germany, Germany, above all."

The mythical state just got its national anthem.

out among them.

Nothing illustrates this better than the Alliance suppression of the Imperial Free City of Krakow, the last piece of free Polish soil on the continent. By the early 1840s Paris had become the principal gathering spot for political refugees from all across Europe; Karl Marx would arrive there by November of 1843. Two years later it had become a hotbed for Polish refugees plotting yet another revolution to regain their homeland.

Previous such uprisings had started in Russia's Kingdom of Poland and were effectively crushed there. This time the conspirators planned to start their revolution with simultaneous insurrections in Prussia and Austria's Polish provinces and later spread it to Russian-held lands.

Alas, their activities were fully documented by the French police, and duly reported to the Austrian and Prussian governments. They easily destroyed the revolts in their provinces, then Metternich secured Prussian and Russian consent for the Austrian conquest of Krakow. Even though the city-state raised an army of 40,000 and had some initial successes, it was defeated and subjugated by March of 1846.

Outside of crushing its own revolt, Prussia took little part in Austria's operations for it had bigger problems confronting it. Two years earlier, in 1844, a major depression had spread through all the states in the German Confederation. Economic development stalled, workers lost their jobs and very quickly, far quicker than would happen in modern times, riots and unrest spread throughout the states.

This meant the police, local militia but most especially the regular armies were used to suppress the riots and maintain what all Germans craved the most: order. In the midst of all this, on July 8th of 1846, King Christian VIII of tiny Denmark added to the woes of all Germans and the Germanies by publicly announcing his plans to annex the principalities which his house had some claim to: Schleswig and Holstein.

Even German Liberals, meeting in the first Landtag – the first united Prussian Parliament – would debate the issue of Denmark's threat. They would have done well to also discussed an even greater future threat to the Germanies, one who also made news in 1846.

After spending six years in a relatively luxurious prison, during which time he wrote a very socialistic book titled *The Extinction of Poverty*, Louis Napoleon Bonaparte finally tired of prison life and executed a spectacularly easy escape from the Ham fortress by disguising himself as a stone mason and joining a work crew. Afterwards it was a leisurely stroll across the Belgian frontier and on to Britain. There he started planning yet another coup attempt, and this time he resolved to be less reckless and more patient.

In reality Louis Napoleon would not have to be *that* patient, for the revolution he saw coming would arrive faster than he or anyone else predicting it could have anticipated. Not even the radicals gathering in Paris would be ready for it, for by 1847 most had been imprisoned or expelled from France. Karl Marx got tossed out by the latest Guizot Ministry some two years earlier, Friedrich Engels followed him to Britain shortly afterwards, the iconoclastic Russian anarchist Mikhail Bakunin left for Switzerland while Heinrich Heine was allowed to remain by virtue of his "celebrity" radical status.

Marx, Engels and most of the other German and eastern European radicals gathered either in Belgium, Brussels specifically, or London. They traveled more between those cities than to their native homelands, and it was in London where their newly organized federation called the Communist League would have its first major conference.

Late in 1847 the League commissioned Marx to write a document stating the beliefs and aims of the organization. Working off a first draft by Engels, he had it ready in the opening weeks of the new year. Though by then events had outpaced the radical philosophers, and the revolution *The Manifesto of the Communist Party* had been prepared for was already breaking out.

1848: A Continent in Revolt

Most contemporary accounts of this momentous event date its start to late February and Paris, when rioting broke out at a Liberal/Reform banquet commemorating George Washington's birthday. This suits Communists and Socialists as, by February 22nd, Marx's manifesto had been released and they could claim credit for sparking the continent-wide insurrection. It suits American historians as they could lay some claim that the greatest hero of the American Revolution helped ignite this one. It even suited the Germans of the period, such as freshman Parliament Member Otto von Bismarck, since the later date proves 1848 was a "French" revolution which spread to the rest of Europe.

In reality all of this is untrue as the wave of revolution had broken out nearly six weeks earlier, and it began in Italy. On January 12th a popular revolt against the hated Bourbon rulers spread from the port city of Palermo to all of Sicily within a few days. By January 27th it had gained the attention of the Italian revolutionary leaders Giuseppe Manzzini and Giuseppe Garibaldi, and jumped the Messina Straits to start an insurrection in Naples.

Now the First Age of Mass Communications, and in particular the telegraph, spread news of the revolts faster and farther than any other time in history. After a brief lull, Tuscany in central Italy arose and proclaimed itself a republic on February 15th. A week later the riots started in Paris after the aforementioned banquet, and from there the conflagration did indeed spread like wildfire.

On February 23rd the National Guard was called out to quell the Paris rioting, and promptly sided with the rioters. Two days later Louis Philippe followed Charles X and abdicated, leaving Paris for the temporary safety of St. Cloud. And two days after that, at Place de la Bastille, the Second French Republic was announced.

At the beginning of March an insurrection in County Tipperary causes the British Government to suspend *Habeas Corpus* across Ireland. Between then and the middle of March the Hungarian legislature begins an open revolt, the Austrian Provincial Diet is overrun by a mob and Vienna descends into chaos. Berlin is swept by rioting *after* a mob gathers at the imperial palace to thank the King for proposing liberal reforms while all of Italy and Sicily are in either open warfare or insurrection. Poles are in revolt in Posen and Krakow, the Chartists are threatening a national strike in Britain and even in Switzerland the federal government unravels after the Catholic cantons threaten secession.

If modern telecommunications technology had existed in this era, had there been 24-hour news cycles, all-news radio stations and television networks, one would have thought the world was coming to an end. That civilization was disintegrating through some mutual compact with mass hysteria.

Indeed it was the end of an era. It was the end of the Age of Metternich; on March 13th he resigned his office and by the next day he had fled to Britain. It was the end of Louis Philippe's reign; after staying on the throne longer than Louis XVIII and Charles X combined, he remained about a week in France before fleeing to Britain as well on March 4th with the discredited Guizot.

Only the Scandinavian countries and those on the Iberian Peninsula seemed immune, and Spain and Portugal were exempted from the socialist/Liberal tide because they were too exhausted from the decades of coup attempts and civil wars. And in the midst of all those conflicts, their despotic monarchs had indeed been successful in holding back the future.

Scandinavia, on the other hand, was a rather different story. True, the Kingdom of Sweden and the Grand Duchy of Finland had grown apprehensive over events taking place in the rest of Europe, and very much hoped it would pass them by, but Denmark saw opportunity in the chaos and strife. It saw a chance to take what the great powers had unjustly denied it after the last great European cataclysm had ended 35 years ago.

On March 22nd King Frederick VII, son and successor to Christian VIII, and the ultra-nationalistic Eider-Dane Party declare their intent to take Schleswig and Holstein as Danish troops crossed the southern border. On the very same day, in Berlin a revolutionary mob parading the dead from the previous week's rioting is stopped in its tracks by reports of Denmark's invasion. In Frankfurt au Main a pan-national German revolutionary parliament is also effectively checkmated by the news and adjourns to a later date.

All across the Germanies the news is treated in pretty much the same way; insurrectionist fervor is transmuted into nationalistic wrath. The new catchphrases from Marx's manifesto are replaced by the cry "Germany, Germany, above all!" And the cry was sung to Josef Haydn's old imperial anthem melody to form: "Deutschland, Deutschland über alles." The rest of Europe may be deposing its monarchs and forming republics, but the Germans were marching to war.

Denmark: The War in a Storm

Most contemporary historians treat this incident, if they mention it all, as either comic relief in the middle of a hurricane, or recklessness to the point of insanity. But if Denmark and its leaders were crazy, they were crazy like foxes for they started the war with three great advantages: One, they were operating directly on their southern border with extremely short lines of supply and communications. Two, their main opponent, the Prussian Army, was tied down all across the Germanies with military treaties to the other states in the Confederation. And three, the Danes had a navy while the Germanies had none. Even though it was small, if you have something and your opponents have nothing like it, then you have what could be a decisive advantage.

In fact the first army the Danes met was neither Prussian nor professional. A corps of students from the University of Kiel, augmented by radical volunteers from the other Germanies, joined untrained, inexperienced recruits of the invaded principalities to form a citizen army. They had revolutionary zeal and a patriotic spirit – they thought they were fighting the first battle for a united Germany. They were all but annihilated by Danish troops who were better trained, disciplined, organized and equipped.

The Prussian Army, entrusted by both Berlin and Frankfurt with conducting the war, moved more slowly. In a land that had railroads since 1837, the Prussian and all other German armies still deployed the same way they had since Napoleonic times – via forced marches on military roads. Which meant men, horses and equipment often arrived worn out at their destinations; friction can be as great an enemy to an army as attrition.

Add to the mix confusion as orders to many units were changed or countermanded while in-transit, since not every radical responded to the call for unity. On April 6th, only five days after it convened, a pan-Germanic constitutional parliament in Frankfurt collapses when its most extreme members realize they are not going to get the republic they want. The German Confederation armies are thus forced to deal with both revolutions and a conventional war attempting to capitalize on them.

Europe: The Storm Outside Intensifies

For a time, during the opening weeks of April, it appeared as though the storm might just be subsiding. In Britain the threatened Chartist demonstration/national strike fizzles out on its appointed day, April 10th. Though not before the Duke of Wellington performs one last duty for his country by accepting the command of the military force organized to stop it.

In Paris the Second Republic focused on restoring order and organizing general elections; Karl Marx was even invited to return and found much to his liking. In Rome Pope Pius IX granted liberal concessions and in Frankfurt a popular parliament was to meet and draft a pan-national constitution. Then the storm clouds, never completely gone, boiled back with a vengeance.

By mid-April the German constitutional parliament had dissolved and insurgents were preparing to fight government troops. The Pope renounced his concessions and created an alliance with Austrian forces in northern Italy. The revolt in Naples was being ruthlessly suppressed and Garibaldi had returned to his city with his "Red Shirt" brigades. Hungary, after gaining near autonomy from Vienna, finds its own Serbs and Slavs preparing to revolt. And even in Paris the leftists are agitating after the elections failed to give them what they wanted.

The storm broke anew from mid to late-May with open civil wars in France, Austria, Hungary, the Papal States, Frankfurt and Baden. This time it was not only between Liberal revolutionaries and Royalist forces but, especially in France, between Moderate Liberals and Radicals.

On the Italian peninsula a three-way battle formed between Charles Albert's Kingdom of Sardinia fighting *both* Austria in the north and Naples in the south. Giuseppe Garibaldi allied his Red Shirt brigades with King

Albert – it would be an uneasy alliance – and the Pope sided with Austria.

In France the Liberal Reformers in charge of the Second Republic gave the ex-Royalist General Louis Eugene Cavaignac virtual dictatorial powers to end the fighting. The menacing tone of the opening to Marx's *Manifesto*, and especially the phrase "the spectre of communism" had indeed served as a unity call, though not exactly the way he intended.

Most notably in France, but also across the rest of Europe, it united Moderate Liberals with Conservatives, Royalists and even some Nationalists against their common enemies: Radicals, like Marx himself, and Anarchists, like Mikhail Bakunin. On the left there was no similar move to unity as communists and socialists fell out over petty squabbling, and pure animosity with the anarchists; Marx, for example, detested Bakunin.

Many of the foreign contingents still fighting in France decided it was high time to leave. Engels joined a column of German radicals who crossed the border to carry the revolution into Frankfurt and Baden. There, Prussian and Baden troops slaughtered most of them and scattered the rest, though in his memoirs Engels appears to have enjoyed it, especially becoming a celebrity refugee in Switzerland.

The Germanies and the False Peace of Malmö

Leftist insurrections in Freiburg, Kandern, Frankfurt au Main and over a dozen other locations kept the German armies, and in particular the Prussian Army, tied down in operations other than the war with Denmark. And in most cases these other operations were not merely riot control exercises but pitched battles.

At Freiburg the leftists constructed trenchworks which had to be stormed and at Kandern the army commander was shot from his horse while he was negotiating with the Radicals; after they finished cheering they were routed and slaughtered. These operations lasted throughout April until mid-May when Prussia could finally lead a strong coalition against Danish positions.

In Frankfurt au Main the Federal Diet finally convened, an event celebrated throughout the Confederation. At the same time France was being consumed by civil war and Austria appeared to be descending into anarchy, the Germanies were responding to the chaotic times with order and statecraft.

By the beginning of June the Diet had agreed to create a Confederation Navy to answer the Danish advantage, and responded to the pan-national cries for unity by ordaining the new central executive office of Imperial Vice Regent, the Reichsverweser. Instead of becoming the republic the Radicals and Socialists wanted the Germanies had taken another step toward becoming a unified imperial state.

And while Frankfurt laid the foundations for the future, by quickly electing Archduke John of Austria to the position of Reichsverweser, Berlin went about doing what it did best: conducting a war. Though by the end of July the all-but-forgotten German-Danish War was not going well.

Militarily the course of events could scarcely have been better. The coalition army, actually mostly Prussian and Saxon troops, gained victories at Dannewirk and Oversee and stood ready to roll back the outnumbered and outgunned Danish Army. However, if "the spectre of Communism" was scaring the hell out of most European monarchs, then the spectre of foreign intervention was haunting Berlin. The little bully had big friends.

Fearing this cabinet war in the middle of a hurricane would only further spin events out of control, an alliance of Great Britain, Russia and a very nervous Sweden put pressure on the combatants to accept a truce and agree to negotiate an end to the crisis. They did not wish to reward Denmark's aggression, but they also did not want to see German troops carry out their generals' wishes to reduce every Danish village, town and city to ashes in retribution for the damages done to the principalities and the German coasts by the Danish fleet.

While Friedrich Wilhelm IV and other German sovereigns received the new Imperial Vice Regent in grand ceremonies, negotiations quietly began in the city of Malmö in Sweden. A treaty was signed on August 26th, providing for a seven months truce, the return of all prisoners-of-war, the disbanding of the Schleswig-Holstein Army and joint rule of the disputed lands by both Prussia and Denmark.

Most Germans were dumbstruck by the news, and the Federal Diet repudiated the treaty. Still, the Prussian delegation brought it to a formal vote in early September, where it was formally rejected and the new-formed German Ministry under the Imperial Vice Regent resigned, never to be resurrected. What could have been an important step toward German unification was stillborn.

It's hard to believe a peace treaty could cause such problems, but worse was to come. Legislatively at least, calmer heads did prevail for a second vote was taken on the Malmö Treaty by September 17th and this time it got accepted. The immediate response was a call by Radicals to dissolve the Diet and the South German states, curiously the ones who did not have troops actually in the war, began a revolt.

The very next day, two conservative leaders from the Diet, Prince

Lichnovski and General von Auerswald, are seized and lynched by a Radical mob at the Frankfurt city gates. There's wild cheering throughout the streets over this "victory" – until it is realized, far too late, that the two had been part of a delegation heading out of the city to meet a Prussian Army column.

Ironically enough on the same day, September 18th, another Radical mob similarly attacked and killed Emperor Ferdinand of Austria's personal military commander in Hungary. On the bridge separating the cities of Buda and Pesth, General Lamberg got dragged from his carriage and torn to pieces. What was left of his body was eventually hung in front of imperial ministry buildings.

The response from both Prussia and Austria was pretty much the same: to unleash the dogs of war. By September 20th Prussian troops had Frankfurt under martial law. By September 24th they were defeating insurrectionist columns at Staufen near the Swiss border, and the Diet was reinstated at Frankfurt. In Austria, with the best units of its army fighting the Kingdom of Sardinia in Italy, the war against insurgent forces was not going nearly so well – a Bohemian revolt had pushed Austrian troops out of Prague and a Hungarian column had driven the royal family from Vienna.

The Approaching Hour of Louis Napoleon

By the end of June, southern England had become a crowded place for Royalist refugees. Louis Philippe and Francois Guizot arrived in Newhaven on March 4th, Metternich appeared in London in April and even the Hohenzollern Crown Prince arrived later in the month. His efforts at clearing the Berlin streets of rioters in mid-March had earned him the nickname "the Cartridge Prince," and for his safety the family decided to send him to Britain.

All of this may just have made Louis Napoleon Bonaparte feel time had come for a change in scenery. With little other apparent reasoning he arrived in Paris at the end of June, just as the heaviest fighting was ending. For Cavaignac and the moderates trying to hold the infant republic together this distraction could scarcely have come at a worse time. They quickly asked him to leave, preparing to expel him from the country, but with uncharacteristic discreetness he departed after meeting with some of his followers.

The discreetness continued through July and August with France preparing for a new round of elections and appearing the very model of stability, while the rest of the continent was consumed by war. From Sicily to the Swiss border all of Italy was wracked with battles as Sardinia fought Austria, Naples and even the Papal States for Italian unity. Austria appeared ready for disintegration with ethnic groups fighting each other and the central government. And finally the German Confederation had conventional war in the north and civil war in the south.

The September elections were peaceful, by all accounts fair, and rewarded Louis Napoleon with wins in no less than five departments/districts out of 840 constituencies. With further uncharacteristic adroitness he declined to serve as a deputy in the new National Assembly, but declared himself a candidate for President in the next round of elections set for November. His hour had arrived.

His opponents were General Cavaignac and the politician/poet Alphonse de Lamartine, and they never stood a chance. For a dozen years the Bonaparte Prince had tried to use his uncle's stature and legend in the most obvious and amateurish ways to gain power. His 1836 coup attempt just happened to coincide with the completion and dedication of his uncle's most famous architectural monument, the Arc de Triomphe. The attempt in 1840 tried to take advantage of the greatly anticipated return of Napoleon to Paris. And in the interim he published an idealized account of his uncle's career: *Napoleonic Ideas*.

Now, all the glories of his family's rehabilitated and burnished name fell on him almost without asking. Even his earlier fiascoes became advantages as they were committed against the now-reviled Louis Philippe. Far more effective than any political party, for there was no Bonapartist Party pushing his candidacy, Louis Napoleon had achieved what every politician running for high office could hope they would become: a national phenomenon who transcended class and political distinctions.

While there were some people, such as Radicals, who voted for Napoleon because he was not the dictatorial Cavaignac. Most people voted for his because of his name, because they felt he offered stability and because in carefully-worded speeches he offered something for every class. In the end, out of roughly seven million votes cast, five million went to Louis Napoleon Bonaparte: the first, and soon to be only, President of the Second Republic.

Austria: Reversals of Fortune

Unlike Prussia and the German Confederation, who were weathering the storm of revolution far better than any other region, the Austrian Empire seemed ready to unravel and disappear in the spreading anarchy. At first Emperor Ferdinand tried to ride the tiger and granted reforms, especially to Hungary. But events there, as in the Italian provinces, the Polish, Czech and Slavic regions, were flying out of control by the middle of the year.

Then the Emperor reversed his actions late in September and declared the Hungarian parliament dissolved. The immediate result of this was Hungarian rebels took control of Vienna and the royal family fled to Olmütz. There he counterattacked by ordering the general who had crushed the Bohemian revolt in Prague, Prince Alfred Windischgrätz, and the commander of Croatian forces in Hungary, Marshal Josef Jellacic, to rendezvous outside of Vienna.

In Italy the victories of Marshal Johann Wenzel Radetzky, one of the last heroes from the Napoleonic Wars still in service anywhere, over Sardinia and its insurgent allies at Custozza and Milan, allows an armistice to be signed with Charles Albert. By the middle of October the link-up between Windischgrätz and Jellacic is effected. They begin the investment of Vienna on October 23rd, and wheel around to counter a Magyar army advancing from Hungary on the 28th.

Between the end of October and the second week of November there are a series of furious battles in and around Vienna. The city was bombarded, the Magyar army defeated and Austrian troops took the city by storm; those rebels not killed in combat were given summary courts-martial and executed. By the 1st of December operations around Vienna had ended and the royal family returned to the imperial palace. But the year of revolution proved too much for Ferdinand I.

On December 2nd he formally abdicated in favor of his brother, Archduke Francis Charles. Surprisingly, no one had bothered to ask him if he wanted the crown, and he turned it down the same day it was offered. The Hapsburg family convened an emergency council and by December 3rd declared the 18 year-old son of Francis Charles would be the next emperor. Franz Josef I would be one of the longest-serving monarchs in the Hapsburg line; he would also be the next to last.

Prussia: The Last Liberal Battle

The "humiliation" of the Malmö Treaty and the suppression of revolts in the southern German states finally proved too much for the Moderate Liberals in the Prussian Parliament. In early October, with operations south of the Main River ending and troops from the Denmark front starting to return, it passed a resolution ordering all officers to leave Army service out of sympathy to the German democratic movement.

This met with little success, as did repeated attempts by Radicals to accost the returning troops as they entered Berlin and other Prussian cities. Parliament succeeds in forcing the Minister of War from office, but after this King Friedrich Wilhelm IV refuses any more concessions or reforms and by mid-October he dissolves the rest of the cabinet forced on him.

He appoints Count Friedrich von Brandenburg to form his new cabinet and, with a threat by some Parliament members to call out Berlin's Municipal Guards to depose him, he dissolves the Guards on October 31st. The newly returned Prussian Army carried out the order with few incidents, which left Parliament with few options to respond.

On November 15th they thought they found an answer to a King many believed "will not listen to the truth." They issued an edict for people not to pay their taxes. Within hours Friedrich Wilhelm responds with his own royal order dissolving Prussia's Parliament and proclaiming a Royal Constitution will be written by a new legislative body, Chambers, on February 24th of next year.

Effectively checkmated at every turn the Liberals, never a cohesive force in Prussia or any of the other Germanies, saw their democracy movement collapse. Bureaucratic Liberals chose to stick with the Stein and Hardenberg traditions of working with the crown to achieve some reforms. Moderate Liberals either dropped out of politics altogether, changed political affiliations or emigrated to Britain and the United States.

As for the Radicals, many of those not in prison also emigrated, just not as far. Disappointed by the changes in France, disillusioned with the Germanies, some still thought revolution had a chance in Austria and followed their heroes, like Federal Diet member Robert Blum, who joined the rebels in Vienna. This would be a dangerous move as, shortly after Austrian troops retook the city, Blum was among the first executed by firing squad.

1849: The Second Year of "The Year of Revolution" Begins

With the matter settled in France and the German Confederation, or so everyone thought, the focus of insurrection activities shifted to the Austrian Empire and the Italian peninsula. By January 1st the Austrian Army commanded by Windischgrätz and Jellacic had crossed the Hungarian border at the Leitha River and were advancing on the cities of Buda and Pesth. This forced the Hungarian secessionist government to withdraw from the cities and retreat into the mountains of northern Hungary. On January

5th, 1849, Austrian troops entered the cities.

For a few weeks it all appeared quiet, as if the "Year of Revolution" had truly spent itself. Then, at the beginning of February, the storm returned in a week with King Charles Albert declaring a resumption of the Austrian-Sardinian War (on February 1st), the defeat of the Austrian Army at Hermannstadt by a Polish/Hungarian force (on February 4th), a revolt in Tuscany drove Duke Leopold into exile and Rome formally deposed Pope Pius IX as its ruler and declared itself a republic (both on February 7th).

Revolution was back and, as if anarchy needed company, the Treaty of Malmö lapsed on February 26th with Denmark announcing it was readying for war. This time the German Confederation made a more organized response with the mobilization of Prussian, Saxon and Bavarian troops. And two days earlier, Friedrich Wilhelm IV convened the new Chambers in Berlin and ordained it to create a "constitutional charter" by January of next year.

Emperor Franz Josef did not wait that long. On March 4th, after Austrian victories at Essak and Kapolna, he annuls the old Hungarian and Austrian constitutions and issues a new one declaring the whole Austrian Empire is one indivisible country and constitutional monarchy.

This meant the welter of nationalities in the empire would all officially be equal. And to all except the most radical German this meant unity with Austria would be impossible. Whether it was the "Rechtsstaat" or "Ständestaat," the future united Germany was for Germans only. It was not to include Hungarians, Czechs, Slavs, Serbs, Poles, Croatians, Italians or any of the other two dozen races contained in the Austrian Empire.

The Danish-German War: Round Two

While Italians, Poles and Hungarians energetically battled the Austrians throughout February and March, Denmark took its time restarting its war with the Germanies. Not until April 3rd, when it commenced operations by shelling Alkton Island, just off the peninsula's Baltic Sea coast.

Denmark's tiny but vital navy carried out the attack and, two days later, moved farther south to coordinate with the Danish Army in an attack on Eckenfoerde. It was here, in this narrow inlet, that military history was made when Prussian shore batteries engaged the battle group. Using rifled-barreled muzzle-loaders and ballistically-shaped shells, they sink the ship named after the monarch who started events rolling toward this war: the *Christian VIII*.

Before the engagement is over, it, the pride and flagship of the Danish

Navy, goes down along with the frigate *Gefion* and one smaller warship. The decisive defeat of wooden-hulled ships by shore batteries using modern weapons would start naval architects thinking of ways to protect them: especially Dupuy de Lôme in France and the Swedish-emigré John Ericsson in America.

After this disaster the war was seemingly lost for Denmark. By April 13th Saxon and Bavarian troops overwhelm Danish positions at Dueppel, and a week later Prussian soldiers with Schleswig-Holstein volunteers occupy the Jutland Peninsula to deliver a stinging defeat at Kolding. And then, on April 23rd, Friedrich Wilhelm IV rejects the "pig crown" and the constitutional monarchy it represents when it's offered by the German National parliament. He withdraws the Prussian delegation from Frankfurt, and ignites a wave of armed revolts across the Germanies.

From the last week of April until early May there are uprisings in Hesse, Baden, Würtemberg, the Rhine Provinces of Prussia and the Bavarian Palatinate. The King of Saxony flees the capital of Dresden and Prussia begins recalling troops from the battlefront.

On May 7th the Danes attempt to take advantage of the growing chaos by launching an attack from their fortress at Fridericia. However, there were still enough Prussians on the front lines to defeat the column and push its remnants back into the fortress, where what is left of the Danish Army is invested.

Austria: The Last Campaign of the Holy Alliance

At around the same time Prussia was curtly dissolving the German National Parliament by taking over all conduct of the Danish-German War, the youthful Emperor of Austria was meeting Czar Nicholas I in Warsaw, then the capital of Russia's Polish kingdom. Franz Josef had called for the meeting to invoke those articles of the Holy Alliance where the signatory crowned heads would come to each other's defence if threatened by internal revolt.

With civil wars raging throughout his realm, and a war with the Kingdom of Sardinia still to be concluded, Josef badly needed outside help to maintain his throne. And while Russia was the least effected of all the major powers by the "Year of Revolution," Nicholas I was an imperial absolutist and had already crushed a liberal uprising, the Decemberist Revolt of 1825, on his own accession to power. He despised the liberal movements and reforms sweeping through Europe, he even hated Friedrich Wilhelm's newly-decreed Constitutional Charter, and eagerly wanted to crush the contagion before it reached his domain.

Two weeks after their rulers met, and in the city where Napoleon Bonaparte codified his greatest victory, Russian and Austrian forces arrived in Pressburg (Bratislava) and began preparing the invasion of Hungary. By mid-June they were on the move and, while the Hungarian Army tried to stop it, the columns from Pressburg soon linked up with the rest of the Austrian Army.

On June 28th the coalition took the city of Raab, Hungary while Franz Josef looked on. Three days later, at Waitzen, the Hungarian commander General Goergy wins what proves to be the final victory by Hungarian forces. From here until the middle of August there is only retreat and surrender. It is during this time that the Austrians gain a significant prize when they captured Mikhail Bakunin. He would be held for two years until, in 1851, the Austrian court sentenced him to death, then handed him over to Russia's tender mercies.

Napoleon Shows His Imperial Side

For the first few months of his rule Louis Napoleon Bonaparte kept up the pretense of being a good republican President. Back in January the pretender to the Spanish throne, Don Carlos, is arrested by French officials as he tried to cross the southern border to join the newest Spanish revolution, in Catalonia.

However, by April he had launched a naval expedition to restore Pope Pius to rule over Rome. In so doing he commits the worst crime the leader of a republic, or a democracy, could do: he went to war against another republic. By the end of the month Giuseppe Garibaldi is forced to fall back on Rome to help Mazzini against French siege operations.

By early June the siege arouses republican opposition throughout France to Louis Napoleon's rule. When the Chamber of Deputies refuses to impeach his ministry, a new round of uprisings begins in Paris, Lyons and Marseilles. They manage to spread to other cities before the army puts them down.

With internal opposition effectively suppressed, Louis Napoleon orders the siege to enter its final stages. On June 14th the bombardment of Rome starts. On July 3rd expedition troops enter the city, the French commander gives Garibaldi and five thousand of his followers safe passage from Rome. However, once outside its confines, the Red Shirts are attacked by Austrian and Neopolitan troops. Most were killed or captured but Garibaldi, unlike Bakunin, managed to flee into temporary exile in New York City.

On July 14th, approximately eight months after Pope Pius IX had been smuggled out of a city in revolt by the Bavarian ambassador, he returned to Rome, and immediately launches an Inquisition against his surviving opponents. Though he is grateful to the French, their troops will garrison the city for another 22 years, Pius begins using his alliance with Austria as a counter-balance to Louis Napoleon. He endorses Franz Josef's assault on the Venice Republic, and two weeks later Austrian forces entered the city.

As for Louis Napoleon, his imperial ambitions temporarily assuaged, he returns to the facade of a republican ruler. He begins planning major construction projects, ones that will turn Paris from a filthy, claustrophobic medieval city into something what Ludwig I of Bavaria rebuilt Munich into: a city with widened streets, public squares and outdoor lighting. Paris was not the first municipality to be called "the City of Light." But Louis Napoleon will make it the greatest.

The German-Danish War: Another Reversal of Fortune

Prussia's decision to take over all conduct of this war in mid-May could not have happened at a worst possible time. In addition to losing, almost overnight, all its allies on the battlefront, it had to dispatch units all across the Germanies. By the end of month the Prussian Army was engaged in crushing resurgent uprisings in virtually every German state it had treaty obligations.

From Saxony, next door, to Bavaria in the extreme south its army was again being forced marched along military roads, being separated into ever smaller units and often spending days out of touch with higher commands. Once again friction and confusion were superseding attrition in wearing down an army facing many little enemies instead of one.

And Denmark bided its time. Its May 7th operation had been less disastrous than premature. Its generals waited until most of the forces investing Fridericia were Schleswig-Holstein volunteers and not professional troops. It waited until July 5th to launch a new offensive. One which nearly succeeded in breaking out and inflicting a huge defeat on the remaining German forces.

Some 28 guns and 1,500 prisoners were taken, and 3,000 German dead were left on the battlefield. For Prussia the incident would be the last straw breaking its overextended back. It had no navy to speak of, the German Confederation had only just started building a coalition one, and its army was being worn down suppressing revolts throughout the Germanies, many of whom openly hated its new constitutional charter as too "liberalizing" an influence on their populations.

And then there were Denmark's allies. To the alliance of Russia, Sweden and Great Britain Louis Napoleon added France. The war in Sicily had ended back in April with the Kingdom of Naples victorious over the Sicilian Republic. France had crushed the Roman Republic a few days earlier. Austria was about to conclude a peace treaty with Victor Emmanuel II, the new-crowned King of Sardinia, and with its Russian ally was finishing off the Hungarian revolt. The wars across Europe were ending, and the major powers wanted this Danish one to end as well.

The combatants returned to Malmö and by July 10th Prussia, not the German Confederation, signed a treaty which ended the war. It made Holstein a Danish province and split the control of Schleswig between the two with a five-man ruling council. Nobody got exactly what they wanted, though Denmark received more than it deserved, as did Prussia. Throughout the Germanies it, rightly or wrongly, was blamed for the loss of the war and the loss of the two principalities.

1850: The Third Year of "The Year of Revolution"

At least the year 1850 began well enough for Prussia. On January 31st Friedrich Wilhelm IV presented the new constitutional charter to its parliament and easily got it adopted. By February 6th he swears his oath to it in a formal ceremony.

Taken on its own, Prussia's new constitution was a progressive, modestly liberal, in the Stein-Hardenberg tradition of Bureaucratic Liberalism. Instead of the very radical, for the times, equal suffrage law it created a three-class suffrage system that weighted and divided votes according to income. What the country got was a constitutional monarchy with mixed powers and the old order largely intact.

Unfortunately, almost no one in the rest of the German Confederation took it well. The more reactionary states resented, even feared it as too liberal, which to them was a hated word in any context. The more progressive states resented it because it did not go far enough. And everywhere people noted it was so much like the previous year's national unity constitution – actually, it was not – that they wondered why it and the "pig crown" of a unified Germany had been rejected by Prussia.

But mostly it was hated because it was Prussian. Because it showed Prussia determined to go its own way and drag the rest of Germany with it. And it did not help that Prussia had not only lost a war to a much smaller power but lost sacred German soil to it as well.

Then, on the other hand, there was Austria. It had just finished waging a successful series of wars in Hungary, northern Italy and its Polish and Czech provinces. The names of its successful commanders – Marshal Johann Wenzel Radetzky, Ludwig von Benedek, Alfred Windischgrätz and Josef Jellacic – were well-known and celebrated. No one talked about Prussia's commanders. Not even "Cartridge Prince" Wilhelm, the King's brother, or the rising star of its army's command staff, Helmuth von Moltke. Then again no one talked about the vital aid Russia gave to Austria...but when your star is rising why quibble about the details?

The Humiliating of Prussia

It began the same week Prussia celebrated its new constitution. In early-February Austria's ministers convince Hanover to withdraw from the alliance of North German Powers. Later, when Saxony withdraws, only Prussia would be left. By the end of the month the kings of Bavaria, Würtemberg and Saxony sign a joint agreement calling for a restoration of the German Confederation.

Between mid-June and early-July the last sputterings of the German-Danish War served to further embarrass Prussia. A volunteer army starts a revolt in Holstein and spreads to Schleswig. However, under threat from Britain, France and Sweden, Prussia must refuse them aid. It all ends with a defeat by the Danish Army at Idstedt. An unremarkable battle except for the appearance of William Russell of *The Times* newspaper. The Age of the War Correspondent had arrived.

Later in July the Bundestag reconvenes in Frankfurt and Prussia's latest failure only serves to confirm its loss of political control and influence. Austria is in charge and calls for the reassembly of the old Confederation.

This reality gets reinforced some two months later with the crisis in the Duchy of Hesse-Cassel. Its Archduke and Prime Minister are forced to flee after their attempt to illegally impose new taxes sparks insurrection. They appeal to Frankfurt to restore them to power, the revolt leaders appeal to Berlin for support, and Prussia responds first by sending troops from Baden.

However, Austria and the rest of the Confederation side with the Archduke and, in early-October, Emperor Franz Josef meets the Kings of Bavaria and Würtemberg in Bregenz, Austria, a border city on the eastern shore of Lake Bodensee. There they decide to force Prussia out of both Baden and Hesse-Cassel. Josef then went on to Warsaw where he met again with Czar Nicholas I and, in spite of the arrival of Prussia's Prime Minister

Friedrich von Brandenburg, he secures Russian support for the coalition.

What followed, between the end of October and the end of November, was a humiliating disaster for Prussia. Both she and Austria mobilized their armies, on November 8th the vanguards of the respective forces skirmished inside Hesse-Cassel where a single Prussian horse is killed. Under threats from seemingly every quarter: Austria, Russia, Bavaria and several other German states, Prussia withdraws her troops.

On November 21st Austria's ambassador to Berlin, speaking on behalf of the restored German Confederation, demanded the withdrawal of all Prussian forces from Hesse-Cassel and Baden, and for it to be completed in 48 hours. Eight days later, on November 29th in Olmütz, Austria, the humiliation was codified in a treaty many Prussians called "the Shame of Olmütz."

At the stroke of a pen almost all of Prussia's remaining military alliances throughout the Germanies were dissolved. Everywhere its army was ordered to march back to its borders; from now on its forces would only be allowed to operate in conjunction with the rest of the Confederation. Not since the Tilsit Treaties had been imposed on it by Napoleon Bonaparte some 43 years earlier had Prussia been so humiliated. The coda to all this came approximately a year and a half later at a conference of Great Powers in London.

There the succession problem to Danish rule was settled, even though the German Confederation refused to recognize it. But the Confederation was forced, by Austria and Prussia, to accede to the conference's demand to sell off the navy it had started in 1848 at public auction.

The Death of the Second Republic

For France and Louis Napoleon 1850 was a relatively quiet year. Plans not only for the rebuilding of Paris but the completion of the city's fortifications begun by Louis Philippe were being formulated, with the energetic Baron George-Eugène Houssmann gaining Napoleon's favor. However, increasingly virulent attacks by the press were gaining his ire and by the end of August he enacted new press restrictions.

From here until the end of the year the political crisis his measures sparked only grew worse. Finally, on January 3rd of 1851, Napoleon's Ministry is forced to resign. He responds by dissolving the Assembly and removing the very republican General Changarnier from command of the Paris garrison.

These are the opening shots of a slow-motion, two-stage coup d'etat, covered by a year-long political turmoil. The National Assembly successfully fights its dissolution, Napoleon counters by making public appeals and meeting privately with royal conspirators. Most of it amazingly subtle for a man who once thought he could conquer France by wading ashore with a pet eagle on his arm. By December 1st all elements are in place.

Under the guise of an informal holiday reception at the Elysée Palace, Louis Napoleon meets the princes, generals and other conspirators. At 5:00AM the following morning army units moved out of their barracks and fortresses to positions in Paris and other major cities. Leading opposition members of the National Assembly are arrested, newspapers and other printing presses are seized to begin the mass manufacture of proclamations announcing a favored tactic of Napoleon's uncle: a national plebiscite, to be held on December 14th. The National Assembly is again dissolved, and this time it's done by troops.

Almost at once pro-Republic demonstrators pour onto the Paris streets. Napoleon tolerates them until the morning of December 4th when he orders the army to restore order; by the evening nearly a thousand have been shot. Three days later the Assembly brazenly tries to meet in opposition. This results in 180 more members being arrested and on the same day two lists of names are released: the first is for a "consultive" committee to advise the President, the second is an "enemies list" of individuals to be exiled.

With few disruptions the plebiscite is held a week later and the results announced on the 21st: Napoleon wins a ten year term by a better than 11 to 1 ration and is authorized to issue a new constitution. Like his uncle, he moves swiftly to capitalize on his victory. On New Year's Day of 1852 he is reinstalled as President of France at Notre Dame Cathedral. By January 10th he banishes 83 members of the old Assembly and on the 14th his new constitution is made public. It creates a new governing body, the *Corps Legislatif*, and gives all real powers to the President.

Just over a week later, January 22nd, Napoleon issues his first demonstration of his new powers. By Presidential Decree all lands and estates of the Orleans family are confiscated. Newspapers in France cannot publish without a government sanction. The beloved phrase "Liberté, Fraternité, Egalité" is forbidden and in public squares everywhere liberty poles are cut down. At month's end, as a new round of elections are announced for February 29th, prominent opponents to Napoleon are being escorted to the Belgian border while 600 others were taken to Le Havre for transport to Devil's Island. Stage one of his coup is complete.

Stage two began after the February elections seats almost all of the government's candidates. At the beginning of April Baron Haussmann is given 80 million francs to begin the rebuilding of Paris while Napoleon goes on a triumphal tour of France. The Second Republic is dead in all but name. To thunderous applause the one country in Europe to have gained democracy from "the Year of Revolution" was throwing it away.

The final discarding of the name would come some eight months later, when the Senate is reconvened in a special session to consider the resumption of the French Empire. Its answer was to order yet another national plebiscite and on November 21st, and by a ratio of better than 30 to 1, voters approve of what most realize is just a name change. And on December 2nd, on the anniversary of the first stage of his coup, the President of France completes it by being installed as Emperor Louis Napoleon Bonaparte III.

1853: The Winners and Losers of "The Year of Revolution"

It was not quite what anyone had hoped or feared, or forecasted. None of the Communist or long-simmering nationalist movements which had flared to life back in 1848 had succeeded. Everywhere they had been crushed, suppressed, compromised. Or, in the case of France, abandoned. And their leaders, who in reality could agree on nothing except how they hated the old order, were scattered – or worse.

Karl Marx and Friedrich Engels were in foreign exile, as were Victor Hugo and Louis Blanc, one of the first modern socialists. At least their surroundings were far better than the hundreds consigned to the forsaken hell off the French Guyana coast, or imprisoned in France like Pierre Joseph Proudhon, one of the founders of the anarchist movement. His co-founder, Mikhail Bakunin, had been sentenced to death by the Austrian court, though had later been turned over to the Russians for exile in Siberia.

Louis Kossuth, once the Prime Minister of a breakaway Hungary, was an exile in America with 20,000 of his countrymen. They were joined by Giuseppe Garibaldi and hundreds of thousands of Italians, Germans and French. They either fled to avoid arrest or because they had grown disillusioned with defeat and turmoil.

At their birth, the Communist and Anarchist movements suffered their first grand failure. They were scattered, imprisoned, unpopular and fought bitterly among themselves. But they were not destroyed and, though it would take decades, their movements would rebuild.

Among the countries involved there were also winners and losers. For its size the greatest winner was Denmark. It never suffered any socialist uprisings and, through the machinations of its big power allies, got to keep its territorial conquests. Likewise Great Britain could be judged the biggest winner among the major states. Its Chartist Movement had dissolved amid the disgrace of its fraudulent giant petition. But, to borrow a phrase from the Duke of Wellington, "it had been a near run thing."

Considering how The Year of Revolution started, the most unlikely winner was Austria. More than once the unraveling of its empire seemed like a forgone conclusion. However, with its young, energetic emperor and the timely intervention of its Holy Alliance partner, it defeated all its enemies and emerged the dominant power among the Germanies. Though even in the glow of victories it had started sowing the seeds of eventual downfall. At the same time President Napoleon made public his new constitution, Emperor Franz Josef announced he was abolishing the right to trial by jury and most other liberal reforms in his own country's constitution. The move shocks most of the other members of the German Confederation. They begin to wonder if Austria should be the dominant power of the Germanies.

Having gained then lost democracy, France was easily the biggest loser in The Year of Revolution. Conversely, and in a supreme example of irony, the biggest individual winner was its now imperial ruler, who had gone from exile to monarch of one of the most powerful nations on earth. With his enemies, royalist, republican and socialist, either dead, scattered or in prison, he would now make France stable and great.

To do this, Napoleon would use his public works projects and overseas conquests. And he would also use what the Roman Emperors employed: bread and circuses, public pageants, and the public did not have long to wait. Barely two months after becoming emperor, on January 30th of 1853, Napoleon III married the Spanish Countess Eugénie Marie de Montijo de Guzman. Shortly afterwards, and almost as a perfect cap piece to the wedding cake, the other crowned heads of the major powers recognized him as the sovereign of France.

And finally there was Prussia. Overall it weathered the years of turmoil and revolt better than any other major power except for England and yet, it had been humiliated and driven from its position as the dominant Germanic power. Its army had not only been driven from the battlefield, it had been driven out of almost every military alliance it once held with other German states. Even its vaunted "wonder weapon" of 1848 had proven a failure: the world's first bolt-action, breech-loading rifle, the Dreyse Needle Gun, used a paper cartridge which apparently could not stand up to the rigors of warfare.

And yet, Prussia had not been destroyed. Unlike the conditions imposed by the Tilsit Treaties, she did not lose half her territory or population, nor was she forced to cut her army in half. Not defeated in any battle, the Prussian Army had been worn down by fighting on too many fronts and repeated deployments across the Germanies. More importantly her industrial and technological base, which would not be ignored today, survived unaffected.

In the midst of their rejoicing, Austria and the German Confederation were tying themselves ever closer to Prussia. Headed by Otto von Bismarck, a Prussian delegation arrives in Vienna to negotiate Austria's entry into the Zollverein, the Pan-Germanic, and Prussian-dominated, trade alliance. By April Austria signs an agreement to be part of the Zollverein for 12 years.

A year earlier the Postal and Telegraph Union, also Prussian-dominated, extends its services to the other states in the Confederation. And for the future there is the German National Railway System, which Prussia will dominate and not just administratively. In the Ruhr valley city of Essen, a Prussian industrialist is forging one of the major links of tomorrow's united Germany. Thin, tall and eternally-excitable, Alfred Krupp was turning his family's steel business into a world-leader through the manufacture of cast-steel railroad wheels, rails, axles and suspension systems. And already he was trying to interest the Prussian War Ministry in something as revolutionary as the Dreyse Needle Gun.

As for the War Ministry, it too was busy. Freed from the obligation to garrison troops all over the German Confederation, they were creating a new Prussian Army. And with its obligation to participate in a Confederation-controlled navy now gone, Prussia was free to develop one of her own. And it would not have long to wait to see what the other major powers were doing in these areas.

The peace Europe wanted to enjoy after more than five years of revolt and turmoil would prove short-lived. In May of 1853 Montenegro rises against Turkish rule. Austria quickly moves to be its protector, frustrating Russia's long-standing ambition to dominate the Balkans, though only temporarily. On July 7th a Russian Army of 80,000 invades Turkey's Danube principalities of Moldavia and Wallachia. Almost at once the British and French fleets arrived in the Dardanelles to support Turkey. By the end of the month there is a Great Powers conference in Vienna to resolve the crisis. But it only delays the inevitable – on November 1st Czar Nicholas I formally declares war on Turkey.

The Crimean War has begun.

Chapter V: Europe, 1859 - 1860 – The Balance of Power Shifts

"Not the least of the qualities that go into the making of a great ruler is the ability of letting others serve him."
-Cardinal Richelieu (1585 - 1642)

The Crimean War and Its Innovations

IN THE ANNALS of military history the Crimean War is synonymous with the words "catastrophe" and "disaster," the latter of which has its roots in Middle French and is derived from Marshal Francois Canrobert's observation that "the British fight as (Queen) Victoria dances."

In reality there was enough incompetence, mismanagement, arrogance and stupidity to besmirch almost all the participants, though it fell to the British to get an epic poem written about the most spectacular of theirs. What has been less written about were the advances and innovations to come out of the conflict, or who were its real winners and losers.

The innovations practically came with the start of the war. On November 30th of 1853, the Russian Navy caught a Turkish squadron of seven frigates and four smaller ships by surprise in Sinope harbor on the Black Sea. Using modern explosive shells, the Russians virtually annihilated the squadron; only one small steamer escaped.

And, as if armor plating on warships needed further emphasis, roughly two years later the first use of ironclads in warfare took place. On October 18th, 1855, the French Navy – not the Union and Confederate Navies on March 9th, 1862 – inaugurated armored ship warfare with the deployment of *Lave, Dévastation* and *Tonnant*: armored battery ships of 1,400 tons displacement, mounting 18 fifty-pound smoothbore cannons and protected by 4 inches of iron plate. They attacked the Russian fortress at Kinburn on the Crimean Peninsular. With negligible damage and two crewmen killed they bombarded the fort into surrender, allowing the rest of the British-French fleet to land their troops.

Less successful was the first use of cast-steel cannon by the British during the siege of Sevastopol. Even though such artillery had been used by Sweden's great warrior-king Gustavus Adolphus during the Thirty Years War more than 230 years earlier, it was distrusted because the metal, while much lighter than wrought iron or bronze, was brittle. And unfortunately British casting methods had not improved much in the interim. The casualties among their artillerymen were appalling; at times they surpassed the toll among their Russian targets.

The use of photography was introduced to the battlefield, as was the first wave of war correspondents, led by the already experienced William Russell of *The Times*. The telegraph was employed, mostly for sending reports, and even the train had its first use. And not only for transporting British and French troops to their embarkation ports but in the Crimean Peninsula, where a Russian railroad was built of Krupp steel.

And, after reports and photographs of the horrific conditions endured by those soldiers were published, some thought was finally given by various military services to improving sanitation and medical care. Perhaps the one true hero to emerge from this blighted war was the heroine Florence Nightingale. Having studied nursing techniques and operations throughout Europe during the previous decade, the British government recruited her to tend the wounded in two hospitals set up in Scutari, outside of Istanbul, Turkey.

Arriving with a mere 38 nurses, the "Lady with the Lamp" found conditions so vile as to be criminal. She fought them, as well as the lack of personnel, lack of equipment, the indifference and incompetence of Lord Raglan and his staff. Aided by the French, another *Times* correspondent named Thomas Chenery and a timely letter to Raglan by Queen Victoria, she won most of her battles. It is no small irony that Fitzroy Raglan, and his even more incompetent Adjutant-General J.B. Estcourt, were to die within a few days of each other in June of 1855 of cholera.

France and Crimea

It is a curious historic anomaly, and probably a cultural prejudice, that Crimea is largely known as an "English" war when, outside of Sardinia, it had the smallest number of troops engaged in the fighting. Almost from the outset France had twice as many troops in the primary theater of operations. They were better equipped, and on the whole better lead.

It's also an anomaly that Marshal Jacques de Saint-Arnaud so passively ceded command of the allied coalition to Lord Raglan. Though this may have been due to his age and already frail health, he too would die in 1855. But other sources claim it had to do with imperial orders.

Napoleon III was, at the start of this war, the newest of the major power rulers. With still another display of uncharacteristic tact and discreetness he allowed Britain to take the lead in diplomatic activities and overall military command. Further he did not participate in any of the operations, even though he apparently wanted to. Bonapartist involvement in Crimea would be limited to his fastidious, fussy cousin, Prince Louis Napoleon, as a division commander.

Partly this occurred because all the theaters of operation in this war were at the other end of the continent. And the Emperor did not want to leave his new domain, nor travel so far away from it, for any length of time. But mostly it happened because he wanted to prove he had outgrown his reckless youth – his days with the Carbonari revolutionaries, or when he thought he could conquer France by wading ashore with a pet eagle. Napoleon III wanted to show he was a mature member of Europe's ruling elite. And because of his tact and overall conduct of French forces, he largely succeeded.

France would emerge as the biggest winner among the major powers from the Crimean War. To be sure, it suffered its own blunders and had almost as many casualties as the British. But it fielded twice the men and, in comparison to its senior partner, had a superbly equipped army and navy. The Crimean War would be its stepping stone to becoming the dominant land power of Europe.

As a footnote to its achievement, the one country that could claim greater success from the war was its tiny ally of Sardinia. Also called the Piedmont, it was Napoleon III who, in yet another sign of his maturity, persuaded its king to join the war. Victor Emmanuel's declaration came in the final months of 1854 when, compared to the bloody and inconclusive combat raging at Inkermann and other battlefields, it seemed like a victory. A Napoleonic one.

Sardinia dispatched ships and 15,000 troops, roughly a division, to the Crimean Peninsula. On August 16th of 1855 it was these troops who repulsed a Russian breakout sortie from Sevastopol, turning the tide in the long siege of this city. It was a victory which resounded around Europe. It forged a closer alliance between Napoleon III and its indispensable

Premier, Count Camillo di Cavour. It also served to further embarrass the power that would be the major loser of the war.

Crimea and the Germanies

Austria was the one combatant power not to have sent forces to the Crimean Peninsula. After only recently regaining the upper hand in the German Confederation and maintaining its dominant power status in Europe it was Austria who ended up the biggest loser in a war where it took little active part in. Not Russia and not Turkey, who pretty much retained their pre-war positions. And not even Great Britain, whose wretched performance brought down the Aberdeen Ministry and initiated much needed military reforms.

It had not started out this way. In 1853 the Great Powers had convened a conference in Vienna to resolve the crisis. When this failed, Czar Nicholas I visited both Franz Josef and Friedrich Wilhelm IV and got them to remain neutral in exchange for a promise not to cross the Danube River. When Russian troops did so in March of 1854 it cracked the Holy Alliance and Prussia and Austria entered a secret agreement to mobilize if Russia moved against the Balkans.

While France and England went to war, and Turkey held off Russian attacks in Moldavia and Wallachia (in the west) and Silistria (in the east) the German powers remained aloof – until Austria signs a treaty with Turkey to liberate the two Danube principalities from Russian control. Its hand had been forced by the imminent arrival of British and French troops in the Black Sea port of Varna, in what is now Bulgaria.

On June 21st, 1854 these forces move against the Russian troops occupying Moldavia and Wallachia. It's the only major operation Austria participates in, fighting is minimal, the Russian Army quickly retreats across the Danube and Pruth Rivers. And the Holy Alliance is forever shattered by the action.

Concurrent with this a British and French fleet arrives in the Baltic Sea in early July. Ostensibly there to bombard the Kronstadt Fortress guarding the entrance to St. Petersburg, it is also in the area to 'persuade' Prussia and Sweden into joining the coalition. However, this would have been easier to accomplish had the fleet succeeded in its original goal and, after more than a month of bombardment operations, it humbly retired. The wooden-hulled ships had learned the lessons of the Danish and Turkish navies and did not press their attacks too close to the fortress. Perhaps the outcome might have been different had France's ironclads been used, but at the time they were still under construction.

Prussia and Sweden easily resisted the persuasion to join; for Austria it was another matter. By the end of the year her Italian rival was preparing to join the war and again she felt her hand being forced. To neutralize Sardinia's action Austria signs a further treaty, this time with France and England, to defend Moldavia and Wallachia, and to not negotiate separately with Russia.

The rest of the German Confederation sees this as Austria pulling them into a war whose blunderings and carnage were being widely reported. At the same time, they begin admiring Prussia for resisting the Anglo-French intimidation and maintaining its neutral stance. But the so-recently humiliated country was not entirely staying out of the Crimean War. It did something far more subtle and largely ignored by the others. Prussia was learning.

Following its own long tradition, and some of the lesser-known precepts of Karl von Clausewitz, the Prussian Army had military observers and advisors on both sides of the conflict. They did their usual studies: of tactics, the performance of men, weapons, logistics, communications and medical systems. And they studied something more, something unique to Clausewitz's theories – they studied "friction." The fatigue, the breakdown of equipment, the minor errors, the bad luck, the transitory good luck no one took advantage of, the failure to inspire or command, all of which thread together to produce disasters – of which there were many in Crimea.

This blighted war does not end until March 30th, 1856. Not until after the death of Nicholas I and the installment of his son, Alexander II, as the new Czar. Not until after the fall of Sevastopol to the coalition armies, in September of 1855. After this Austria cannot move fast enough to urge Napoleon III to convene a peace conference, which he does in Paris.

The treaty signed on March 30th returns most of the conquered lands to their original owners, ensures the freedom of navigation on the Black Sea to all commercial ships, and sets up a new league to replace both the Holy Alliance and the Quintuple Alliance. The Concert of Powers is broader than either as it allows in both Turkey and Sardinia. Europe hopes, once again, this will bring peace. But the groundwork for the next war is already being laid.

1856 - 1859: Build-Up to the Franco-Austrian War

Count Camillo Benso di Cavour – of all the politicians and national leaders of the 19th Century, it is Cavour who comes the closest to the perfect embodiment of the political ideals of his countryman, Niccolo Machiavelli. The guile, cunning, bad faith, duplicity were all there, plus a brilliant sense of timing. And it was on display before the ink had scarcely dried on the Treat of Paris.

In April of 1856 Cavour signs a statement on Austria's mismanagement of its central and southern Italian provinces, just as the peace conference is about to close in Paris. France quickly supports his charges, as does Great Britain. With the Concert of Powers seemingly against her, Austria promises to make major changes.

From May to August Emperor Franz Josef visits his Italian provinces, announcing a general amnesty in Milan and relieving one of Austria's most famous warriors, Marshal Johann Josef Wenzel Radetzky, of his governorship. He is replaced by the Emperor's younger brother, the progressive and liberal-minded Prince Ferdinand Maximilian Josef, who arrives with his bride Carlotta, the daughter of Belgium's King Leopold I, and promises to lift Austria's restrictive measures and return confiscated estates to their owners.

Cavour emerged victorious. He forced Austria's hand and made Sardinia and King Victor Emmanuel the protectors of Italy. Even more amazingly he managed to serve the interests of both the organizer of the peace conference, Napoleon III, and the leader of Prussia's delegation to it, Otto von Bismarck.

For the rest of the year and into 1857 Cavour made contact with both Garibaldi and Mazzini and made plans for them to raise guerrilla forces for the coming war of liberation in Italy. He secures the covert help of both Napoleon III and Bismarck for this endeavor, all the while keeping his contacts with the notorious revolutionaries a secret in turn from them.

The other members of the Concert of Powers might have uncovered or stopped the intrigue. But neither Russia or Turkey were interested so long as the fate of the Danube principalities were being negotiated by the Powers. As for Great Britain, its attention was most decidedly elsewhere in the world.

At the beginning of the year she had wars in Persia and China, where the French were also involved. Then, in February, disturbances began among the native troops in its Army of Bengal. Mostly over the use of animal fat in newly-issued rifle cartridges, there were also unfounded rumors about forced conversions to Christianity. By mid-year the fortress at Delhi had been occupied by mutineers and insurrection was spreading to the Upper Provinces of India. The Sepoy Rebellion was underway.

It would not be until the beginning of 1858 that the future of Moldavia and Wallachia were decided. By then Cavour's plans with Napoleon III for war with Austria were well-advanced. They nearly derailed when, in March, revolutionaries from the Papal States attempted to assassinate Napoleon with bombs in a Paris street.

For a time it looked like the secret alliance might unravel, but Cavour used his skills to turn the crisis to his advantage. He claimed England was responsible for the plot. He succeeded in convincing the Emperor, the French government and civil population. His deceit mended the relationship, but it also fed a wave of Anglophobia that threatened French relations with Britain – and forced the Royal Navy to come up with a response to squelch the anger.

As this was starting, on April 19th, 1858, Franz Josef issues an ultimatum to Sardinia to cease support of all rebel organizations n northern Italy. Now, Austria is viewed as the aggressor and is actively playing into Cavour's willing hands. He calls for a meeting with Napoleon III and three months later, at the spa resort in Plombieres, France, they hold an extraordinary conference where nothing is written down.

Based on *ex post facto* sources, the participants agreed to the following: that Sardinia would continue to incite Austria toward war, once it started France would intervene and force Austria out of its Italian provinces. As a reward France would receive Nice and the Savoy region around it and lastly relations between the two royal families would be established the old-fashioned way: by the marriage of Prince Jerome Napoleon, another of Napoleon's cousins, to Victor Emmanuel's young daughter, Princess Clotilde.

The only three people who knew the full extent of the agreement were Napoleon III, Cavour and Victor Emmanuel. Napoleon told none of his ministers the full details while Cavour kept Garibaldi and Mazzini equally in the dark – especially about surrendering Nice to France since the city was Garibaldi's birthplace.

It was a dangerous, complicated, high-stakes deception on several fronts that Cavour played. At any time a moment's indiscretion, a bit of bad luck or stupidity could have unravelled it all. But he played the game close to the vest and played it well. On New Year's Day, 1859, Napoleon III summons the Austrian ambassador to his palace and issues a "war threat." A few weeks later Victor Emmanuel II opens his parliament in Turin with an ultimatum to Austria on northern Italy.

The countdown had started.

The War that Almost Doesn't Begin

The immediate response to these ultimatums and war threats was a financial panic in France. True, she had done well in the Crimean War against Russia – but there France had been part of a grand alliance of other major powers. Now, her only ally would be Sardinia and they were taking on Austria: a humbled, castigated empire that was still the dominant land power in Europe.

The next response had Russia and Great Britain proposing a Concert of Powers conference to settle the "Italian problem." Napoleon III warms to the idea and Cavour begins to fear his grandly designed plans are crumbling. By the end of February Franz Josef accepts the idea of a conference, but demands Sardinia disarm its troops.

Britain responds that both Austria and Sardinia should disarm. In spite of rising Anglophobia in his country, Napoleon accepts the proposal and telegraphs Cavour to do the same. Finally, at the beginning of April the very despondent Premier – his own secretary feared he would commit suicide – decides all is lost and to give in.

More cables are sent, national leaders appear to be fascinated by the now widespread technology, but Austria takes its time responding and in the end decides to snatch defeat from the jaws of victory. On April 26th Franz Josef formally rejects England's second proposal and demands Sardinia immediately disarm. Three days later Austrian troops are crossing the Ticino River south of Milan and the war that almost did not begin was underway.

Initial fighting was confined to Sardinian and Austrian forces in northern Italy. The early victories were all Austria's, but then its army lingers fatally in the Po River valley east of Milan. It does not move to take Turin or to engage either the gathering Sardinian or French armies in turn. And while Austria tarried, Camillo Cavour stepped his plans into high gear.

On May 1st Napoleon III declared war on his ally from the previous war, and eleven days later arrives in the port city of Genoa with a major expedition as another crosses the Alps in the beginning of a grand pincer movement. Cavour signals Garibaldi, Mazzini and other rebel leaders, who spread revolt throughout northern and central Italy.

Everywhere Austrian regents and petty monarchs allied to them are driven out. Prince Maximilian flees his governorship – later he will not be so prudent – and the Austrian Army finally moves to crush the Sardinians before either French expedition can arrive at the front. On May 20th a seesaw battle starts in Genestrello on the Po River. The Austrians take the town but, in its first direct use in warfare, the French arrive by train and take it back.

The next day Garibaldi's Red Shirts attack an Austrian cavalry column in force at Varese, Lombardy. They are driven off, then counterstrike the following morning on Lake Como where they seize ships and carry out harassing operations all along the lake's shore. In doing so they tied down an entire Austrian corps, allowing a Sardinian-lead force to cross the Sesia River and defeat the Austrians on their own at Palestro.

Once again the next day, May 31st, an effective counterattack had the Italians in danger of losing Palestro – until Canrobert's corps arrives and he achieves what eluded him in Crimea: a clear cut victory. His men capture most of the Austrian artillery, then he makes a joint attack with Victor Emmanuel's own brigade to take the lone bridge over the Brida River, forcing the Austrians to fall back to Robbio. Three days later, on June 3rd, another French corps crosses the Ticino River and takes the town of Turbigo. Now the Austrians are in danger of being out-flanked, setting up the first great battle of the war.

Magenta and the Rising Star of Marshal MacMahon

The general leading the corps which now so imperiled the Austrian Army was one of France's most experienced field commanders. Marie Patrice Maurice de MacMahon started his combat career in 1837, at the Battle of Constantine in Algeria. During the Crimean War he commanded French forces at the protracted Battle of Malakoff Tower, and in the interim lead a successful campaign against the Kabyle tribe back in Algeria.

On June 4th, 1859, he was pushing his corps as fast as he could to reach Magenta and the nearby village of Buffalora. Due west of Milan, they held the two most important bridges over the Ticino River and combat had started between the over-extended Austrians and French troops who had just arrived by train. The local Austrian commanders received orders from Marshal Francis Giulay to blow the bridges, but were forced to hold them until the powder casks to do the job could be brought up by a woefully inefficient transport corps.

Despite their dire situation, they managed to hold off four assaults, even when Algerian Turcos and Napoleon's Guards regiments were thrown in. The Austrians got several regiments of reinforcements and now endangered the French vanguard. They turned their right flank, and defeat seemed certain when the thunder of cannon announced the belated arrival of MacMahon's corps.

Hours behind schedule, he links up with Marshal Niel's and

Canrobert's units. In joint operations they storm the important positions at Magenta, Buffalora and nearby Marcello. All are taken, though it's not until after nightfall when the train station and rail yard in Magenta are captured by MacMahon's troops.

On the following day Italian reinforcements arrive for the French, Austrian reinforcement do not, and Giulay is forced to realize not only is Magenta lost but Milan is indefensible. Under an orderly, fighting retreat conducted by General Ludwig von Benedek, the Austrians withdraw and both Napoleon III and Victor Emmanuel II enter the liberated city in triumph on June 8th.

For his role in the historic victory, Napoleon elevates MacMahon several grades to Field Marshal and gives him the title of the Duke of Magenta. Empress Eugénie declares magenta to now be the official court color and it becomes the instant fashion in Paris. For Austria the loss of prestige is disastrous. Three days later, on June 11th, Emperor Franz Josef leaves Vienna for the battlefront hoping to rectify the situation. He still has a powerful army in northern Italy and more reinforcements are arriving, but a greater disaster is in the offing.

Solferino: Napoleon III Wins His Waterloo

Even traveling by train, it takes Franz Josef five days to reach his army's headquarters in Verona, where he relieves Giulay of command and assumes personal command of the war. He finds his army in northern Italy harried and in retreat, and his provinces in central Italy in revolt while the Sardinian and French navies are blockading Venice with a threat to land troops.

Since there was little he could do about the naval situation, at the time France was the only country in the world to deploy ironclad warships, Franz Josef concentrated on the ground situation before him. He pulls most of his units inside a heavily defended area called "the Quadrilateral of Fortresses," bounded by the forts in Mantua, Verona, Peschiera and Custozza. Here he concentrates six corps, the equivalent of 12 divisions, and splits them into two armies. His staff prepares to launch a decisive attack along a broad front with the date for its commencement set at June 25th.

However, the preparations for the offensive are noticed by French and Italian scouting parties, leading Napoleon and Victor Emmanuel to hastily assemble their forces, also six corps, and strike first. On June 24th, along the Mincio River running due south from Lake Garda to join the Po River, the slowly advancing Austrian front is attacked by the coalition French and Italian armies. The front is eight miles long, extending from San Martino on the left to Modelo on the right, with nearly 350,000 men involved. Close to the center is a mountain town with a dominant church tower, the Spia d'Italia, which will give the battle its name: Solferino.

The largest land battle in Europe since Waterloo – in fact, it's the same size as Waterloo – begins at 2:00AM with artillery duels and the clash of vanguard forces. By dawn there is heavy fighting along the entire eight-mile battlefront. What Franz Josef had hoped would be an unstoppable offensive became a defensive battle for his armies. Momentum had already drifted to the French.

Admittedly, in the middle of the various engagements, it did not always seem that way. They were universally seesaw battles over the all-important villages and high-ground. Modelo, on the right flank, falls to the French and is immediately attacked by Austrian cavalry. Robecco is a small village that falls and gets retaken several times. On the left flank, General Benedek's corps drives the Italians from the San Martino heights then holds off their repeated assaults. But it is the middle where the momentous battle is eventually decided.

In the center of the Austrian line two corps under Franz Josef's personal command holds Cavarina, Cassiano and most critically Solferino. Between daybreak and noon there are NINE assaults up the slopes to Solferino by French troops, and all are driven back with heavy losses. Just before 1:00PM Napoleon III decides to personally lead the tenth assault with his Imperial Guards. This too is stopped by what are now exhausted Austrian troops, until a new French hero appears: General Francois Achille Bazaine.

His fresh division rallies the retreating Guards, resumes the attack and, with the aid of artillery brought up behind the infantry, enters Solferino. The wild fight that develops is dubbed by the Italians "furia francese." As at Palestro and Magenta, "furia francese" is a style of infantry attack where speed, agility, individual initiative and small group actions were favored over rigid line advances. After several hours the Spia d'Italia is taken by Bazaine's men, Solferino is in their hands and the Austrians are falling back to Cavarina. The Austrian battle line is broken.

The long-threatening sky finally opens up with a heavy thunderstorm which only further disrupts the collapsing line. Franz Josef is forced to order a retreat and it's only because of rear guard actions by officers like Benedek, plus a wheeling charge by Hungarian cavalry, which prevents the retreat from becoming a rout. The casualties are almost exactly the same as 44 years earlier: 24,000 dead for the losers versus 18,000 dead for the victors. Only this time the victors are the French and their allies. Napoleon III has managed to do what his legendary uncle could not – he has won his Waterloo.

The War's End

The magnitude of the losses stagger both sides and yet, neither is broken. The Italians and French advance on the "Quadrilateral of Fortresses" with the Italians investing Peschiera and the French moving against Verona and Mantua. On the Austrian side fresh divisions were arriving from the north and east. In a week both sides would be ready for combat, but the Franco-Austrian War was almost over.

In reality neither side wanted another battle. For Austria another battle, and another defeat, carried the possibility of re-igniting revolution in the empire. For France another battle, and another victory, brought the likelihood of a wider war with the German Confederation joining Austria. Already there were rumblings in Hungary and Garibaldi, denied cooperation with French forces because Napoleon detested him, threatened to take his guerrilla war into the Tyrol region between Austria and her Italian provinces. This would all but invite German intervention and it forced Napoleon's hand.

On July 9th he sends word to Franz Josef and the two quickly agree to an armistice. Two days later the emperors meet at Villafranca, just southwest of Verona. Just like Napoleon Bonaparte and Czar Alexander I at Tilsit almost 52 years to the day earlier, they negotiated without any other leaders or monarchs present. Not King Victor Emmanuel or Prince Maximilian, nor Count Cavour or even Pope Pius IX. It would be Napoleon III and Franz Josef who would decide the fate of Italy.

They agree France will get Nice and the Savoy, something already agreed to by Cavour at the Plombieres Conference; Austria retains Mantua and the Venetia/Venice, its central Italian provinces and got Modena and Tuscany restored to their deposed monarchs. Sardinia gets to keep the Lombardy region and its capital, Milan. Lastly, they agree to the establishment of an "Italian Federation," which would include all Italian states, even the Austrian-held provinces, and be presided over by the Pope.

The Villafranca Treaty pleases neither the Italians, the Austrians nor the Pope. When it is ratified in Zurich later in the year it's denounced by all parties who did not negotiate it. Cavour resigns his Ministership, though not before shipping 10,000 muskets to the rebels in Modena. Mazzini and Garibaldi plan to liberate all of Italy, in much the same way Simon Bolivar liberated Spanish South America, and create a national republic.

Even Pope Pius IX objected to the terms of his proposed rule, especially the potential loss of his sovereignty over his Papal States. And throughout Italy the leader who had been hailed as its liberator was now reviled as a traitor to its cause. But Napoleon III had obtained most of what he wanted from the brief war. It now remained for those he hated the most to get the rest.

The Fate of Italy

The emperors thought they had decided Italy's fate with their treaty. But it really was only one, Franz Josef, who actually thought so while the other tacitly let the Italians do it for themselves, and he did not have long to wait.

The Villafranca Treaty stayed in force for a lot shorter time than most such agreements. By Christmas Eve of 1859 the French government had discovered a secret treaty between Austria and the Pope over the proposed European Congress to settle the Italian Federation. This allows Napoleon III to not only break Villafranca and further embarrass Austria, but to take on the Clerical Party in his own country.

In January, 1860 Count Cavour is recalled to his office and, with the hated treaty no longer in force, started organizing plebiscites across the northern Italian states. For a time Austria threatens to mobilize its army, until Britain and Prussia persuade her not to do so.

During the first two weeks in March the plebiscites go smoothly. France gets what it agreed to at Plombieres while Parma, Modena, Tuscany and Lombardy vote to join a united northern Italy. Garibaldi, whose birthplace had voted to join France, had grown disgusted with the power politics of both Victor Emmanuel and Napoleon III. He threatened to take his Red Shirts to Genoa, but Cavour persuaded him to take his rebels south instead. To Sicily.

Some 11 months earlier, just after the Battle of Magenta had been decided, the tyrant king of Naples died. Ferdinand II was replaced by his weakling son who continued his anti-Italian policies. It did not take long for the rumors of insurrection to start drifting on the air. When their steamers arrived at Marsala on May 11th, Garibaldi's "Thousand" are received in triumph. After so many failures over the previous 26 years, his hour had finally come.

Between mid-May and late July Garibaldi fights a series of battles across Sicily, taking Palermo, Milazzo and gaining the open support of Victor Emmanuel. On August 3rd he sends the combined North Italian fleet into Naples harbor as Garibaldi crosses the Straits of Messina. The Neopolitan fleet readily changes sides; the conquest of southern Italy is on.

By September 6th King Francis II and his Queen are allowed to sail into exile as Garibaldi is proclaimed Dictator of Naples. With the aid of an army sent from northern Italy, the remaining Neopolitan forces are routed and besieged. Their last defeat comes in early-November when the Capua garrison falls to Garibaldi and Victor Emmanuel enters Naples in triumph.

Only the garrisons in Messina and Gaeta on Sicily remain, and when they surrender, by March of 1861, Garibaldi turns his conquests over to Victor Emmanuel. They are the heroes of what is now proclaimed as the united Kingdom of Italy. But the man who's truly responsible for their achievement is on his deathbed and knows the dream is still not complete.

Count Camillo di Cavour dies in Genoa in early April, 1861, after receiving news of the last garrison's surrender. Venice remains under Austrian rule and Rome is still controlled by the Pope, and guaranteed by the French troops stationed there. Italy is not yet complete, but given time and Prussian military success it will be.

The Rise of France

With the acquisition of Nice and Savoy, France got back something it had dearly wanted for 45 years – its Napoleonic Era borders. The region had been lost as punishment for Napoleon Bonaparte's One Hundred Days back in 1815. Ever since then Frenchmen had considered it to be as much a natural part of their country as the provinces of Alsace and Lorraine. Now his nephew had kept the promise to restore it, and brought with it something of even greater importance.

For 45 years the dominant military land power in Europe had been Austria. Most of the dead from Waterloo still laid where they had fallen when the shift took place from France to what was the largest empire inside Europe. Now, its status already diminished from its actions during the Crimean War, Austria had suffered staggering losses on the battlefield, lost all its Italian allies and provinces except one, and had most of the other Great Powers aligning against it. France was back as the dominant land power and Napoleon III wanted to see it stayed that way.

As wildly popular in his country as he was unpopular in Italy, he began a series of ambitious programs to maintain France's newly-won-back status, and even to challenge the supremacy of the one Great Power still ascendant over it. But to challenge Great Britain meant taking it on in the one arena no one had dared to confront it since Trafalgar.

Even before the Franco-Austrian War had begun, Napoleon III launched a new naval building program. What began with shallow-draft, coastal battery ships moved up to true ocean-going ironclad warships with construction contracts for Dupuy de Lôme's *Gloire*-class frigates. The name-ship was launched at about the same time as the Villfranca Treaty got ratified. Its sisters *Invicible* and *Normandie* soon followed and were superseded by more ambitious ships.

The *Magenta*-class was an ironclad version of the standard capital ship of the last two centuries: the two-decker line-of-battle-ship. They were included in a program to construct no less than 30 ocean-going ironclads and 11 armored battery ships. Which was but one part of Emperor Napoleon's plans to gain superiority over France's old *ennemi héréditaire*.

In 1859 he approved of a far more challenging construction project than the remodeling of Paris or the building of its new sewer system. With the Khedive of Egypt, he signed a treaty to undertake the building of Ferdinand Marie de Lesseps' plan for a Suez Canal.

Britain immediately recognized the naval program and the canal plans as a challenge to its position in the world. She responded with a counter-program to the former and bitter, if impotent, protests to the latter. And yet, as this 19th Century arms race was just starting, she, Spain and Austria decided to cooperate in what would prove to be Napoleon's most perilous scheme.

Since 1838 French rulers had been involved with and fascinated in Mexico. Early in that year Louis Philippe demanded the Mexican government pay reparations for injuries and property losses suffered by French citizens during the recent revolution. When Mexico refused a naval blockade resulted, culminating in the bombardment of Vera Cruz and San Juan de Ulloa in late-November. An agreement on the reparations is signed in March of 1839, but the interest in influencing, controlling and ultimately acquiring the unstable and weakly governed country continued.

Approximately 20 years later yet another revolution brought into prominence the one great statesman of modern Mexican history: Benito Pablo Juarez. In 1858 he established a new political party with a solid set of liberal principles and by 1861 had been elected President. At about the same time, Napoleon III decided the moment had come for him to demand repayment of all the loans the previous Mexican governments had taken from France. To demand indemnities for the high taxes and property confiscation those same previous governments had inflicted on French and other foreign businesses.

He did it now because his imperial ambitions demanded more foreign conquests. Because he had never been, and never would be again, quite so popular in France. Because he wanted to replace the new world territory his uncle had sold away at a bargain basement price some 60 years earlier. And because the one country which would effectively stop him, the one with the Monroe Doctrine and an army and a navy to back it up, was destabilizing and fracturing into conflict. The American Civil War was about to command the world's stage.

Chapter VI: 1864 – The Danish-German War, Round Three

"There is no little enemy."
(French proverb)

The New King and Future Kaiser

IN 1861 PRUSSIA'S Regent and *de-facto* ruler finally became its king when his long-ailing older brother died. The "Cartridge Prince" was now Wilhelm I and one of his first royal acts was to request a second and more complete tour of the Gusstahlfabrik steel works from its owner, Alfred Krupp.

For the steel maker, who had fought a long and bitter feud with the War Ministry in Berlin over his cast-steel cannon, this was heaven sent. He organized such a thorough and extensive tour that some members of the royal entourage, such as the new Minister for War Emil von Roon, thought it a flagrant imposition on the King's time.

King Wilhelm I did not, and he led his distressed, impatient entourage through the grimy complex of steam hammers, furnaces, forges, power presses and fitting shops. He dutifully studied the displays arrayed for him, took a genuine interest in the wooden models of future Krupp cannons and, at the end of the day, he watched the casting of a new artillery piece.

The final hours of the tour have been described as a scene from Dante's *Divine Comedy*, or of Vulcan's forge for the gods. Wilhelm watched the whole process, even as his dress white uniform grew stained with the grit of the foundry. He emerged with a new heart, made of Krupp steel, and a resolve to end the decade-long bickering his friend had to put up with from the War Ministry. Even if it meant overruling von Roon, which he would do, the King would see his army equipped with Krupp cannons.

It also helped that he planned major military reforms, increasing conscription and enlarging Prussia's standing army. And it especially helped when, within the year, he would recall his ambassador from Napoleon III's court and make Otto von Bismarck both his Foreign Minister and President of the King's Cabinet. But first, Wilhelm and the other monarchs of the German Confederation were about to do something of even greater importance to the future German armies: they would send their observers to America.

The Germanies and the American Civil War

Most of the major powers sent military officers as observers to America's Civil War, particularly after the First Battle of Bull Run indicated it would not be the "Ninety Day War" that had been advertised. While Britain took a genuine interest – after all it had colonies bordering the area of conflict – many of the other countries only sent a perfunctory contingent. And some, like Russia, Austria and Turkey, scarcely sent any at all.

The Germanies were different. It was not just the Prussians – Moltke sent a full Observer Corps – but also the Saxons, Bavarians, Hessians, Hanoverians, even Würtembergers and Badens. Nor did they confine their activities to touring the front lines, visiting the occasional field headquarters and setting up shop in the war departments of Richmond and Washington, D.C.

The Germans studied the aspects war which most other observers scarcely acknowledged. They studied the sinews of war: the extensive use of railroads, especially by the Union side, the use of telegraphs for the transmission of all manner of orders, the sanitary corps, the hospital services, the commissariat departments. Even the military prisons and war graves registration.

They noticed and studied seriously what the observers of other countries dismissed with derision, even contempt. In particular, British and French officers ridiculed both the Union and Confederate use of cavalry. They discounted it as fighting "like mounted infantry" and for that there were Dragoons, perhaps the most disrespected of all classes of cavalry.

The Germans saw things differently. They watched and reported, on the effects to both sides, of the daring cavalry raids and sweeps by commanders like James "JEB" Stuart, Philip Henry Sheridan, Nathan Bedford Forrest,

Chapter IV: 1848 – The Year that Changes Everything

"Nothing is more terrible than ignorance in action."
-Johann Wolfgang von Goethe (1749 - 1832)

1841 to 1847: Build-Up to Conflagration

THE YEAR 1848 is commonly referred to as "The Year of Revolution," though in actuality it lasted a lot longer than one year and contained more events than revolutions. Historians often depict it as a wildfire spreading across Europe and the analogy is quite appropriate. However, no wildfire could burn with this intensity without a sufficient buildup of kindling, and that only accelerated in the last eight years prior to ignition.

Across Europe the general conditions which contributed to this were, first and foremost, the full tidal effects of the Industrial Revolution. They swept away the last remnants of the feudal system in country after country, causing major population shifts from rural to urban areas, exacerbating pre-existing inequities and creating whole new problems of its own.

Concurrent with this was the rising tide of popular expectations for some type of democratic reform, if not independence, in their countries. But most such hopes, from the Chartists in Great Britain to the Magyars and Poles of eastern Europe, would be dashed by the ruling governments. For these, though no one knew it at the time, were the waning years of the Age of Metternich. And increasingly, his activities and the actions of the Holy Alliance partners were being directed more and more toward keeping the titled heads of Europe on their thrones than preventing war from breaking

George Armstrong Custer, John Hunt Morgan and Benjamin Grierson. While the first two were generals who commanded forces up to corps strength and developed new tactics and strategies, it was the latter two who attracted special interest.

John Hunt Morgan was a Confederate brigade commander who carried out the longest-ranged cavalry operations in history: the 1,000-mile raid through Kentucky and middle-Tennessee in July of 1862, the destruction of Union rail lines around Nashville a month later and culminating with a raid across the Ohio River in July, 1863. This one swept hysteria and destruction across Ohio and Indiana until Morgan and most of his men were finally captured.

While his exploits, including a subsequent escape from a Union POW camp, captured popular imagination and headlines, it was Colonel Benjamin Grierson's operation in Mississippi that attracted the most attention in reports to the War Ministries throughout the German Confederation.

One of the finest horse soldiers in the Union Army, Grierson proposed to General Grant a plan to disrupt Confederate supply lines to Vicksburg in April of 1863. With 1,700 men he rode down the entire state of Mississippi, a distance of over 600 miles, in 16 days. They destroyed some 50 miles of railroad track on three different lines, burned rolling stock and rail depots, fought nearly a dozen skirmishes which lured an infantry division and most of the state's depleted cavalry into a futile pursuit.

It may not have matched the distances traveled, or the amount of damage done, by either Morgan or Forrest, but in the end it proved to be the most important cavalry operation of the war. It disrupted supplies to the Confederate forces in Vicksburg on the Mississippi River. And when the city fell to Grant's army, on July 4th, it was on the same day as Robert E. Lee's defeated Army of Northern Virginia began its retreat from Gettysburg in Pennsylvania. The Confederation States of America had just suffered the twin thunderclaps of defeat from which it would never recover.

Round Three Begins

Four and a half months later, on November 15th of 1863, the third and last round of the Danish-German War began with the death of the ruler who started the first two rounds some 15 years earlier. King Frederick VII died in Copenhagen and the very next day, before his son could even be installed as Christian IX, the citizens of Schleswig and Holstein proclaimed Duke Frederick of Augustenburg to be their ruler, and unite as a single duchy.

Both sides in the coming war react swiftly to the events. On November 18th King Christian IX signs a new constitution annexing Schleswig, just as Bismarck reaches an agreement with the Austrian ambassador for a Prussian-Austrian Alliance. By December 7th the German Confederation gives its consent to the alliance and votes to join it to counter the mobilization of the Danish Army and Navy. Just over two weeks later, on December 23rd, an initial contingent of 12,000 Saxon, Prussian and Hanoverian troops enter Schleswig-Holstein and cause the Danish Army to retreat.

As with the earlier rounds of this war, Denmark called in her trump card early. She appealed to the Concert of Powers for intervention, but this time the response would be different. This time France was fully involved with Napoleon's Mexican Expedition and he was in the midst of delicate negotiations with his former adversary: Austria. In a bid to have Franz Josef join him in a secret alliance against Prussia, Napoleon III privately offered the Mexican Crown to his brother, Archduke Maximilian and the former governor of Austria's lost Italian provinces.

Denmark turned to Russia, but Czar Alexander II had troubles of his own. Early in 1861 he had emancipated 47 million Russian and Polish serfs. Far from begin greeted with celebration, the end of serfdom sparked insurrections and uprisings across the Russian Empire. Three years later they had still not all been suppressed, and Czar Alexander could not be interested in any foreign crisis begging for intervention.

Finally there was England and its Prime Minister, Lord Henry Palmerston, who initially lent a sympathetic ear. He hinted at assistance, but he had wars of his own to fight in New Zealand and on the Northwest Frontier of India. And then there were the events in North America, which occupied too much of his time. In the end all he could do was allow the Danish government to purchase a virtually complete Confederate Navy ironclad from its British builders, and commission it as the *Danmark*. She would be one of only four ironclads to see service in the Danish Navy.

In the meantime German forces were gathering, and their conditions were different as well. This time Austria, desperate for a victory in any war, joined the German coalition. This time, following the example set by the U.S. Military Rail Roads department, there would be no forced marches. Almost everyone and everything arrived as close to the battle front as possible by train. This time the Prussian and Austrian navies would combine to provide an effective counter to the Danish fleet. This time the Dreyse Needle Gun would be ready for combat.

On February 1st, 1864, an additional 25,000 Prussian troops and 20,000 Austrian troops crossed the Eider River, joining the earlier contingent. The next day they attack Danish forces along the Schlei River. It's the first full-scale engagement of the war and sets the precedent for it; the Danes are forced to retreat.

For the next three months the Danes would only know victory at sea, with commerce raiding on the Baltic and North Seas. On land, it was a catalog of disasters. By February 5th the Danes are forced to evacuate their principle defensive position on the frontier of the Jutland Peninsula: the Dannewirk Fortress.

Over the next two weeks the Danish Army is scattered. Part of it is overtaken by the Austrian corps and is forced to surrender at Oversee. Most of the rest reaches the imagined safety of the Sundewitt Peninsula and is invested there by the beginning of March. Two weeks later, after they had regrouped, the combined German corps invades Jutland itself and lay siege to the cities of Veile and Fridericia.

By the middle of April, after a six-week siege, Danish forces on the Sundewitt are stormed and captured; another 5,000 men and 118 guns are lost. By the end of April, Fridericia is evacuated and falls to the German coalition. For Denmark nothing is going right, until London.

Denmark Catches a Break, and Squanders It

The Concert of Powers conference over the Danish-German War opened in London at the beginning of March. Austria, Prussia and the German Confederation stalled for time and get plenty of it, until the collapse of Fridericia. After that Palmerston's government finally starts to move and negotiates a truce called the London Protocol.

The cease-fire began on May 9th, 1864; the German-Austrian coalition honors it but Denmark violates the conditions of the Protocol, especially with regards to continued commerce raiding. It invites the response of May 28th, a series of sharp attacks all along the front lines by German and Austrian forces.

Veile quickly falls and there is a general retreat of Danish forces up the peninsula. At sea a combined Austrian-Prussian fleet sweeps away the commerce raiders; the last and most notorious is captured on June 19th. However, the Danish ironclads still exist and, since the first Prussian ironclad is still under construction in a British shipyard, Denmark hoped they could still turn the tide.

Already, on June 9th, the schooner-rigged monitor *Rolf Krake* engaged Prussian shore batteries as German forces invaded the Als Peninsula. Armed with four 68-pound smooth-bores in two turrets, she is unable to stop the advance though it's hoped she can join up with the other three ironclads to decide the battle.

Alas, those ships (the *Dannebrog, Danmark* and *Peter Skram*) were too deep-drafted to even attempt inshore operations. On June 29th the *Rolf Krake* attempts once again to stop a Prussian attack on Als. And once again she fails, this time the peninsula is taken with over 4,000 men lost while the Prussians only suffer light casualties.

This proves to be the last battle of the war. With her army depleted and scattered, her navy rendered ineffective and none of the Great Powers willing to intervene on her side or threaten the German-Austrian alliance arrayed against her, Denmark this time accepts a truce worked out in London.

The War's Aftermath

Most historians have named this conflict the Danish-Prussian War yet, considering the active participation of Austria and the other German states, it is more accurate to call it the Danish-*German* War. Its Prussian-oriented aspects only become apparent after the fighting ends and the negotiations start.

It's Prussia and Austria who negotiate the terms of the treaty with Denmark and the Concert of Powers. The German Confederation and Schleswig-Holstein were not represented, nor did their representatives sign the subsequent peace treaty in Vienna on October 30th. Only the monarchs attended: King Christian IX, King Wilhelm I and Emperor Franz Josef I.

Christian was forced to cede Schleswig and the city of Lauenburg to Prussia while Holstein passed to Austrian control. Denmark's southern border followed the Kongeaa river, some 46 miles north of its present location, which a 1920 plebiscite would permanently fix.

The treaty's terms were humiliating for Denmark. It ended forever her territorial ambitions to the south, something her rulers had nurtured as a national goal since the end of the Napoleonic Wars. But neither was the treaty everything Prussia wanted either.

Schleswig and Holstein would not be united under the rule of Duke Frederick of Augustenburg. In a later treaty, the Treaty of Gastein signed on August 16th of 1865, Prussia is forced to ante up six million marks for the purchase of Lauenburg while the naval base at Kiel and the Rendsburg Fortress on the Eider River are to be operated jointly by Prussia and Austria for the German Confederation. For a lesser man in the positions of Prussia's Foreign Minister and President of the King's Cabinet, these terms would have been unacceptable, insulting and perhaps even the cause for another war. But Otto von Bismarck took them in his stride, for they could be used in the service of a far more important goal.

The Rise of Prussia

Militarily humbled by Denmark and her Great Power allies over a decade earlier, and politically humbled by a resurgent Austria at the same time, Prussia was finally getting back her status. The nation of officious bureaucrats, stuffy professors and military martinets who observed wars but did not fight them was returning to her dominant position among the other Germanies.

Partly, it is the result of being patient, letting Austria get caught in her cynical manipulations during the Crimean War and paying the price for it. And partly discreetly aiding Sardinia to lure her into a second war where she was resoundingly defeated and lost important territory to a new Prussian ally.

But mostly it came about because of those bureaucrats. They ran the Zollverein, the economic heart of the German Confederation, and largely staffed its Zollparlament. They ran the Postal and Telegraph Union, by now the central nervous system of the Germanies, and they ran the increasingly dominant Prussian State Railways. If nothing else were done, Prussia would eventually unite Germany through her industry and bureaucracy. But there was also her military.

A laughing stock some 14 years earlier for being characterized, unfairly, as the giant who lost a war to a tiny adversary, she now got some attention from the world's other Great Powers. Some, although not a lot, as one of history's great confluences diverted attention elsewhere. Actually, to several elsewheres.

At the same time the Danish-German War was ending, the American Civil War had reached a crescendo. On August 5th of 1864 Admiral David Farragut initiated the Battle of Mobile Bay, a three-week campaign that would see the capture of the last major blockade-running port in the Confederacy. On September 1st John Bell Hood evacuated what remained of his Army from Atlanta, allowing it to fall to General Sherman after a siege of nearly three months. And three weeks after that, on September 22nd, Philip Sheridan crushed Jubal Early's army in the Shenandoah Valley of Virginia, crowning the Union's most successful operation in what had been a very hostile region.

Farther to the south, Napoleon's Mexico Expedition was running into serious trouble after beginning so promisingly. Archduke Maximilian Josef had agreed with Napoleon back in March, at about the time the German-Austrian coalition army was invading Jutland, to accept the title of Emperor of Mexico. He departed Europe with much ceremony, and extra force of mercenaries and a fortune in other people's money.

However, from the day he arrived in Mexico, Maximilian encountered trouble and it would only get worse in the coming years. Napoleon had his attention divided between Mexico, the setbacks with the Suez Canal's construction, military operations in Indochina and increasing political opposition at home. For the Emperor and his army there was precious little reason to devote much time to Prussia's success in so short a war.

Great Britain also paid scant attention. Its war in New Zealand, the third in 20 years, was still going strong and a serious rebellion was fomenting in Jamaica. British bankers had a major financial stake in Mexico and there were still the problems of Britain's unofficial involvement in America's Civil War.

For Prussia, this lack of interest would actually be a godsend. Her growing competency with the new technologies of war, specifically the railroad and telegraph, were in part ignored because the other Great Powers were rather slow to appreciate them. Great Britain, for instance, would not use the railroad to directly transport troops to a combat zone until 1870, when Colonel Garnet Joseph Wolseley commanded the Red River Expedition in western Canada to suppress the rebellion of Louis Riel. This was long after its use had been established by French, American and Prussian-lead armies. And some historians think the only reason Wolseley used a train in 1870 was his assignment to Robert E. Lee's headquarters some eight years earlier, as a military observer.

And then there were the technologies and tactics that Prussia was developing entirely on her own. The infantry weapon invented by Johann Nikolaus von Dreyse was the world's first true breech-loading, bolt-action gun – the first long-barrelled, musket-type weapon to be called a rifle.

As with Alfred Krupp's cast-steel, breech-loading cannon, the Dreyse Needle Gun had a long and difficult development. Its first use, in the first two rounds of the Danish-German War was little short of disastrous due to its waxed-paper cartridges not standing up to field conditions. Some 14 years later, and an all-important change to a thin-walled cardboard cartridge, and the Dreyse finally proved its worth.

It was not just its vastly increased rate-of-fire where the weapon got validated – the Sharps carbines and Spencer repeaters of the U.S. Civil War had already done that – but the manner in which it was used. Muzzle-loading muskets required their users to stand in order to reload, but breech-loaders allowed them to crouch or even lie down.

Firing from such a prone or crouching position presented a much smaller target to the enemy, while pouring continuous fire into them. It was unnerving, and when combined with rapid, agile advances making use of whatever advantages the local terrain offered, it was devastating.

Incredibly no other Great Power, not even Austria, chose to notice this. In fact, Austrian reports from Denmark took note of how much ammunition the Prussians used and not how effective their attacks were. But it would not be long before they, and the other Great Powers, would be forced to acknowledge. For the next war Prussia would fight would be directed at them.

Chapter VII: 1866 – The Last "Cabinet" War

"Be as rude as you like about this army of lawyers and
oculists, but it will get to Vienna just as soon
as it likes."
-General Charles Denis Sauter Bourbaki (1816 - 1897)

1865: A Year of Peace, and Preparations

1865 WOULD BE a unique and relatively brief moment of peace for most of the world. The American Civil War was sputtering to its official end on April 11th. For Great Britain the New Zealand War was also coming to an end, the Jamaican Rebellion had been contained, the Indian Frontier quieted down and for the time being there were no wars in China.

Except for France, the other Great Powers were also enjoying a period of calm. In Russia the peasant uprisings were largely over and peace reigned between Prussia and Austria. If only Bismarck, Roon and Moltke could have enjoyed it. Instead, they had other plans.

Even though their treaty with Austria and Denmark ordained that the naval base in Kiel was to be operated under joint administration for the German Confederation, Wilhelm I and his cabinet wanted it for Prussia. They had their first ironclad, the *Arminius*, and more were being built. But Kiel lay inside Holstein and Holstein was governed by Austria.

Undeterred, Prussia moved her principal Baltic Sea naval base from Danzig, present-day Gdansk, to Kiel. A crisis loomed, until Wilhelm proposed a conference with Franz Josef. The resulting Treaty of Gastein solidified the terms of the peace treaty ending the Danish-German War.

Kiel and the Rendsburg Fortress would continue to be operated jointly on behalf of the German Confederation.

But Bismarck, Roon, Moltke and others did not agree that it settled matters. In the Prussian Parliament, where he had won hard votes to increase military spending and the size of the Landwehr (the militia), Bismarck knowingly forecast, "the great questions of the time are not decided by speeches and majority decisions, that was the error of 1848 and 1849, but by blood and iron."

Blood and iron, *blut und eisen*...it was a favorite phrase of Bismarck; he used it many times. But this time, at the end of September of 1865, it marked the countdown to yet another war. And this one would decide forever which power would dominate the Germanies.

1866: How to Force a Crisis

The beginning of the new year found Prussia discreetly casting around for allies in its coming war. Bismarck and the rest of the king's cabinet wisely decided not to approach any of the other German states. Not Bavaria, not Würtemberg, not even Saxony or Hanover. Instead they chose the newest state in Europe, the one that remained incomplete and had been betrayed by Napoleon III: Italy.

By April 8th Bismarck had concluded a secret treaty with Italy for an alliance against Austria. Due to her nervousness, the treaty would only remain in force for the next three months, and Bismarck immediately set about making the most of it.

The next day, he had the Prussian delegation to the Frankfurt Diet propose changes to the German Confederation's constitution and that the question of Schleswig-Holstein should be treated as a national issue and not as something to be decided by monarchs. With Wilhelm's consent, he effectively undercut the recent treaties signed with Franz Josef.

On the same day, April 9th, Roon and Moltke began mobilizing Prussia's huge standing army and activating its Landwehr. Austria responds by asking for negotiations and seeking support among the other Germanies. Weeks of apparent inactivity follow; the life of the secret treaty was more than half over by the time Bismarck issues a detailed circular on the future of Schleswig-Holstein and the changes to the German Confederation on May 27th.

He wanted the issue to be settled by a national convention whose members would be directly elected by the people of each state attending it, and not selected by the various rulers. This was a direct slap at the autocratic style of rule Franz Josef exercised in Austria, and had long been repellent to many Germans.

To Bismarck's mild surprise Austria agreed to it, and King Ludwig II of Bavaria also consented, though only so long as Austria and Prussia agreed not to attack each other. Events were not going exactly as he had planned, but again Bismarck took it in stride, and cabled the Italians. It was time for them to start doing their part.

A few days later Italian Prime Minister Alfonso Lamarmora advised Napoleon III of his country's agreement with Prussia. And, as both the Prussian and Italian governments expected, the Emperor promptly communicated the information to the Austrian ambassador. Within a day Vienna offered to cede the Venetia provinces to Italy if she will break her treaty with Prussia. When Italy refuses to do so, Austrian reinforcements are rushed to the area. And Bismarck uses this response to claim Austria has broken the Gastein Treaty.

Events now spiral out of Austria's attempt to control them. On June 1ˢᵗ the Austrian governor of Holstein convenes a meeting with local estate holders over contingencies for the crisis. It's a technical violation of the Treaty that only further serves Prussia's claim. On the same day Franz Josef makes a weak attempt to end the crisis by suggesting the German Confederation's Diet, or Bundestag, should resolve the issues. This, however, had already been rejected by Berlin, and in any event neither peace nor the Confederation had long to live. The war that would be measured in weeks was but a week away from starting.

June 7ᵗʰ is the unofficial start to the Austro-Prussian War with the "invasion" of Holstein by a Prussian Army corps lead by cavalry general Baron Edwin von Manteuffel. It is not until June 12ᵗʰ that a large-scale contact is made with Austrian forces, which promptly retires from the field with the Duke of Augustenburg. On the same day Austria protests the invasion to the Confederation, claiming it violates the 11ᵗʰ Article of its constitution, under which member states could not levy war against one another, and calls for a vote to mobilize the armies of other non-Prussian states.

Two days later an irregular and disjointed vote in the Bundestag approves the Austrian measure. Prussia immediately counters by dissolving the German Confederation and drawing up new articles for its constitutional charter, which exclude Austria and Holland from the list of member states. The next day, June 15ᵗʰ, Prussia issues ultimatums to Saxony, Hanover and Hesse-Cassel to recant their votes in Frankfurt, de-mobilize their forces and remain neutral for the duration of the conflict. When they refuse the *Bruderkrieg*, the Brothers' War, is on.

Prussia Attacks, and Routs

The first outright victories in the Seven Weeks War went to Prussia, but
they were not over Austria. By June 22nd Hanover, Hesse-Cassel and the
Saxon capital of Dresden are all occupied by Prussian troops. Saxony
appeals for help and, even though the Confederation is officially dissolved,
it assigns Bavaria and Austria to respond. They begin organizing a
Confederation Army consisting of units from Bavaria, Baden, Würtemberg,
Nassau and Austria. However, it will never take to the field as Prussia has
already won the "Battle of Mobilization" and with it will go the war.

The first major battle of the war uniquely does not occur in Prussia,
Austria or any other German lands. It takes place at Custozza in Northern
Italy where the Italians blow a chance at victory. They have superior
numbers over the Austrian forces in the area, but they disperse instead of
concentrating, proving one of Helmuth von Moltke's most quoted remarks:
"a mistake in the original concentration of the Army can hardly be made
good in the entire course of the campaign." The Italians suffer a serious
defeat and the war will be nearly half over before they can make good their
losses.

Three days later, on July 27th, a Hanoverian corps of 22,000 men is
outflanked and checked by a Prussian force less than half its size, just
10,000 men. One of the secrets of the Prussian victory is Moltke's use of
the telegraph to send orders to his field commanders. Though it did not
originate with him, or even the Union and Confederate armies in the U.S
Civil War, he was turning the use of modern communications from fanciful
experiment into a science. The next day the Hanoverians are forced to
surrender, then get paroled on their pledge to remain neutral.

Like his Italian allies, concentration of force was a problem Moltke
also nervously faced. Even using all available rail lines he had to detrain his
three armies of 326,000 men across a broad front of 250 miles. He got
further handicapped by imperial "requests" even a Chief-of-Staff could not
ignore. In order not to appear as openly as an aggressor, Wilhelm I delayed
the Prussian Army's deployment, using up valuable time. Further, the royal
fear that the province of Silesia could be threatened by an Austrian advance
lead Crown Prince Friedrich Wilhelm to "request" that he move his army
to the southeast. Reluctantly, Moltke agrees to it.

As a result of the necessity to deploy his armies so broadly, there were
multiple engagements with Austrian forces over a relatively short period of
time. Between June 28th and July 1st the Austrians were encountered at
Hühnerwasser, Turnau, Podol, Gitschin, Trautenau, Nachod, Skalitz and
Schweinschadël. All of these battles were at division or corps strength and

were hard, sharp fights. In only one of these, Trautenau, did the Austrians emerge victorious, but they had suffered three times the casualties and in the end were unable to hold the ground theyhad won.

At all the other engagements they were repulsed with heavy losses and pushed back, and the reasons were always the same. The Prussians were more disciplined and aggressive, they were trained to use their rifles for massed, sustained fire and not just as a mount for their bayonets. In the middle decades of the 19th Century most Austrian officers still believed in the Napoleonic-era "charge...l'outrance" tactic: an all-out, to-the-limits cavalry or infantry charge which all earlier phases of any battle had lead up to.

It was a daring, high-stakes maneuver which usually worked, especially in the era when the principal infantry weapon was the muzzle-loading, smooth-bore flintlock musket with an effective range of just 50 to 60 yards. The situation changed greatly when the principal weapon became the percussion cap, rifle-barrel musket with an effective range ten times (500-600 yards) the previous one. This was proved at Magenta and Solferino, but the Austrian Army did not take notice. Now the Dreyse Needle Gun added a higher rate-of-fire and easier operation to the already greater reliability and range.

The results were devastating to the army which had neither learned the earlier lessons nor how to use the latest technologies of war, lavishing and squandering its funds on salaries to incompetent officers and a corrupt bureaucracy. They had grown so devastating that, by the evening of July 1st, the commander of the Austrian Army cabled Franz Josef: "I request urgently of your Majesty to come to a peaceful settlement. A disaster for the army is unavoidable."

Alas, the Emperor refused. He even sent a response demanding to know, "has a battle taken place?" For Field Marshal Ludwig August Ritter von Benedek, his fate, the fate of the army he commanded, the future of his nation and the Germanies was about to be decided in the rolling forests and farm fields between the Königgrätz fortress and the town of Sadowa.

The Battle for the Future of Germany

Königgrätz, also called Sadowa and even called Chlum, was a battle which should have gone to the defenders. The Austrians, despite the inferiority of their weapons and field tactics, had superior defensive positions and a large army holding them. Marshal Benedek had arrayed the army in three corps: the center with 44,000 men, the left wing with 51,000 men and the right with 55,000 men. 450 field guns, mostly brand-new 8-pounder, rifle-barreled bronze muzzle-loaders, were distributed among the three corps. Finally, there were another 47,000 infantrymen, 320 cannons and 11,500 cavalrymen held in reserve. On paper a formidable army, but not this one.

This army had just suffered a rapid series of defeats at the hands of a better-equipped, more aggressive foe. One its exact location and strength it could not pinpoint. This was due to the broad front over which the Prussian armies had deployed, and particularly with Crown Prince Friedrich Wilhelm's army only just emerging from Prussia's Silesia province, much farther east than expected. On the eve of battle Benedek's reconnaissance patrols could not give him accurate information on his opponent's disposition of forces.

A greater problem for the Austrian Army lay in its own internal politics and this one went all the way to the top. Field Marshal Benedek had more than earned his rank, he had distinguished himself as a regimental commander in Italy during the battles between 1848 and 1850, then as a corps commander during the Franco-Austrian War. He had been hand-picked by Austria's military legend, Marshal Johann Wenzel Radetzky, to succeed him as army commander. To those who respected Benedek he was the "Austrian Bayard", after the 16th Century French general Pierre Seigneur de Bayard, who gained lasting fame for his bravery and chivalry.

Unfortunately, most of those who held Benedek in esteem were in the armies that had opposed him. Far too many Austrian officers held him in contempt for Benedek was a Magyar, the dominant ethnic group of Hungary, and they were damned if they were going to be commanded by a Hungarian peasant. This would be especially true for the generals who commanded the corps on Benedek's wings, Austrian aristocrats Count von Thun and Count von Festetics.

Most of July 2nd was spent marshaling and deploying the countless regiments, batteries and squadrons of cavalry on each side. By nightfall it had begun to rain, masking Prussia's final movements, but also hindering the dispatch riders sent out from Moltke's field headquarters. The coming battle would not go exactly according to plan for either side.

The rains continued on the morning of July 3rd, and for many the first sign that battle had been joined was to realize they were not listening to thunder or an approaching heavy downpour but cannonades. Benedek was still riding to his command post when initial contact took place: a Prussian cavalry advance to the Bistritz River at Sadowa. Austrian artillery and a Jaeger battalion had driven the cavalry regiment off the bridge crossing the river. The Prussian commander, Prince Friedrich Karl, counterattacked with an infantry assault and an artillery barrage of his own. The most important German battle since Napoleon was defeated at Leipzig had started.

By the time Benedek reached his command post he found one of his two aide-de-camps quite overjoyed, though not because of the battle's progress. The other had just been sacked by Franz Josef for incompetence. It took a while for his staff to find out what was happening, and for the moment the battle had started in Austria's favor.

Austrian infantry had withdrawn to the Swiepwald Forest northeast of Sadowa, an excellent defensive position in which they were decimating Prussian troops, despite the superiority of the Dreyse Needle Gun. And here the battle might well have been decided. Only one of Moltke's two armies had been engaged, the defensive positions the Austrians held negated Prussia's advanced weapons and aggressive tactics, and their use of artillery proved at least as good as their enemy's.

Here Prussia's gamble for dominance among the Germanies, after so brilliant a beginning, could have ended in failure, along with the careers of Bismarck, Moltke and Roon. A united Germany might have remained a dream, an endless debate between academics over "Rechtsstaat" versus "Ständestaat." Napoleon III's French Empire might have lasted longer than it did. But hubris and a belated arrival would set the path for all their fates.

From their lofty positions on the wings overlooking the battle, Thun and Festetics were rapidly growing restless. All the fighting was occurring in the Austrian center, hot and sharp but it had nothing to do with them. For two men so highly connected with the imperial court this was intolerable, even dishonorable, and they were not about to let an aging Magyar Ritter tell them what to do. Shortly after 10:00AM they moved their corps out of their defensive positions and toward the Swiepwald Forest, where the Prussian Seventh Division had managed to fight its way in and get trapped.

Wave after wave of white-uniformed Austrian troops swept into the forest, but this time its dense growth aided the Prussians. Furious bayonet charges could scarcely be mounted, and massed fire from the Dreyse Needle Guns produced appalling casualties. In the tiny village of Cistowes all the officers and over half the enlisted men of two Austrian regiments were killed. The casualty reports and his corps commanders' disobedience reached Benedek at the same time. He angrily ordered two corps to move and cover the gaping holes in his defensive lines. Then, just after 11:30AM, he received the message that turned him pale: the unlocated army of Crown Prince Friedrich Wilhelm had been found, advancing on the empty lines of his right flank.

The Crown Prince could scarcely believe his luck, yet he had his Guards regiment advance up the hill slowly. Until they found the lines empty, and a rush was ordered to take the nearby undefended Austrian batteries. When this ended, the Austrian right flank had been turned; all that remained now was the fighting to exploit it.

Benedek desperately tried to rally his exhausted, confused and dispirited army. The decimated units which had nearly taken back the Swiepwald were ordered to abandon the forest and attempt to regain the heights lost behind them. When the Prussians took Chlum, a village in the middle of the Austrian center, Benedek refused to believe it, until he nearly died on his own reconnaissance sortie to find out if it was true.

He ordered an attack by one of his last remaining intact corps, it nearly succeeded in retaking Chlum capturing the Prussian division inside it when a corps from Friedrich Wilhelm's army swarmed the village and outflanked the Austrian units around it. As a final, futile, gesture a battery of Austrian light field guns rushed onto a nearby hill, unlimbered and opened fire. They easily fell within small arms range, and a thousand Needle Guns replied, wiping out the entire battery. When Prussian cavalry reached its location they saw nothing could stop their army's advance.

Benedek ordered his broken, exhausted army to fall back to the Königgrätz Fortress, located some six miles behind the front lines, at the confluence of the Elbe and Adler Rivers. Part of the Adler had been diverted around the ramparts of the fortress and was controlled by a series of sluices, falls and locks. When the army appeared at its gates, along with reports of the Prussians hard on its heels, the fortress commander ordered the sluice gates and locks opened. It would be the capping disaster to the day's catastrophe.

The moats quickly filled and the outlying fields began to flood. The panicked survivors scrambled for the single-lane causeway leading to the fortress. It became clogged with desperate men, pushing caissons, limbered cannons and even carts filled with wounded into the rising waters. Officers shouting orders in a dozen different languages tried to force some discipline into the chaos but it proved useless. The Austrian Army inflicted its final defeat on itself; after July 3rd it would not attempt another offensive operation. The Austro-Prussian War, barely more than two weeks old, had been won.

After Königgrätz: Four Weeks of Mopping Up

No one quite understood the enormity of the defeat. William Russell, by now a celebrity in his own right for his reports on the Crimean War and Sepoy Rebellion, wrote a lengthy article wondering exactly how the

Austrians were defeated and underestimating their casualties by over 40%. He also wrote "it would not astonish me to hear it was more." But on being told the Austrians had lost 44,000 men, not the 25,000 he thought, he was astonished indeed.

In its terrible numbers Königgrätz surpassed Solferino. Austria's casualties alone surpassed the total casualty numbers of the earlier battle, while Prussian casualties were half of what the victorious French and Italians had suffered: 9,000 killed and wounded versus 18,000. Königgrätz stunned Austria, who quickly started peace negotiations. It shocked the world. It just took a little time for its impact to settle in on the other Germanies.

Prussia had been able to field four armies under its mobilization plans, but used only three at Königgrätz. The fourth, called the "Army of the Main" (River), stayed inside German Confederation territory to deal with the Bavarian and Confederation armies. It did this mostly by continually outmaneuvering the other troops, forcing them to retreat, and allowing the momentous news from Austria to settle in. Finally, on July 16th, the "Army of the Main" entered Frankfurt, where the German Confederation received its death knell.

Back in Austria, the unfortunate Benedek got one last chance to redeem his army and give his Emperor a better bargaining position in the peace talks. However, what he scraped together was a dispirited, intimidated force. As with the Bavarian and Confederation armies, the Prussians outmaneuvered rather than engaged the Austrians. They did it for political reasons – from Wilhelm I and Bismarck on down they wanted the *Bruderkrieg* to end with as little further loss of life as possible.

Largely, they were successful; the Prussians used confusion and friction to wear down an already beaten opponent. Just under three weeks after Königgrätz, on July 22nd, they were compelled to engage the Austrian Army at Blumenau, on the road to Bratislava and Vienna. The battle had scarcely begun, Blumenau was taken and the capture of Bratislava all but assured when news arrived to both sides of a truce.

For Benedek, as well as his army, it meant an inglorious end. Sacked soon afterwards and replaced by Archduke Albrecht, Austria's most loyal soldier found himself facing a closed-door court-martial whose outcome had already been ordained. The Austrian court was not about to find two of its members guilty of yet another crushing defeat. After being stripped of his honor and rank by this royal kangaroo court, Ludwig von Benedek would be stripped of his dignity when his personal valet stole his medals. He would die a broken man.

Lissa, and the Wrong Lessons Learned

In the other theater of operations for the Seven Weeks War, Austria won what amounted to a consolation prize victory: Lissa. On land the campaign for the Venetia province had degenerated into a complete fiasco for the Italians. With his army suffering a string of defeats, Victor Emmanuel II turned to his navy to reverse that tide.

After France and Great Britain, the nation which had invested the most in building a modern navy was Europe's newest: Italy. By 1866 it had spent an impressive 300 million francs to construct, in her own yards as well as French, British and American ones, a fleet of 14 ironclad and iron-hulled capital ships. These included the _Affondatore_, one of the world's first iron-hulled turret ships and only just completed in its British yard.

However, the admiral of this fleet, Count Carlo Pellione diPersano, proved reluctant to take his ships to sea. It needed a royal demand by Victor Emmanuel himself to get Persano moving, and he elected to attack the Austrian-held island of Lissa in the Adriatic Sea. It's difficult to see how attacking this target would relieve the problems Italy faced on the Venetian front; nevertheless a fleet of four frigates, three gunboats, one corvette, a hospital ship, five dispatch/communications cutters and two transports laden with assault troops set sail for the island.

In an era when no navy in the world possessed more than two dozen ocean-going ironclads, it was a powerful battlegroup. And the _Affondatore_ led it, easily the most powerful and modern warship in either the Adriatic or Mediterranean Seas. Nothing with a wooden hull could stand up to it, but the stone forts at Port San Giorgio and the other towns on Lissa did.

Their bombardment of the island began on July 18th and continued through the next day with few results, except that the _Formidabile_, one of the first ironclads in Italian service, received so much damage it forced her to retire. On the 20th Count Persano was waiting for a morning haze to burn off before resuming the bombardment when the Austrian fleet of seven ironclads, all its navy had in commission, and a wooden-hulled steam frigate hove into view. The first major naval battle between European powers since Trafalgar, and the first in history to use ironclad fleets, was on.

Right from the start the Austrians were in a superior position: they were in formation whereas the Italian ships were scattered. Persano ordered his ships, minus the hospital ship and troop transports, to form a battle line. Then he ordered the inexplicable, the transfer of his flag from the _Re d'Italia_ to the _Affondatore_. This created a gap in the hastily formed line, through which the Austrian ironclads steamed.

Their commander's own orders had effectively cut the Italian fleet in two, now a wild melee resulted where Persano's new orders were either ignored or misunderstood because not every ship had seen the transfer. Ships began individual duels rather than attempt a coordinated fight. The *Affondatore* decided to take on the sole unarmored ship in the battle: the 92-gun, two-deck line-of-battle ship the *Kaiser*. The Austrian flagship, the *Ferdinand Max* engaged the *Palestro* and *Re d'Italia* in turn.

When their gunfire proved ineffective, the *Ferdinand Max* was not equipped at the time with its full complement of 48-pounder smoothbores, they resorted to ramming. The *Affondatore* in particular was equipped with an enormous ram, 26 feet long, which she tried to use several times on the severely mauled *Kaiser*. Each time Persano broke off the attack and the ships scraped past each other, causing more damage.

The *Ferdinand Max* fared better with her ramming attacks. She actually did strike the *Palestro* and *Re d'Italia*, though initially without doing major damage. As the battle intensified the *Re d'Italia* took a disabling shot aft, in her steering gear. Dead in the water, she was approached again by the *Ferdinand Max* and rammed amidships on the port side. She sank within two minutes, taking most of her crew with her.

From there on the battle was firmly in Austria's favor. The *d'Italia*'s sistership, the *Re di Portogallo*, was rammed by the damaged *Kaiser* and lost all her hatch lids to her port side guns, had 60 feet of side armor displaced and a field gun was swept overboard. At least she got to retire from battle, the *Palestro* was not so lucky.

Struck by heated shot while trying to aid the *Re d'Italia*, she was taken in tow by another Italian ironclad. Her captain, displaying more courage than Count Persano, flooded the magazines then stayed on board to fight the fire with his crew. But a ready store of loaded shells exploded, destroying the *Palestro* and killing all except 19 of the crew.

The *Don Juan d'Austria* engaged the *Affondatore* and forced her to retire with damaged funnels, upperworks and a dangerous fire below decks. The *Regina Maria Pia* was set on fire by explosive shells and, as a fitting end to the battle, accidentally rammed her sistership, the *San Martino*. To be so soundly trounced by an already defeated enemy – Königgrätz had occurred a full 17 days earlier and the preliminary truce was only two days away – proved little short of a disaster for Italy. And, as if things could not possibly go worse for Count Persano, his flagship would sink at her moorings during a storm on August 6th.

Naval tacticians and architects the world over, except perhaps for the legendary Alfred Thayer Mahan, immediately seized upon Lissa and learned the wrong lessons from it. Since ramming had apparently been more effective than naval gunfire alone, it became the preferred tactic for sea battles. For now until early in the 20th Century virtually all capital ships would be built with ram prows.

It would even go so far as the construction of armored ram ships, similar in design to the ill-starred *Affondatore*: slim, low-profiled vessels with few guns and prominent, projecting bows. It also captured the public's imagination. Admiral Wilhelm von Tegethoff, commander of the Austrian fleet, became his nation's one true military hero from the conflict and got a promise from Franz Josef that a new ship would be named after him. And four years later a former Paris lawyer published a novel starring the most fabled fictional warship in history. The futuristic *Nautilus* submarine, of Jules Verne's *20,000 Leagues Under the Sea* would sink the ships it encountered by ramming.

It is no small irony to note that the science-fiction writer, *not* the naval architects or admirals, was the one who seriously considered there might be problems with ramming a modern, mechanically-powered warship into the side of another. All those highly complex, and therefore delicate, propulsion systems, not to mention the increasingly mechanized armaments, would be subject to damage on both ships. But only Verne foresaw some of these problems and came up with ingenious solutions to mitigate them. Some of which would be re-invented in the Nuclear Age, and no one would remember the writer who first created them.

The real lessons to be learned from Lissa, the effectiveness of end-on fire, the superiority of rifled guns over smoothbores and explosive shells over solid shot, would take a little longer to be appreciated – even when they had been demonstrated some 13 years earlier at Sinope. That, however, had been the Russians over the Turks; Lissa was one European power against another and both were equipped with the latest warships. It would take time for the real lessons to be learned; what would not take much time was the spectacularly short ascendancy of Austrian naval power.

The Death of Austria

As big as Lissa was, and there would not be another naval battle like it until 38 years later at Tsushima Straits, it did not stem the tide of defeat for either combatant. At least for the Italians their disasters were all reversed by the actions of their allies: the Prussians and, with yet another small touch of irony, Napoleon III. For Austria, there would be no such reprieve or reversal of fortune.

Two days after the victory at Lissa the truce between Austria and

Prussia was declared. Four days after that, on July 26th at Nikolsburg in Austria, a preliminary peace treaty was signed while negotiations continued towards the permanent treaty. And it was not just with Austria that Prussia negotiated, it was all the other Germanies as well as Italy and France. Bismarck, Wilhelm I, Roon, Moltke and the corps of diplomats and officers under their command were going to see that those who had humiliated Prussia with the "Shame of Olmütz" were going to get payback.

Roughly a month later, on August 23rd, the final peace treaty between Austria and Prussia was signed in Prague. It demanded a modest war reparation from Austria, who gave up all claims to Schleswig-Holstein and withdrew from the German Confederation. Neither would she be allowed to join any future confederation of German states. Austria, with its huge, multi-ethnic population, had forever lost her German identity and by the middle of the following year it would lose so much more.

Between October and December of 1866 Austria ceded Venice and the territory surrounding it to France. And Napoleon III, honoring a separate treaty with Victor Emmanuel, turned the acquisition he had so long desired over to Italy. Now the only Italian territory left to Austria was the port of Trieste at the head of the Adriatic. From here Austria had hoped to build a powerful fleet, but that would not be.

With the degrading treaties capping a string of defeats, the future of Franz Josef's throne was in doubt. Even his own younger brother, the by-now besieged Emperor of Mexico, plotted against him. Alas, the new year only brought more troubles and even tragedy for the House of Hapsburg. By the June of 1867 Maximilian Josef was dead and the Mexican Adventure lay in ruins, an unmitigated disaster for two empires, three emperors and a host of financial backers. Königgrätz was not the last nail in the coffin of Austria, events half a world away were, and Franz Josef would be forced to do what he once considered detestable in order to survive.

In mid-year he travels to Pesth, the ancient capital of Hungary, where he's given an ornate coronation ceremony. In addition to Emperor of Austria he is crowned King of Hungary and, like the Czar, an official dual monarch. The Austria Empire is no more; it's the Austro-Hungarian Empire and the change goes far beyond just the name.

Franz Josef signs a new constitutional charter in the presence of Hungarian deputies and magnates. A Magyar Ministry is formed for the joint rule of the empire and the dual monarch also signs the Act of Grace, an official amnesty for all who attempted nationalist insurrections in the past. The new Ministry and Diet have real powers, and they use them immediately to quash imperial ambitions. Hungary is not interested in building a bigger navy, fearing it will only lead to more international entanglements and war. Naval construction grinds to a virtual halt in the Austro-Hungarian Empire, even as it becomes part of the arms race among the other Great Powers. The hero of Lissa would not get a ship named after him for another ten years.

Bismarck Ascendent

As the Battle of Königgrätz swung decisively from murderous stalemate to outright Prussian victory, one of Moltke's staff turned to Otto von Bismarck and said, "Your Excellency, you are now a great man. But if the Crown Prince had come too late you would now be the greatest villain." To which the consummate Anglophile replied with a version of Wellington's famous phrase from Waterloo: "Yes, it was a close run thing."

Close run indeed. Had Königgrätz gone the other way, had Benedek's subordinate commanders not been so stupid and Crown Prince Friedrich Wilhelm been so fortunate, then Bismarck, Roon, Moltke and even their King would all be minor figures in history – footnotes whose ambitions exceeded their abilities. But fortune had yet again favored the bold and Bismarck especially set out to make the most of it.

Before the *Bruderkrieg* he had been universally unpopular, and never more so than in Prussia itself. In its aftermath he became equally acclaimed, some even started talking of him in terms of being the new Barbarossa, and the smoke had scarcely cleared from the battlefields in Austria, Italy and the southern Germanies when he set about proving it.

Bismarck supervised his diplomatic corps in simultaneous negotiations with Austria, Italy, France and the other Germanies. While the treaties with Austria were accorded priority, the others were equally far-reaching. The treaties that got the Venetia province ceded to Italy further cemented the alliance between it and Prussia. Bismarck also knew it would frustrate Napoleon III, whose catalogue of woes for the year was only increasing. However, the treaties with the other German states would prove to be the most important to the long-cherished Prussian dream of forging a united Germany under its dominion.

Of the states that had opposed Prussia in the *Bruderkrieg*, Hanover was dealt with more harshly than the others. The imperial free city, which had also been the home of British kings for 123 years (until 1837), was completely annexed by Prussia. Its powerful army, for its tiny size, got absorbed into the Prussian Army and its royal house could no longer be an opposition power to Prussia's ambitions. The larger states were dealt with more leniently, though it still proved to be an iron hand carefully wrapped in a velvet glove.

Small tracts of land and war indemnities were taken from various states, particularly Bavaria and Hesse, and what remained of the old German Confederation was split in two. All states north of the Main River joined the new North German Confederation, dominated by Prussia. Bavaria, Baden, Würtemberg, Hesse and the smaller states south of the Main formed the theoretically independent South German Confederation. However, all German states were still part of the Zollverein, still part of its Zollparlament, as well as the Postal and Telegraph Union. And in the all-important area of transportation, Prussian State Railways extended its influence and control.

None of this going to the victor in what proved to be Europe's last "cabinet war" was unexpected. In fact it was rather tame compared to earlier such wars where entire regions, provinces and millions of people would change hands. It would be underneath all this, in a confidential and parallel set of negotiations, where the essential links in the creation of a united Germany were being forged.

All German states were cajoled, wrangled, but not threatened, by Bismarck and his diplomats into signing alliances that they would place their troops under Prussian command in time of war. Some were persuaded to join because it meant access to modern weapons. Other states, such as Bavaria, were more reluctant and negotiations continued into the new year.

Time, in this case, worked to Bismarck's benefit, and he had Napoleon III as an unwitting ally. In greatest secrecy he circulated a proposal Berlin had received from France in May of 1866, on the eve of the *Bruderkrieg*: for Prussia and France to jointly appeal the Concert of Powers for a congress on the issues of Schleswig-Holstein and the Venetia Province. And, once they engineered its failure, they would form an offensive alliance against Austria and declare war.

The proposal was brazen, craven, particularly since Austria had become France's partner in Mexico, and showed just how dangerous and reckless Napoleon III could be. And Bismarck very shrewdly used it, plus the crises of the new year, to persuade even the most reluctant German states to join his secret alliance. Friedrich Barbarossa was preparing for the day when Germany would call upon him to defend her.

The Weapon of the Future

The world finally took notice of the breech-loading, bolt-action Dreyse

Needle Gun and raced off to build its own versions of it. The French, for instance, hurried the Chassepot rifle from development to deployment. But the Dreyse was not the weapon to have made its operational debut at Königgrätz. That had occurred some 16 years earlier, however, there was another which did make its debut in the *Bruderkrieg*. And, like the Dreyse during the first Danish-German War, it was not an auspicious one.

Shortly after the end of the final Danish-German War Wilhelm I personally instructed Roon to order 300 of the new cast-steel, breech-loading cannons that Alfred Krupp had been trying to sell for over a decade. In early 1866, after successful field trials, a much larger order came from Berlin: 162 four-pounders, 250 six-pounders and 115 24-pounders, most of which were ready by the time the Bruderkrieg began.

At Königgrätz roughly half the Prussian cannon were Krupp's breech-loaders. Mostly, they performed well...until repeated firings revealed a flaw in the breech design. The angles of the breech-block slots were wrong. Gas and flame could leak around the block, especially in the long and heavy duel with Austrian batteries. Many four-pounder and six-pounder guns had burst during the battle, maiming and killing their crews.

Roon wanted to declare the new weapon a failure and scrap the survivors. Krupp suffered what amounted to a nervous breakdown and thought about going into exile. In fact he did flee to Berne, Switzerland for over a year. Though before he left, posted literally at the train station in Essen, Krupp sent a letter to Berlin offering to replace all the earlier batches of cast-steel cannons free of charge.

Subsequent reports from the field proved it was the breech mechanism and not the steel barrels which failed. The design would be improved, but Alfred Krupp still despaired over the Bessemer process for casting the barrels. For 15 years, since he first bought a license for it from Sir Henry Bessemer, he tried to make the process work, but it never became really profitable.

Then, a German engineer working in England, Karl Wilhelm Siemens, perfected an open-hearth furnace design which took impure iron ore and turned it into high-quality steel. The first company he offered it to was Gusstahlfabrik in Essen. The exile, who had since moved on to Nice and the French Riviera, suddenly had a reason to return home.

Now, Krupp's cannons would be lighter, stronger and better designed. Their ranges and rates of fire would improve even more so over their muzzle-loading opponents and, with enough training and new procedures, so would their accuracy. The explosive shells that had proven so deadly at Sinope and Lissa, when they actually hit something, would also be improved. Alfred Krupp was well on his way to becoming "der

Kanonenkönig," the Cannon King, and his dream, actually his obsession, was on its way to becoming a war-winning weapon.

All that was needed was a war for it to win.

Chapter VIII: The Final Crises

"A great empire and little minds go ill together."
-Edmund Burke (1729 - 1797)

Imperial Dreams Meet Cold Reality

IT WAS NOT supposed to happen like this.

In the aftermath of the Franco-Austrian War everything appeared set to go France's way. She had regained her status as Europe's dominant land power, something she had not enjoyed since the zenith of Napoleon Bonaparte's reign. And with the building of the Suez Canal and the new ironclad technology she was the world's leader in, France looked poised to challenge the all-important naval supremacy of the one power greater than her.

At the beginning of 1860 Napoleon III stood at his own zenith of popularity. It coincided with his bravery on the battlefield – one could not really call his reckless charge at Solferino successful – and the wave of Anglophobia which followed in the wake of the assassination attempt on his life. Count Camillo di Cavour had convinced the French government that the Italian subversives responsible, lead by Felice Orsini, were financed by Great Britain. It suited Cavour's purpose in securing French aid for the unification of Italy. Now Napoleon used it for his own ends, and no one has ever found any evidence that England was ever involved in the attempt.

He initiated an ambitious construction program for the building of 30 ocean-going ironclads and eleven armored battery ships, culminating with the incredible *Magenta*-class double-decked line-of-battle ships. At least that is the way it all looked on paper and in the mind of Napoleon III. The problem was reality could not give him what he wanted.

The program proved far beyond the financial resources of the French Government and the capabilities of the nation's shipbuilders. In the end, the *Magenta* and its sister ship *Solferino* were completed, at the then prohibitive expense of six million francs apiece. They were impressive, even majestic-looking, ships but they would be the only ironclads ever built with two gun decks. They were unstable, which hampered their maneuverability, speed and ability to take heavy seas. And they were hopelessly obsolete from the day they were launched.

Britain did not sit still for the not-so-subtle threats to her global dominance. Some six months before the *Magenta* was launched, *HMS Warrior* slipped down the ways at Ditchburn and Mare in London. Nearly 50% longer and over one-third heavier than her French rival, she was faster, more maneuverable, carried heavier guns and had an all-iron hull instead of iron plates bolted to a wooden one. Soon joined by her own sistership, the *Black Prince*, they were intentionally assigned to the Royal Navy's Channel Fleet.

They had been designed by the great naval architect Isaac Watts to beat any ship afloat or under construction. What the Royal Navy quite unintentionally got were two ships that could beat any *fleet* in the world. What they could not outgun – and there were precious few ships who could match their broadside combination of 68-pounder and 110-pounder cannons – they could outrun and outmaneuver. They were given the joint nickname "the Black Snakes of the English Channel," and were every bit as era-changing as *HMS Dreadnought* would be some two generations later.

To be fair, the French Navy did *start* construction of the world's first iron-hulled warship. The *Couronne* had its keel laid some three months before work began on the *Warrior*. However, with technical problems encountered in her building and mounting costs, she would end up almost as expensive as *Magenta* or *Solferino*, and she could not be launched until nearly the same time as *Black Prince* slipped down the ways. And the French got a ship one-third lighter, over 50% shorter and with a much lighter armament than her British rivals.

At least she would be as nearly long lasting as *HMS Warrior*. Converted to a gunnery training ship 20 years later, the *Couronne* would be hulked in 1910 and remained afloat until finally scrapped in 1932. *Warrior* would survive a collision with *HMS Royal Oak* in 1868, both were heavily damaged, and nearly ended her days as an oil pipeline pontoon in Milford Haven in Wales. Rescued from oblivion in 1979, today she is one of the few surviving warships of her age. A tribute to her sturdy construction and luck, which in her day Louis Napoleon III was enthusiastically squandering.

North America in Turmoil

It was not supposed to happen this way either.

Imperial France's disastrous fascination with Mexico began long before Napoleon took power. Back in 1838 Louis Philippe instigated a brief war with Mexico over the payment of reparations to French civilians caught in the country's unrest. Since then both Philippe's and Napoleon's governments extended a series of loans to Mexico, most of which disappeared through mismanagement, graft and corruption. Then, in 1858, its fortunes appeared ready to change with the appearance of Benito Juarez, the new political party he lead and the government he formed. Alas, Napoleon could not let that happen.

From 1859 to the end of 1861 he had to bide his time on Mexico while he fought the Franco-Austrian War and acceded to, though did not want, the unification of Italy. After 1860 he attempted to mend his relations with Great Britain, by cooperating with British forces in their third war with China and agreeing on a free trade commercial treaty advanced by then-Finance Minister William Gladstone.

He also waited for events in North America to fall his way. In Mexico they did not, much to his irritation, with the defeat and exile of General Miguel Miramon by Juarez on December 22nd of 1860. The general had been the Clerical Party's presidential candidate and a major French ally, though he would still prove useful at a later date.

In America events went much more to Napoleon's liking as the long-building national crisis lead to a four-way presidential election in the fall of 1860. Abraham Lincoln received just under 40% of the popular vote, Stephen A. Douglas got 29%, the former vice-president John Breckinridge got 18% and the last Whig party candidate John Bell won 13% of the votes. In the Electoral College Lincoln won a comfortable 180 out of 303 votes with most of the rest going to the southerners Breckinridge and Bell. It was the perfect recipe for the dissolution of the republic; by December 20th South Carolina passed its ordinance of secession. The countdown to civil war had begun.

The shelling of Fort Sumter, by coincidence in South Carolina, did not begin until April 12th of 1861. By then almost no one in North America or

Europe doubted there would be a civil war in the United States. The problem was: which one would it be? At the time consensus both domestically and internationally was for a short conflict.

Most enlistments in the Union and Confederate armies were only for 90 days, and popular sentiment on both sides held it would just take a few encounters to send either Billy Yank or Johnny Reb "skedaddling" for home. However, after the First Battle of Bull Run, Wilson's Creek, Lexington (Missouri), Ball's Bluff, Port Royal and dozens of smaller battles the answer became obvious: the war would be a long and ruinous one.

This suited Napoleon III perfectly. Though like the British he worried about what the famine of Southern cotton would do to his textile industry, something which actually would not hit until late in 1862, he began planning to take advantage of the turmoil. He knew better than to attempt anything on his own however, on November 8th of 1861, the Union Navy presented him with the perfect opportunity to forge a grand alliance: the *Trent* Affair.

On that day a Union sloop, ironically named the *U.S.S. San Jacinto*, intercepted the British steamer *Trent* just after it left Havana. The Confederate diplomats on board it, James Mason and John Slidell, were arrested and, though the ship was allowed to proceed, the incident touched off a major diplomatic crisis. Prime Minister Palmerston embargoed critical supplies of saltpeter to the Union, threatened a diplomatic break with it, threatened to recognize the Confederacy, and even hinted at war until calmer attitudes prevailed.

Even so, the anger this crisis generated in both England and Spain, who also felt insulted because the *Trent* had originally sailed from its Cuban colony, provided Napoleon with ready-made allies for his long-dreamed adventure.

The Invasion of Mexico

At the beginning of 1862 demands were issued by the all three allies to Mexico for repayment of the debts she owed them. By the end of January French, British and Spanish warships had arrived at Vera Cruz on Campeche Bay, where they landed their troops with little opposition.

It was a blatant violation of the Monroe Doctrine, which Great Britain had supported since its creation, but none of the powers involved, nor any other nation in Europe, thought there would ever again be a United States of America to enforce it. There were few statesmen who believed the North would win, that the Union would be restored, and because of this Mexico and Juarez felt they had to submit.

On February 19th the three invading powers signed the Soledad Convention with the Mexican government. European troops were permitted to occupy the towns of Cordova, Orizaba and Tehuacan, and a schedule of debt payments planned. The belligerents seemed to have obtained what they wanted, until Napoleon's ambition grew insatiable.

By early-April he has shipped in more troops and starts demanding changes to the Convention. His actions alienate his allies, who suddenly decide his adventure is not worth what they might be risking. Union fortunes in the American Civil War had revived. They captured Nashville on February 25th, *Monitor* fought the *Virginia* to a draw on March 9th and Henry Halleck's armies won the momentous Battle of Shiloh in early April: the first battle in the Americas to produce the casualty figures approaching those of Waterloo or Solferino.

Spain feared the Union, the Confederacy, or even both would seize Cuba from them, which had been a U.S. goal since the start of the 19th Century. Britain similarly feared for her Canadian colonies, also a U.S. desire, as well Bermuda and the Bahamas. It would be enough for them to consider there might just be some teeth in the Monroe Doctrine after all, and they departed on virtually the same day France declared war on Mexico.

On April 12th, to wild cheering on the streets of Paris, the declaration was made public. For Napoleon III this should have been a moment to savor; he would not be this popular again until the end of July some eight years later, when he would leave Paris to personally take charge of the French armies preparing to invade Prussia. This time he had the army on the other side of the Atlantic and would have to go it alone for now if he wanted Mexico.

On the same day in Mexico City, Juarez called upon all men, all patriots, to resist the French invasion. To reinforce this message, and a portent of the bitter fighting to come, he had one general who had been negotiating separately with the French arrested, court-martialed and shot. For the next three weeks Mexican guerrilla bands, responding to Juarez's call to arms, attacked but were easily driven off by French forces under Comte Charles de Lorencez. But on May 5th, at the city of Puebla de los Angelos, the French Army suffered a defeat in bitter fighting with the Mexican Army. Later a violent tropical thunderstorm forced them into a general retreat to Orizaba.

For the summer, as George McClellan's Peninsula Campaign lead to the pivotal Seven Days' Battles, and later the Second Battle of Bull Run, the French had to fight just to maintain their foothold on the Mexican coast. They fought yellow fever, malaria and guerrillas, of which the first two killed more than the later, and set up a provisional government in Vera Cruz.

General Juan Nepomuceno Almote headed the government, along with General Marquez and the followers of President Miramon. They raised an army, levied taxes on the residents of Vera Cruz and other occupied cities, but little else happened until General Elie Forey arrived with additional troops and warships. Among them was the *Normandie*, sister ship of the *Glorie* and the first ironclad to make a trans-Atlantic crossing. And she was quickly put to use.

On September 24th, between McClellan's victory at Antietam and the announcement of the Emancipation Proclamation, major operations resumed in Mexico with an attack by guerrillas on French/Mexican lines near Vera Cruz. The Battle of Tejeria proved to be an easy victory for General Forey, who afterwards assumed command from Comte Lorencez, and went on the attack.

Within a fortnight he moved his coalition forces out of Cordova and Orizaba to take both Jalapa and Medelin. The *Normadie* led the naval squadron in the bombardment and capture of Tampico, a major harbor further up Mexico's Gulf Coast and soon to become an important French base. By December Forey had captured Tehuacan and Admiral Louis Bouet-Willaumez, after taking another French squadron on a long voyage into the Pacific, attacked the port of Acapulco. This denied the port as a possible base for aid from the Americas and made Napoleon's Mexican Adventure a two-ocean war. At the end of the year the French Army was advancing again on Puebla de los Angelos, on the road to Mexico City.

1863: Siege and Success

The new year began with the world's attention focused on the United States, where the Emancipation Proclamation became law on January 1st, and the other side of the world, to China where a 30-year-old captain from the British Army's Corps of Engineers took command of a mercenary army for Governor Li Hung Chang of Kiangsu Province. Charles George Gordon and his men would shortly become famous as "Chinese Gordon" and the "Ever Victorious" army as they suppressed the Taiping Rebellion over the next two years.

This is perhaps fortunate for Napoleon III as his army is defeated and nearly routed on its second approach to Puebla de los Angelos. Located in a mountainous region intersected by deep ravines, the city would be difficult to invest and it took Forey until the middle of March to achieve this. However, once the siege began, it became impossible for the rest of the Mexican Army to break it.

At Puebla the French Army found itself facing another Saragossa. Another city that, like the one in northern Spain during Napoleon Bonaparte's Peninsular War, was surrounded and resisted to the bitter end. "Guerra y cuchillo," *war to the knife*...it was the way the Mexican Army and civilians fought, even as Fort Hidalgo and Puebla's San Algier quarter were taken by the French. And especially when a relief column under General Ignacio Comonfort tried to break the siege.

Beaten back twice with heavy losses, it finally retreated to Mexico City. In mid-April the forces holding Puebla de los Angelos capitulated to the French, though not before they dismantled or spiked their cannons, broke or buried their small arms, blew up their munitions magazines and burned whatever else could be of value to the French. Their uniforms in rags, over 12,000 soldiers surrendered; among them were 26 generals and 1,000 officers of lower ranks. The back of organized resistance to the invasion was broken. The road of Mexico City lay open to the French.

In spite of this, they took their time advancing to the capital. First they had to replace their commander again. For his victory at Puebla, Elie Frederick Forey received a promotion to Marshal of France and Francois Achille Bazaine assumed command of all French forces in Mexico. And then there were delaying actions by guerrillas as Juarez decamped his government to San Louis Potosi, deep in the country's central plateau region.

Not until June 5th, around the same time as Robert E. Lee makes the fateful decision to embark his Army of Northern Virginia on its Pennsylvania Campaign, would Bazaine lead his coalition army into Mexico City. For Bazaine his hour had come, he was the most popular soldier in France. Though he did not know it, he had reached his career high-point, his moment in the sun. From now on his endeavors would only end in defeat.

However, the future certainly did not look that way to anyone on his staff or in France. Perhaps it should have, had someone bothered to look into the recent past. Just 16 years earlier General Winfield Scott had landed an army of 12,000 men at Vera Cruz during the Mexican-American War. In a campaign lasting a little over five months, from April 8th of 1847 to September 14th, he fought his way to Mexico City over the same route and captured it – a third the amount of time the French took under Lorencez, Forey and Bazaine, and without suffering a single major defeat.

But no one did for they were busy creating an imperial future for Mexico. By the end of June a provisional government had been set up in Mexico City with General Almonte, General Salas and Archbishop Labastida as its ruling triumvirate. They ceded Sonora Province in northwestern Mexico to France, reviving both the monarchy and the nobility. What they needed next was a European ruler to make it all legitimate. And Napoleon III would find a willing partner in a former enemy.

Enter Maximilian

For many historians and students of history it's always been something of a mystery why Austria and the House of Hapsburg permitted Franz Josef's younger brother to become the Emperor of Mexico. Much less why Ferdinand Maximilian Josef would accept it. He had already failed at ruling one foreign land, namely Austria's Italian provinces, and had apparently found a home as the head of its navy. Ordering the ironclads that would one day win Lissa.

On the other hand, his chances of gaining the throne from a brother only two years older than himself, and had just celebrated the birth of a second son, were rather remote. There is also much evidence Maximilian disapproved of his brother's autocratic ruling style, and admired Prussia and its Stein-Hardenberg tradition of progressive monarchy. He even admired Czar Alexander II's emancipation of Russia's 47 million serfs.

At first reluctantly, he met with French envoys and Mexican exiles, and soon becomes taken with the idea of establishing a progressive monarchy in the New World. For Napoleon III there was no reluctance in drawing Austria into what many others already considered a risky adventure. Ever since the end of the Franco-Austrian War he had been seeking a way to compensate Austria for the loss of most of its Italian territories. Now this desire became wedded to his need for a partner in Mexico.

The mere mention by the Lincoln Administration of the invasion being a violation of the moribund Monroe Doctrine had been a major reason for the withdrawal of Spanish and British forces. But Napoleon knew there was little love lost, or respect for, the American republic in the Austrian court. He knew that, back during his rise to power, a little-known incident had nearly incited war between Austria and the United States.

On June 21st, 1853 a Hungarian refugee traveling on an American passport had been arrested by the Austrian consul in the port of Smyrna, present-day Izmir, on Turkey's Agean coast. Austria suspected Martin

Koszta of aiding the Hungarian insurrection, which it had crushed nearly four years earlier, and certainly aided many Hungarian exiles emigrate to America. The only U.S. warship in the eastern Mediterranean, the sloop-of-war *U.S.S. St. Louis*, got wind of the arrest and arrived in port. Its captain demanded the release of Koszta or he would send in the Marines to free him. The French consulate intervened and within hours took custody of the prisoner, then released him to the ship's officers.

It should have ended there but Austria protested. She protested to the U.S. government, and Congress responded by giving the captain of the *St. Louis* a medal. She issued a circular letter to the other courts of Europe, but none of their titled heads took much notice; more pressing matters between Russia and Turkey demanded their attention. She hinted at war and this is where the British Minister to the Hapsburg Court explained to them the status of the North Atlantic: that it was a British "lake" and the Royal Navy would not countenance any transgression by a hostile power seeking war with its most important trading partner.

Now, as the fate of the United States was being decided on the rolling hills of Pennsylvania, Napoleon opened negotiations with the only European power more autocratic than his to establish a monarchy in North America. However reluctant Maximilian may have been, the idea soon won him over. By the end of the year, when Austria and Prussia were negotiating an alliance against Denmark in their coming war, he signalled his willingness to join the scheme. By the end of January, 1864, as their armies and navies are deploying, Napoleon formally offers the crown of Mexico. Maximilian accepts.

At a time when Maximilian should have been commanding the Austrian fleet in its first successful combat operation in centuries he left for Paris. There, in early March, he signed an agreement with Napoleon III to become the Emperor of Mexico. Bankers in London and Paris advanced him over 200 million francs to establish his empire, and additional Belgian mercenaries joined his entourage. The only discordant note to be struck occurred as he left the continent; on April 4th the United States Congress took time out from the Civil War to vote against recognizing Maximilian as the legitimate ruler of Mexico.

From Farce to Debacle

On May 28th, 1864, the same day the Danish-German War resumes with Prussian and Austrian attacks across the Jutland Peninsula, Emperor Maximilian and Empress Carlotta arrive at San Juan d'Ulloa on Mexico's

Gulf Coast. They get a formal, dignified, reception from Bazaine and Provisional Government officials. However, from Mexican civilians the response is open hostility. And from now until June 15th of 1867 that would be the one constancy of his reign.

Barely two weeks later, while still setting up his court in Mexico City, Maximilian is forced to deal with the first of many financial crises. And this one, like so many of the others, is brought about by the increased demands of Bazaine, the Belgian mercenaries, and the French Foreign Legion, which was the largest contingent of French troops serving in Mexico at the time.

Marshal Francois Achille Bazaine, hero of Solferino, awarded the Grand Cross of the Legion of Honor for his previous year's conquest of Mexico City, now set himself to the task to tarnishing his honor and reputation by repeatedly looting Maximilian's treasury and issuing barbaric orders. The most notorious of these were the organizing of "counter-guerrilla" bands of Mexican criminals to fight Juarez's forces. The atrocities they commit in the name of the new Emperor of Mexico gain him, in an age of seemingly endless conflict sweeping the world, a reputation for evil and cruelty.

His special envoy to Washington D.C. fails to even gain an audience with Lincoln or Secretary of State William Seward. His overtures to President Jefferson Davis of the Confederate States of America meet with scarcely more success. Mostly they revolve around trans-shipping southern cotton through Texas to France, but they come to nothing for two reasons.

Tactically, the Confederacy had been split in two a year earlier with the surrender of Vicksburg on the Mississippi and Mobile Bay; the last port blockade-runners could use east of the Texas ports would fall on August 5th, just over two months into Maximilian's reign. And politically, Davis wanted something more than money or gold for southern cotton. He wanted diplomatic recognition for the Confederacy. At least by Mexico, and especially by France. But Napoleon would only act in concert with Britain, and Britain chose to wait until the northern states' November elections, when, according to most observers during the summer of 1864, the Democratic "peace" candidate General George McClellan would oust Lincoln.

Since Maximilian's empire remained under French control he was forced to hold off on these schemes during the critical early months of his rule. By the time the northern elections had been decided, and the impossible had happened, he had fallen into yet another financial crisis and created a political one for himself.

To replenish his treasury Maximilian proposed the sequestration of most church lands in Mexico by his government. The move brought him some support from the Liberals still in the Mexican legislature, though he hesitated enacting it before gaining the Pope's consent.

By December he had his answer when the Papal Nuncio arrived in Mexico City. Not only did Pius IX reject Maximilian's plans for the Church's extensive real estate holdings, he condemned all his other liberal reforms, demanded restoration of the holy orders, demanded the complete transfer of public education in Mexico to the Catholic Church and the exclusion of all other religions from the land, including all Protestant denominations.

Maximilian had seriously misread the support he received from Mexico's Clerical Party, and the Vatican's support for his throne. He withdrew the sequestration plan as ordered, but again he misread Pope Pius. The private letter the Nuncio delivered was not just a confidential correspondence with a list of suggestions. It was a take-it-or-leave-it ultimatum, no negotiations. And when he refused to enact the other dictates, Maximilian began to lose support of the local clergy and the Clerical Party.

1865 began with even more desperate schemes being hatched. To reduce the extravagant expenses of his mercenary army, Maximilian opened negotiations with a delegation of Confederate Army generals, shortly before Lee's surrender at Appomattox Courthouse. It arranged for the direct transfer of 25,000 Confederate troops in Texas to Bazaine's command and for General Sterling Price to recruit farther afield for Mexico's imperial army.

The promise was the Confederate soldiers would serve for a fraction of the pay given to the Belgians, and demonstrate better discipline to boot. But it never came to pass as the Union Army got to the Rio Grande River rather sooner than expected. As for General Price, he managed to recruit enough men and families to establish an exile colony in northern Mexico by the summer of 1865. Named Carlotta, after the Empress, it would attempt to grow cotton for the French market – right in the middle of prime guerrilla country.

Following Lincoln's assassination, by the respectful distance of about three months, Maximilian tries yet again to establish diplomatic relations with the United States. However, William Seward is still Secretary of State, and the Johnson Administration refuses to even grant an audience to his envoys. This insult is followed by one that will cause even graver injury: by August recruiting offices for Juarez's Mexican Republic Army are opened in New York, Boston and other northern U.S. cities.

Even before American recruits begin arriving in the field the increase in guerrilla activity brings Maximilian to sign the infamous "Bando Negro" decrees on October 3rd. They declare all armed republicans to be outlaws and, if captured, summarily executed. Ten days later, in Mexico City, rebel commanders General Gonzalez Ortaga and General Salazar are executed under them.

As news of the decrees, and the massacres they spawn, spread to Europe and America, Maximilian becomes even more isolated and Washington decides it has to act. By February of 1866 General Philip Sheridan, commander of the Military Division of the Gulf, has massed a one million man army on the Texas side of the Rio Grande. His orders are to invade Mexico and aid Juarez if the French do not leave. But first, a diplomatic ultimatum will be issued.

In early April the U.S. ambassador to Napoleon's court tactfully warns him that France must leave Mexico or President Johnson will declare war. The rumors and threats of war are rife in Europe, on virtually the same day Bismarck is concluding Prussia's secret treaty with Italy against Austria, and Napoleon issues a threat of his own.

Shortly after this the British ambassador arrives in his court, to do what his counterpart to Franz Josef's court did some 13 years earlier, and to advise that *Warrior* and *Black Prince* would steam up and be ready to sail before the French fleet could leave port. A few days later, Napoleon advises both governments that the French Army, and even the French Foreign Legion, would leave Mexico by no later than November 1st of the following year.

However, he does not inform Maximilian until May 31st of France's decision to leave, or of Bazaine's orders to advance him no more funds, and to incorporate the Belgian mercenaries into the French units. Nor did he send the news by trans-Atlantic cable. Napoleon sent it as a personal letter; it would take nearly a month to arrive in Mexico City.

Exit Maximilian

Napoleon's bombshell sparked furor in the Mexican imperial court. Maximilian threatened abdication as his first response. The commander of his mercenaries resigned in protest and they mutinied when word got out of the orders. Maximilian might have carried out his own threat were it not for the arrival of more bad news, this time by telegraph: Prussia had declared war on Austria.

In these two crises Maximilian came to see opportunity. After Austria's initial victory at Custozza over the Italians, she experienced nothing but defeat at the hands of the Prussians. Even now he could see if they defeated Austria, his brother's throne would be in jeopardy. But he needed to hold onto Mexico if he was to have a chance at succeeding Franz Josef, and for that Maximilian needed money. At the beginning of July Carlotta is on a ship for Europe to secure more funds for her husband.

By the time she arrives the Seven-Week *Bruderkrieg* between Austria and Prussia is over but its consequences had yet to subside. None of the German courts would receive her; they were too busy dissolving their old Confederation, forming two new ones and dealing with Prussia as the dominant power in their midst. The Hapsburg court would not grant her an audience; her brother-in-law likely suspected what was being schemed. Nor would the Italian, Spanish or Greek monarchs.

Pope Pius IX *did* give Carlotta an audience, though only to tell her he would not reconsider the hated sequestration plan. Finally, in desperation she turned up in Paris, where Napoleon III kept her waiting an extraordinarily long time. Empress Eugénie brought her to the court to plead her case, which she concluded by getting on her knees and begging for the Emperor's charity, much the same way Queen Louise of Prussia humiliated herself to his uncle, some 59 years earlier.

And, as Louise did not save Prussia from the Tilsit Treaties, Carlotta could not save her husband's throne from the nephew's decision. In frustration she shouted at him, "What folly! I forgot that in my veins flows the blood of the Bourbons, and that I am dealing with an adventurer, a Bonaparte!" Then she fainted and had to be carried from the court.

Eventually her brother, the newly-installed King Leopold II of Belgium, took her into his care as she had suffered a nervous breakdown. She would never see her husband again. Carlotta would spend the rest of her days in Château Bonchant, just outside of Brussels. It would be years before she would learn of the events that followed in Mexico.

By the beginning of 1867 the situation for Maximilian had deteriorated markedly, as had the situation for his brother. Austria's defeat in the *Bruderkrieg*, the resurgent nationalism in Hungary and its loss of influence among the Germanies had put Franz Josef's future on the Hapsburg throne in doubt. Maximilian's court friends advised him that a resolute stand against Juarez and his army, even if it ultimately resulted in defeat, could gain him a far more important prize.

The problem was both Napoleon III and the Mexican Republican Army had other ideas. In early January Napoleon delivers a final betrayal when he informs Maximilian that his failure to render the latest payment of 25 million francs to Bazaine released France from all its obligations to Mexico. The French Army's withdrawal date advances from November 1st to whenever it could evacuate to the naval bases at Tampico and Vera Cruz. As it did so, it handed over most positions to the Republican Army.

Between the end of January and the beginning of May, as it accepted surrendered positions from the French Army, Juarez's army defeated Maximilian's in a series of battles – so many defeats that there were enough mercenaries to form "foreign legions" under Mexican command. Maximilian evacuates Mexico City by the end of April, but is unable to reach Vera Cruz. He's trapped in the La Cruz Cloister in Queretaro where, after a final battle on May 15th, he and his remaining entourage and officers surrender to the Republican Army.

Exactly a month later, on June 15th and after a brief trial by a military court, Emperor Maximilian, former-President Miguel Miramon and other imperial officers are executed by firing squad. By the time of his death he had already become a footnote in history to his own family. And especially by Napoleon III, who had already moved on to another crisis and another assassination attempt.

Luxembourg

Like the Alsace and the Rhineland provinces, Luxembourg was one of those mostly Germanic territories France had long coveted and sometimes actually owned. This had not been the case since the Treaty of Paris signed on April 12th of 1814, which shrank France back to its 1792 borders. But in early February of 1867, with the last act of the Mexico Debacle bringing disrepute to his prestige, Napoleon decides to shift public attention from it by creating a crisis with Prussia over its garrison in Luxembourg.

The garrison was nothing new, it had occupied the fortress almost since the end of the Napoleonic Wars. Even when Luxembourg had been Dutch, and then Belgian, territory the Prussians had held the fortress as a bulwark to the western defences of the Germanies. Now, France presented the little Grand Duchy as a threat to its security, and demanded its surrender.

Perhaps if Napoleon had understood how his accusation and demands were viewed in Berlin, Munich, Dresden and other German capitals he might not have made them. Since the end of the *Bruderkrieg*, some five months earlier, the realignment of the Germanies had not gone exactly to Berlin's, meaning Bismarck's, plans. Nor Moltke's or Roon's for that matter, but now the French Emperor gave all a heaven-sent opportunity to achieve them, and act with diplomatic restraint to boot.

Throughout February and into March Bismarck confers with the North German Bundestag on the Luxembourg Crisis, as well as Bavaria and the

South German Confederation. Then, in early April, he does something which catches Napoleon off-guard and demonstrates a previously unseen subtlety: he proposes a Concert of Powers Conference in London.

Austria, wanting revenge for the tragedy in Mexico, readily agreed with last year's enemy. England, always eager to knock its greatest rival, also agreed. Italy, still not forgiving Napoleon's betrayal of its national unity dreams, agreed as well and Russia's acceptance made Napoleon's acquiescence inevitable. A month later the major powers plus Holland and Belgium meet in London where they take one week to craft a treaty which ends the crisis.

On virtually the same day as Maximilian surrenders to the Mexican Army, the treaty is signed. It makes Luxembourg a neutral state whose sovereignty is guarantied by the Powers and the Prussian garrison is withdrawn. Napoleon is forced to be content with much less than he had wanted while Bismarck, Moltke and Roon get an added incentive to complete their secret alliances with the other German states, and the re-equipping of their armies with Krupp cannons and Dreyse rifles.

Suddenly, the world was at peace. A relative peace to be sure, but at least the European powers were not threatening each other. Even Napoleon busied himself with ventures other than his usual intrigues: on June 1st he opens the long-planned International Exposition of Paris. He plays congenial host to King Wilhelm I and his Queen, Bismarck and Moltke, the very people he desired to make war against just a few weeks earlier, and will meet under very different circumstances some three years later.

The Sultan of Turkey also arrives, as does Czar Alexander. And five days later, while riding with the Czar in Paris, Napoleon narrowly escapes yet another assassination attempt when a Polish national shoots at both of them. Peace would be very troubling for the Emperor.

Decline and Revolt

Try as he may, Napoleon would not be able to put Mexico behind him. Not only was it an international disaster of the first magnitude, it also became a financial and domestic political one. Thousands of investors wanted their money back, though only a few of the banks and powerful individuals would see anything of what they had thrown away. The rest found sympathetic ears in the national press and Corps Legislatif, which only weeks before had debated the question of war with Prussia over Luxembourg.

For years political opposition to Napoleon III had been nascent in

France, held in check by his military successes and a good economy. Now the French economy had begun faltering, most of Napoleon's ambitious public works projects were completed, and all his victories were in the past. His promises for greater press freedom and political reforms went largely unfulfilled, so the Corps struck back with the best weapon they possessed.

They slashed Napoleon's budget requests, especially in light of Mexico and the small victories in China and Indochina for the large expenditures made. Not even the success of the expedition he sent to Rome, where it routed yet another insurrection led by Giuseppe Garibaldi, gave the Emperor any relief from his political troubles.

By the middle of 1868 his decline had grown so great he was powerless to stop the latest revolt in Spain, either the 34th or 35th since the monarchy's restoration in 1814, from being one of the few successful ones. Queen Isabella II, over whom several revolts and civil wars had already been fought, finally lost the Spanish Army's support by choosing the wrong lover from its officer corps.

This time the revolt was widespread with juntas established across the country and all of Andalusia rising against her rule. The one major battle between loyalist forces, under the Marquis de Novaliches, and the revolutionary army commanded by Marshal Dominguez y Serrano, then the President of the Senate, occurred in late-September just outside of Cordova in southwestern Spain.

With the defeat of the loyalist army all organized resistance to the revolution ended. Empress Eugénie's voluble protests to the contrary, this time there would be no French intervention. Unlike 45 years earlier, when Louis XVIII sent "a hundred thousand sons" to aid the restoration of the imbecilic and reactionary Ferdinand VII to his throne, the French had learned one lesson. They would not put his despotic daughter back on the Spanish throne and Napoleon III did not have the power to compel it.

Instead Isabella fled to exile in France while Spain completed her revolution. However, this revolution was not a modern one, in the post-1848 sense of the word. There were no socialists, communists or anarchists; none of this would exist is Spain until late in 1871 when Karl Marx's son-in-law would arrive in Madrid after the suppression of the Paris Commune. Once it had been set up, the provisional government of Marshal Serrano began to modernize the country. Most important would be the selection of the right progressive, liberal monarch for the vacant throne. The process would drag on for over two years, and lead to the Hohenzollern Candidature.

The Final Crisis

It is no small irony of history that, had Maximilian heeded Bazaine's last warning and evacuated Mexico with him some two years earlier, he would have likely been the leading candidate for a throne the Hapsburgs had lost to the Bourbons in 1700. But he did not and the process wound its way through a number of lesser candidates, all of whom either declined or were rejected.

Several candidates had been French nobles, and throughout 1869 Napoleon harbored dreams that the throne his uncle Joseph had lost in 1813 would be regained by a Frenchman. He had an ally in the Spanish provisional government, Army Commander-in-Chief Juan y Prats Prim, who kept reassuring him of it. As late as the Spring of 1870 the general had a long conference in France with the Emperor on the subject. But when he returned to Madrid, Prim found the rest of the committee had made a new selection: Prince Leopold Hohenzollern of Sigmaringen, one of the smallest of the German states.

The Spanish thought they had found the perfect candidate. He was young, energetic, a member of a distant branch of the Prussian royal family as well as related through his mother to Queen Hortense of Holland, Napoleon's mother. And he was Catholic and an army officer to boot. An initial polling of Spain's Constituent Assembly indicated he would win the formal election. On July 3rd the Prince himself publicly announced he would accept the throne if the Assembly voted for him.

Leopold's candidacy had a lot of recent history behind it. For the last four decades there had been a steady trickle of German nobles becoming monarchs of foreign lands. In 1831 Prince Leopold of Saxe-Coburg became Belgium's king. A year later Prince Otto of Bavaria accepted the throne of Greece. And of course there was Prince Albert of Saxe-Coburg who, in 1840, married Queen Victoria of England, which made Belgium's King Leopold Victoria's uncle. Even Prince Leopold's older brother had recently become heir to the Romanian throne so this new choice had a lot of favor for it – except from the French.

This time the French press, who had been busy denouncing Napoleon, enthusiastically joined him in attacking the candidate, the reasons for his choice and who actually did the choosing. Almost no one in the press corps, the Corps Legislatif or Tuileries Palace believed, or really wanted to believe, that the Spanish government had honestly blundered into choosing someone so offensive to them.

Outside of France the German states and the governments of England, Italy, Belgium and Holland wondered what madness had possessed them.

Some suspected the whole crisis to be a conspiracy by Napoleon and General Prim to justify a war against Prussia which Berlin was now trying its best to avoid.

Wilhelm I disapproved of the choice but, in keeping with the articles of the North German Confederation, he could not forbid it. Taking the hint from the most senior member of his extended family, Prince Leopold promptly withdrew his acceptance. A few days later Wilhelm left Berlin for the resort spa of Ems in western Prussia, considering the crisis over.

But Napoleon would not let it go. In days he had gone from being detested tyrant to the defender of French honor. He had not been this popular in years, not since the early days of the Mexico Invasion, and he instructed his ambassador to Berlin to keep pressing the matter with a new list of demands. And as Count Benedetti traveled to Ems for his repeatedly demanded private meeting with Wilhelm, other French ambassadors contacted the Foreign Ministries of Bavaria, Baden, Hanover, Saxony and other German states to see if any would form an alliance against Prussia.

Unfortunately for Napoleon, his intelligence service had been rather too enthusiastic in reporting the discontent with Prussian dominance across the Germanies. To be sure there were plenty of malcontents and particularists who desired Austrian dominance instead of Prussian and anti-imperialists who wanted neither. But few were in any position of power and none chose to ally themselves with an empire obviously maneuvering an invented crisis toward war. As events began cascading into the conflict Napoleon desired they were already spinning out of his control.

Oblivious to all this, Ambassador Benedetti had two meetings with Wilhelm where he read him the new riot act of French demands. Not only did the King of Prussia have to absolutely guarantee that Prince Leopold would not accept the Spanish offer, he had to further guarantee no other Prussian noble would be a candidate to its throne. Demands were also made to the future of Belgium and Luxembourg, which Napoleon coveted along with the Rhineland provinces.

Wilhelm agreed to none of this and curtly dismissed the ambassador. And when Benedetti demanded a third meeting with the King the Prussian court dismissed him from its service. All this was contained in the famous Ems Telegram the King sent to Bismarck, who happened to be having dinner in Berlin with Moltke and Roon when it arrived on July 13th. Here, translated verbatim, is the original telegram:

His Majesty the King has written to me:

"Count Benedetti intercepted me on the promenade and ended by demanding of me in a very importunate manner that I should authorize him to telegraph at once that I bound myself in perpetuity never again to give my consent if the Hohenzollerns renewed their candidature.

I rejected this demand somewhat sternly as it is neither right nor possible to undertake engagements of this kind [for ever and ever]. Naturally I told him that I had not yet received any news and since he had been better informed via Paris and Madrid than I was, he must surely see that my government was not concerned in the matter."

[The King, on the advice of one of his ministers] "decided in view of the above-mentioned demands not to receive Count Benedetti any more, but to have him informed by an adjutant that His Majesty had now received from [Leopold] confirmation of the news which Benedetti had already had from Paris and had nothing further to say to the ambassador.

His Majesty suggests to Your Excellency that Benedetti's new demand and its rejection might well be communicated both to our ambassadors and to the Press."

In its day much was written about how these three rewrote the telegram, giving it a more inflammatory tone to ensure war would break out and then releasing it without Wilhelm's permission. The truth is this conspiracy myth had been fabricated and mostly perpetuated by Bismarck's critics, especially post-war French historians. Here is the text of the released version:

"After the news of the renunciation of the Prince von Hohenzollern had been communicated to the Imperial French government by the Royal Spanish government, the French Ambassador in Ems made a further demand on His Majesty the King that he should authorize him to telegraph to Paris that His Majesty the King undertook for all time never again to give his assent should the Hohenzollerns once more take up their candidature.

His Majesty the King thereupon refused to receive the Ambassador again and had the latter informed by the adjutant of the day that His Majesty had no further communication to make to the Ambassador."[*]

The reality of the day, in the middle weeks of July of 1870, is that the paths to this war were now racing to their inevitable junction. After its generations-long gestation, it had just days to go before being born.

---

[*] Primary Documents, FirstWorldWar.com. Original source of translation unknown.

The Ems Telegram, which Wilhelm had already given his permission to release, would not be the only message the three dinner guests sent out that night. Bismarck sent orders for all other German governments to be contacted; the secret treaties and alliances he worked on for the last three years were now activated. Moltke and Roon concentrated on military matters. Moltke on mobilizing the Prussian Army and calling up its Landwehr reserves while Roon contacted the war ministries of Prussia's closest allies to mobilize their forces.

But these were not the first mobilization orders to be sent out. On July 8th, a day *before* Count Benedetti had his first meeting with Wilhelm, Napoleon III ordered two army corps to be readied for immediate movement: one under Francois Bazaine and the other under the new French Minister of War, Edmond Leboeuf. By July 12th the first column of French troops marched through Paris on their way to the eastern frontier.

Two days later, shortly after Berlin released the contents of the Ems Telegram, the French Navy received orders to commence blockade operations against German ports. Bismarck countered by sending out a general warning to all German merchant shipping to seek shelter in neutral ports. On the next day, with the French press railing over the insults in the Ems Telegram and the dismissal of Count Benedetti, both the Corps and the Senate met in extraordinary session at the Palace of the Corps Legislatif.

"Prussia has forgotten the France of Jena and we must remind her!" thundered the elderly Senator Guyot-Montpayroux at the start of the session, and the tone of his rhetoric was taken up by Prime Minister Olivier Emile Ollivier. In a fiery speech he repeated the lists of insults Prussia had heaped upon France and French Honor. He repeated the threat she supposedly represented to France – surrounding her, investing her, with German princes on foreign thrones. He then asked for a declaration of war and a budget of half a billion francs "to safeguard the interests, the security and the honor of France!"

Both measures passed by overwhelming votes, but they were not unanimous. The republican leaders Jules Favre, Louise Thiers, Leon Gambetta and a few others abstained their votes. They were not particularly anti-war – pacifism had yet to become a serious political movement – and from all evidence they did not like Prussia any more than Napoleon.

What they feared was either a protracted war, which could devastate France, or that Napoleon would win decisively. He would humble Prussia, take control of the German states and repeat his uncle's greatest achievement: becoming the new Charlemagne of Europe. He would be unassailable, and the dream of a French republic would be dead for generations.

In Prussia, Wilhelm I did not leave Ems until the 15th, the same day the French declared war. The formal declaration would not reach Berlin until July 19th, and shortly before that Wilhelm opened his own extraordinary session of the Prussian legislature with a call for war. This time the vote in favor was unanimous and all parties supported the budget vote of 120 million thalers for the military. The North German Confederation and the South German states followed soon thereafter with their own declarations.

The war that would decide the future of France, Germany and the world had begun.

Part II – The Franco-Prussian War

"The vicissitudes of fortune, which spares neither man
nor the proudest of his works, which buries empires
and cities in a common grave."
-Edward Gibbon (1737`- 1794)

Chapter IX: The War Leaders – France Versus Germany

"Pay attention to your enemies, for they are the first to discover your mistakes."
-Antisthenes (c.445 - 365 B.C.)

Into War

THIS UNFOLDING CONFLICT brought together two unique sets of national leaders. By their training, demeanor and lifetime experiences one set had become qualified to win the first modern war in history, and the other destined by their own special circumstances and arrogance to lose it.

If their material positions had been reversed it would not have mattered. If the Germans had the Chassepot Needle Gun and the Mitrailleuse, and the French the Dreyse and Krupp's breech-loading artillery it would not have changed the outcome, though it might have produced different casualty figures.

It would not have mattered because the Germans, especially the Prussians, would have learned to master the technology, while the French would have been content that the mere possession of such advanced weapons was mastery enough. And the same would be true of the other, more mundane, technologies both sides would employ on such massive scales.

The quality of France's new weapons could not be questioned, but the quality of its leaders should have, and if Louis Napoleon III had truly been a student of his uncle he would have. His uncle's greatest resource, his greatest weapon throughout all the wars that bore his name had been his marshals. Bonaparte understood the supreme value of good commanders, and his nephew should have remembered the following quote from him:

> "The Gauls were not conquered by the Roman Legions but by Caesar. It was not before the Carthaginian soldiers that Rome was made to tremble, but before Hannibal. It was not the Macedonian phalanx which reached India but Alexander. It was not the French Army that reached Weser and the Inn; it was Turenne. Prussia was not defended for seven years against the three most formidable European powers by the Prussian soldiers but by Frederick the Great..."

Emperor Versus Kings

The problems with French leadership begin right at the top, as does the advantages in leaders among the Germanies.

To be momentarily fair to Charles Louis Napoleon III, he did last more than twice as long on the throne as his uncle. Modern Paris, with its broad geometric avenues, public squares, public lighting, prominent train stations, advanced sewer system, modernized defences and even an underground canal, is largely his doing. As is the greatest French engineering achievement, the Suez Canal, which had finally opened just eight months earlier. The first true mega-projects of the modern age were done at his instigation.

He put Italy on the road to unity, something that without French help would have been a bloody, protracted affair ending in the ruination of every Italian kingdom from the Alps to Sicily. He got Nice and the Savoy region restored to France by right of lawful conquest, but this is largely where his attributes end.

Much has been written in full-length biographies of his recklessness, his ruinous follies, his deceit in dealing with allies, adversaries, and even his own countrymen. Perhaps these behaviors befit the heir of history's consummate opportunist, but after more than 20 years in power he was without any real allies and his court filled with the corrupt and sycophants.

His one real ally in all his follies and betrayals was his wife, Empress Eugénie. Many accounts from the period identify her as one of the main driving forces behind the crisis over the Hohenzollern Candidature. And French newspapers began using in public a nickname formerly mentioned only in private: L'Espagnole (the Spaniard).

That she had been a major influence on his reign had always been accepted, especially during the Mexico Disaster. Now, between the events of the last few weeks and those over the next month, the newspapers would begin looking on her as a foreigner with undue influence over France. People would begin comparing her to the still-infamous "Austrian Whore" – Marie Antoinette.

On the German side Wilhelm Friedrich Ludwig Hohenzollern could scarcely stand in more contrast with his adversary if he had planned it that way. Prior to his accession to power, Napoleon spent most of his life either in exile, in prison or on the run from the authorities. Wilhelm spent most of his early life either in service to his country, or preparing to succeed his brother.

Born in 1797, 11 years before his adversary, he was old enough to see his parents and country defeated and humiliated by the first Emperor Napoleon. He entered military service before turning 15 and took part in the campaigns that united and liberated the Germanies. After 1815 he stayed in the army and, in 1840, became the governor of Pomerania, a province in northeastern Prussia on the Baltic Sea coast.

Eight years later he commanded the Berlin garrison in suppressing the city's first wave of rioting during the "Year of Revolution." He earned the nickname the "Cartridge Prince" both for his aggressive tactics and one of the earliest uses of the Dreyse Needle Gun. However, it made him very unpopular, a flashpoint for the later waves of rioters, and he spent his only extended time away from his country.

After nine months of exile in England, Wilhelm returned to be elected to the Prussian National Assembly, though he took no active part in politics as he assumed command of Confederation forces defeating an insurrection in Baden. He advocated Prussia joining Russia's side during the Crimean War, a move which would have seen that blighted war turn into a continent-wide conflagration.

Fortunately, the government did not take up the initiative and soon Wilhelm had a more important duty to perform. With his childless older brother growing senile, he receives the reigns of government on October 23rd of 1857. By October 9th of the following year he's declared Regent and on January 2nd, 1861 he is crowned King Wilhelm I.

Unlike Napoleon III, at first his rule in unpopular. He accepts counsel from his ministers and generals, and gradually becomes everything the Emperor is not. He leads his country into two successful wars, Prussia becomes the dominant power among the Germanies and the rising star of Europe. But he is careful not to alienate or insult the leaders of those other German states.

His sincere efforts to maintain cordial relations with the other kings, princes, dukes and arch-dukes now stood him well in the war and the crisis leading up to it. When Wilhelm told Count Benedetti he could not and would not even try to stop any Prussian or German noble from becoming a candidate for the Spanish throne, the French thought him evasive, even deceitful. The Germans saw him respecting the authority and independence of the other monarchs and, most important, willing to go to war over it.

Whereas France would experience nothing but failure in recruiting allies, even when it went father afield to Austria-Hungary and Denmark, Prussia would experience nothing but success in those it approached. In fact, in many ways the first successful blitzkrieg operation in modern warfare was the diplomatic offensive Prussia launched with the release of the Ems Telegram.

The other German monarchs could have said no, many did have problems with what they termed Prussian arrogance and imperiousness, but they chose to imbue those in Prussia's chief ministers and not in its ruler. King Johann Wettin of Saxony, King Karl I of Würtemberg answered the messages sent out by Bismarck almost immediately. The only major German state anyone had possible reservations about was Bavaria, and King Ludwig II Wittelsbach.

Known alternately as "the boy king who died a virgin" or "the virgin king who liked little boys," the odd behaviors and questionable sanity of Ludwig were well-known amongst the German aristocracy. When he delayed his government's reply the rest worried. However, Bismarck's release of a secret treaty proposed by Napoleon III just before the Austro-Prussian War started apparently brought him around. In the end he authorized the mobilization of Bavarian forces, two full corps plus reserves, then returned to his castle-building and other activities.

Wilhelm continued his cordiality to the battlefield; when he joined the mobilized armies he brought a royal entourage with him. Many of the other monarchs, except for the castle-builder, joined him in this retinue attached to Moltke's headquarters staff. This was not merely an enlarged version of a royal hunting party with Wilhelm as its host. They were there to oversee the conduct of the war, and he was the head of a coalition.

By comparison, when Napoleon went into the field he only took his son, the Prince Imperial, with him. And he did not go to oversee the French Army's conduct, he joined it to take direct command, much like his uncle had done some 60 years earlier, though without his military genius or great wealth of battlefield experiences.

Bismarck Versus the Midgets

The Prussian minister most imbued with the "crimes" of arrogance and imperiousness by all those other German rulers was, of course, Count Otto Edward Leopold von Bismarck. Strictly speaking he was not Prussia's Prime Minister, or the equivalent of France's succession of Premiers and Dictators during this time period. He held more power in the dual positions of Governor of the King's Cabinet and Foreign Minister.

In the former role he fought hard battles with both houses of the Prussian legislature, the House of Deputies and House of Nobles, to reform and modernize the army. At times he closed one of the Houses and used other strong arm tactics to get the programs and budgets he, Roon, Moltke and King Wilhelm wanted passed by the government.

In the latter role he had to run a complex, and unique, two-track foreign policy. One track was for Prussia's relations with the other European Powers and the rest of the world. The second track managed relations with the other German states and it is here where Bismarck, even more so than his treatment of the Prussian legislature, got the reputation for being stern, arrogant, even imperious. But he almost always succeeded in getting what he felt Prussia needed. And even if other Germans resented him for what he did – he would never enjoy the kind of popularity most American politicians crave – most respected him for the success he achieved.

By comparison the French opponents the tides of history pitted against him were political and statecraft midgets. The first of them, at least in the immediate period leading up to the Franco-Prussian War, was Premier Olivier Emil Ollivier, one of the last direct appointments to be made by Napoleon III.

Once, about a decade earlier, Ollivier been part of the republican opposition and attacked Napoleon bitterly. Then, starting around 1863, the Emperor began cultivating a better relationship by giving him a lucrative, temporary appointment. And gradually he seduced Ollivier away from the opposition until, in January of 1870, he made him Premier.

Once a friend of men like Thiers, Favre and Gambetta, he now fought with them in the Legislature and usually lost. While not without some abilities as a politician, he would only be successful and popular for these few brief weeks in July. Once the French Army started losing, he would be cast aside by Napoleon, who appointed from the field Comte Charles Guillaume Antoine de Palikao.

His tenure in both this office and as War Minister, where he replaced General Edmond Loboeuf, would be less than a month. An elderly cavalry officer and a veteran of the colonial wars in Algeria and China, de Palikao would have been better suited to be Minister of War than Premier. In either office he did not get much of a chance to prove himself as the disaster that engulfed France swept him out of both positions by the first week in September.

His replacement, in the chaos which followed the disintegration of the Second Napoleonic Empire, was the first President of the Third French Republic: Louise Adolphe Thiers. A man who had once been exiled by Napoleon, during the coup which destroyed the Second Republic, would take the reigns of government in the midst of a collapsing war effort. Easily the most capable of the leaders to oppose Bismarck, Thiers would last no longer in office than his imperial predecessor. Even with the dictatorial powers given to him, he could not stop the investment of Paris, where he wanted to stay but could not, while another took control of the government.

Whereas Thiers was a dictator in all but name only, Leon Michael Gambetta was actually given the title in early October; in the 19th Century the word "dictator" did not carry the same pejorative connotation as it does today. However, apart from his novel method of escaping a besieged Paris, he would do little else that proved helpful to his country.

Even though he had been one of the opposition leaders who opposed the war, he insisted on the "Guerre à Outrancé" policy that would see army after army of half-trained and poorly-equipped troops sent against the Germans. Who in almost every instance destroyed them.

After five months of near-endless failures he finally had to negotiate with Bismarck and Roon. Once the initial treaty had been concluded, Gambetta resigned his post and fled into temporary exile in Spain. He would return after a few months and have an eventful post-war career in the French government, which ironically would end up serving Bismarck's post-war interests.

Roon and Moltke Versus the Unfortunates

General Graf Albrecht Emil von Roon was one of the other ministers associated with Prussian arrogance and imperiousness. While similar charges against Bismarck were at least partly unfair – most accounts describe him as a courtly gentleman – Roon *was* stern, arrogant, short-tempered and uncompromising.

He proved this way even with his allies in King Wilhelm's cabinet, such as Bismarck and Helmuth von Moltke, and seemingly always this way with others like Alfred Krupp. He was a driven personality – the only person he yielded his unbending views to was Wilhelm I – and to many of his colleagues he had acquired the nickname of "Ruffian Roon."

As a strategist many staff and field commanders considered him a comedian, as a tactician something worse. But he was honest, and ran the least corrupt and most efficient War Ministry of any of the European powers. When Roon came into office in 1859, the scandals of the British Army in Crimea, not to mention the Sepoy Rebellion in India, were still making news. Then came the stories of the disasters the Austrian Army inflicted upon itself in Italy during the war with France. And later there would be reports of the Union and Confederate armies of the U.S. Civil War and the French in Mexico.

All of these Roon had studied, and their lessons and their warnings had been absorbed into the Prussian Army. And the man most responsible for this, one of the few he honestly respected and would even accept contrary views from was Marshal Helmuth Karl Bernhard von Moltke. The third partner in the political-military triumvirate – Roon and Bismarck were the others – who would take Prussia from a humiliated power to the unifier of the Germanies and possessor of the world's most powerful army.

The longest-serving of the three, Bismarck got his office in 1863 and Roon in 1859, Moltke was appointed by Wilhelm I in 1857, immediately after he became *de facto* Regent from his increasingly senile older brother. Born in Prussia in 1800, Moltke received his initial training in the Copenhagen Royal Cadet Academy and served in a Danish infantry regiment.

In 1821 he transferred to the Prussian Army and received a commission as a lieutenant. Like Bismarck he had a facility for languages and soon learned French and English. He had a great interest in the natural sciences, especially topography and geology, and began devising military applications for them. His language abilities were an advantage he would use throughout his life. In the early 1830s he supplemented his meager officer's pay by translating, in the astonishing short time of 18 months, the entire nine-volume set of Edward Gibbon's *The Decline and Fall of the Roman Empire*. Later, especially in the 1850s and 1860s, he would directly read the reports of battles in foreign wars without waiting for them to be translated.

And, unique for a Prussian officer, not only did he read up on foreign battles, he experienced them. Between 1835 and 1840 he was an advisor and military observer to the court of Sultan Mohammed II in Istanbul. In 1839 he took to the field to observe the Ottoman Empire's campaign against the Egyptians in Syria. When the Ottoman commander failed to follow his advice and defeat resulted, Moltke took personal command of the Turkish artillery and covered the retreat.

Back in Prussia he wrote about his experiences in the Ottoman court and became a popular author. Now a celebrity as well as an experienced officer, he received a series of staff appointments, culminating in his 1857 selection as chief of the Prussian Army's general staff. He would remain in this position for 31 years, the longest-serving chief of the army in modern Germany's history, and revolutionize warfare in ways that would shortly astound the world.

In the Imperial French government the positions of Minister of War and Chief of the Army were combined into one office. In theory this could have lead to greater efficiency, but this would never be borne out in practice. Partly this is the result of Napoleon putting a series of mediocrities into the office and the overall dismal state of the French Army.

Perhaps the one man who could have changed some of this never got a chance to match his abilities against Roon and Moltke. Marshal Adolphe Niel recognized the shortcomings, failures and corruption in the army and was willing to do something about it. He did not see his job as being a Napoleonic yes-man and supporting the Emperor's fantasies of possessing the most powerful army in Europe. He wanted to give Napoleon III that kind of force, and began instituting reforms almost from the day he entered the office.

Alas, he died in 1869. His replacement was General Edmond Leboeuf, who fell in line with his indistinguished predecessors. An artillery officer who did perform bravely in the Crimean and Franco-Austrian Wars, he became Napoleon's aide-de-camp and head of the Artillery Bureau shortly thereafter. He lead the Selection Commission that decided on the Chassepot rifle, and because of the procedural troubles the stain of corruption followed Leboeuf to his new office.

While he did continue some of the reforms initiated by Niel, they were not pursued with enough vigor and they had run out of time. What would have needed years to achieve any change were overtaken by Napoleon's opportunism. When Leboeuf told his Emperor that "the army is ready to the last buttons on its gaiters" for the coming war he knew he was lying, but did not want to incur imperial wrath.

Instead, what Leboeuf got was the imperial boot from his office after the disasters of August and replacement by de Palikao. In turn the Government of National Defence, headed initially by Thiers, replaced him with a civil engineer from a family of naval officers: Charles Louis de Saules de Freycinet, who would head the War Ministry until the end of the conflict.

Outside of Marshal Niel, de Freycinet was probably the most capable individual to head the ministry in years. Had he its pre-war resources and enough time, he might have created a formidable enough war machine to effectively counter what Roon and Moltke had created.

Unfortunately de Freycinet, like the overall Government of National Defence, had inherited a disaster where time and resources ran out. In the end logistics broke down, the armies disintegrated and the French government had more to fear from the Communards in Paris than the Germans in the field.

After the suppression of the Paris Commune de Freycinet would leave the government, but he would not stay out for long. Elected senator in 1876, he went on to become one of the longest-serving politicians in France and live to the astonishing age of 105.

The French Military Commanders

Marshal Marie Edme Patrice Maurice de MacMahon: The descendant of an Irish Jacobite family who fled Britain after the fall of the House of Stuart in the late-17th Century. MacMahon graduated from the Saint-Cyr Academy in 1825 as a cavalry officer and saw his first combat in Algeria, as did most other French Army officers of his generation.

In 1837 he gives distinguished service at the Battle of Constantine and is promoted to regimental command. He gets his first division in 1855, when he's recalled to France for the Crimean War. By September he's on the peninsula, leading his division in a renewed assault on the Malakov Tower batteries, a key position in the Russian defences of Sevastopol.

MacMahon's division occupies the Tower, but their achievement is imperiled by the failure of British forces to take the nearby Redan lines. "Dead or alive, I will hold my ground," is his answer when his commander warns him to retire. They manage to hold on, giving victory to what could have been a massive replay of Balaclava.

Two years later MacMahon returns to Algeria to suppress a revolt of the Kabyle tribes. He is so successful he's given command of all French land and naval forces in the colony. And two years after this, in 1859, he's again recalled to France, this time as a corps commander in the Franco-Austrian War.

His timely arrival at Magenta, where he saves the corps of Marshals Canrobert and Niel from defeat, and his intervention at Solferino, where he saves Bazaine and Napoleon himself, rewards him with the title of Duke of Magenta and the rank of Field Marshal. These are his crowning achievements on the battlefield; he would not know their like again for the rest of his military career.

In January of 1861 MacMahon gets a further reward when he leads the French delegation at the coronation of Wilhelm I in Berlin. Here he meets all the leaders he will later encounter under more trying circumstances at Sedan.

By 1864 he is back in Algeria as governor of the colony. For the next six years his career is uneventful. He fights no major battles, which allows Bazaine to become the new military star of Imperial France because of his conquest of Mexico. On the other hand, when Mexico becomes a nightmare it's MacMahon's career that shines brighter because it is not stained with disaster.

Early in 1870 he is brought back to France by Minister of War Edmond Leboeuf, who acceded to Niel's dying wish to put the best soldier in the French Army in command of all its field forces. In that sense MacMahon is the equivalent of Moltke, though he was not part of Napoleon's cabinet and had little influence on policy.

What he could do was complete Niel's reform of the French Army's command structure. As much as he could do so without imperial interference, he put the right men, the most experienced officers, in the best positions for their talents. On the eve of war it became one of the few real advantages the French Army held over the coalition of German ones arrayed against it.

Sure, there had been a number of joint field exercises held between the Prussian Army and its North German Confederation partners. But how they would function as a cohesive whole in actual combat had yet to be seen. This was the one real unknown facing the massive war machine Roon and Moltke had created.

Marshal François Achille Bazaine: Born, in 1811, to a family with a long and distinguished history of French military service, Bazaine studied at the Polytechnique School of Paris before entering the army as an infantry officer. Between 1831 and 1837 he serves in Algeria, then he's sent to Spain and commands a French Foreign Legion unit in the suppression of yet another Carlist uprising.

After two years in Spain he returns to Algeria in 1839 to join an expedition against Morocco. For several years afterward he serves as military governor of the Tlemcen Province, until the Crimean War. There, he commands an infantry brigade and wins notice for his organizational abilities. After Sevastopol falls to the British and French, Bazaine is made its governor until the end of the war.

Three years later he's given command of an infantry division in the Franco-Austrian War. It's his men who rally the retreating Imperial Guards after Napoleon's brazen assault on Solferino fails and he is in danger of being captured. He wins fame as one of the heroes of the Emperor's greatest victory, but even greater success is in store.

Barely two years afterwards Bazaine is one of several divisional commanders who participates in the invasion of Mexico. In April of 1862 he assumes command of the faltering campaign from Marshal Forey and completes the much-delayed drive to Mexico City. This is his crowning success; he becomes the most popular soldier in France and an imperial favorite, until August of 1870.

However, by the end of 1862 Bazaine's reputation begins getting tarnished. He regards Mexicans as little more than uncivilized animals and enacts barbaric measures to suppress Juarez and his republican forces. The most notorious measure is the creation of "counter guerrilla" bands out of criminals and bandits. While they achieve some success, they ambush and kill the Republican General Ignacio Comonfort in mid-1863, their murderous rampages would have devastating long-term consequences for Mexico.

In the short term Bazaine's corruption and cruel tactics undermined Emperor Maximilian's throne virtually from the moment he set foot in Mexico. Almost single-handedly he emptied the treasury the unfortunate Archduke brought with him. The laws Bazaine encouraged him to enact, especially the infamous "Bando Negro" decrees, are ultimately used against him. Maximilian is tried under his own decrees and executed.

In the meantime, Bazaine returns to France a wealthy man and still one of Napoleon's favorites. Though both Niel and MacMahon would have liked to cashier him from the Army, they are forced to retain him. At the beginning of the war he commands the Third Corps at Metz with five divisions under his control.

Marshal François Certain Canrobert: The same relative age as MacMahon, he entered the Saint-Cyr Academy the same year his friend graduated from it, and came out an infantry lieutenant in 1828. From that year until 1839 he is in combat almost continually in Algeria. Back in France he's assigned to the Foreign Legion to form units out of refugees from the latest Spanish revolt.

In 1841 Canrobert returns to Algeria and Morocco, where he fights for another eight years. By 1850 he's in France in time to support the future emperor in his two-stage coup against the Second Republic. He becomes an imperial favorite and is rewarded three years later for his support by being appointed a division commander in the expedition force heading for Crimea.

Within a year and half, with Marshal Jacques St. Arnaud on his deathbed, he assumed command of all French forces on the Crimean Peninsula. Having already been successful in the battles of Inkermann, Alma, Balaklava and Eupatoria, Canrobert found himself in an unwinnable one with the inflexible and ignorant Lord Raglan.

For two months they argued over whether there should be an immediate assault on Sevastopol at all, much less how to conduct it. Even though the French had twice as many troops on Crimea as the British, they ceded operational control to Raglan and Canrobert got replaced with General Pelissier.

Still, for his successes in the war Napoleon III promoted him to the rank of Marshal in 1856. In the Franco-Austrian War he is the Emperor's personal aide-de-camp and overall commander of the French Army. He also has corps command at the battles of Magenta and Solferino where his skill and tenacity are major contributors to victory.

However, shortly after the war he falls out of imperial favor and retires from active service to become a full-time Senator. Canrobert escapes the taint of the Mexico Disaster and, on the eve of the war, is recalled to duty and given command of the Sixth Corps at Châlons with five divisions.

General Pierre Charles de Failly: First sees combat in the Franco-Austrian War and, fortunate for him, is not sent to Mexico. Instead he gives Napoleon III one of the few military successes he can enjoy in the late-1860s – de Failly commands the expedition sent to Rome to defend the Papal States against yet another uprising led by Giuseppe Garibaldi.

The campaign sees the first use of the Chassepot Needle Gun, which is so effective it easily routs Garibaldi's forces and convinces Napoleon that his army has developed a war-winning weapon. Now an imperial favorite, de Failly gets command of Fifth Corps at Bitsch with four divisions.

General Felix Charles Douay: Serves in both the Franco-Austrian War and Mexico with his older brother, Charles Abel Douay. Both become generals and while the older brother has more extensive service, including the Crimean War, it's Felix who gets a Corps command: Seventh Corps at Belfort with four divisions. Charles Abel is a favorite of Marshal MacMahon and is retained at 1st Corps as commander of its 2nd Infantry Division. It is this corps and this division which will first see significant combat on August 4th.

General Charles Denis Sauter Bourbaki: The son of a Greek immigrant family, he first sees service in the Crimean War, then in the Franco-Austrian War at the Battle of Solferino. He serves in various staff appointments and gains the all-important imperial favor. At the start of the war he is the commander of the Imperial Guard.

One of the most highly desired commands in the French Army, the Imperial Guard is no mere ceremonial unit, but a corps-strength elite force of two infantry divisions and one cavalry division. To serve in it was a high distinction, to command it even more so.

Uniquely, Bourbaki was one of the few senior-rank French officers to appreciate the new strength and combat-prowess of the Prussian Army. His concerns did not interfere with his posting, but it is not known if he communicated these to anyone except MacMahon.

General Louis-Jules Trochu: Like Bourbaki, Trochu was one of the younger generation of army officers. He graduated from Saint-Cyr in 1840 and spent ten years in staff positions in Algeria. During the Crimean War Trochu was aide-de-camp to St. Arnaud and a Major General in the Franco-Austrian War.

In this war he should have had a field command, at least divisional if not corps, but those coveted positions only went to officers who had Napoleon's approval, and Trochu was out of imperial favor. Skill, leadership and bravery did not mean much in the Emperor's court when you openly spoke your mind and disdained bribes.

Instead, Trochu got command of the Paris garrison and its extensive fortifications. As the troops flowed through Paris on their way to Châlons, Metz, Belfort and other points east, he could not have helped feeling history was passing him by. However, Trochu's hour would come. History, and the German armies, would find him.

General Charles Auguste Frossard: Was an officer who played the political game the right way. The former chief of Napoleon's household and governor of the Prince Imperial, Napoleon's 14 year-old son, he got command of 2nd Corps at St. Avold with four divisions.

General Comte Louis Paul de Ladmirault: One of the few nobles with a senior position in the army, Ladmirault held command of the Fourth Corps at Thionville with four divisions.

The German Military Commanders

Prince Friedrich Karl Alexander Hohenzollern: The son of Prince Karl and nephew of Wilhelm I, he followed the tradition that all Hohenzollern princes were automatically enrolled in the Prussian Army's officer cadet corps. Unlike the other cadets the princes all received personal instructions from some of the army's highest-ranking and most experienced commanders. This was due to the fact that the princes were expected not to lead just divisions or corps but entire armies. As Moltke himself put it, "the military commander is the fate of the nation."

And in fact Helmuth von Moltke would be the principal instructor to Prince Friedrich Karl in his later years. The first great influence on his military career was General Friedrich von Wrangel, to whose staff the prince would be assigned in 1848, shortly after his 20th birthday and just before the start of the First Danish-German War.

In the Battle of Schleswig he took to the battlefield rather than remain at headquarters and his direct leadership materially aided in liberating the principality. By 1849 the Treaty of Malmö had enforced its false peace, but Friedrich Karl still found action with the Baden Campaign against the radicals. He did not take part in the Second Danish-German War – it was over with too quickly – and spent the next 15 years of peace, at least for Prussia, studying war.

He studied reports from other conflicts, especially Crimea, and from Moltke he learned the sciences of topography, geography and meteorology. He studied the new technologies of telegraphy and steam railroads, and how they could influence the conduct of war. By 1863 he was ready, the Prussian Army was ready and King Christian of Denmark signs a new constitution permanently annexing Schleswig to Danish rule.

In the Third Danish-German War Friedrich Karl would again be under von Wrangel's command and this time took a division into the field. He leads the assault on the fortress at Dueppel, on the Sundewitt Peninsula, gaining 5,000 prisoners and 118 artillery pieces. At the end of the war he's leading a corps command of Prussian, Saxon and Hanoverian troops in the assault on the Als Peninsula.

Two years later he led the Second Prussian Army across the border into Austrian-held Bohemia. His tally of victories at Liebenau, Turnau, Podol, and Münchengrätz lead to Gitschin where he linked up with the Army of the Elbe commanded by General Karl von Herwarth. And this led to Königgrätz, where Friedrich Karl's army attacked the Austrian center while Herwarth's army hit the left flank and Crown Prince Friedrich Wilhelm's First Army engaged the right.

In spite of the heavy losses his army suffered – the heaviest of the battle – Friedrich Karl held most of the important center positions until the Crown Prince's First Army made its belated arrival, turning a bloody stalemate into a war-ending rout. In the four weeks that followed the victorious armies out-maneuvered the broken Austrians until a truce was signed just as the last battle, at Blumenau, had begun.

The *Bruderkrieg* had scarcely ended and the laurels and accolades were still falling on the commanders' heads when Friedrich Karl began writing reports on the drawbacks and deficiencies he encountered on the battlefields, especially Königgrätz. Officials in Berlin opposed what he submitted, in spite of his rank, title and combat experience. But he resolved to make his views known, for the good of his army and country.

A few weeks later an anonymous pamphlet on the problems the Prussian Army had encountered in the recent war and the reforms needed to correct them, appeared in Frankfurt au Main. It created a sensation, and even then its author was widely believed to be the Prince, though it would be years before he acknowledged authorship.

Nonetheless Friedrich Karl got the results he wanted when Moltke read the pamphlet and approved his reforms. Four years later most had been put into place and the Prince was in command of the Second Army with six corps of troops from a dozen different German states including Prussians, Saxons, Hessians and Hanoverians – in all a total of 14 infantry divisions and four cavalry divisions.

Crown Prince Friedrich Wilhelm Hohenzollern: The oldest son of Wilhelm I and heir to the throne of Prussia. Born three years after his cousin, Friedrich Karl, in 1831, and just missed out serving in the first two Danish-German Wars. However, by the third he had become a corps commander and oversaw the siege of the Dannewirk Fortress among other operations.

In 1866 Friedrich Wilhelm, like his cousin, was an army commander. Due to communications problems his First Army would be the last to engage the Austrians at Königgrätz. But the delay proved heaven-sent, for he arrived at exactly the right location, at exactly the right moment in the battle and had the boldness to fully exploit the abandoned Austrian trenchworks on the right flank.

The Crown Prince turned a stalemated battle into an era-ending, decisive victory which lifted Prussia into the dominant position among the Germanies. It would have been a fitting pinnacle to any general's career, but for Friedrich Wilhelm it would not be the last.

Less than a year later, he and Moltke would be touring the Alsace and

Lorraine provinces, as an elderly Professor of Geology and one of his students. They conducted their own rambling tour of the terrain around Strasbourg, Metz, Weissenburg and as far west as Toul. They picked an occasional plant, or took a cutting from one, for their herbariums. But mostly they studied the land.

In the guise of performing geologic surveys – they even took rock and soil samples – the two studied the topography of each location they visited. They studied the local fortresses, or in the case of Metz the fortress complex surrounding the medieval city, and where possible chipped samples of the concrete and stone work from the outer walls.

Moltke and Friedrich Wilhelm took notes, later to be turned into detailed maps, of the roads, railroads, canals and telegraph lines that ran across the landscape. And later, in Berlin, they and their staffs would work out plans for an invading army to attack each location and what a defending army might do. On the German side of the Rhine they and their Prussian, Saxon, Baden and Bavarian officers spent weeks reconnoitering the land in more open surveys. By the war's beginning the German armies are the one force ready for any contingency.

And by then Friedrich Wilhelm would be commanding the Third Army with 12 divisions of infantry and two cavalry divisions. Third Army included the two Bavarian Corps, an army in their own right, plus divisions from Hesse, Nassau, Würtemberg and Baden.

General Karl Friedrich von Steinmetz: Easily the most unique of any senior officer to serve on either side of the Franco-Prussian War. Born in 1796, Steinmetz is not only older than the two Princes, he's older than Bismarck, Roon, Moltke and even Wilhelm I. He is the only Napoleon Era officer still on active duty, one of the last living links between Napoleon Bonaparte and Louis Napoleon III.

Steinmetz's entire life had been the Prussian Army. At the age of ten, in the year of Jena and Auerstädt and Prussia's greatest defeat, he is enrolled in the Culm Military School. In early 1812, at the age of 16, he's ordered to Berlin to serve on the corps headquarters staff of General Hans Ludwig Yorck. Less than two years later Steinmetz is commissioned as a lieutenant and serves in the battles of Königswartha, Dannigkow and Bautzen where, having received a serious leg wound in the previous battle, he fought the entire engagement on horseback.

He goes on to fight most of the battles in 1814 and enters Paris with the victorious allies after Napoleon's first abdication. Steinmetz is recuperating from additional wounds when Bonaparte begins his One Hundred Days and is unable to participate in either Ligny or Waterloo. For the next 35 years he serves as a staff officer at various commands without seeing combat until 1850 and the brief clash between Prussia and Austria.

In fact Steinmetz is in the middle of it as he's the newly-appointed commandant of Cassel where the only skirmish of the crisis occurs. He is not involved in direct combat during the Third Danish-German War but finally, in 1866, he returns to the field as a corps commander in the *Bruderkrieg*.

In late June, in the astonishingly short time of four days, his corps engages and defeats two Austrian corps and, at Skalitz, a force nearly twice his size. His aggressive fighting style, his skillful use of cavalry and his third triumphant victory leads to him being called "the Lion of Skalitz." Because of his victories, and his unique status, Steinmetz becomes the Prussian court's favorite commander, even over the Crown Prince and Prince Friedrich Karl.

At the start of the war he's given the prestigious command of the First Army. It consists exclusively of Prussian divisions, six of infantry and two of cavalry. Though it's the smallest of the three front-line armies it is also the best equipped, the most combat-experienced and, at least on paper, the most formidable. Much was expected of it, especially by Steinmetz. Perhaps too much.

Crown Prince Friedrich August Albert Wettin: The oldest son of King Johann of Saxony and heir to the Wettin throne, his lifelong military education and service closely parallels that of the Prussian princes. Born in 1828, the same year as Prince Friedrich Karl, he served briefly in the First Danish-German War, in 1848. He would not see combat again until 1866, when he commanded the Saxon army corps attached to the Austrian Army in the *Bruderkrieg*.

Impressed by the fighting skills, honor and wonder weapons of the Prussians, he slowly accepts the alliance with them. At the start of the Franco-Prussian War he commands the Saxon Corps attached to Friedrich Karl's Second Army, though it would not be long before he gets an army of his own.

Grand Duke Friedrich Franz II: Ruler of the Grand Duchy of Mecklenburg-Schwerin, he serves in the Prussian Army in all three Danish-German Wars and later in the Austro-Prussian War. Together with Generals Werden and Canstein, he organizes the Fifth, Sixth and Seventh armies, composed of mostly Prussian Landwehr units and reserve formations from other states. While the Seventh would be held along the Baltic Sea coast, to guard against a rumored Danish-French alliance and a threatened amphibious invasion, the Fifth and Sixth would eventually be committed to the war.

General Baron Edwin Hans Karl von Manteuffel: The younger brother of Baron Otto Theodor von Manteuffel, a senior politician in Wilhelm's cabinet, his first combat service is in the Third Danish-Prussian War. In the *Bruderkrieg* he's a division commander, and by the start of the Franco-Prussian War he commands the East Prussian First Corps. Though he is only one of many corps commanders in the German coalition armies, fate and arrogance would make him one of that machine's highest-ranking field commanders.

Chapter X: Battle of the Military Gods

*"The art of war is simple enough. Find out where
your enemy is. Get at him as soon as you can.
Strike at him as hard as you can and as often
as you can, and keep moving on."*
-Ulysses Simpson Grant (1822 - 1885)

A Revolution in the Offing

OF ALL THE revolutions in warfare the coming conflict either introduced or perfected, the most sweeping would ironically be the least discussed, at least in most modern accounts of the war. Perhaps this is because the revolution had not just been sweeping but a full-bore tide that swept one of the most prominent and celebrated military men of the age into obscurity, and elevated an unknown who had been dead for over a generation to the status of a legend.

Writing on military strategy and tactics has probably been an ongoing endeavor since the first invention of language. Mostly this involved military leaders writing accounts or journals of their campaigns, Julius Caesar's *Commentaries on the Gallic War* being an excellent example. However, few of these accounts actually dissected what made warfare successful. A systematic analysis of the strategy, tactics, weapons, logistics, industries and politics involved in its conduct had been attempted many times. But turning the study of warfare from an art to a science would have to await the 18th and 19th Centuries, and the arrival of the Military Gods who tried to make sense of it all.

The Age of Jomini

On the 24th of March, 1869 an era-ending event took place in the Paris suburb of Passy. Baron Antoine Henri de Jomini, one of the youngest, and one of the last surviving generals from Napoleon Bonaparte's *Grande Armee* died quietly just a little over two weeks after celebrating his 90th birthday. For many his passing marked the true end of the Napoleonic Era, though that would not actually happen until the following decade with the deaths of Steinmetz and the other remaining veterans of the emperor's wars. Rather, another age passed with the Baron's death – his own. The Age of Jomini.

The age began 71 years earlier, when a 19-year-old Antoine Jomini secured an appointment to an army headquarters staff. This was not a life preordained for him – he was no baron, and his title would be conferred on him some nine years later and he was not even a French citizen. He was Swiss, the son of the mayor of Payerne in the western Vaud canton. He could have lead a privileged and relatively safe life in politics and banking but he chose a military life. As did many others in Switzerland for at the time, the year 1798, the republic no longer existed as an independent country but a puppet state under French control.

1798 was a year of relative peace in Europe, coming just after Napoleon's first great string of victories which redrew the map of Europe and had him proclaimed the Hero of the Centuries, at least by the French. 1798 would also be the year of Napoleon's first great military disaster, but that took place in Egypt and did little to tarnish his image.

Despite the local lack of combat Jomini did his duties surprisingly well. By the age of 21 he had been given command of a Swiss battalion, just as Napoleon returned to Europe and took part in a coup which removed the Directorate from power. By May of 1800 he was at war with the Holy Roman/Austrian Empire and fighting raged all around Switzerland.

After nine months of operations and another string of victories, Napoleon signed the Treaty of Lunéville, ending the war between France and Austria and making him the arbiter of the Germanies. With Europe again briefly at peace Jomini was discharged from service. He returned to banking and soon discovered he had an even greater love than military service...writing about it.

Between 1804 and 1805 his first major work, the four-volume *Treatise on Grand Military Operations* is published, and comes to the attention of Michael Ney. Then one of 18 newly-minted Marshals in the French Army, he's impressed with its clarity and quality, and accepts Jomini as a volunteer aide-de-camp – just as the peace Lunéville established four years earlier is evaporating and Europe is plunging into war.

In a momentous year of combat operations Jomini serves on Ney's staff during the Austerlitz campaign. His accomplishments, and a chapter from the *Treatise*, come to Napoleon's attention and he commissions Jomini as a colonel in the French Army while Ney promotes him to his principal aide-de-camp.

The resulting Peace of Pressburg did not end conflict, by September of 1806 Prussia and Saxony had signed a secret alliance with Russia and were mobilizing their armies. Jomini, without being privy to the intelligence reports Napoleon received, foresaw war with Prussia and wrote about it. This impressed Napoleon, as did Jomini's knowledge of Friedrich the Great's operations in the Seven Years' War, and it got him a position on Napoleon's own headquarters staff.

For his services at the battles of Jena, Auerstädt and Eylau he's awarded the Cross of the Legion of Honor. It's after the Tilsit Treaties that Napoleon makes Jomini a Baron and promotes him to Ney's chief-of-staff. In the peace which followed, the cordial relations between Emperor Napoleon and Czar Alexander extended to a number of French officers, and this included Jomini.

In this age it was not unusual for highly-valued officers to be offered commissions in more than one country's military. Among the German states it was very common, and even the American naval hero John Paul Jones accepted a commission in the Russian Navy of Catherine the Great. Jomini accepted his commission from Alexander, though not without some misgivings by Napoleon and enmity from Napoleon's own chief-of-staff, Marshal Louis Alexandre Berthier.

Still, the Emperor needed Jomini if he wanted to get the most out of his best field commander. Aggressive and brave to the point of being reckless, Michael Ney needed a calming influence and this proved to be his Swiss chief-of-staff. From Austerlitz to Friedland the two worked well together, with Jomini even getting Ney to command and not just lead.

This relationship would be strained almost to the breaking point in the next campaign the two would embark upon: the Peninsular War in Spain, which began a year after the Tilsit Treaties were signed. This grueling conflict nearly destroyed one of the most important teams in Napoleon's command structure. He resolved it by promoting Jomini to General of Brigade, and allowing him to accept a similar rank in Russian service.

While it did fix one problem, a year later it created another when Napoleon broke his peace with the Czar and fatefully declared war on Russia. With Jomini now a general in both armies this put him in a dangerous position. If he served in one but got captured by the other he could then be executed as a traitor. If he refused to serve at all then both sides would have the right to imprison him – and where in Europe could he hide from the two most powerful men in the world?

Jomini tried to resolve this by taking a non-combatant command in a line-of-communications unit. Here he was reasonably safe from capture by the Russians and Napoleon could not object. However, Louis Berthier did and he pushed Napoleon to treat Jomini with far less civility and respect. Even when he rendered valuable service in the horrific retreat from Moscow, and later rejoined Ney's staff for the battles in central Germany, he still received poor treatment from the Emperor and his antagonistic chief-of-staff.

The final, full break came after the Battle of Bautzen. While it ended in French victory, it did not gain all that had been expected of it, and Berthier chose to lay the blame for this on Jomini. He had been late in handing in some staff reports from Ney's command. Berthier got him arrested and his name removed from the promotions list. In the general truce which followed Bautzen, from June 4th of 1813 to July 20th, Ney removed the charges but the end had come. Jomini resigned his commission in the French Army and joined Czar Alexander's staff as his newest aide-de-camp.

For the next two years he took part in operations against his former friends and commander, though not in direct combat. Jomini did not participate in the actual invasion of France by the allied armies, from December 22nd of 1813 to April 30th of 1814, but he take a role in the lengthy negotiations at the Congress of Vienna.

During Napoleon's brazen One Hundred Days campaign he helped mobilize the Russian Army, which was still in-transit through Bavaria when Waterloo finally brought the Napoleonic Wars to an end. Jomini did accompany Alexander I to Paris for the signing of yet another peace treaty. There he participated in one of the last acts of the passing era: he tried in vain to secure clemency for Michael Ney, but his friend was found guilty of treason and executed on December 7th of 1815.

This nearly cost Jomini his commission in the Russian Army, and won him little respect from the other, surviving, French generals. Many of his former colleagues considered him a traitor, claiming that in his service to the Czar he betrayed troop numbers, unit dispositions and battle plans of their army. This plus the Russians demobilizing most of their army sent Jomini into semi-retirement in his native Switzerland.

There he rewrites another early work into an impressive, multi-volume set: *History of the Campaigns of the Revolution*. It's successful and is quickly followed by an even more popular work, the first major Napoleonic biography: *Life of Napoleon*. Published in 1827 it was unlike earlier biographies, which were mostly the "Napoleon I knew" memories of other generals. Jomini's work was the first serious attempt to examine his life and achievements.

By now, the 1820s, the harsh feelings against Jomini had softened, thanks in large part to Bonaparte himself, who wrote from his exile on St. Helena that the charges of betrayal were completely unfounded. And he even forgave Jomini for his change of sides, stressing that he was a Swiss national, not French. And there came another, growing, reason for his success – he was back in demand.

Jomini's officer's commission in the Russian Army had never been rescinded and as early as 1823 Czar Alexander made him a full general and the principal military tutor to his son. By 1827 the son had become Czar Nicholas I and had wars with both Persia and the Ottoman Empire. Recalled to active duty, Jomini participates in the siege of the Black Sea port of Varna. When it falls in 1828, one of the few Russian successes in the wars, it would be the last military operation he was personally involved in.

Officially, he retired from the Imperial Russian Army in 1829, though he stayed on to help organize its staff college, which opened in 1832 as the Nicholas Academy and would have that name until the Bolshevik Revolution of 1917. Shortly after this Jomini settled in Brussels, where he would remain for the next 30 years writing his monographs, pamphlets, open letters and treatises on military history, military art and strategy and tactics.

By the end of the decade his voluminous writing made him the most renowned military thinker of his age. In many ways he became history's first true strategist, and was very widely read. Military academies from West Point and the Virginia Military Institute to Saint-Cyr and of course the Nicholas Academy taught him. Even Britain's Sandhurst Academy eventually used his books. All this proved especially true of his enduring classic, *Summary of the Art of War*, though there was more to Jomini than his writing.

As his father had done for him, Czar Nicholas appointed Jomini the principal military instructor to the new Cesarevitch, his son Alexander, in 1837. Some 16 years later the internationally respected Jomini entered the world of diplomacy as an emissary from Nicholas' Court to the British and French governments over a growing rift in the Quintuple Alliance.

On the questions of who would protect the Christians living in Jerusalem, the Ottoman Empire had granted that duty to a European power, and the status of Montenegro, Moldavia and Wallachia were creating dangerous tensions between Turkey and Russia. When Sultan Abdul Majid chose France for the duty over Russia it brought in the European Powers, and sent Jomini out on his mission to relieve the crisis.

Alas, the path to what history would call the Crimean War had taken on a life of its own and Jomini's mission failed. For the balance of the war he remained in St. Petersburg, a military advisor to first Nicholas and then, when the Cesarevitch became Czar in 1855, to Alexander II. And when he launched a new peace mission Jomini was again involved. This time it proved to be successful, another treaty was signed and the war ended in 1856.

Shortly afterwards, he returned to Brussels, though he lived there for only a few more years. In 1859, and some accounts say on Napoleon III's request, Jomini moved to Passy and within months had written a battle plan for the Emperor on the imminent Franco-Austrian War. It's not known how closely the actual conflict followed the plan but at Solferino, at the replay of Waterloo, it was a Napoleon who won.

In his last years Jomini was in frail health, and still he wrote. One of his final published works was an essay on the 1866 Austro-Prussian War and the importance to future warfare of the breech-loading, cartridge rifle. And on the day of his death the future of warfare was approximately a year and a half away.

The Life of Clausewitz

The success and renown Jomini enjoyed would not only be due to his wealth of experiences or his productive pen, but to several accidents of history. One was Napoleon Bonaparte never wrote a book or major treatise on his philosophy of warfare. Another was how relatively few of Napoleon's really good generals survived the Napoleonic Wars. But the biggest accident of history Jomini benefitted from would be the death of his only real rival some 38 years before his own passing.

Karl von Clausewitz was born a year after Jomini in 1780 near Magdeburg, Prussia and, unlike his rival, had a military life almost predetermined for him. With a retired army officer for a father, he would be inducted into the Prussian Army by the age of 12. A year later, 1793, he had his first combat experience against the French, the same year Napoleon got his baptism of fire.

In 1801 he entered the newly opened military academy in Berlin where his studies spanned the ages from Alexander the Great and Caesar to Friedrich the Great and Machiavelli. After graduation he returned to active duty in time for the ruinous alliance with Russia and Saxony, and the joint declaration of war on France.

Clausewitz would be captured at the Battle of Prenzlau, one of the more minor engagements in the wake of Jena and Auerstädt. During the year he spent in prison he pondered the questions of how the most respected and vaunted army in all the Germanies could be so easily and repeatedly defeated by a man they all despised. By the time of his release he had some ideas about what went wrong, and how to fix them.

In Berlin he became the private instructor to the Crown Prince, and department head under the reformers Scharnhorst and Gneisenau. For five years he worked at both rebuilding the Prussian Army and educating the future Friedrich Wilhelm IV. For the latter he wrote what became his first published work, a treatise called the *Principles of War* that discussed the relationship between offense and defence, and when to make the change from one to the other.

In the former he wrote a study on Napoleon's future course of action. Clausewitz predicted he would fail if he invaded Russia, due to the distances involved, the severity of its winters and the improvements to its army. In 1812, one the eve of Bonaparte's invasion, Clausewitz and number of other Prussian officers refused to participate and deserted to the Russian Army. For the next two years he served in various staff positions, eventually as chief-of-staff to an infantry corps.

When the Russians pursued what remained of the *Grand Armee* into German territory, Clausewitz stepped forward to become chief negotiator and convince the Prussian government to change sides. This proved to be more difficult than anticipated. Even though General Yorck, then commanding a Prussian auxiliary corps in Lithuania, had signed a "neutrality agreement" allowing a Russian Army to march though his territory to engage the French, his king vacillated.

Friedrich Wilhelm III took three months in the beginning of 1813 to negotiate an agreement with Clausewitz and the Russian representatives. Even when he finally declared war on France, on March 13th at Breslau, his hesitant call to arms and inept mobilization meant Clausewitz would stay in Russian service until the end of the year.

Ironically this would mean that for a brief period, between the end of July, 1813 to the beginning of 1814, Clausewitz and Jomini served in the same army against Napoleon. It is unknown if the two ever met during that time. Certainly Jomini never mentioned doing so in all his extensive writings, though he would have much to say on Clausewitz's theories.

By early 1814 Clausewitz is back as a general in the Prussian Army, where he participates in the invasion of France. Napoleon's One Hundred

Days finds him busy mobilizing the Prussian Army and coordinating it with the other German armies. However, he does not participate in the final battles of the Napoleonic Era.

He stays in the post-war Prussian Army, rising to the rank of major general in 1818, at the relatively young age of 38. Soon afterward he's made a *Direktor* in the War College in Berlin. Here he spends the rest of his life reorganizing and improving the army, training future generations of its officer corps. Among his last students would be that impoverished young officer who chose the Prussian Army over the Danish Army, Helmuth von Moltke.

Many officers and his wife, Marie, urged Clausewitz to assemble his voluminous lecture notes, study papers and pamphlets on various military subjects into an organized collection for publication. He had only just started this task when, in late 1830, he was detached to the Prussian Army's Observer Corps and commanded the delegation sent to Russia's Polish Kingdom to report on the growing civil war there.

Easily the bloodiest outgrowth of France's July Revolution, it would be in Poland where Clausewitz contracted cholera and returned to his home in Breslau. There he died on November 18th of 1831, a few months after his 51st birthday and with the momentous volumes which would be his greatest achievement uncompleted.

It fell to Marie von Clausewitz to assemble, edit and get a publisher for her husband's work. *Vom Krieg/On War* would eventually span ten volumes, published between 1832 and 1837, of which the first three became the most popular and the most studied. Though, for the next 38 years, it would only be the Prussians and other Germans who would read Clausewitz while the rest of the world worshipped Jomini.

Battle of the Gods

Though he is only dimly remembered today, no one should underestimate the stature or importance of Baron Antoine Henri de Jomini in his age. To cite but one example from those days, U.S. Army officer Henry W. Halleck is reputed to have earned his first stars because of Jomini.

A gifted cadet who graduated near the top of his class at West Point, he initially learned of Jomini through the courses of Dennis Hart Mahan, who taught at the academy for nearly 50 years in the 19th Century. Halleck was fluent enough in French to translate Jomini's *Life of Napoleon* into English and later, in 1846, published his own book on military strategy. *Elements of Military Art and Science* is essentially a translation and re-editing of

Summary of the Art of War and several other Jomini texts.

Halleck's version became a textbook at West Point, and virtually every active-duty army officer in the U.S. Civil War knew his name. By 1861 he had left the service to become a lawyer in California, but then joined the Union Army, received a promotion to Brigadier General and replaced the insubordinate John Charles Fremont as commander of the Department of Missouri.

From there "Old Brains," a nickname reportedly not used in Halleck's presence, progressed rapidly to commander of the Western Department, to General-in-Chief of all Union Armies and finally stepping aside from that position to become Chief-of-Staff in favor of an officer who had once been his subordinate: Ulysses S. Grant. Not bad for a career that started with a Jomini translation.

By comparison, Clausewitz would not achieve this kind of popularity or impact until long after his death, and his writings would need to eclipse those of his rival in order to do so. Perhaps this is something Jomini perceived, for in the years immediately following his untimely death it would be Jomini himself who most frequently raised the name of Clausewitz outside the German states.

It would not be in respect or admiration, for as early as 1838 he saw Clausewitz as a threat and tried to diminish him. In that year he released an updated version of his masterwork, *Summary of the Art of War*, which contained a new prologue. In it Jomini was obsequiously complimentary to Archduke Charles of Austria, admittedly the best general the Austrians had in the Napoleonic Wars, but had little good to say of Clausewitz.

His writings were "unfinished sketches," his writing style "vagrant" and "above all too pretentious for a didactic discussion, the simplicity and clearness of which ought to be its first merit." Worse than that, Clausewitz stood guilty of Pendantry: of using language so learned and accurate as to imply insult on all those lesser mortals, the readers, who did not write the "Great Work" in the first place.

Add to this he was an "unscrupulous plagiarist" who pillaged his best ideas, theories, and observations from his predecessors or Jomini himself. And who, if he had only but read Jomini's earlier works – something Clausewitz probably had to do in order to steal from them – likely would not have bothered to set pen to paper. It is interesting to note that the standard English translation of *Summary*, published in 1862, did not include this prologue material. First, because it did not contain anything really new and second, because Clausewitz was so little known outside of continental Europe the translators probably wondered what all the erudite nastiness was about.

By the summer of 1870 all that would be changing as the army steeped in Jomini prepared to clash with the armies honed on Clausewitz. And which strategist was the better one? To be honest, both wrote in such opaque styles, with Jomini diving into ambiguity and Clausewitz philosophically dense, that they are difficult to understand.

The old joke about Jomini, that you did not read him so much as decipher him, could also be said of Clausewitz. To this day military scholars will pour over their works like monks with medieval manuscripts, gleaning them for new insights and revelations.

The problem with Jomini is he took Napoleon's relatively simple tactics and made them, made everything, complex and ambiguous. To the point that when he described how artillery fire should be directed at one point on the enemy's front lines, it's not known if he, or Napoleon, meant a strong point or a weak point.

For Clausewitz his problem was the deep philosophic nature of almost all his writing. Many have wondered why but it is basically due to when and where he had been educated. In the early 19th Century, the time he attended the Berlin military academy, the "Sturm und Drang" movement had reached its high point. Immanuel Kant still lived, Goethe was in his prime and Schiller, Hagel and the Schlegel brothers were still active, as were so many other philosopher-poets. In a land where you could hardly throw a stick without hitting one, it's not difficult to see how Clausewitz became one himself.

And in his deep, ponderous writing he concluded warfare and politics were essentially the same. That for a war to achieve its aims it must remain under the direction, but not the personal control, of political leaders. That "war is the continuation of politics by other means." It's his most famous quote, the maxim he is best remembered for. But more important to the conduct of warfare, in his writings Clausewitz develops the concept of "friction."

Probably originating with his thoughts on how his army could have been so easily defeated at Jena and Auerstädt, "friction" became defined as the building avalanche of personnel fatigue, equipment breakdowns, logistics failures, communications errors, bad weather, bad luck and lack of leadership which lead to defeat. Clausewitz stressed its study, not only in post-battle reports of their own engagements but in sending out observers to other conflicts. In fact, the Prussian Army would be one of the few to take this activity seriously, sending out some of their best officers instead of incompetents, large teams instead of just one or two individuals and having staffs back home to study their reports.

By comparison, Jomini spent relatively little time in his texts divining how armies lost battles. If you followed his maxims, used the right percentages of infantry, cavalry and artillery for a given situation, the right geometric formations for either attack or defence and kept your interior lines of operations intact then you should be victorious.

Clausewitz also wrote extensively on the importance of good morale and motivating belief in the cause the nation and its soldiers are fighting for. Jomini did not ignore this, though he did pay it rather scant attention, apparently thinking it to be the province of brave, qualified commanders to instill it in their men. He gave little thought to the idea of building morale from the nation up. Perhaps this is an advantage only a country defined as "less a state with an army but an army with a state" could properly develop.

There were a few topics which Clausewitz did not spend much time on and Jomini did. The biggest is the tools of trade of any military force: weapons. Clausewitz hardly wrote on the matter, apparently taking it as a given that weapons and advancing technology were part of the permanent groundstate of warfare and did not need much explaining. Jomini did otherwise.

Another was sea power. Perhaps this is because few wars in central Europe were ever decided by naval battles, though an extensive study on the relationship between Trafalgar and Austerlitz may put this into doubt. Again, Jomini did otherwise, writing fairly extensively on the use of navies, but mostly from the standpoint of amphibious operations.

However, in the coming war sea power would play a minor, though at times interesting, role. And at any rate, the two great strategists did have an influence on the man who would mold naval theory into a globe spanning, global dominating, force.

The son of West Point lecturer Dennis Hart Mahan, who did so much to spread the influence of Jomini to America, broke with family tradition and enrolled at Annapolis. He graduated second in his class of 1859, and would go on to serve in the Union Navy at Port Royal and later blockade operations.

Some 20 years afterwards Alfred Thayer Mahan would join the U.S. Navy's newly-established Naval War College, where he would lecture on the history and theory of sea power. These would eventually be edited and refined into books, over half a dozen volumes in all, that would have a profound impact on the development of the modern navy. Theodore Roosevelt, Winston Churchill, Franklin Delano Roosevelt, Jacky Arbuthnot Fisher, Heihachiro Togo, Alfred von Tirpitz, Isoroku Yamamoto and all the senior commanders of the U.S. Navy since the beginning of America's rise to world power status have been students and supporters. And it was Tirpitz who proclaimed him "the Clausewitz of the Sea," demonstrating the final eclipse of Antoine Henri de Jomini.

Chapter XI: Opposing Forces – Opposing Weapons

"In anguish we uplift
A new unhallowed song:
The race is to the swift;
The battle is to the strong."
-John Davidson (1857 - 1909)

The French Army on the Eve of War

IF GENERAL EDMOND Leboeuf had been truthful with Napoleon III in those fateful July days, that the French Army was not ready for war, more than just the Emperor would have scoffed at such an outrageous claim, for on paper the Army did appear to be an impressive force.

It could have been even more so had Napoleon found the time to pull in troops from his empire's vast overseas territories. But such would the rush of events that only units from Algeria and the Papal States could be used, and most of them, like General Emmanuel de Wimpffen and his men, would not arrive until after hostilities had started.

In metropolitan France the Army had a total aggregate of approximately 1,350,000 men. There were roughly 405,000 officers and men in the active duty army, over 400,000 in the reserve, about 509,000 in the National Guard and over 30,000 pontoniers, a special engineering corps devoted to building pontoon bridges. And there was a further force, the *Garde Mobile* of an estimated 600,000 men. A vast reserve militia nearly half the size of the regular army and with little organization other than a skeleton force of mostly retired officers.

The active duty and reserve personnel were organized, at least at the start of the war, into 26 infantry divisions, eight cavalry divisions with a further three cavalry divisions held as a strategic reserve. Each of the seven fielded army corps had a reserve artillery command of four to eight batteries, and the reserve cavalry divisions were complemented by a further 19 artillery batteries held as the Great Reserve.

In addition to this massive force there were the sizeable garrisons of the Paris fortifications, and those at Lyons and Metz. And the National Guard had a basic organization of 318 infantry battalions and 123 artillery batteries, all of which would be activated and incorporated into the regular Army.

Each infantry division was nominally composed of 4 infantry regiments, the classic divisional "square," a Chasseur battalion and Division Artillery Command with two batteries of four-pounder cannons and one Mitrailleuse battery. The cavalry divisions were more varied formations with anywhere from four to seven regiments of mixed cavalry units: Mounted Chasseurs, Hussars, Cuirassiers, Lancers and Dragoons. Roughly half the cavalry divisions had their own artillery commands of one or two batteries of light field guns.

The Chasseur battalions assigned to each division, even the cavalry divisions, were light infantry units who did not go into the field with the same heavy equipment packs or weapons as the line infantry regiments. There were several reasons for this: first, they were used on local reconnaissance for the division. Second, the battalion provided dispatch runners to maintain communications with corps command and other divisions. Third, it would act as a screening force to cover the movements of the regular infantry and artillery. And fourth, the Chasseurs provided a mobile emergency reserve to fill any gaps in the front line.

All of this conformed to what Napoleon Bonaparte, and Antoine Jomini, prescribed for a modern field army. And yet, there were severe problems in this outwardly impressive force. Marshal Niel saw it, but died before he could do much about it. Leboeuf saw it, and apparently ignored most of the problems in the hope they would just go away. MacMahon, de Failly, Canrobert, the Douay brothers, Bourbaki, Trochu and the dozens of other competent generals knew it and tried their best to deal with the problems. But it was quite beyond their means to deal with problems which were, in reality, decades in the making.

Going straight back to the days of the French Revolution, *levées* or annual drafts were used to fill the enlisted ranks. And starting around the 1830s, when France was at relative peace and prosperous, the grey market of draft substitution became a burgeoning industry. In reality this practice had existed since the Revolution and its *levée en masse* but now, with even radical politicians like Guizot saying "everyone should be rich" and France engaged in a series of ongoing wars in Spain and various colonies, the idea of military service had grown rather unappealing, especially for those in the growing middle class.

For a few thousand francs – like any industry the price varied over time – anyone could hire a substitute to answer a draft notice. For the most part, those who engaged in it were career soldiers looking for a boost in their meager pay. What it created was a permanent underclass, neither desperately poor or especially well-off, rotating in and out of service in the Army, Navy and Foreign Legion, who at least paid a little better.

And not terribly well-educated either, which down the years lead to a more serious problem. If the middle class had a growing aversion to military service, leaving it to the poor and career soldiers to take their places, then the upper class developed a positive loathing to the fulfillment of their traditional military duty: manning the officer ranks.

For every Canrobert, Trochu, Comte de Ladmirault and Douay brothers who felt it was their duty to follow family tradition to enter the military, for every MacMahon and Bourbaki who sincerely felt they owed a debt to their adopted homeland for the gift it had given their families, there were hundreds who felt no particular attachment to France, much less a desire to serve it.

With Saint-Cyr, the Polytechnique School of Paris and other military academies not turning out nearly enough lieutenants to meet the army's needs it was decided to increase field promotions from the ranks of worthy Non-Commissioned Officers. This had the advantage of accessing a pool of already trained, combat-experienced talent who had good rapport with the other enlisted ranks.

However, the French Army only went partway to creating the kind of officers a modern army needed. In an age when the advances of the Industrial Revolution were being increasingly harnessed to the engine of war, these new officers needed something more than a brief commissioning ceremony and a party afterwards. For one thing, most of them were illiterate.

There was no Officers' Candidate School, a distinctly 20th Century innovation, no courses at a military academy or a war college – the latter institution did not even exist in France at the time – for these men. The doors to Saint-Cyr and all other such academies were closed to them. In spite of the need for more officers these were still elitist institutions, and would remain so well into the next century.

Gone were the days when a virtually unschooled, illiterate man like Francisco Pizarro could become a great commander. Apparently this notion had not yet sunk into the French Army, for in the war to come the Germans would be astonished at how many lieutenants and captains they would capture who could not even read or write their own language.

The Armies of the Germanies

For a coalition force from so many separate states, the Prussian-lead German Army showed surprising uniformity. Surprising at least to the French, for Napoleon III and his command staff had hoped for discord, even insurrection, as Prussia gathered the armies of the other Germanies under its command.

But it should not have been. For that recent period of history, between the "Shame of Olmütz" and the end of the Austro-Prussian War, where Prussia was forced to cut its military alliances with most of the other German states, had been an aberration. The real history, the enduring history of centuries, had been one of a network of alliances between Prussia and many of the smaller states.

In truth only the middle-power German states of Saxony, Würtemberg, Baden and Bavaria could maintain true armies, at least two corps or better, on their own. Most of the other Germanies could at best field a division or two, and often not even that. Most of these smaller states: such as Hesse, Anhalt, Mecklenberg-Schwerin, Strelitz and Oldenburg, had long been integrated smoothly with Prussian forces at the corps and divisional levels.

Barons, Counts, Dukes, Grand Dukes, Princes and Crown Princes from across the Germanies served as brigade, division, corps and army commanders. And not just of their own native or national units. After all, it would be Grand Duke Friedrich Franz of tiny Mecklenberg-Schwerin who would eventually command the Sixth Army.

As these armies mobilized they fielded a force of just under 950,000 men. The North German Confederation brought around 448,000 active-duty personnel, Landwehr reserves of 165,000 and 153,000 garrison troops. The South German States, principally Bavaria, Baden and Würtemberg, contributed 108,000 active-duty troops, over 36,000 reserves and 37,000 garrison troops.

On paper an inferior force to the French Army by over 400,000 men. However, this presupposes the French could actually deploy the numbers they claimed – in reality many reserve and National Guard units were under-strength. And, more important, the German armies would bring with them more than twice as many field artillery pieces, over 2,000 versus around 960.

The composition of the German divisions and corps were also markedly different from their French counterparts. All the infantry divisions had the then-standard compliment of four regiments, but all other units were attached to the divisions on an as-needed basis. Usually this included a Jäger battalion, a cavalry regiment, a Field-Pioneer company of combat engineers and anywhere from four to six batteries of mixed field artillery, usually two light and two heavy batteries.

The cavalry regiments universally assigned to the German infantry divisions were either Hussars or Dragoons. They were used to conduct reconnaissance and screening operations. And in the case of the Dragoons, who were mounted infantry, they could be sent on independent operations, such as the deep-penetration raids practiced by Union and Confederate cavalry during the American Civil War.

Also used for reconnaissance, and sharp shooting, were the Jäger battalions. These were composed of game wardens, professional hunters and mountain guides. They knew the art of concealment, how to use the lay of the land to move without being seen, and especially the very refined art of long-range sniping.

Unlike their French counterparts, the German cavalry divisions were not saddled with light infantry units, the Chasseurs, in their organization, which in practice were not always mounted. Most of their subordinate regiments were either Hussars, Cuirassiers/light cavalry and Uhlans. The Uhlan regiments were lancers and, like the Dragoons, capable of independent operations. Soon, their name would be applied to all German cavalry units, and strike fear in the French Army and civilians alike.

At the corps level the German armies also differed from their counterparts by having a Commanding Engineer assigned to each headquarters staff. His duties included the coordination of the Field-Pioneer companies attached to the infantry divisions, often with entrenching tool columns or light bridging trains.

More importantly, these officers oversaw operations of the pontoon-bridge columns and the train battalion attached to the corps artillery formation. These, when coordinated by the Engineering General on each Army headquarters staff, gave the German armies a unique mobility capacity not matched by the French Army, whose Military Train Command numbered less than 9,000 men – a fraction of the personnel assigned by the German armies to this crucial task for any military force in the Industrial Age.

Dreyse Versus Chassepot: The Supposed Wonder Weapons

Though it had been adopted by the Prussian Army as far back as 1841 – one of the country's responses to the Egyptian Crisis of 1840 – and first used operationally in 1848, it would not be until the *Bruderkrieg* of 1866 that the world would finally notice the Dreyse Needle Gun and proclaimed it a wonder weapon. The truth was breech loading repeater rifles and carbines of much better designs had been used in a war concluded just a year before, though little notice was paid to them.

The American Civil War was the first major conflict where breech-loading weapons had been successfully used in any quantity. Christian Sharps' single-shot rifles and carbines were very popular among the Union Army cavalry regiments and specialist "skirmisher" units. The seven-shot Spencer carbines with metal cartridges were even more popular, and by 1863 most of the Union cavalry had re-equipped with them, but their range and accuracy were not up to the standards set by the muzzle-loading Springfield musket.

The Dreyse Needle Gun changed all that. Use of the Sharps and Spencer weapons had not gone completely unnoticed, especially by the military observers of Prussia and the other Germanies. The Dreyse was improved, its paper cartridge replaced by a more robust waxed cardboard one and its breech mechanism refined, though its leakage of hot gases after heavy use would never be solved.

THE PRUSSIAN NEEDLE-GUN.

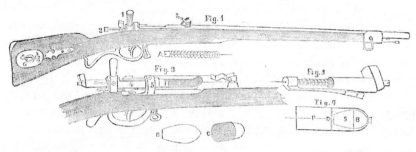

Fig. 1.—1. Lever that locks in cylinder; 2. Needle drawn back ready for projecting into cartridge. Fig. 2.—3. Chamber for cartridge; 4. Cylinder holding needle-case; 5. Cylinder that passes under band; 6. Trigger that pushes on spring, F, in Fig. 3. Fig. 3.—Case containing needle: F, spring lifted by trigger, 6, in Fig. 2. Fig. 4.—Section of cartridge: P, powder; D, detonating powder in hole of sabot; S, sabot holding the ball; dotted line shows passage of needle on to detonating powder at D, through the gunpowder, marked P. A, needle in spiral spring; B, ball; C, sabot containing ball; D, detonating powder at end of sabot.

By the time of the *Bruderkrieg* the Prussian Army would be universally equipped with a single-shot rifle that fired a heavy bullet and was accurate to 600 yards. It was the first such weapon used on so vast a scale, and the string of victories it helped create would push development of similar weapons among the other European powers.

In 1866 the British War Office, which had been content to just modify existing Enfield muskets into Enfield Snider breech-loaders, established a committee to produce the first true rifle for the British Army. And in the same year the French War Ministry responded by ordering into production the center-fire breech-loader its Controller of Arms, Antoine Alphonse Chassepot, had under development since 1863: the now-designated Model 1866 rifle.

Like the Dreyse, the Chassepot was a needle gun, meaning it used a long needle in its firing mechanism to detonate the cartridge's primer rather than a short, stubby pin. Both were bolt-action, center-fire weapons which used a cardboard cartridge and a heavy, 11mm, bullet. However, this was where the similarities ended.

THE CHASSEPÔT.

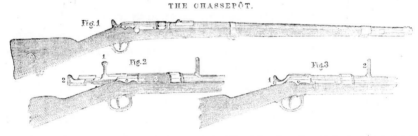

Fig. 1.—Chassepôt Rifle: breech closed. Fig. 2.—Ready for reception of cartridge: 1. Lever for opening and locking breech; 2. Head of the plunger, containing needle for exploding cartridge; 3. Chamber for cartridge. Fig. 3.—Rifle loaded and closed: 1. Plunger drawn out ready for explosion of cartridge; 2. Sight raised for long range.

The firing mechanism Nicholas von Dreyse developed was not only unique, it actually defied logic, as he located the primer cap at the base of the bullet instead of the cartridge's base. This necessitated a long, elegant firing needle, prone to fouling and damage. Antoine Chassepot not only put the primer at the cartridge's base, he also solved the gas leakage problem by placing a rubber knob on the bolt's front end. It did the job, though the knob would need replacing at regular intervals.

Effective sealing not only made the Chassepot a much safer weapon to fire – soldiers did not have to worry about getting their faces or hands burned – it also improved muzzle velocity. With an 85-grain powder charge, much larger than the powder charge in the Dreyse cartridge, it had a 20% flatter trajectory and an amazing effective range of 1,600 yards, nearly three times that of the Dreyse rifle.

Superior designs were available to the Prussians; the brothers Paul and William Mauser were developing a metallic cartridge rifle...but they were Würtembergers and at any rate there was a need to re-equip all the German armies with standardized weapons following Prussia's success in the *Bruderkrieg* and the new treaties she had signed with the other states.

At the same time the Chassepot had given a remarkable demonstration in its baptism of fire outside of Rome. General Pierre de Failly's expedition to stop yet another insurrection had easily routed Garibaldi's "Red Shirt" forces. It convinced Napoleon III and most of his generals that they had a potential war-winning weapon on their hands. By the beginning of 1870 all active-duty, reserve and National Guard units had been re-equipped with the Chassepot. But it would not be able to win the coming war on its own capabilities. Ironically, the French Army *did* have a weapon that could.

The Premature Weapon of the Future

In 1868 Richard Jordan Gatling, an American inventor, sold to France two examples of the newest model of his famous rapid-fire weapon. Soon, when no orders were forthcoming, he feared the French government would steal his design and manufacture it without buying a license. In reality he did not have to worry; the French War Ministry had just bought his weapons for field trials against their newest creation: the Mitrailleuse.

Developed in deepest secrecy, the 19th Century equivalent of Black Project status, the Mitrailleuse has been described by most historians as a 25-barrel Gatling Gun. This is a misnomer – all weapons based on the Gatling design had rotating barrels and a continuous feed ammunition system.

The Mitrailleuse had fixed barrels and a manual breech loading mechanism which used a copper plate drilled out to hold 25 metallic cartridges. A far simpler design than the Gatling Gun and with a slower rate of fire – about 120 rounds a minute. Roughly the size and weight of a four-pounder field gun, it held the potential for being the perfect infantry support weapon and by the summer of 1870 virtually every infantry division in the French Army had a Mitrailleuse battery.

The problem was no one knew how to use it. The cloak of secrecy wrapped around this weapon and its development was extraordinary for its time. The imperial edict authorizing its production remained secret and only those directly connected to the program were even allowed to see a completed Mitrailleuse weapon. Many of the companies involved in its production did not know what they were producing components for, or how many were being built.

Few field exercises were held with the weapon, tactics for its use were never thought out, even training programs for its maintenance and repair would be extremely limited. When they finally got issued to the divisions they were given to the field artillery units, who used their standard tactics of siting them in the open and *en battery*. The notions of concealed positions and overlapping fields of fire, much less single weapon deployments, would not come until much later and far too late.

And ironically, for the secrecy wrapped around the project, it proved relatively easy for Prussia's intelligence service to discover and track the development of the Mitrailleuse, for its original designers were not French. Louis Christophe and Joseph Montigny were *Belgian* ordnance engineers who designed the weapon, even built a few, for the defence fixed installations like their country's fortresses. And then there was the Gatling Gun purchase, which the Prussian government learned of when it bought a few for its own test purposes.

The God of War

Napoleon Bonaparte called artillery this and in a way it was his secret weapon, for he became the first great commander to fully understand its deadly capabilities. He used Jean Baptiste de Gribeauval's system, whom he studied under as a young artillery officer, to standardize weapon sizes, build improved gun carriages and caissons, introduce instruction manuals and use tangent scales and elevating screws to improve accuracy.

The result was half the battlefield casualties he inflicted upon his enemies were caused by artillery. Interestingly, the next highest percentage was caused by bayonets and not musket fire, though it would be infantry small arms that replaced artillery as the Queen-of-Battle in the decades following the Napoleonic Era.

By the American Civil War, studies of battlefield casualties showed nearly 75% were caused by small arms fire. The improved accuracy, reliability and greatly increased range caused by rifled barrels, percussion caps and the conical bullets of French Captain Claude Minié, and American armorer James H. Burton had wrought this. But it would all soon change.

In the aftermath of Königgrätz and his creation's relatively minor failures, Alfred Krupp had become pitifully apologetic and deeply depressed. "Ruffian" Roon was determined to scrap the steel breech-loaders and turn back to bronze muzzle-loaders. But in this post-war battle he would be outgunned by Moltke, Prince Friedrich Karl and Crown Prince

Friedrich Wilhelm, all of whom had either first-hand experience with Krupp's revolutionary cannons or had read all the field reports.

And they had the King's ear, who determined to have the most powerful army in Europe and believed in Krupp's "children." After all, had he not watched one being born? And they had Krupp himself who, from his exile, offered to replace all the earlier weapons with ones of improved design and, thanks to the new Siemens process, would be cast from superior metal.

Exhaustive trials by the Artillery Test Commission at the Tegel Range proved this and orders came flooding in from not just Berlin but Dresden, Munich and all the other capitals of the Germanies to Gusstahlfabrik in Essen. Krupp had to build new factories to accommodate all the new work and his improved artillery had even better range, accuracy and durability.

They also proved lighter, not just to the earlier model cast-steel cannons but dramatically so when compared to their bronze and wrought-iron competitors. For the typical four-pounder and six-pounder guns this meant they needed fewer horses to pull them and fewer men in their crews. Which meant artillery units in the German armies could be increased by 50% or more.

By contrast the French Army, convinced from the Emperor on down that the weapon of the future lay in the hands of their infantrymen, kept most of their artillery distinctly in the Napoleonic Era. This began with Napoleon III who, like his uncle but with much less justification, fancied himself an artillery expert. He published two books on the subject, the first of which, *Manuel d'Artillerie*, had been in print for 35 years and was the standard manual for his army since his rise to power.

As with the Mitrailleuse, he even ordained the weapons to be used. All field artillery pieces were bronze muzzle-loaders called "Napoleons" because the Emperor supposedly designed their pattern. They were heavier, had slower rates of fire, required more men and horses and had dramatically shorter range. The average "Napoleon" four-pounder had a maximum range of around 1,600 yards, just under a mile, while a Krupp four-pounder had a maximum range of over three miles.

The capabilities of German artillery would soon astound France, and the rest of the world, but it should not have. First, there were the extensive field reports from Königgrätz and other battles of the Austro-Prussian War that mentioned half the Prussian artillery were breech-loaders. Second, the year after the war French officers were in Belgium to observe its army on maneuvers. And they witnessed their newly-purchased batteries of Krupp four-pounders being put through their paces. Their reports were insightful, detailed, and quickly forgotten once they were filed with the French War

Ministry.

And third, in the same year, in the middle of the Luxembourg Crisis and the start of the Paris Exhibition, Alfred Krupp himself was trying to interest Napoleon III in ordering his guns. At the time "Ruffian" Roon still had not conceded to re-equipping the Prussian Army with his breech-loaders and Krupp obsessively looked for business anywhere. Fortunately for him, his reputation and Gusstahlfabrik, his proposal and detailed brochures were filed away and forgotten, just like the Belgian reports. Schnieder's new factory would produce the French Army's cannons, not Krupp, and sometimes the greatest cloak of secrecy is your enemy's own arrogance.

In the one concession to the modern age the French Artillery Corps did use explosive shells with timed fuses. But the clockwork timers only had two settings, and occasionally did not function properly. German artillery shells would use percussion cap fuses, simple, rugged and reliable.

The Navies: The Forgotten Forces

There is little written on naval operations during the Franco-Prussian War, mostly because almost none took place. However, this did not mean there was no potential for such activities, or that absolutely nothing happened.

One of the unique features of the coming war is its complete lack of allies on either side. The Germanies had little need for any – they were their own allies – though Italy quietly supported them. France, on the other hand, actively courted other countries. Napoleon III sent his ambassador to the Hapsburg court and, while its Saxon-born Chancellor von Beust was sympathetic, Emperor Franz Josef had had enough with Bonapartist intrigues, especially after Berlin released the contents of a proposed secret treaty Napoleon himself had offered to the Prussians in June of 1866...just before the start of the *Bruderkrieg*.

Belgium, also due to the contents of the stillborn treaty, remained coldly neutral, as did Holland, Great Britain and Spain. Denmark, on the other hand, did express some interest and plans were begun in Paris for an amphibious operation on the Danish-Prussian North Sea coast.

The French Navy put its Marine regiments on alert while it sortied most of its ironclad warships in late-August. Only the *Magenta* and *Solferino* among the capital ships remained in port, ready to act as flagships for the proposed invasion. The deployed fleet, especially the new *Provence*-class frigates, were given two duties: blockade the German ports and patrol off neutral ports like New York City, Liverpool, Cadiz and Naples in the hopes of catching German merchant ships trying to make it to safe havens.

With a fleet of 55 ironclads and over 230 unarmored steamers, the French had little to fear from the Germanies. Only Prussia had ironclads and a navy of any size. But its fleet had scarcely a tenth the warships of its opponent and, apart from a few gunboats patrolling international waters, most would remain in their ports like the British-built *König Wilhelm*, laid up in the Jade Estuary with defective engines.

France planned to conduct more offensive operations on the North Sea front. The problem was most of its ironclads had drafts too deep to maneuver among the sandbars and spits spread along that shore. They only had seven coastal ironclads, the largest of which, in a supreme irony, was the *Rochambeau*.

At over 7,000 tons and 377 feet, roughly the size of a World War II-era light cruiser, she carried 14 guns and had originally been named *Dunderberg* by her builders, Webb Shipyards of New York City. She was American-built, for the Civil War, but not completed until after its end. In 1867, the year the United States and France nearly went to war over Mexico, her builders sold her to the Marine Nationale, who rearmed her with French guns. She would be the largest ship in the only major naval operation of the coming war.

Chapter XII: Mobilization

"All delays are dangerous in war."
-John Dryden (1631 - 1700)

Europe's Zeitgeist at the Start of the War

WHILE NOT UNANTICIPATED – the Luxembourg Crisis of 1867 had given ample warning – the swift rise from confrontation over who could be a candidate for the Spanish throne to declaration of war shocked almost everyone except for the immediate participants. Unlike Luxembourg, there was no time for a Concert of Powers conference. No intermediary could forestall this, not even Pope Pius' letter to the two crowned heads had any effect, though the very Protestant Wilhelm I treated it with much more respect than did the nominally Catholic Napoleon III.

Beyond the shock, the general mood of Europe was apprehension. It is not only Thiers, Favre and Gambetta who feared the Emperor would repeat his uncle's greatest achievement and become the new Charlemagne. Luxembourg and even Belgium feared being annexed by France who, as the anticipated victor, gave every indication it would take as much Rhineland territory as it wished.

Friedrich Engels, who now fancied himself a military strategist as well as a revolutionary theorist, wrote articles for the London newspapers predicting the war would be long, bloody and mostly take place on German soil. He would only be right on one of those counts. Karl Marx, who had become something of a celebrity after the publication of *Das Kapital*, this time picked Prussia to support; he had supported Austria in 1866. He got the council of the First Communist International to issue a proclamation supporting Prussia in its "defensive" war against Bonapartist France. Again, like Engels, he thought the war would be fought on German territory.

There were few who thought otherwise. This was the age before the events of 1914 and 1939. Before the Guns of August, before Verdun, before Blitzkrieg and the technologies which could most efficiently carry it out. This was the age when few *really* thought of the Germans as one people, let alone one country. The past had given little evidence to think differently.

Yes, there had been times when a grave crisis had united the Germanies into a single, reasonably cohesive, military force. It had happened, more or less, under Friedrich the Great during the Seven Years' War and again in the War of Liberation during the Napoleonic Era. And yet, after each such event, the Germanies had returned to the ground state.

However, the ground state had changed over time. In 1800 there had been 360 separate countries and sub-national entities. By 1815 this had been reduced and fixed at 38. After 1866 it shrank to 36 with the removal of Austria and Holland. And over the decades since its creation, the Zollverein had worked its magic. The Germanies were more economically united than ever before; the Prussian State Railways and the Postal and Telegraph Union only served to further the cohesion it started.

Militarily, all of Prussia's successes were discounted by the outside world. Its victory in 1864 had been against a tiny foe who battled overwhelming odds. And at any rate, it had been overshadowed in the public mind by the American Civil War and France's disaster in Mexico. True, the Prussians had beaten and humbled the Austrian Empire in the amazingly short span of seven weeks in 1866. But then again almost anyone could beat Austria and nearly everyone had, even the Mexicans.

What the outside world had completely overlooked, had not yet come to terms with, was *how* the Prussians defeated the Danes and the Austrians. True, the Dreyse Needle Gun did receive a lot of acclaim. But the French had a better rifle and nothing adventurous or exciting could be found in mastering the chatter of telegraph keys or the metallic clank of railroad wheels.

Well, perhaps not so completely. In the months leading up to the final crisis it became apparent to many governments a war between France and Prussia had grown inevitable, and they took steps to prepare. Great Britain reduced the number of its warships visiting European ports, lest they get caught in a sudden blockade. President Ulysses Grant gave one of his best friends, who had been so shabbily treated by President Andrew Johnson, one last gift for an old soldier. He appointed Philip Henry Sheridan as Senior Military Attaché to the Hohenzollern Court, where he quickly became a favorite guest of Bismarck, Moltke and King Wilhelm himself.

And on the personal level, when the war correspondent William Russell got his orders from *The Times* to head for the continent, he chose Berlin over Paris. This time, unlike four years earlier at Königgrätz, he did not want to be reporting on a war from the losing side.

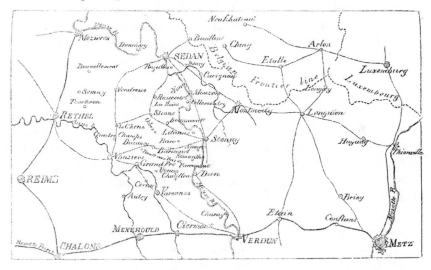

Opening field of operations

France Mobilizes, and Loses the First Battle

For a population which had for years mistrusted and despised its monarch, the French seemingly shed it all overnight and rallied to the flag and the Emperor. In Paris, on streets that once held protest marches, wildly cheering crowds gathered to escort columns of soldiers as they marched out to the city's train stations for deployment to the east. And yet even here, even now, something was subtly different.

For the last dozen years and more the official national anthem of France had been "Partant Pour la Syrie" a pious hymn to a medieval knight setting out on the Crusades. Supposedly written by Napoleon's own mother and energetically pushed by Empress Eugénie, it quickly got replaced by another song – one which had once been banned by Charles X and suppressed by Napoleon III for being too republican.

However, his own uncle had called it "the Revolution's greatest general" and no one in France had forgotten its lyrics. As they marched to their trains the soldiers and their civilian escorts sang a patriotic song of stirring militancy. They sang the song of their fathers and grandfathers. They sang "La Marseillaise."

Only at the Emperor's official departure would "la Syrie" be prominently played, by an army band. On July 28th, nearly two weeks after war had been declared on the 15th, Napoleon and his 14-year-old son departed from the Paris suburb of St. Cloud on a luxuriously appointed train. They were bound for the fortress-city of Metz, where the largest part of the French Army was assembling. And already, disquieting reports were reaching the Emperor about his army. Deployment had not gone nearly so well as had been planned.

None of Napoleon's troops got to travel in nearly so fine a style as he did. The problem was some troops did not get any train at all. Some units got orders to go to the wrong stations. Others were at the right stations, but either their trains did not arrive or they were filled with other troops when they did. Still other trains arrived at the wrong destination, or showed up with the wrong rolling stock for the transport of horses, supplies and heavy weapons.

Even when everything went right with the rail trip, problems still awaited the units at their destinations. Some stations lacked the proper off-loading facilities, others had the facilities but no wagons, carts or lorries, then a long, low horse-drawn wagon with no sides, for transport to the assembly areas.

Depots did not have the supplies the arriving contingents needed, or in some cases any supplies at all. Food, for both men and horses, proved to be the biggest problem the mobilizing army faced. At some bases and depots the food stocks had been sold off by greedy and corrupt officials, at others they were left to spoil by incompetent ones.

This meant the army that prided itself as being the most modern in Europe had to, in many cases, fall back on what armies since the days of antiquity did to replenish themselves: they foraged. While this was easy enough for horses to do, men could not eat grass and too many units quickly went from bartering for food to seizing it from local residents. This stood in marked contrast to when the Germans arrived, who were mostly civil and usually paid for what they took.

Reports of the unfolding disaster needed time reaching the right authorities because of another paralysis: France's national telegraph system could not handle the sudden increase in traffic flow – in effect, a 19th

Century version of information overload. Neither it or the nation-wide railway system had ever been put through a large-scale exercise or dress rehearsal. Not even how they connected or interacted with military authorities had been rehearsed. Before the first shots had been fired the Clausewitz concept of "friction" claimed its first casualties.

On top of all this Napoleon III himself delivered another crippling blow when he arrived at Metz a day after his departure from Paris. At Empress Eugénie's urging he committed a far graver mistake than choosing the wrong the flag or national anthem. Marshal MacMahon had scarcely received him at headquarters when the Emperor appointed himself commander of the Army. On an imperial whim, in a single stroke, he destroyed the one true advantage the French Army possessed going into this war: a unified national command structure – no coalition, and everybody knew everybody and their capabilities.

Now, a man who never took a single course at a military academy, let alone graduated from one, took command of the army and the war effort. True, Louis Napoleon had an eclectic variety of combat experiences, from insurgent operations with the Carbonari in Italy to attempted coups and the infantry charge at Solferino. He had written two books on artillery, an idealized biography of his uncle and thought himself an expert on all military subjects.

But none of this adds up to a real military career. Not for someone leading a company or a regiment, let alone commanding the largest fielded army in Europe – and especially one facing the logistical and communications morass the French Army had created for itself. Given time MacMahon, his staff and subordinate commanders could have worked it all out. Now, they had to restructure the chain of command, MacMahon dutifully becoming a subordinate himself, and respond to the new edicts of Napoleon III. And all the while the time they so desperately needed dribbled away.

The Germanies Show How It's Done

Across the Rhine there could scarcely have been a more stark comparison. The armies, corps, divisions and regiments of three dozen separate states were rapidly gathering. Not smoothly, not easily but competently. Plans had been worked out in advance, then tested in exercises instead of just being reviewed. Extra trains, train crews and telegraphists were put on duty by the Prussian State Railways and the Postal and Telegraph Union.

Trains were late, but did not go missing. When wagons and other transport did not show up, others were requisitioned. If units ended up in the wrong location, they did forced marches to the right one. Food stores did not go missing or were found spoiled. All of this went much better than it did for the French because the Prussians had been here before.

In 1864 and again in 1866 the Prussians had actual wars to practice what they had learned from the American Civil War and even the Franco-Austrian War. The results, the mistakes, were studied and solutions tried instead of being ignored in the hope they would not happen again. Even if the solutions did not work something perhaps more important was learned: that mistakes and failures would happen, would always happen, and it was better to be prepared for them than be paralyzed by them.

As the German troops gathered at the train stations and left their cities they too sang songs. They sang "Watch on the Rhine" and the old Haydn anthem to the lines of the August von Fallersleben poem. It had been sung before, in 1848 as an appeal to Germans to stop fighting amongst themselves and unite. Now it was sung as an appeal to unite and fight a common external enemy. They sang "Deutschland, Deutschland Über Alles."

And when the troops reached their bivouacs and temporary corrals in the central Rhineland provinces most were still singing, as opposed to grumbling about the lack of food or other supplies. And the units did not get misplaced or lost. With great efficiency the divisions of the First Army, commanded by Steinmetz, detrained and assembled at Wittlich, a town just east of the Moselle River on the border with Luxembourg. The Second Army, under Prince Friedrich Karl, gathered at the towns of Homburg and Neunkirchen near Saarbrücken on the French border. The Third Army, lead by Crown Prince Friedrich Wilhelm, arrived at Landau and Rastatt, some 50 miles northeast of the border fortress of Strasbourg.

As extensive as they were, the limitations of the Prussian rail network meant there just were not enough locomotives and rolling stock to bring the Fourth Army to the front. Also, there was another reason to keep it deeper inside German territory. Everyone, not just Friedrich Engels, believed the war would initially start on German soil. So Moltke and his command staff decided to keep the Fourth Army in reserve for the time being. That caution led them to one big blunder at the start of the war. With everyone so sure of where its opening phase would be fought, they decided none of their corps or division staffs would be issued maps of France.

Moltke's initial strategy was to draw the French into the Saar region, at this time not quite so industrialized as it later became, and pulverize them there with his armies before going on the offensive and actually invading France. When this would happen he could not be certain, and telegraphed that answer to Berlin when Roon demanded one. But already, the initiative in this war was slowly ceding to the Prussian-lead coalition. And it would be from Berlin, not the Saar, and Bismarck, not Moltke and his armies, that the first really crippling blow would come.

Taking the Wind Out of the Napoleonic Sails

On July 29th, the day Napoleon III arrived at Metz, Chancellor Bismarck released a diplomatic skeleton from his closet. The release had been politically-timed to do the maximum amount of damage to the Emperor's prestige. But when it came unbidden from his own hand then the political opportunist has no one to blame except himself.

Some four years earlier, in May of 1866, in the midst of not only the build-up to the *Bruderkrieg* but the Mexico Crisis as well Napoleon sent a secret proposal to the Prussian government for an alliance against Austria, his erstwhile partner in Mexico. The protocols of the proposed treaty were as follows:

First: Should the Congress of the Powers assemble, Italy to have Venetia and Prussia the Duchies(meaning Schleswig-Holstein).

Second: Should the Congress disagree, alliance offensive and defensive will be made between France and Prussia.

Third: Prussia to open hostilities against Austria within ten days after the dissolution of the Congress.

Fourth: Should no Congress meet, Prussia to attack Austria within thirty days after the signature of the present treaty.

Fifth: Napoleon to begin hostilities against Austria as soon as Prussia begins, despatching 300,000 men during the first month across the Rhine.

Sixth: No separate treaty shall be made by either power with Austria. When a joint treaty is made, the following are to be the conditions: 1.) Vienna to go to Italy. 2.) Prussia to select German territory at will for annexation, the number of inhabitants not to exceed 8,000,000 of souls; the territory thus acquired to become part of the Kingdom of Prussia, without federal rights. 3.) France to have a liberal share of the Rhine provinces.

Seventh: A military and maritime allegiance to be made between France and Prussia, to which Italy may be a party should she so desire.[*]

---

[*] *The Great War of 1870 Between France and Germany: Comprising A History of Its Origins and Causes, the Biographies of the King of Prussia, the Ex-Emperor of France and the Statesmen and Generals of the Two Countries, the Financial, Social and Military*, by L.P. Brockett. Pg.145 - 146. c.1871

Nor was this a one-off attempt by Napoleon III at a Franco-Prussian treaty. There were repeated modifications he made to it. Restoration of the 1814 Luxembourg border became an obsession, meaning that the Grand Duchy would no longer exist after being re-absorbed by France. Belgium's absorption by France, and Prussia's of the southern German states were also discussed in the modifications. All of which Bismarck had released in a circular to the press and the courts of the neutral powers.

The wretched brazenness from a ruler already infamous for such tactics shocked most of Europe. It marked the end of any feeble hope for a French-Austrian alliance and Denmark, seeing that its alliance would not compel the larger one and could end in its destruction, quickly broke off negotiations.

Bismarck executed one of the shortest and most successful diplomatic offensives in modern times. It left France isolated among the European states and in public opinion. Only later, after the fall of Napoleon and the rise of the Government of National Defence, would she acquire some small measure of sympathy from the rest of the world.

Skirmishes

Even as the armies on both sides were still assembling, a series of minor engagements had started along the border and elsewhere. On July 19th the French made the first incursion when a small force of infantry, probably Chasseurs, raided a custom-house near Saarbrücken; German soil had been invaded.

The next day the first skirmish between the opposing forces resulted in a French soldier being shot by a Prussian fusilier. On July 23rd a reconnaissance party of German cavalry crossed the border at Saar-Louis, a town northwest of the custom-house attack, and headed south, first to St. Avold and later in the day due west towards Metz. It achieved some intelligence value, but started something far greater. The Legend of the Uhlans, the Prussian Lancers who would seemingly be everywhere in the coming war, and very nearly were, had been born.

A more sizeable engagement, again near Saarbrücken, took place on July 26th with the French Army being driven back across the border. The 27th was a traditional day of fasting and prayer held throughout the North German Confederation. Curiously, the French respected the religious observance; no additional border incursions were made. In fact, in the days that followed, activity trailed off.

This is probably because Napoleon had arrived at Metz on the 29th, and dropped his bombshell that he would be taking personal command of the French Army. Time was needed to change the chain-of-command in order to facilitate the Emperor's whims. Compared to all the other problems it faced, this one would be easy for the army to resolve. And when activities resumed it would, however briefly, take the initiative.

Paris: The Party Before the Storm

It seemed almost from the day of his departure, Paris was no longer Napoleon III's city. There is a measured ingratitude in this, for it had been the Emperor who had transformed it from a crumbling, crowded and disease-ridden medieval city into the first modern metropolis: the City of Light. And on those broad avenues and squares, and under all that public lighting he had built, a strange party took place, hand in hand with the preparations for war.

The partygoers not only sang "La Marseillaise," they brought out the equally-suppressed tricolor flags, though for the time being they respected the white Bourbon flags flying from the public buildings. They did not respect – and this would prove one of the few things they shared with their Imperial government – and hated the Prussians.

Not the Germans in general but the Prussians specifically; mixed in with the strains of a suppressed anthem and other songs were the cries of "onto Berlin" and "death to the Prussians!" These were, unknown to the cheering mobs, the last days of an age when Germans would be thought of as only an ethnic group and not a nationality. Just like the government they so detested, many in the mobs held onto the surrealistic hope some of the other German states would ally with them.

Had not Bavaria been one of France's most reliable allies during the Napoleonic Wars? Were not Würtemberg and Baden largely Bonapartist creations? Many Parisians, with incredible naivete, believed most of these smaller states wanted to throw off the yoke of Prussian dominance so recently imposed on them, at least from their less-than-knowledgeable point of view.

Even some who were Germanophiles persisted and expounded on this bizarre notion. Edgar Quinet, a writer and historian who had been politically active during "the Year of Revolution" period, and who had translated the works of "Sturm und Drang" philosopher Johann von Herder, returned to Paris almost as soon as Napoleon arrived in Metz. In 1852 the Emperor had exiled him for anti-Jesuit, anti-Church, writings. He spent the years since then in Belgium, some of the Germanies, and especially in Switzerland. And from the moment he arrived he joined the bizarre celebration and went on a delusional tear on France's coming victory and alliance with southern German states.

The great Victor Hugo, who famously called the Emperor "le petit Napoleon," and whose long exile since 1851 had largely been self-imposed, made plans to return to Paris as well. He too believed in the coming French victory, which is rather curious, since he hated the man. At least Thiers, Favre and Gambetta realized such an event would make Napoleon III Europe's new Charlemagne. But for seemingly everyone else, there willingly existed a serious disconnect between the pending success on the battlefield and the increase in imperial power.

It was rather like an inversion of the old children's tale, *The Emperor's New Clothes*. Everyone wanted to see the splendor in victory, no one wanted to acknowledge the ugly, naked truth that would confront them should the victories come to pass. Until it closed, Parisians flocked to the Louvre. Even as other, smaller, artworks were being packed and transported to the naval arsenal at Brest for safekeeping, they came to see Jacques Louis David's monumental *Napoleon at Saint Bernard's Pass*.

Too big to be safely and quickly moved, in a perverse way it captured the mood of the times, as did the idealized Napoleon paintings of Antoine Horace Vernet and his son Emile Horace Vernet. Mostly ignored, in those momentous days, was a similarly monumental painting at the Louvre: Theodore Géricault's *Raft of the Medusa*. Shunned for now, its hour would come.

A more dangerous perversion the euphoric mood created came over the question of evacuation. Except for the artwork, almost no one left Paris. Few seriously believed the city faced any threat. An invading German army would have to fight its way through the fortifications of Strasbourg, Metz and Verdun. And then there were the defences of Paris itself. The latest improvements to its centuries-old fortresses were started during Louis Philippe's reign, though they had since been allowed to fall into disrepair.

But now they were commanded by Trochu, one of the few generals to have a good reputation with the public. And at any rate, who wanted to be anywhere except Paris when the war was won? Emile Zola stayed, as did most of his other writer friends. Gustave Flaubert feared he would not get back from the provinces in time. And for a former lawyer and playwright now was no time to leave Paris. His most successful "romantic adventure" novel had recently been published: *20,000 Leagues Under the Sea*.

For the writer who foretold so much about the future, Jules Verne could see nothing except a terrible victory for France.

Chapter XIII: First Blood, and the Initiative is Lost

"What we anticipate seldom occurs; what we least expect generally happens."
-Benjamin Disraeli (1804 - 1881)

The French Army "Reforms" and Attacks

HOWEVER LIMITED HIS military abilities were, Napoleon III moved quickly to reform and deploy his forces in anticipation of crossing the Rhine. He had barely been at Metz for a day when he ordered the fielded corps to advance to the frontier. The response he got surprised him; all the marshals and generals protested that the breakdowns in logistics and communications made such a deployment impossible.

Typical of his past behavior, he ordered the advance anyway, then wrote a letter to Eugénie. He told her of the chaos and mismanagement he found, who had betrayed him and that he would yet continue until victory. In the meantime, the demoted MacMahon took command of the First Corps at Strasbourg. The Second Corps, still commanded by Charles Frossard, moved farther to the northeast, to St. Avold near Saarbrücken. The Third Corps, still under Bazaine, remained at Metz though with fewer divisions. Fourth Corps, commanded by Comte de Ladmirault, stayed at Thionville, on the Moselle River near the Luxembourg border.

Pierre de Failly's Fifth Corps, due to the breakdowns, was now deployed at both Saarguimines and Bitche, just south of Saarbrücken. Canrobert's Sixth Corps remained at Châlons, far to the west near Reims.

Felix Douay's Seventh Corps lay spread between Belfort and Besancon, along the Swiss border. Finally, Charles Bourbaki's elite Imperial Guards Corps had just moved to Metz.

By the beginning of August it had become obvious the French Army would not be crossing the Rhine to invade the South German States of Bavaria and Baden. The deployments and skirmish activity indicated an attack much further to the north. Where the less-imposing Saar River marked the border between France and the Germanies: Saarbrücken.

On August 2nd, with Napoleon III and his son in attendance, the three corps of Frossard, de Failly and Bourbaki attacked the border town with its garrison of three infantry battalions, four squadrons of cavalry and one artillery battery. It took the overwhelmingly large French command all day to rout the garrison from the town, after which they were congratulated by the Emperor for a great victory.

When the news reached Paris the crowds became delirious with joy. German soil, more accurately Prussian soil, had been invaded and the victory treated as the harbinger of greater conquests to come. In another letter to Eugénie, Napoleon spent more time describing how their son had weathered his first battle than in its success. By nightfall seemingly everyone in France was confident of further victories, except for their army command staff.

By the following morning they realized the problem they faced. Due to their logistical morass and confused leadership, the French Army had been deployed across a front almost 90 miles wide. Three German armies, with more men, more artillery and more cavalry, were apparently deployed on a front about a third as long. And, to add to their troubles, French command did not know where.

A rumor of 40,000 Prussian troops marching across the frontier to the north of Saarbrücken caused the French left wing to be reinforced. Contradictory orders were issued to Bourbaki's Imperial Guard, and delayed the fortification of the Spicheren hills behind Saarbrücken. And the appearance of German forces, in reality a few local militia units, in the Black Forest area near the Swiss border caused Douay's Seventh Corps to remain spread over the Alsace.

Tactical paralysis, in addition to all their logistical woes, had set in. It compelled Napoleon to split the French Army into two commands. MacMahon took control of the First, Fifth and Seventh Corps while Bazaine got the Second, Third and Fourth with the Sixth Corps being called in from Châlons. Having two armies in the field instead of one did not resolve any of the threats or problems they faced, but everyone hoped it would make subsequent operations less ponderous. It would not.

The First Real Battle

On August 3rd the one partial success the French Army achieved occurred about 50 miles west-southwest of Saarbrücken. An infantry division, supported by a detached cavalry brigade, from MacMahon's First Corps at Strasbourg secured the French border town of Weissenburg on the Lauter River. Its railway station was an important asset, for either the invasion of the Germanies or the invasion of France. And Moltke determined his armies should have it.

On the morning of August 3rd he had already given orders for them to move out of their assembly areas. This would lead to the first real battles of the Franco-Prussian War, and one near-disaster that should have been as paralyzing to the coalition armies as the logistical and communications morass the French Army had inflicted upon itself.

By daybreak on August 4th the vanguard of Crown Prince Friedrich Wilhelm's Third Army was advancing on a comparatively compact front between Lauterburg, near the junction between the Lauter and Rhine Rivers, and Weissenburg about a dozen miles to the east. A Bavarian infantry division made first contact with General Charles Abel Douay's Second Infantry Division. A sharp fight erupted along the town walls and Château Geisburg on the heights overlooking it.

The defensive positions and the capabilities of the Chassepot favored the French, until some 30 field guns were brought up and shelled the town, its rail station and the chateau. Unable to get reinforcements, while the Bavarians were joined by corps-strength formations, Douay ordered a retreat as early as ten in the morning.

It would not be until early in the afternoon that an orderly one could be effected. Under continuous, heavy artillery fire Charles Douay was killed and all discipline broke down soon afterward. The Germans routed the Second Division, which lost over 800 killed and wounded plus 1,000 prisoners and a battery of field artillery.

For the first time the Mitrailleuse guns were used in combat, but the wonder weapon achieved little in the way of anticipated results as the Krupp breech-loaders quickly silenced them. So complete was the rout that the Army's Fourth Cavalry Division lost all contact with the surviving remnants as they fled to the west.

Weissenburg would prove to be the true harbinger of the war's future course of action. With some interesting variations, the battles would begin with an infantry fight and the French would hold their own, even take the initiative, until German artillery came into action. Defeat would be followed by cavalry pursuit, which often turned it into a rout. While not every battle would develop this way, it would become depressingly familiar to the French.

The German Crisis

For such destruction to be wrought upon their enemy, the German armies did have to actually engage them. And from August 3rd to the 5th there occurred an incident that could have, should have, led to a complete paralysis of the First and Second German Armies. If anything, it should have been more damaging than what the French Army had faced for over two weeks as it came on the very commencement of combat, when initial tactical movements were so critical.

Moltke had arrayed his three armies in a very deliberate manner. The two largest, the Second and Third, were deployed in exactly the area he expected the main French invasion to take place. The First Army, the smallest, he located farther to the north, on the frontier with neutral Belgium and Luxembourg. From there, once the French Army had committed itself to an assault in the Saar region, First Army would sweep down from the north and part of the Third Army would flank the invasion force from the south. Together they would encircle it, and with the Second Army annihilate it. All that had to happen for this plan to be executed was for the French to do what Moltke anticipated, and what they wanted to do.

But after Saarbrücken French tactical and logistical paralysis meant a new plan had to be hurriedly executed, and to First Army commander Friedrich von Steinmetz it looked as though he would be left out of the picture. Moltke gave him orders to advance no farther than Tholey, some 20 miles north of the border town. Instead, he arrogantly demanded that if it were to be liberated then it should fall to First Army. He complained to King Wilhelm, who had arrived at Moltke's headquarters with his huge royal entourage back on August 2nd, about this, then pushed his leading divisions down the St. Wendel-Ottweiler Road.

This lay straight across Prince Friedrich Karl's line-of-march. When units of the First and Second Armies encountered each other a first-class disaster was in the making. The nightmare of two armies hamstringing each other within a dozen miles of the front was only avoided by the skill of the division and regimental commanders, some very heated telegrams from Moltke and an order from the King himself. But the order only restated that Moltke issued military commands and said nothing of Steinmetz's proposals.

After a day's delay, during which Moltke devised plans to trap and destroy the French at Saarbrücken, Steinmetz sent his Seventh and Eighth Corps into the Saar. Not in the encircling maneuver towards Saarlouis as Moltke dictated, but due south for Saarbrücken. They would again entangle themselves with the vanguard of the Second Army, and force Moltke to do the last thing he wanted...launch a blind frontal attack on an entrenched enemy.

A War on Two Fronts

While the Prussians blundered into each other, the French exhausted their troops in pointless forced marches, often in the rain. Finally, on the morning of August 6th, combat erupted on two fronts some 40 miles apart: Wörth/Woerth, about ten miles southwest of Weissenburg and the Spicheren Heights west of Saarbrücken.

On the preceding night General Charles Frossard concluded his Second Corps to be too exposed in Saarbrücken. Without permission he fell back to the hills of Spicheren Heights, just inside France. Behind him were the French Army's Third, Fourth and Fifth Corps, plus the Imperial Guard Corps. With the Heights having received some fortifications, and all those corps ready to support him, Frossard felt his new position fairly secure.

In front of him were the cavalry scouts of Friedrich Karl's Second Army, already reconnoitering the drilling grounds of the local reserve unit, and behind them could be seen the divisions of First Army's Seventh Corps. Farther behind, and beyond sight, were the Second Army's lead divisions. The armies were again entangled, the disaster Moltke feared was in the offing.

Woerth, on the Sauer River and at the foot of the heavily forested Froeschwiller Ridge, had become filled with the wounded and survivors of Weissenburg in its aftermath. They, and their relief troops from the rest of MacMahon's First Corps, treated the defeat as a fluke and not a portend of the future. Still, they blew the bridge across the Sauer just to be sure.

The problem was the area of the Froeschwiller Forest had already been heavily surveyed by German cavalry patrols in the final days of July. They consisted of just an officer with two or three men instead of full cavalry squadrons – something officers from across the Germanies had learned during the American Civil War. Especially one young Würtemberg captain, who got surprised by French police dining with his men at an inn near Woerth. For the dashing aristocrat this was not the first time such brazen acts caught the attention of his superiors; there was that near-capture by Confederate forces in Virginia. Nor would it be the last for Count

Ferdinand von Zeppelin.

At Spicheren the battle started when Uhlans from Second Army's 5th Cavalry Division took fire at the Heights from what they thought to be the rear guard of a retreating formation. At Woerth it was skirmishers from a Silesian Jäger battalion who waded the Sauer and found the town mostly abandoned. Initial combat lasted just half an hour, though by then artillery on both sides had joined in.

Spicheren quickly developed into a corps-level engagement with Frossard's Second Corps trying to fend off one division after another sent against their positions. Eventually, all the divisions of First Army's Seventh and Eighth Corps, along with Second Army's Third Corps were committed to a battle raging over steep slopes, heavy forests and even the massive buildings of an iron works plant.

Frossard, through most of the day, grimly held on to his positions. He had no intention of retreating, if he did so then the town of Forbach behind the Heights would surely fall. And, unknown to the Prussians, the town and its rail station were the great storehouse of supplies for the planned French invasion of the Saar.

The Battle of Woerth also grew into a corps-level engagement with Crown Prince Friedrich Wilhelm arriving at the front to find the battle he had not wanted already occurring. Instead of obstinately ordering a disengagement, he accepted the situation and commanded the Eleventh Corps to support the Fifth, already fighting, and summoned the two Bavarian Corps and the Würtemberg Division. To a battle he did not want, the Crown Prince committed virtually his entire army.

The same would not happen at Spicheren because the paralysis Moltke feared had come to pass. First and Second Armies were fully entangled, and new units found it nearly impossible to reach the front lines. The battle would have to be decided by the three corps and some 29 cavalry squadrons from various commands already in the area.

The French should have won this battle. Frossard had most of the best positions and four corps behind him in addition to his own. Should have and yet did not, and what lost it for them would be the very slowness in which the Prussian corps commanders fed their divisions into the battle. No one in the French chain-of-command really believed the situation was growing worse until well after it had. And then there were the field guns.

Chassepots and Mitrailleuse batteries could outrange the Dreyse, but the Krupp four-pounders and six-pounders swept everything before them – especially after the Prussians took a key position, a spur off the Heights called the Rotherberg, by mid-afternoon. The infantry assault had been costly; its own commanding general died as he reached the spur's plateau.

But soon afterwards a battery of eight four-pounders were hauled up to the plateau and began pouring fire onto the other French positions.

Even so, repeated assaults failed to turn either French flank or push them from other locations. In fact by 6:00PM it seemed as though the entire Prussian right wing began collapsing when a French counterattack turned one of the assaults into a rout. Though by then the Prussians had won Spicheren – Frossard telegraphed Bazaine that he had to retreat. He cited a lack of supplies, a need to bring his widely dispersed units under tighter control with the approaching night, and Prussian units had been spotted in the hills above Forbach.

The Battle of Woerth ended rather differently. The town itself had been taken before Crown Prince Friedrich Wilhelm arrived and Field-Pioneer battalions had thrown pontoon bridges across the Sauer. Bavarian, Hessian and Silesian gun crews limbered up their field pieces and rushed across the bridges to join the infantry regiments hotly engaged with the divisions of MacMahon's First Corps.

Their arrival, along with a number of cavalry regiments, came not a moment too soon. Repeated infantry attacks and counterattacks did little except wear down the units involved. Then, the French right wing launched a massive attack on what they believed were exhausted troops, and three cavalry regiments under General Michel charged down the slopes of the Froeschwiller Ridge south of Woerth.

Both were done with a flare and *élan* worthy of Napoleon Bonaparte. *Furia francese. Charge à l'outrance.* And if they had been done in any battle during the Napoleonic Age they might have carried the day. But this was the first modern war in history, and they ran straight into modern, breech-loading small arms and artillery.

The cavalry charge, over 1,000 horses strong, hit a German infantry formation at the moment it had been wheeling to the right. They were without cover, at their most vulnerable, but they formed a firing line and shredded the charge with rifle fire. The horsemen who actually broke through were met by Hessian Hussars at the village of Morsbronn and virtually annihilated. To use Moltke's antiseptic phrase they "disappeared from the field."

The infantry charge managed to do a little better; they drove out the forward-deployed elements, until they ran into the artillery. At a range of less than 500 yards they opened fire, stopping the charge by inflicting massive casualties. With these attempts over, MacMahon's Corps ceased offensive operations. They were no longer trying to win the battle; now they fought to avoid being invested, and either destroyed or forced to surrender.

By mid-afternoon his command had been reduced to a pocket of one square mile in area. Every division had suffered heavy casualties, ammunition supplies became critical and German artillery seemingly covered the entire ground with fire. To the north and east Bavarians were closing in. To the south Prussians stormed through the blazing houses of Elsasshausen village and could not be stopped. Only to the west, where the cavalry of the Eleventh Corps and the Würtemberg Division had yet to completely close the encirclement, was there a chance for escape.

At 3:30PM MacMahon ordered the last of his reserves to be used. The regiments of light cavalry, Cuirassiers, were sent south to stop the Prussians while eight batteries of carefully husbanded field guns were brought out to answer the German artillery. But the Cuirassiers only delayed the Prussians, and met the same fate as Michel's *charge à l'outrance*. They "disappeared from the field." In the remarkably short time of an afternoon, First Corps repeated the British disaster at Balaclava twice – and at least with the Light Brigade there were over 500 survivors. The batteries fared only a little better, with their crews picked off by sharpshooters after firing just a few rounds.

About half an hour later, with all resistance collapsing, MacMahon ordered what remained of First Corps into a general retreat to the west. Since the Würtemberg Division had not completed its latest deployment, they managed to break through to the town of Reichshoffen, where MacMahon found reinforcements from de Failly's Fifth Corps just arriving.

They had been ordered in the morning without apparent urgency. Now, instead of being used to outflank and surprise the Germans, they could only briefly hold off the pursuing cavalry and Würtemberg Division before joining the general flight from the Froeschwiller Ridge. They would fall back to the town of Niederbronn and its railway station, where news of the defeat would be telegraphed to Metz, the other corps commands and the rest of France.

The Battles Behind the Lines

Neither side had anticipated, planned for, or wanted the Battles of Spicheren Heights or Woerth. Both sides suffered from paralysis, indecision and mistakes. Both sides suffered roughly the same number of casualties, but in the end it was the French who retreated and the Germans who won. But, for most of August 6th it did not look that way to Moltke at his headquarters.

Against all the odds, the paralysis caused by Steinmetz pushing First

Army into the line-of-march of Friedrich Karl's Second Army did not produce disaster. The victory that resulted could hardly be called clean or decisive: the Prussians took 4,500 casualties, the French only 2,000 killed and wounded. But the French also lost their prize, Saarbrücken, lost 2,000 more men as prisoners of war, and lost all the equipment and supplies they had stockpiled at Forbach for the invasion of the Saar.

Woerth produced more evenly balanced casualties: over 10,500 for Friedrich Wilhelm's Third Army and 11,000 for the French First Corps. But again, MacMahon's command lost over 9,000 more as prisoners as well as 2,000 horses and all the artillery, caissons, wagons and other equipment a corps of five divisions would bring into the field.

Confusion reigned supreme on both sides, and brought about largely by their chains-of-command. Steinmetz was largely the cause on the German side, he even fatuously claimed he did what he did "in the interests of the Second Army." Friedrich Karl thought different and he had given authority to the commander of his vanguard division to clear First Army off the roads. Fortunately, the division and corps commanders at Spicheren did not translate the antagonisms of their superiors into actions which would have crippled their combat effectiveness.

At Woerth the confusion started with the Crown Prince's orders the day before that all units under his command were not to seek combat on August 6th. A larger part of his army had yet to cross the border and he wanted it fully deployed before engaging in any major battles. Instead battle found his army, and his Fifth Corps commander took it on his responsibility to continue and expand the fight.

When Friedrich Wilhelm arrived at the front line headquarters he instantly realized this was an engagement too big and too serious to break off. Still, its accidental nature meant he could not bring in all the units he wanted, or when and where he wanted them. He and his commanders were forced to react to events and seize the unfolding opportunities. In this sense they were more like Napoleon Bonaparte and his legendary staff than was MacMahon and his – who, by the afternoon, were no longer fighting to win as trying to keep defeat at bay until reinforcements arrived.

And throughout the day Moltke could do little but sit and fume at his headquarters as his grand strategies were dashed by arrogant subordinates and chance events. At least by the evening he could begin work on unraveling the chaotic condition of his First and Second Armies.

The same would not be happening for Napoleon III at his headquarters in Metz. Throughout the day he received fragmentary reports from both battlefronts, copies of the telegrams from MacMahon and Frossard asking for reinforcements, though without any real urgency, and then there came the reports of additional enemy activity all through Alsace province and the Moselle region of Lorraine.

Ever since the victory at Saarbrücken, French High Command had been bedeviled by these reports and the indecision and paralysis they caused. They kept the Comte de Ladmirault's Fourth Corps at Thionville, north of Metz, and Felix Douay's Seventh Corps no closer to the fighting than Strasbourg, though at least it was closer than Belfort.

And a new dimension could now be added to these often errant and exaggerated reports: loss of communications. In squadron-sized units or smaller, Uhlans, Dragoons and other German cavalrymen infiltrated the countryside. They cut telegraph lines, blew sections of railroad tracks and bridges, ambushed French reconnaissance patrols and raided whatever targets of opportunity presented themselves. For all the headaches he dealt with, Moltke at least did not have to contend with this.

For a successful army on the attack, these pinpricks would be no more than nuisances. To an army confused about the enemy's location, ineptly commanded and already afflicted with communications and logistical problems they produced a paralysis of their own: fear. The Legend of the Uhlans was being established. Soon there would be reports of them appearing as far west as Paris, as far south as Lyon. By the end of August 6th Napoleon called for a general retreat of all forces along the frontier with the Germanies.

The Rout After the Rout

Certainly no such order would be necessary for the remains of MacMahon's First Corps. At the town of Niederbronn its remnants met up with General Guyot de Lespart's infantry division from Fifth Corps. From there it would have been possible to fall back to the northwest, to Bitche where de Failly had a corps headquarters and a supply center. However, the route back took them too close to the Prussian border for safety and, after sending his Emperor a stark report on what happened, MacMahon ordered a retreat to Ingwiller and Saverne in the southwest.

Without having seen any fighting, Bitche was abandoned. De Failly's Fifth Corps left behind artillery supplies, ambulances and even its own funds in an effort to lighten and speed the march. They also left men behind. Farther to the west, at the border town of Sarreguemines, the brigade stationed there for local defence would eventually get absorbed into Frossard's Second Corps.

Largely intact, and scarcely having been blooded in combat, de Failly's corps fell in with MacMahon's in a stampeding retreat. To pursue them, Friedrich Wilhelm ordered up one of two cavalry divisions in his army, the Fourth. Prince Albert of Prussia drove his command throughout the night, giving it only three hours of rest before daybreak, then pushing on until making contact with the French rear guard at Steinberg.

By then Felix Douay's Seventh Corps, which had since moved up from Strasbourg, joined the retreating mass. This should have stiffened their resolve, given their morale a boost; they could have made a stand, for when the Fourth Division's advanced column appeared they were without any infantry support of their own. Instead, their appearance only renewed the impulse to flee.

MacMahon's rout did not end until his First Corps reached Neufchateau, southwest of Nancy and over 130 miles from Froeschwiller, where it finally boarded trains for Châlons. Fifth Corps received confusing orders to march in several different directions until reaching Chaumont and also taking trains for Châlons. And Seventh Corps took the most circuitous route, boarding at Bar-sur-Aube and moving through Paris before arriving at Reims, just northwest of Châlons.

For much of that time the army was out of contact with Napoleon, who had multiple troubles of his own. First he ordered Canrobert to bring his Sixth Corps from Châlons, then contradicted the order and sent him back. He next ordered Trochu to form a Twelfth Corps from the best personnel of the Paris defences and to transport them as soon as possible to Châlons as well.

After this, on the morning of August 7th, Napoleon and Minister of War Edmond Leboeuf left Metz on a train for St. Avold to discuss with Bazaine what could be done to stem the German invasion, especially in light of MacMahon's full flight with his army. Then, they learned Forbach and its supplies had fallen to the Prussians and the location of Frossard's Second Corps was unknown. All this left St. Avold threatened and the three decided the best course would be to continue the general retreat and eventually collect the entire army at Châlons.

Napoleon III returned to Metz in full mental and physical collapse. Initiative had been lost, entire corps could not be found, reports had Prussian and other German forces seemingly everywhere, and all hope of gaining allies in this war had evaporated. Far from recreating the glory days of Austerlitz or Jena, it looked as if Imperial France was about to relive the disaster of 1814.

Chapter XIV: The World Turns Upside Down

"We shouldn't maltreat our idols, the gilt comes off
in our hands."
-Gustave Flaubert (1821 - 1880)

Paris: Party Interrupted

THE INITIAL VICTORY at Saarbrücken received wild cheering on the streets of Paris. For virtually the last time, Napoleon III was universally popular with the civil population. Almost no one noticed it had been made by an overwhelming force against a small garrison – except perhaps the newly-appointed Governor of Paris: General Louis-Jules Trochu. He knew an easy victory when he saw one, and worried over the reports he read of massive coalition armies massing in the Saar and Bavarian Palatinate, when he was not busy refurbishing the long-neglected Paris defences. Then came the news of Weissenburg.

At first the official reports treated it as another victory. By the time the press revealed the truth, the news of Woerth and Spicheren had started to come in. Throughout the day of August 7th the city stood in shocked silence as the contradictory and often exaggerated reports came in.

Frossard's Second Corps had gone missing, then it was destroyed. MacMahon's First Corps lost a great battle, his own telegram said so, but had joined up with de Failly's Fifth Corps to counterattack. Then, all contact was lost with both. Douay's Seventh Corps had left Strasbourg to reinforce them, then contact with it ended as well. Paris would not remain silent for long.

The next day the demands started. For the end of Napoleon's reign, the establishment of a republic, a *levée en masse* to draft the armies necessary to crush the Prussians. Unrepentant royalists wanted senior Leftists and Liberals arrested, and Emile Ollivier thought this might be a good idea. Jules Favre urged the arming of all draft-age Parisians, which he would later come to regret.

Remarkably, the head of the Imperial Government while Napoleon was in the field, Empress Eugénie, kept her head and rejected all of it – though she did agree to send Trochu to Châlons with his newly-formed corps and to bring the Corps Legislatif into session. On the following day both it and her accepted the resignation of Ollivier, and his replacement by Comte Charles de Palikao as both Premier and Minister of War.

The Press and those Leftists who had advocated pacifism and feared where militarism would lead their country for the last two decades and more suddenly changed their tune. France was in peril, it did not matter that their Emperor was responsible. French soil had been violated, something they never considered happening. And instead of trying to understand the realities of modern warfare they revived the glories of the French Revolution.

They recalled 1793, when the National Assembly called for the first great *levée en masse*. The fabled year when: "all young men will go to the front, married men will forge arms and transport foodstuffs. Women will make tents, uniforms and serve in the hospitals and children will tear rags into lint."

Those who a few weeks earlier had rightly feared a French victory would elevate Napoleon III to the status of Europe's new Charlemagne now joined in the drumbeat for war. And not just Favre but Thiers, Gambetta and returning exiles like Quinet and Victor Hugo. The amateurs were preparing for war, and apparently without one of them ever thinking that the glory days they invoked and wanted to relive had occurred nearly eight decades earlier. The world had changed, and so had the art of war in ways Jomini never wrote about and they could not comprehend.

After the Battle: The German Armies

By themselves, the costly victories of Spicheren and Woerth could not and did not win the war. In fact in earlier days, in the Napoleon Era, they would have been considered a stalemate. After such losses the victorious armies would have needed two or three months to replenish, to replace the men and equipment lost and the supplies consumed. But this was war in the Industrial Age, and the coalition German armies scarcely needed much longer than a week to make good their losses and untangle the mess in their own lines.

First and foremost came the task of separating First and Second Armies. Only the victory at Spicheren Heights had saved Steinmetz from being relieved of command. Even then he maintained an unrepentance and arrogance which made relations between him, Moltke and Prince Friedrich Karl absolutely sulfurous. Only with the greatest of difficulty were the command and logistics staffs of the two armies able to separate their units.

Part of the problem lay in the topography. There were only two good roads in the area between Saarbrücken and Saarlouis to the west. As for the rail lines which ran through Saarbrücken, Spicheren, Forbach and on to St. Avold and points west, they had been so badly damaged by the fighting it would take several weeks to repair. Coupled with Steinmetz only sending the barest of information on his location and activities, it made for a grindingly slow advance. And on top of all this, it rained heavily in the days following the two battles, making conditions even more miserable

Nor did the complaints and recriminations stop with the "Lion of Skalitz." About 40 miles to the east Crown Prince Friedrich Wilhelm kept busy with burying all the dead from Woerth – that alone took over a week – transporting the thousands of prisoners to the rear areas for internment and making complaints to the ambassadors of Bavaria and Würtemberg on his command staff about the performance of their units.

Nearly 85% of the casualties suffered by the Third Army at Woerth were Prussian. To the Crown Prince this meant the other German units were not conduction themselves as boldly. While this may have been true, in at least one instance it had a major beneficial effect.

The Würtemberg Division's inability to complete the investment of MacMahon's First Corps did mean its escape. And soon afterwards its exhausted, defeated remnants ran headlong into de Failly's Fifth Corps, who only needed to hear the thunder of German artillery and have a few skirmishes with the pursuing Würtemberg vanguard to be put into flight.

While the two panicked corps were able to outrun the infantry division, which they could have defeated had they made a stand, they did not outrun the Fourth Cavalry Division. And in its turn it kept the stampede going when First and Fifth Corps collided with Douay's Seventh Corps, and a single cavalry attack routed them all until they were south of Nancy. So in the end, by not achieving the destruction of single corps, Third Army pushed MacMahon's entire force out of the theater of operations in one of the most amazing routs in military history.

In fact the German coalition armies lost all contact with the Marshal's army, as did Napoleon's headquarters in Metz. While troubling, Moltke's staff had a more immediate problem with the French Army: they could not locate Charles Frossard's Second Corps, and that unit was still in-theater.

Eventually they did find it – Frossard had not fallen back like the rest of the French Army, he had gone sideways. He pulled his corps southeast to Sarreguemines, where he learned of the far larger defeat of MacMahon, and picked up the brigade de Failly abandoned before retreating to the southwest.

Effectively, the three German armies were out of contact with all the main elements of the French Army. They encountered garrisons, especially when the Crown Prince's Third Army wheeled to the right and marched across some 30 miles of mountainous terrain in detached columns, but little else except for stragglers.

The right wheel had been ordered by Moltke to bring all three armies into a reasonably compact, abreast formation where they could support each other. It would take the Third Army some five days to reach its new position, where fresh troops and supplies awaited it. By the time this was finished, on August 12th, First and Second Armies would be disentangled, another imperial warning issued to Steinmetz to obey high command's orders and what Moltke originally thought might take until the end of the year could at last begin: the invasion of France.

After the Battle: The French Army and Napoleon

However daunting the problems facing Moltke and his command staff were, French high command would have gladly traded the troubles they confronted for them. On the face of it, the defeats of Weissenburg, Spicheren and Woerth did not by themselves add up to an irredeemable catastrophe.

At Weissenburg a single division got surprised and overwhelmed by a superior-sized force. The corps at Spicheren was pushed into untenable positions yet retired in fairly good order. Only at Woerth did a major unit of the French Army suffer a serious defeat and rout. The problem was none of it should have happened. No one anticipated such a turn of events, much less planned for it, and that only began the problems.

Had Woerth just resulted in the destruction and surrender of MacMahon's First Corps then, in theory, de Failly's Fifth Corps and even Douay's Seventh Corps could have counterattacked a substantially weakened enemy in the following days. Instead, almost every unit in

MacMahon's army were routed right out of the theater of operations. Only the brigade de Failly left behind remained in-theater and it serendipitously got picked up by the only French army remaining in the immediate area, Bazaine's army at Metz.

Again, on the face of it, this army still looked to be a formidable force. Most of the losses Frossard's Second Corps had sustained at Spicheren were made good by the acquisition of the "abandoned" brigade. Third, Fourth and Imperial Guards corps' were still in-theater, though scattered. And Canrobert's Sixth Corps was still enroute from Châlons – until the serious problems in this command bubbled to the surface.

Sixth Corps was the first major unit of the Imperial French Army to not be composed of regular troops or reservists but National Guard and *Garde Mobile* units. Their training had been inadequate for decades and their equipment largely non-existent because the Intendance, the logistical branch of the French War Ministry, arrogantly decided it was someone else's business to arm them. This made their notoriously poor discipline even worse, and in the end not even Canrobert's fame, or famous charm, could mold them into a fighting command.

Ordered to Metz, then Nancy, then Metz again only to be recalled each time, the force was finally exchanged for the corps Trochu brought from Paris, but retained the number designation. And suddenly, for this "new" Sixth Corps the Intendance magically found the munitions, equipment and other supplies it needed for the front lines.

And while the problems of collecting the scattered units, regrouping them and replenishment were vexing enough, a far greater one awaited the high command's collective decision: what to do next. Even without Napoleon's daily input, the depression following his collapse had grown quite deep; all manner of plans abounded. Even Moltke, when he was not dealing with his own troubles, took time to consider what his enemy would do next.

Not too surprisingly, all the professionals agreed the best course the French Army should take was to concentrate all available forces at either St. Avold or some point farther south then hit the German armies in the flank when they penetrated deeper into France.

But this excellent, and for a fleeting moment doable, plan ran into a stark political reality: since the days of Cardinal Richelieu the keystone to French military policy had been the defence of Paris. To send the remaining corps out of Metz, Thionville and other fortified cities to some location south of the invaders' expected line of march would be seen by all as the abandonment of Paris.

Politically, no one could sanction the plan. Napoleon, Leboeuf and

Bazaine dismissed it almost as soon as one of them proposed it. Moltke dismissed it as well, though not for political reasons. Instead he considered it unlikely as the French Army had not shown the attitude for such a "vigorous" decision.

Unfortunately, almost all the other plans were politically untenable for much the same reason. Thinking strategically, and proving not to be completely incompetent, Bazaine suggested the next best operation would be to leave garrisons at Metz, Thionville and other forts, then take the remaining forces to Langres where they could easily reunite with the scattered corps of MacMahon's army and crush the invading German armies in a massive flanking maneuver.

This could have been a masterstroke – a daring, high-stakes gamble worthy of Napoleon Bonaparte himself. It would have taken Napoleon III from pathetic loser to reviled traitor to, potentially, the Savior of France. The problem was he could not think past the reviled traitor part for Langres, the major town in the lake region where the Meuse, Marne and Aube Rivers originate, is so far south as to be out of the theater of operations. It would again open the Emperor to the charge of abandoning Paris and he wanted none of it.

Less desirable would be the option of, again, leaving the garrisons and continuing the fall back to Châlons this time. Sixth Corps was already there, and MacMahon's First, Fifth and Seventh Corps' had orders to rendezvous in the city. But Ollivier, in one of his last acts before resigning, sent a very stern warning to Napoleon III that such a fall back would be no less dangerous politically than pulling the army out of the way of the invading Germans.

All this created a vacuum of leadership where the French high command dithered for a week over a range of difficult choices. The saddest irony here is that neither the Emperor, nor his generals or politicians bothered to notice, nor the civil population made to understand, that the Paris of Napoleon III was not the Paris of Richelieu.

He had not just turned it into a City of Light, but had completed the defences ordered by Louis Philippe. It had a ring of 15 forts covering the main approaches to the city, 94 smaller bastions, a moat and a high *enceinte* wall designed to make it difficult for invaders to breech. The great engineering general Vauban could not have created better and, as events would prove, the system would be able to handle a siege by the most modern army in the world.

At the end of a week of dithering the only things decided were Bazaine did indeed have command over the Second, Third and Fourth Corps *and* the Imperial Guard Corps, which Napoleon had insisted on retaining command of, even after Spicheren and Woerth. General Claude Théodore Decaén finally relieved Bazaine of his duties as Third Corps commander, so he could concentrate solely on the pressures of being an army commander. And Edmond Leboeuf was no longer War Minister; Empress Eugénie's Council of Regency had dismissed him and Premier de Palikao took his office as well. For the moment without duties, this would not last for long.

In the absence of any real plan Bazaine – at least he could now give orders without being countermanded by others, fell back to the most politically expedient option. All corps were to form a defensive line along the Nied River, ten miles east of Metz and its fortress complex. Leboeuf would inspect their positions and hopefully get them ready by the time the Germans arrived. Already, there were probes throughout the region, and the Legend of the Uhlans had gone full bloom.

The Legend and the Fear

After August 7th, after Crown Prince Friedrich Wilhelm recalled his cavalry division from pursuing the routed corps of MacMahon's Army, the coalition armies effectively lost contact with all the major units of the French Army. While the various German commands did have the pressing needs to replenish, regroup and disentangle themselves, it was equally vital for them to know the enemy's location.

This was the age, before wireless communications, before aerial reconnaissance, when opposing forces could pass within earshot of each other and never know they were there. To remedy this numerous cavalry patrols were sent out by all commands from division level on up.

Rarely larger the squadron-size, and frequently smaller, they ranged over the countryside, staying off the main roads but aggressively pursuing their objectives of locating the enemy and harassing him – often brazenly and innovatively so with operations reminiscent of the exploits of John Hunt Morgan, Benjamin Grierson, "Jeb" Stuart and Philip Sheridan.

At Thionville one patrol rode up to the main gate of its fortress, which the garrison closed with only minutes to spare. At Metz, patrols openly scouted within a mile of its outlying ring of fortresses. By August 9th their more hostile activities cut the Lunéville to Metz rail lines. On August 12th two patrols crossed the Moselle River south of Metz and began demolition operations on the tracks connecting it to Nancy. In both cases French troops surprised them before much damage could be done, with at least the balance of one patrol being captured.

And then there is the most legendary of these exploits, one which involved little damage to the French but instilled a good measure of fear. Some sources attribute this operation to Count Zeppelin; whoever commanded the cavalry squadron in question showed a great deal of originality as they rode to the southwest, towards the city of Nancy on the Meurthe River.

In each village or town the squadron swept into they informed the stunned inhabitants that the German Army would be there by either nightfall or the following day, often citing a specific corps or division. They would then request billeting arrangements: the best hotels and inns for the commanding officers, schools and churchyards for the enlisted men, stables and barns for the horses and certain fields for gun parks.

As news of this filtered back to Bazaine at Metz and MacMahon, still entraining his corps at Neufchâteau, it had them believing at least one German army was heading southwest. In reality all three armies were drawing into a compact front around a dozen miles wide and approaching Metz.

This operation plus the cutting of telegraph lines, the demolition or attempted demolition of railroad tracks, open reconnoitering in the Metz-Thionville region and probes as far west as Toul and the Verdun road contributed greatly to the tactical paralysis of French Army command on all levels. And it led directly to the legend of the German cavalry being swift, aggressive and omnipresent, ranging the countryside as the vanguard of unstoppable and all-conquering armies.

More than just Lancers(Uhlans) were used on these operations. Other heavy cavalry units, such as Dragoons and cuirassiers, were employed since they could work independently and at long-range. But the name Uhlans would stick, and for the next four decades their tales would be used to frighten children as bedtime stories, and educate soldiers in the slowly developing concept of Maneuver Warfare.

In marked contrast French cavalry operations were far more conventional and timid. Partly this came from command decisions – Bazaine ordered "our reconnaissances should not be aggressive" – but mostly from their own battlefield experiences. For the last four decades the crucible of French cavalry operations had been Algeria, where small units deploying far into the countryside, even squadron-sized parties, was an invitation to disaster.

Marshal MacMahon's own experiences at the Battle of Terchia serve as an example of the perils. Near the end of the engagement the commanding general needed to send an order to a unit some four miles away to change its line of march. Even at that short distance the dispatch rider, Lieutenant MacMahon, was offered a squadron of mounted

Chasseurs for an escort, but he declined.

Less than a mile from the headquarters camp local tribesmen spotted him, and took off in pursuit. As he approached his destination MacMahon noticed a deep ravine running beside its headquarters. To ride his way around the obstruction would mean being overtaken and killed. Instead, he spurred his horse and jumped the ravine. While his mount broke its leg, and had to be destroyed, MacMahon received his commendation.

Reportedly, he also received a stern warning never to do anything like that again. Most French cavalry operations not only involved squadron-sized units of better, they used light infantry to screen them and provide protection. Hence the regiments of Chasseurs assigned to every cavalry division. While this arrangement provided the cavalrymen with some protection, it greatly limited their mobility. And in an age that saw the first evolutions of Maneuver Warfare, it meant French cavalry was not only incapable of providing timely information about enemy movements, it was incapable of giving protection to its own troops.

Fall Back and Advance

Leboeuf did not remain out of work for long. Bazaine gave him the duty of inspecting the new French positions along the Nied River. He quickly discovered they were tactically well-sited but would not be able to withstand the impending blows from a massive German coalition army. If they could not get the various corps from MacMahon's army to regroup at Metz – soon to be a moot point with the severing of the necessary rail links – Bazaine's army would have to retreat to the protection of the Metz fortresses.

Ironically, the massive army Leboeuf and the rest of the French command feared was at least partly chimerical. Without aggressive reconnaissance by their own cavalry, French command had to rely on reports filtering through neighboring countries and other third party sources about the size and intentions of the coalition army.

From the British reporters encamped with the Germans, such as William Russell, they read newspaper accounts of the staggeringly huge movement of men, equipment, horses and supplies from the railheads to the muddy roads of the Saar and the Palatinate and into France itself. They described the roads being choked with troops, artillery and wagons. And yet, all of it moving efficiently to the west.

From Belgium came detailed reports of yet another German army, some 450,000 strong, being assembled and ready to attack. From Luxembourg came the even more ominous warning that every German state had been stripped bare of its military forces, including all Landwehr units, and they were being sent to the western frontier. At least these reports were partly factual, and coincided with an official statement by the Russian government that they would match any mobilization of the Austrian Army with one of their own.

In effect Russia was demonstrating it had Prussia's back in this war – the closest thing either side would get to an ally – and it made sense for the other borders to be denuded of their military forces. Though in reality this would not happen for some time to come.

What actually was chimerical were reports, again from Luxembourg, of an army of 150,000 massing on its borders, between the Moselle and Saar Rivers and ready to descend on the French left wing at Thionville. The reports even named the army's commander as General Vogel von Falkenstein – who did happen to be real, but just a brigade commander in Steinmetz's First Army.

No such force existed but, with all the other calamities raining upon the French Army this one was believed. Empress Eugénie's Council of Regency strongly advised Bazaine to bring Sixth Corps forward from Châlons, just as Leboeuf warned the front line positions along the Nied would not withstand both flanking and frontal attacks.

As a result many of the orders Bazaine had given in the last few days were countermanded. Canrobert got what would be his last order to move his corps from Châlons. And not for Paris, as had been discussed just a day earlier, but to Metz.

All French positions on the Nied River were abandoned, the corps falling back to Metz and the safety of its big guns just as Moltke gave orders for his armies to establish defensive positions at Boulay and Faulquemont. This opened yet another gap between the two forces, though it would not last for long.

The French Army was falling into a trap largely of its own making – it only remained for the Germans to close it. By the morning of August 12th the Uhlans had blown the rail lines connecting Châlons to Metz. Canrobert arrived with all his infantry, but his cavalry division, corps artillery and field service units would remain at Châlons for MacMahon when he arrived.

The trap had been sprung.

Chapter XV: The Disasters at Metz

"Great blunders are often made, like large ropes, of a multitude of fibers."
-Victor Hugo (1802 - 1885)

Battle By Vacuum

TO THE ACTIVITIES of the German cavalry fate added its own crippling blow during the night of August 12th. Heavy rains caused the Nied, and even the larger Moselle, to swell. In low-lying areas they flooded infantry bivouacs and the increased water flow swept away every one of the pontoon bridges, leaving only the three permanent bridges to continue moving the four army corps to the fortress.

The pontonier commanders estimated it would take until the morning of the 14th to repair just four of the bridges, and even then local flooding meant only infantry could use them. Horses, artillery and transport of all kinds would have to use the permanent bridges. Effectively it reduced the area the corps could move through to, at best, three miles wide: the perfect bottleneck.

With diligent staff work this hard task could be done, but it overwhelmed Bazaine's army. Traffic jams spread throughout the area and one permanent bridge, at Longeville-les-Metz, got overlooked in the confusion. Bazaine could not, and in his defence, did not ignore the great dangers inherent in this mess. He warned Napoleon III that, should the Germans appear, it would be better to make a stand, or even take the offense, than be stampeded into a rout like MacMahon's army.

In response Napoleon gave him a report from the Council of Regency. It now thought the coalition armies would bypass Metz with the Crown Prince's army flanking it to the south while the army of Friedrich Karl and Steinmetz would circle north, picking up the imaginary army of Falkenstein, before rejoining the Crown Prince at Verdun.

In reality, Moltke learned of Bazaine's fall back on the night of August 11th. The next morning he ordered his armies, concentrated at last on a front a dozen miles wide, to disperse across a broad one more than 50 miles wide, from just north of Metz to Pont-à-Mousson, some 20 miles below it, and ending at Nancy. It was not what any of the three army commanders, or Moltke himself, had been planning but they responded quickly to the new situation. The French Army had created a vacuum and they were filling it.

At 4:00AM on August 14th those units of Bazaine's army still outside the Metz fortresses stirred from their camps. This time the weather had cleared, and would become swelteringly hot, but the confusion and traffic jams remained. Not only were the bridges over the Nied crowded, so were the approaches to them. Then, 12 hours later, the thunder of artillery rolled across the bottleneck. The Prussians had caught up to the French rear guard.

However, the battle did not begin exactly the way Moltke had wanted or ordered. Steinmetz, chastened by the imperial wrath he brought upon himself, advanced his First Army cautiously. When his cavalry patrols reported traffic jams and the clouds of dust they raised, he refused to order an attack because Moltke had not specifically ordered him to do so.

Fortunately, his subordinates did not feel this way. A brigade commander in the Seventh Corps, Major General von der Goltz, took the town of Colombey and the Château d'Aubigny, then brought in artillery. At the sound of the guns a division in General Decaén's Third Corps broke off their retreat to attack and General Manteuffel brought his First Corps in to support Goltz.

When they heard an engagement had begun, both Steinmetz and Bazaine reacted furiously. They demanded combat be broken off and forbade their corps commanders from responding to calls for help. Nothing of the kind happened, for when Bazaine arrived at Colombey he found it had spread to nearby Nouilly and involved Decaén's entire Third Corps, his former command. Both would be wounded in the battle, and Decaén would be dead by the following day.

Steinmetz arrived rather later, after nightfall and still furious, and ordered his corps commanders to retire to the Nied. But the ground they had just taken was hard won, 5,000 dead and wounded versus around 3,600 for the French, and to abandon it as a kind of no-man's land would have given the troops the distinct impression they had been defeated – or worse, their commanders were incompetent.

General von Zastrow, commander of the Seventh Corps, refused the order while First Corps commander Manteuffel said he would only issue it if Steinmetz came in person to his headquarters. And then there would be the problem of Second Army's Ninth Corps, which had come to the support of Zastrow's divisions and would be left in an exposed position by the fall back. In the end it became a moot point.

Not only did Moltke send his congratulations on a hard battle well fought, King Wilhelm's Royal Headquarters said it approved of the actions and the next day Wilhelm himself visited the battlefield. And in the midst of the cheering troops Steinmetz still fumed, wondering why his earlier insubordination nearly had him relieved, while that of his corps commanders now received such acclaim.

The Engulfing Tide

French command, from Napoleon on down, treated the Battle of Colombey-Nouilly as a victory. The Germans, and most especially the Prussians, had been checked. True, the French Army had lost ground, but the enemy lost more men and had been shown the fierce resolve everyone expected of French soldiers. When he went to bed that night, even Bazaine allowed himself to believe the words the Emperor greeted him with, "you have broken the spell."

The problem was everyone failed to notice the French Army had lost something far more valuable than ground. That could be recovered, time could not. And from the morning of August 15th onward the commanders began to realize they would not be able to evacuate the army from Metz. What had been a tactical success would be a strategic disaster.

At 10:00AM that morning Bazaine gave detailed orders for his army to continue its retreat to the west, to Verdun. Only one road lead out of Metz in that direction, the Gravelotte-Mars-la-Tour-Verdun road, a steep road which wound up the escarpment overlooking the city and the Moselle River. At the heights above the escarpment lay the Gravelotte Plateau, where the road split in two, at Vionville.

It would be over this poorly-policed route that a huge convoy five corps strong, minus one division left to garrison the Metz fortresses, would move. Second, Third, Fourth and Sixth Corps, with all their surviving artillery, bridging equipment, commissariat and medical supplies in some 4,000 wagons would attempt this Herculean task with the Imperial Guards Corps providing the rear guard.

It was a recipe for certain disaster. Along the entire route there were reports of Uhlan scouting parties. When finally given maps of the region by the French Army's cartographical service, the corps staffs found them wholly inadequate and out-of-date. By comparison, and once they arrived from Berlin, the German coalition armies were supplied with modern, accurate maps of France – ones Moltke himself had supervised, and done some scouting for, in the years between 1866 and 1870.

Ironically, it would be Moltke himself who delayed his armies' encirclement of Metz and engagement of the retreating columns. On August 15th he ordered Friedrich Karl's Second Army not to cross the Moselle in force – only its cavalry divisions could probe farther to the west – and for the Crown Prince's Third Army to proceed no further after occupying the compliant city of Nancy.

There were reasons for this. First and foremost, Moltke did not know the exact disposition of the French Army at Metz. He knew a retreat was underway, not that every corps in Bazaine's command had been included in it, and feared a strong counterattack on Steinmetz's First Army. He also could not understand the inertia and timidity besetting his opponent, though as reports from the reconnaissance sorties filtered back he got a better picture of the situation and by noon reversed his orders to Second and Third Armies.

Almost from the moment the new directives arrived, Second Army's two most aggressive corps commanders bolted across the Moselle in hot pursuit of the cavalry divisions they had dispatched earlier in the morning. Lieutenant-General Constantin von Alvensleben pushed his Third Corps across at Novéant, where a permanent bridge had been found intact. A little farther to the south, General Constantin von Voigts-Rhetz sent his Tenth Corps over a pontoon bridge erected at Pont-à-Mousson.

Already their cavalry had made contact with French cavalry on the Gravelotte Plateau. The most advanced units wanted to cut the road to Verdun near Mars-la-Tour, but were held back by their division commander. The French made no effort to push them off the plateau or ascertain their true numbers for Bazaine's army had nearly ground to a halt from congestion on the road and squabbling among its various commands.

The traffic jams quickly grew so bad that Leboeuf, given command of Third Corps after Decaén's death, could only keep his troops moving by going off the road and striking cross country. Comte de Ladmirault, after having brought Fourth Corps down from Thionville, found road conditions so bad he asked if he could switch to the more open one running through Woippy to the northwest.

Bazaine refused this, citing reports of heavy Prussian cavalry activity between Thionville and Metz as a sign the German armies were bypassing Metz to the north. Ominously, he took the fact there were no reports of enemy activity from Novéant, Pont-à-Mousson or Thiaucourt as a sign the Germans had not yet crossed the Moselle in force.

Even when he got reports to the contrary from his Second and Sixth Corps' commanders, Frossard and Canrobert, they were ignored as being nothing more than heavy reconnaissance. Bazaine's laxity on this, brought on in part by his mental and physical exhaustion, would set in motion the next battles, and allow the engulfing tide to invest his army in Metz.

The Battle of Vionville and Mars-la-Tour

Early on the morning of August 16th, Napoleon III came to Bazaine's headquarters to bid good-bye. By all accounts it was a sad affair. Both men were haggard, the few hours of sleep each got did little to rejuvenate them, and both apparently felt they would never see each other again. When the Emperor left, with a major escort of Dragoons and mounted Chasseurs that would see him to Verdun, the distant roll of artillery fire could be heard behind him. The battles at Vionville and Mars-la-Tour had begun.

Just before Napoleon's arrival, Bazaine had sent word he agreed to de Ladmirault's idea to halt a retreat already paralyzed and prepare in place to face the expected German attack. This was easy for the Count to do, his Corps still lay inside Metz. Leboeuf's Corps had bivouaced north of the Verdun road at Vernville, Bourbaki's Guards Corps at the town of Gravelotte while Second and Sixth Corps were spread out between Rezonville and Vionville, the farthest point west the retreat would achieve.

Meanwhile the Germans, in particular Prince Friedrich Karl, finally realized the French Army was retreating to Verdun and, basing its rate of march on his own army's capabilities, figured its vanguard had already reached the Meuse River. This was the next major north-south river in France and the fortress town of Verdun, which dominates the only easy crossing on it for some distance in either direction.

The Prince ordered half of his Second Army: the two Saxon Corps, Fourth and Twelfth, and the Guards Corps commanded by Prince August of Würtemberg, to head due west. The remaining three corps, Third, Ninth and Tenth, were to head north. However only two, the Third and Ninth, were heading to where there actually were French troops: Vionville.

At 8:00AM the cavalry division camped there first spotted an approaching dark mass of soldiers. Incredibly, most thought it to be Ladmirault's Fourth Corps and no one bothered to send out scouts. At 9:00AM artillery fire rained down on them, and for the moment complete surprise had been achieved.

It caused some panic, but not heavy enough to start a rout and it had been launched too soon. It attracted more French troops than German – soon Alvensleben found his Third Corps was not facing the rear guard of a retiring army but the vanguard of an advancing one. He had two full corps immediately in front of him, with elements of at least two more arriving. He sent out riders with urgent calls for help to every corps command in the area, and hoped he could hold his positions until something arrived.

At first his infantry attacks did little except pile up the casualties. An initial attempt to bring field guns onto the bare heights was met with murderous rifle fire. A second attempt proved more successful when 15 batteries, all that remained of the Corps artillery reserve and the divisional commands, were brought to the heights south and southeast of the massed French formations.

Alvensleben judged the only way he could prevent a disaster would be to convince the entire French Army that they were facing an entire German Army. The heavy fire from his batteries helped, as did an infantry attack on Vionville itself and later the nearby town of Flavigny. However, neither could be held and both were soon set ablaze by French artillery.

At this point the French Army could have achieved a major victory, if any of the corps commanders or Bazaine himself had decided that their job would be to *defeat* the enemy. Instead, everyone thought their first job was to prevent the loss of their command, and perhaps reopen the road to Verdun.

Frossard and Canrobert wondered when or where a German counterattack would materialize, and were hesitant to be more aggressive until Bazaine arrived. He ordered a cavalry attack, resulting in the regiment sent out being shredded by rifle fire. As he personally supervised the placement of a battery to prevent a cavalry counter stroke, something a subordinate officer should have done, he was surrounded by German Hussars, then French cavalrymen charging to his rescue. In a wild melee the Hussars nearly captured him, only to be driven off. For the rest of the day Bazaine would be a little more cautious in venturing to the front lines.

Other French batteries that were brought forward also had to deal with German cavalry, especially those hammering Alvensleben's left flank. By 2:00PM his Third Corps had been in heavy fighting for five hours. The last of his infantry regiments were committed, to the Tronville Wood northwest of Vionville; all that remained were two regiments of cavalry.

Commanded by General von Bredow, they were the Magdeburg Cuirassiers and the Altmark Uhlans. They were 800 strong, and Alvensleben gave them the task of silencing the newly established gun line, not unlike the one given to the Light Brigade at Balaclava. And they would ride into the legend – like the war itself a largely forgotten one – of "Bredow's Death Run." The last successful cavalry charge in western Europe.

The General took his time to form up his squadrons, to establish a flank guard, and most importantly he used a natural depression in the land north of Vionville to partially conceal his attack until his horsemen broke out of the smoke a few hundred yards away from the French guns. By then coordinated counter-battery fire had driven most of the infantry screen back from the gun line. The Cuirassiers and Uhlans fell upon the gun crews, killing or dispersing them before continuing up the slope behind the line. There they encountered two brigades of French cavalry and another melee ensued.

Bredow got his men out under heavy rifle fire. Just over half, 420 men, survived the attack, a far heavier casualty toll than at Balaclava but it was a success as the guns were stopped. And then...it seemingly had been all for nothing. A dark mass appeared to the northeast – de Ladmirault had finally managed to get his Fourth Corps out of Metz, and his lead division just pushed the German infantry out of Tronville Wood.

They needed reinforcements, but they had been Alvensleben's last reserve. His left flank was turned, his troops fell back in a fighting retreat as the French infantry crossed the Verdun road and its screening cavalry reached as far as Mars-la-Tour before encountering opposition. Victory at last had come to the French. Ladmirault only needed to crush Alvensleben's corps the same way MacMahon's had been and restore French honor.

And then, Ladmirault chose to delay his assault by half an hour to bring up at least one more division, and did not notice the thickening columns of German troops west of Tronville Wood. It was 3:00PM, and Constantin von Voigts-Rhetz had finally brought his Tenth Corps into the battle.

For the next four hours his divisions supplanted Third Corps and fought a massive seesaw battle with de Ladmirault and part of Leboeuf's Third Corps. Rifle fire shredded an assault by one of Tenth Corps' divisions and routed it. Like Alvensleben, Voigts-Rhetz stopped the threat by sending in the cavalry: a regiment, three squadrons of Dragoons and two squadrons of Cuirassiers.

They cantered through the fleeing survivors, then charged the French infantry. Ladmirault countered it with a cavalry charge of his own. Both sides sent in more squadrons, and in the waning hours of the afternoon heavy and light cavalry units of all kinds struggled in a wild fight which only ended with the onset of evening. The Germans retired to Mars-la-Tour, but the French had a new problem on their left flank where Bazaine had feared a surprise attack all day.

Steinmetz had pushed most of his First Army across the Moselle south of Metz, and now launched his Seventh Corps up the plateau's edge at Rezonville, a town between Vionville and Gravelotte. His attack was paired with one from Second Army's Ninth Corps in about the same area to cause the French to divert their attention. In the gathering darkness Friedrich Karl belatedly arrived and ordered still another assault, from Vionville down the Verdun road back to Metz.

Had all three of these attacks been launched a few hours earlier, they would have had sufficient daylight to rout the battered, exhausted French divisions. As they transpired, they were reasonably successful. The French infantry at Vionville got routed back to Rezonville by a cavalry charge, where still more units were in panicked flight from Seventh and Ninth Corps. But the night made further exploitation impossible, and the two sides had separated by 9:00PM.

The Debris of War

As with the earlier Battle at Colombey-Nouilly, both sides were quick to claim victory here. The French had suffered marginally fewer casualties than the Germans, roughly 14,000 dead and wounded versus 16,000, had battered two German corps and kept most of their positions. The Germans claimed that with the heavy losses from those corps they checked the retreat of the French Army and cut its only real escape route to the west. As always, the real situation proved far more complicated, and a lot grimmer for one side than the other realized.

France's losses could not just be calculated in numbers of casualties, for the army outside of Metz had become the perfect casualty of the Clausewitz concept of "friction." It had started to break down, becoming immobilized from thousands of errors big and small, and would not be given the time to recover.

Given the numbers involved, Bazaine's army should have won outright the battle it just fought. But it was an army in retreat, shocked that its only means of escape had been severed, fearful of where and what the enemy might throw next at it, and commanded by officers who were looking to avoid further losses instead of fighting to win. And after August 16th there were a dwindling number of even those left.

Bazaine himself had nearly been captured. Infantry division General Bataille, cavalry division commander General Legrand and brigadier commander Letellier-Valaze had all been killed. Cavalry brigade commander General Montaigu had been wounded in the final melee of horsemen and was out of the fight, as were many others.

The army's logistics had completely disintegrated, almost from the first sound of enemy artillery. The great host of supply wagons and lorries, not well-policed at the start of the retreat, was thoroughly disorganized. Many civilian drivers had cut their horses from their transports in order to flee. The abandoned, heavily-laden vehicles clogged the Verdun road all the way back to the Moselle. Some were off-loaded to carry wounded, others were burnt and more than a few fell into German hands. Camping gear, tents and food supplies proved especially useful to German divisions who had outrun their own baggage trains.

Frossard's Second and Canrobert's Sixth Corps got no issue of supplies all day, and would receive none until late on August 17th. Ammunition stocks, in particular artillery shells and powder charges, were running low. This forced Bazaine's artillery commander to gather what wagons and lorries he could for a restocking sortie to Metz. In the two miles between Rezonville and Gravelotte were the disordered elements of nine infantry divisions, three cavalry divisions and artillery from all manner of corps and divisional commands.

Shortly before midnight, an exhausted Bazaine sent a stark report to Napoleon. Then he issued orders for his army to fall back to a line running from St. Privat in the north to Rozerieulles in the south and using Gravelotte as its westernmost point. And though they worked through the night, his staff simply did not have the time to work out all the routes and march-tables for a dozen divisions and what remained of their equipment.

If anything, confusion proved greater on the day after the battle than during it. To move just three to four miles the army needed all of August 17th, and by nightfall many units were still not in the assigned positions. Others, such as Canrobert, found his position, and got permission from Bazaine to move his entire corps to St. Privat itself. There, they would enjoy superior fields of fire. But the French line would have no defensive depth to it and in most places they did not have the time or the equipment to construct proper defences.

For the German armies there were no major headaches in their logistics or communications. The corps of Second Army that had overshot the previous battle doubled back and, together with Steinmetz's First Army, gave Moltke a total of six corps to use in deciding the fate of Bazaine's army.

A Hard and Bitter Victory

Gravelotte-St. Privat would be different than all the previous major engagements of the Franco-Prussian War. It would not be something that sprang up while commanders were planning for other battles. This one was expected, and all immediately available forces were brought to bear.

The French had just under 113,000 men and 520 artillery pieces on the field while the two German armies brought over 188,000 men and 732 guns. Against Moltke's superior numbers Bazaine had an excellent defensive line. The terrain in front of his army were long, bare slopes with little cover. Those on his left flank sat atop wooded ravines that cut into the Gravelotte Plateau from the Moselle River valley. Near the center was the deep and steeply-sided Mance Ravine, with the farms along its crest turned into strong points. Only on the right flank did the terrain become less formidable, with no heavy forest or terrain features to hinder a flanking movement.

Ironically, what Bazaine worried most about was his left flank. Partly because of the surprise Steinmetz gave him in the Vionville battle, and mostly because he continued a series of skirmishing actions throughout August 17th which always seemed ready to erupt into a full-scale assault. The best defences were built here, particularly trenchworks, while on the right flank little was done beyond making St. Privat the strong point commanding the slopes.

By the morning of August 18th Friedrich Karl had massed the Second Army between Mars-la-Tour and Rezonville. With little prior reconnaissance by cavalry patrols, he ordered out the Hessian (Ninth), Saxon (Twelfth) and Guard Corps. They were followed by the surviving units of the Third and Tenth Corps, who would be used mostly for artillery support.

Their objective was the town of Verneville, a few miles northwest of Gravelotte, and to turn the French right wing, to flank it and destroy the defensive line that the rear guard of the evacuating army had established over the last day. But Friedrich Karl and Moltke had made two serious mistakes: first, they and the rest of the German High Command still thought most of Bazaine's army had successfully escaped to Verdun. And second, the French right wing did not stop at Verneville but several miles farther north, at St. Privat with Canrobert's Sixth Corps.

Such a mass movement of so densely-packed troops could not go unnoticed. By 9:00AM Leboeuf, at his Third Corps headquarters near Leipzig Farm, could easily see the dust clouds they raised. He sent a warning by dispatch rider to Bazaine's headquarters at Fort Plappeville, one of the largest and best outerworks of the Metz fortress complex.

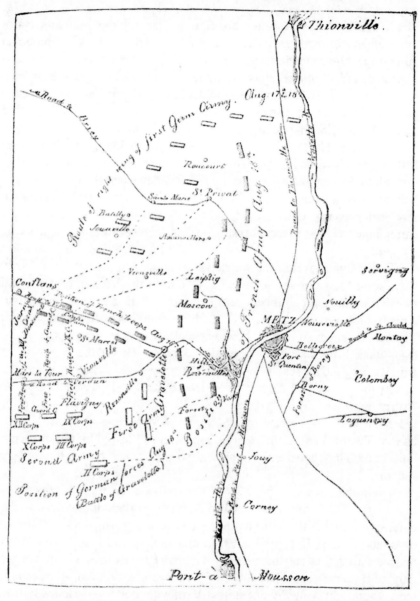

And while Bazaine relayed the message to the other corps commanders,

Frossard to the south and Comte de Ladmirault and Canrobert to the north, he did little else. He did not try to coordinate the operations of the four front-line corps, nor did he warn his reserve commander, Bourbaki and the Imperial Guards Corps, of the impending battle. For most of the day he would be remarkably passive.

By 10:00AM Friedrich Karl saw his situation a little more clearly. Reports from his advancing corps told of French encampments north of their objective. Just how far north had yet to be ascertained, so he ordered the Saxon Corps to move farther north while keeping the Hessian and Guards Corps on the march to Verneville.

Half an hour later Moltke ordered a general attack by both First and Second Armies, at about the same time the Prince realizes Verneville is almost dead center in the French line and its actual right wing was located at St. Privat. He sends urgent orders for his corps to hold off their attacks and change their line-of-march. But it's too late. Hessian gun crews open fire on Leboeuf's Third Corps at 11:00AM. The Battle of Gravelotte-St. Privat had begun.

And both Leboeuf's and de Ladmirault's men responded immediately. While Third Corps opens up with their own cannons and Mitrailleuse guns, Fourth Corps rushed from their tents to flank the Hessian gun line and start volleys of massed rifle fire. To the south, Steinmetz and his Eighth Corps commander, General August von Goeben, took the thunder of the guns as a signal for them to begin their own assault.

The day before Moltke had removed Eighth Corps from Steinmetz's army so he could not cause further trouble. The problem was Second Army had yet to establish its command over the corps. It existed in a kind of "operational vacuum," and Goeben chose to take his orders from Steinmetz. He easily pushed his first brigade through the town of Gravelotte itself, then down the main road into the Manse Ravine.

The problem for Second Army's Hessian Corps was its gun crews had pushed its line too close to the French. At 1,000 yards its fire may have been more accurate, but they were now well within range of both antiquated bronze muzzle-loaders and start-of-the-art weapons like Chassepot and Mitrailleuse guns. For the latter especially the long, barren slopes were an ideal environment; their distinctive growl would be heard all day long.

For the divisions of the Hessian Corps the mutually overlapping protection of infantry, artillery and cavalry broke down. Parts of the gun line were overrun by a French infantry charge and four artillery pieces were lost. Not until the battered Third Corps brought up its own guns and properly sited them did the chaotic situation stabilize. By then both the

Saxon and Guard Corps had deployed farther to the north, and a far greater catastrophe was occurring a little ways to the south.

Mance Ravine – with its deep-cut road, steep sides and complete lack of cover made it an even better killing ground than barren slopes. And this in spite of the artillery assets of Seventh and Eighth Corps arrayed north of Gravelotte. Over 150 four and six-pounders hammered the French positions until nightfall. They turned the farms along the ravine's crest into rubble and still the Germans could make little headway.

Steinmetz, like Moltke and Friedrich Karl, was convinced all he faced were the rear guard units of a retreating army. He sent division after division, even a cavalry division, into the Mance. It only created thousands of casualties, and a catastrophic congestion on the roads leading into the ravine.

At either location a corps-level French counterattack would have turned a disaster into a rout. Yet none materialized as Bazaine refused to unleash Bourbaki's Imperial Guards. Partly this had to do with his ongoing timidity. But he also fell victim to a rare and bizarre event called an "acoustic hollow" where the terrain features, such as those around his headquarters at Plappeville, masked the sounds of battle from both Mance and Verneville. Some 64 years earlier, Marshal Jean Bernadotte marched his army into a similar "acoustic hollow" between the battles of Jena and Auerstädt, with scarcely hearing a rumble of artillery fire.

When Bazaine finally did leave Plappeville, at mid-afternoon, it would be to the south, to inspect the fortress at Mont St. Quentin. There he made sure its guns were ready for the attack he still expected to hit his left wing. He would now be out of communications with all his corps commanders, and in the exact opposite locations from where the fatal blows would land on his defensive line.

Since discovering his mistake, that his lead corps were attacking the French center and not its right wing, Prince Friedrich Karl gave strict orders to the ones not engaged to head north and avoid all contact with the enemy. Moving cautiously, the Saxon Corps took until 3:00PM to get into position and make their attack on the French outpost of St. Marie-les-Chênes.

This small village, just over a mile in front of St. Privat and at the foot of the barren slopes, fell easily to an artillery barrage and infantry attack. Then, the gun line had to be redeployed for the assault to continue on St. Privat itself. Because the Guard Corps had left part of its artillery with the Hessians at Verneville, it was more dependent than usual on the accompanying Saxons. They, in turn, had to move farther north than expected to properly redeploy their batteries, and in this interlude disaster struck.

Crown Prince August of Würtemberg, commander of the Guard Corps, ordered the assault to continue on St. Privat, after hearing its few field pieces fall silent. Some reports suggest he feared Canrobert was moving some of his divisions to aid de Ladmirault's Fourth Corps. Others believe he did it because, like Steinmetz, he was brazen, impatient and wanted victory for himself.

At 6:00PM the Corps' vanguard started up the slope, without waiting for the Saxons, without proper artillery support. Using just their Chassepots and a few Mitrailleuse guns, Canrobert's men stopped the attack dead in its tracks. In 20 minutes nearly a quarter of the Guards Corps were either killed or wounded, including all the officers of the vanguard formations.

If the engagement had ended here, it would have proved Baron Jomini right: the breech-loading cartridge rifle had become the dominant weapon of the modern battlefield. However, just over half an hour later, the true wonder weapon of the then-modern warfare struck – 14 batteries and at almost a right angle to the Guards' positions.

The Saxons were finally in place and struck with an unstoppable fury out of the gathering twilight. What remained of the Guard Corps artillery joined in and crushed Canrobert's Sixth Corps. Without adequate fire support of its own or proper trenches, the corps abandoned the blazing town. Though in the midst of disaster Canrobert did manage to do something most other French commanders could not: he staged a fighting retreat, sent an urgent plea to Bourbaki for aid and even managed to warn de Ladmirault and Leboeuf of the collapse.

Had there been a strong counterattack, the outflanked right wing might have reformed and staved off defeat. Unfortunately de Ladmirault's Fourth Corps, which had been trying to help both Leboeuf in the center and Canrobert to the north was by now exhausted. His men reached their own breaking point when they saw the Saxon breakthrough and panicked. By the time Bourbaki arrived with his elite Imperial Guards, all roads to the front were clogged with fleeing soldiers. Furiously, impetuously...Bourbaki turned his column around and left.

The sight of his retreat would be the last straw for Fourth and Sixth Corps. The panic became a full-scale rout. They abandoned their remaining positions, abandoned their discipline and fled in a tidal wave of fear and exhaustion which even swept up Bourbaki's elite corps. It would not abate until it reached the banks of the Moselle and the gates of Metz.

Ironically enough, and simultaneous with this rout, a similar event took place a few miles to the south, in the Mance Ravine. Steinmetz, still convinced he could win but having run out of intact units to do so, lied to

Moltke and Wilhelm I that he had taken the ravine's crest and begged for the reserves to exploit it.

As it happened the Pomeranian Second Corps, the last unused corps of Friedrich Karl's Second Army, had arrived on the plateau with its fresh columns of troops. Moltke refused but the King, who had since ridden up to Gravelotte, gave his consent and the Pomeranians went in. The lead column had just reached the mouth of the ravine when a wave of men and horses swept around them; eight hours of slaughter had finally broken the men Steinmetz threw into the killing ground. His army was in a rout.

They surged through Gravelotte; the King joined his officers in trying to beat some sense into them with the flat of his sword but the outgoing tide could not be stopped. In fact they did not stop until they reached Rezonville, where many had started from that morning. Wilhelm I and his entourage also retreated to the town, while the Pomeranian Corps took up the abandoned positions inside the ravine to hold back the expected French counter thrust.

But none came. For hours Moltke, Wilhelm and their staffs believed they had been handed a bitter defeat. Not until midnight did they receive news from the Guards and Saxon Corps, that they managed to get the hard military equation right: they pulled victory from the jaws of defeat.

At 3:00AM on August 19th, Leboeuf withdrew his Third Corps from their now-untenable positions overlooking the Mance Ravine and points north. By 5:00AM Frossard had pulled his Second Corps from Rozerieulles and the rest of the French left wing. By all accounts their retreats were orderly and quiet; the Germans facing them would not realize they were gone until daybreak.

The battle had cost the French some 13,000 killed and wounded. German casualties were nearly 60% greater, an astonishing 20,163, of which 900 were officers who Moltke and Roon would now have to scour the rest of the coalition armies to find replacements. They were losses comparable to Solferino and Waterloo and yet the side that suffered the greater number had come out the winner.

The Germans took ground, the French retreated. Instead of being handed a bitter defeat they gained a bitter victory. And, in spite of its great cost, an important one.

Chapter XVI: Sedan

"In private enterprises men may advance or recede,
whereas they who aim at empire have no alternative
between the highest success and utter downfall."
-Cornelius Tacitus (c.55 - c.117AD)

The Strategic Dilemmas of Winning

HAD THE ARMY now entrapped at Metz been given an aggressive, opportunistic commander, such as history's greatest political and military opportunist, then the last three victories would not belong to the German coalition but to France. All had the earmarks of Napoleon Bonaparte's most difficult battles, such as Austerlitz, Marengo and Eylau. He faced a numerically superior enemy, momentum constantly changed, but in the end he took advantage of enemy blunders to win hard, even stunning, victories.

Alas, the French had Bazaine and not Bonaparte at Metz, while his in-name-only nephew had retreated to Châlons via Verdun where he hoped to assemble a second imperial army. And even facing such less-than-competent opponents the strategic situation posed difficult problems for Moltke and his army commanders.

Beyond the immediate ones of clearing the battlefield of the dead, treating the German and French wounded, transporting the thousands of prisoners to internment camps, replenishing the battered divisions and finding replacements for all the casualties, there were the problems of operating a huge force deep inside enemy territory and stuck between two opposing armies. But before handling this, and while his staff worked on the immediate tasks, Moltke had to deal with Steinmetz.

Bismarck, who kept in daily touch with Berlin, said it best, "the people are fed up with Steinmetz's butchery." After the collision of his army with Friedrich Karl's, after his obstinate timidity at Colombey-Nouilly, his performance at Gravelotte was his third strike and should have been the end of his military career. But he was still "the Lion of Skalitz," and the last active-serving officer from the Napoleonic Era. Moltke decided to put him in a position where he could not do much mischief, and it folded in with his decisions on what to do with the coalition armies.

Laying siege to Metz had never been part of his original war plans. None of the three armies he organized could do this by itself, nor could one army on its own defeat the new force assembling in Châlons. By noon on August 19th, in the remarkably short time of less than half a day, Moltke made the decision to split the Second Army in two.

A new army, provisionally titled the "Army of the Meuse," would be commanded by the Crown Prince of Saxony, Friedrich August Wettin. The general who had done so well with his corps at St. Privat, who lead the Saxons on Austria's side in the *Bruderkrieg*, was an astute military and political choice. He got his Twelfth (Saxon) Corps, the Fourth Corps, the Guard Corps, with a repentant Crown Prince August still in command, and the still largely intact Fifth and Sixth Cavalry Divisions.

The remaining corps of the old Second Army, four in all plus two cavalry divisions with a reserve division, were combined with the three corps of Steinmetz's First Army to form the investing "Army of Metz." Many of these formations, especially the Third and Ninth Corps of the Second Army and the Seventh and Eighth of First Army, were heavily battered over the last four days and only partially operational.

However, their Field Pioneer and train battalion units were intact and put to work with the others in the new army building their own works around the Metz complex. They would need to build not just their own fortifications but rail lines to replace those severed by the siege.

Prince Friedrich Karl was given command of the new army, and Moltke very deliberately made Steinmetz subordinate to him. He also gave him a free hand to deal with the "Lion of Skalitz" any way he saw fit should a new incident happen. Finally, Moltke sent orders to Crown Prince Friedrich Wilhelm's Third Army to change its line-of-march.

Since crossing the Moselle River, back on August 15th, the Army had obeyed the commands Moltke then gave it, more or less. It easily occupied Nancy, then Bayon and Lunéville two days later. At Toul and Verdun the fortresses were shelled as the battles across the Gravelotte Plateau were raging, but they did not surrender.

Instead, when the new orders came for Third Army to prepare to move northwest for Châlons and Reims, Friedrich Wilhelm left small observation forces at the two fortresses until siege guns could be brought in. Meanwhile, his cavalry patrols spread into the region between the Meuse and Marne Rivers, the imposing Argonne Massif. The dominant geologic feature of central France, its heavily forested mountains had few good roads running through them and was generally thought to be a serious hindrance to any invading force.

But Moltke and Friedrich Wilhelm had toured the region years earlier, as vacationing geology professors, and acquired knowledge they since disseminated through the Prussian command staff to the other German forces. Moltke realized his armies would need a few days to prepare, to finish replenishment and especially for Friedrich Karl's army to complete a proper investment of Metz. After their reorganization was complete, he set the date for the advance to begin on August 23rd, far ahead of what the French expected or hoped would happen.

The Strategic Mistakes of the Losers

When Napoleon III arrived at Châlons on the night of August 16th, he stepped from the train to find Comte Charles Antoine de Palikao had wrought a minor miracle. He had indeed assembled the substantial components of a new imperial army. The corps of MacMahon's original army: the First, Fifth and Seventh, were arriving by train from Chaumont, Belfort and Paris. Their equipment and horses had been replaced, and their ranks filled with recruits from the 1869 *levée*.

To this de Palikao added the "new" Twelfth Corps, made up of the lone division originally assigned to watch the Spanish border, the French Navy's Marine regiments formed into a second infantry division, a third from the garrison troops brought from Paris by General Trochu, and a cavalry division reasonably equipped with regiments of Lancers, Cuirassiers and Chasseurs.

The "Army of Châlons" could even boast a cavalry reserve of two newly-formed divisions and all its corps had full artillery reserves. In total it had 130,000 men and 432 field guns, including Mitrailleuse batteries. No small achievement for so short a time, it proved that the War Ministry's Intendance could perform miracles of competency.

Given time, this army could have been trained and regimented into a combat force equal to either of the invading German armies. The problem was it did not have months or weeks to carry this intensive process out. It scarcely had days to do everything needed to make it an operational field army. And for that you did not just need a Napoleon Bonaparte but a Louis Berthier and an Antoine Henri de Jomini.

Unfortunately none of these men, no one like them or even approaching their caliber, were to be found at Châlons or Reims. And the Intendance's miracle of competency ended at the Reims railway station. Supplies piled up but the organization's staff did not have the size to catalog and distribute it. Foraging parties often would go away empty-handed and some vital items, such as medical supplies, did not get delivered at all.

Shortly before Napoleon's arrival, Trochu returned to hand over more Paris garrison staffs and the division from the Spanish border to General Barthélemi Lebrun, a former senior aide to Leboeuf. The next day, August 17th, Trochu attended a unique conference with Napoleon III, MacMahon, the commanding general of the *Garde Mobile* and Prince Louis Napoleon, the former division commander from the Crimean War and the most recent arrival at Châlons.

Initial reports from the Battle of Vionville-Mars-la-Tour indicated a French victory, and yet Prince Napoleon found them disturbing. If Bazaine's army had won, why did it need to fall back on Metz and was the road to Verdun still cut? Called by Trochu the "only Napoleon who counts," the Prince also warned his cousin of the nascent revolution back in Paris and something needed to be done to quell it. He pushed for Trochu to take back the *Garde Mobile* units, 18 battalions worth and be appointed the Governor of Paris.

Almost everyone at the conference supported these ideas, though the reluctant Emperor wondered if the Empress and her Council of Regency should be consulted first. Again, the Prince spoke up and put some backbone in his cousin. "Are you not the sovereign?" he asked, then demanded: "This has got to be done at once." And by the end of the day Trochu had collected the battalions for the return to Paris as its new Governor.

The conference had also decided that MacMahon would take the "Army of Châlons" back to Paris as well. There, under the guns of its fortresses and bastions, and behind its moat, it would be free to maneuver and recruit from the public. It would also end the threat of revolution and yet, the newest reports from Metz were even more troublesome. By the following day the situation would change yet again.

On August 18th one of Bazaine's aide-de-camps arrived at Châlons and briefed Napoleon III and the officials on what they should expect from Metz. Once again initial messages came in reporting the Germans had attacked the new French defensive line. And then, the last telegraph lines out of Metz were cut. The battlezone fell silent, and everywhere panic set in.

From Paris came a storm of messages. The Council of Regency demanded to know why Trochu had returned to the city with the ill-disciplined *Garde Mobiles*, especially when de Palikao and Eugénie sent him to Châlons to get rid of him. From the Senate and Corps Legislatif came the warnings, and in some cases threats, that if Metz fell then the imperial government would follow it. August Rouher, came in person a few days later to urge that the newly-formed army must be sent to rescue Bazaine. And from all points came reports of Uhlans being spotted. Some on the Marne River just below the army's headquarters.

But MacMahon, after seeing his army perform in the field for just a day, decided this would be impossible and convinced Rouher, the Emperor and Prince Napoleon. Then the news of Gravelotte-St. Privat arrived, along with Bazaine's message that his army was still intact and he intended a breakout to the northwest. Toward either St. Ménéhould, on the Aisne River, or Sedan on the Meuse.

This changed everyone's plans. To fall back on Paris now meant abandoning an army still willing to fight, and abandoning Paris meant saving the imperial throne. MacMahon reversed himself and collected his army at Reims as he prepared to strike east. Empress Eugénie's wrath struck Rouher, just after he submitted drafts for an imperial proclamation on the fall back to Paris, and on Prince Louis. Of Rouher little more would be heard and as for the Prince, the "only Napoleon who counts," he went on a forlorn diplomatic mission to Italy. This meant the only royal consul Napoleon III would have from now on was Eugénie.

At Reims the "Army of Châlons" would stay only a few days, collecting what supplies it could and rounding up the stragglers. More reports of Uhlans came in and this time they were true, on August 24th Friedrich Wilhelm's reconnaissance patrols had reached Châlons and found it deserted. By then his Third Army was due east of the base, at Commercy on the Meuse, and heading northwest. As for the "Army of the Meuse," Friedrich August already had it in the field and heading north. With all three armies on the move the race to destiny had started.

Field Maneuvers

Since Roman times the Argonne Massif had been a formidable barrier to any army, and the Romans knew it. The few good roads which cut through the region, such as the Metz-to-Verdun road so recently fought over, were originally Roman roads with foundations and drainage systems. They would be vital to the deployment of the German Armies in the coming days, particularly when rainstorms swept the region, turning most of the other roads into mud rivers.

Columns slowed, in some cases overlapped when forced to use the same road, but there were few traffic jams, not even in the forests where nobody, not even the smallest cavalry patrol, tried going cross country – not with woods so thick you could not walk ten feet in any direction in a straight line. Only on cultivated land was there such room, and farms were scarce throughout the region.

This actually had more impact on the "Army of Châlons" than on either of the German Armies. Before leaving Reims, on August 25th, MacMahon advised his troops to draw at least four days of rations from the available stores. But the Reims railroad station held even fewer supplies than the one at Châlons. The foraging parties quickly became pillaging expeditions, who soon found there were not enough farms in the region for an army so large to live off the land.

Less than a day after leaving the city, MacMahon found himself forced to veer off his line-of-march by almost 90 degrees, and head due north to Rethel on the Aisne River and its rail station. Other than the pressing need for supplies it made no sense, though at least it gave MacMahon access to a telegraph and his army would not be discovered for another day by Uhlan patrols.

On August 26th, shortly before these reports got back to his field headquarters, Moltke had to deal with a potentially serious event back at Metz: Bazaine was attempting a breakout. Three days earlier he had sent Napoleon III a message, via courier, that his plans were finalized and the operation imminent. Friedrich Karl's investment of the city and all its fortresses had by no means been fully implemented. There were weak spots, and the French thought they found one on the lower Moselle.

The operation might have worked, had the lead units not been so obvious, had planning not been so amateurish, had fate not played another trick, and the Germans not installed a field telegraph system linking all their bases and observation posts surrounding the city. Orders went out just hours before the operation was set to begin, prompting Bazaine's Chief of Artillery and the garrison commandant to request an urgent meeting.

General Soleille warned the army only possessed enough artillery munitions for one battle while Commandant Nordeck threatened the city would fall if the army left, and with it Bazaine's career. Unbelievably, he had not considered any of this and at 4:00AM countermanded his orders. By then the lead divisions were jammed on the pontoon bridges crossing the

Moselle, and the German observation posts in the breakout area had already been attacked.

And on top of it all, the rain which plagued the armies in the Argonne came down on Metz as well. The river threatened to wash away the bridges, artillery and wagons became stuck in the mud, and Friedrich Karl sent battalions from Third and Tenth Corps to block the attempt. The posts were quickly recaptured and, after Bazaine held another meeting with all his corps commanders, he cancelled the operation. Some of the French troops would not return to their barracks until 26 hours later.

By then the "Army of Châlons" suffered an embarrassment of its own when cavalry from Felix Douay's Seventh Corps skirmished with a Saxon cavalry patrol at Grandpré, due south of Sedan. Fearing the entire German Army would be falling on him, Douay deployed his corps rather than continue moving it east. MacMahon sent in First Corps to back him up and for nearly a day the "Army of Châlons" ground to a halt, all for a skirmish with a single cavalry patrol.

Not only was this as embarrassing as Bazaine's fizzled breakout, in the end it would prove fatal. While the French were stopped the Germans kept moving, bringing their armies closer and MacMahon still did not know he faced two coalition armies, not one. By now Napoleon III and his generals realized there were *three* German armies operating in their country, not two.

Like Moltke, they correctly estimated no single army could lay siege to Metz. But unlike Moltke they never considered splitting the largest army in two, combining one half with the smallest army to prosecute the siege and send the other half into the field with the remaining intact army. Even though they had made contact with its cavalry, the French still did not know the "Army of the Meuse" existed.

In 48 hours they would know different.

Beaumont and the Doom of Empire

By the time Douay realized his mistake and got his corps moving again, de Failly's Fifth Corps had a brief, sharp cavalry fight with the same Saxons a few miles north at Buzancy. While both sides retired, the incident was part of a pattern of encirclement both MacMahon and Napoleon III were viewing from their field headquarters.

Behind them, Châlons and Reims were occupied by German forces. In front, the towns of Dun and Stenay on the Meuse River were also reportedly occupied and from all points south came more reports of a massive German army emerging from the Argonne passages. The Emperor agreed with his general that they had to abandon their eastward march and move the army north to a defensible position. They telegraphed their intentions to Paris, and got back a response that sealed the fate of the Empire.

Both the Empress and de Palikao demanded they maintain the march. To abandon it would mean abandoning Bazaine and Metz, and this would bring down the government. Further, Palikao stressed the German forces MacMahon had encountered or heard about were nothing more than harassing forces with the largest concentration still investing Metz. To this he reiterated earlier messages of the invaders suffering from low-morale, no food, dysentery, mutiny among the reserves – the beginnings of the ludicrous flights of fancy the Parisians would soon believe of the Germans.

MacMahon got the reply at 1:00AM on August 28th, and by daybreak Napoleon agreed with his Empress and Premier; perhaps if his cousin had been with him events might have gone differently. The previous day's decision was reversed, the army would continue east until it reaches the Meuse, then follow the river south to Verdun, relieve it, then continue to Metz and catch the German host between the hammer and anvil of the two French armies. Of such fantasies are disasters created.

Throughout the 28th, and its rain, the "Army of Châlons" marched under the continual, unnerving gaze of Uhlan parties who did little to conceal themselves. Apprehension grew especially in the two southern corps, the Seventh and Fifth as they followed one another to the Meuse. Just north of them the First and Twelfth Corps began scouting for other crossings along the river should Dun and Stenay be held.

By August 29th French cavalry patrols reported it to be true and MacMahon ordered the entire army to wheel north, toward Mouzon and Remilly. Except that Fifth Corps did not receive the change, the dispatch rider heading for de Failly's headquarters ended up captured by German cavalry. The first inkling they had of trouble happened when its lead cavalry formation came to a rise overlooking Nouart, the last town before the Meuse, and discovered the Twelfth Saxon Corps, deployed and waiting.

After the volleys of rifle fire came the artillery exchange, then the cavalry charge and de Failly frantically deployed his corps for a fight that lasted until nightfall. Casualties for both sides totaled around 600 and Fifth Corps withdrew to the north, to the slopes around the village of Beaumont. The thick woods and moonless night meant it took the French troops six hours or more to reach their destination. By dawn most had only been asleep a few hours, and their camp a haphazard mess.

At noon on August 30th the camp finally began to stir. Cook fires were started, and the French decided to eat before posting sentries, emplacing any field guns or Mitrailleuse batteries, or saddling any cavalry horses. Half an hour later one of the divisions from the Saxon Fourth Corps appeared at the edge of the southern woods. Corps commander Gustav von Alvensleben had given orders for no fighting to begin until all units were in place, but this was too good of an opportunity to let pass.

The Battle of Beaumont began in much the same way as Vionville-Mars-la-Tour, with a single German division attacking a French corps. This time, however, the corps was not the vanguard of an advancing army but the flank of a retreating one. This time help did not take most of the day to arrive. To the other division of Alvensleben's corps was added the lead division of the First Bavarian Corps, emerging from the woods on their right. Corps from both the "Army of the Meuse" and Friedrich Wilhelm's Third Army would attack together.

In Beaumont de Failly's Corps never recovered from the attack, though initially it responded like a swarm of angry bees. But apart from a few infantry regiments and artillery batteries they were confused, disorganized bees. While their rifle fire and a gun line north of the village checked the Saxon advance, they were flanked by the Bavarians and forced to retreat just after 3:00PM.

About a mile further north de Failly had established good positions, and with some assistance he could have made a determined stand, but the other corps commanders could render little help. First and Twelfth Corps had already crossed the Meuse at Mouzon, and Douay's Seventh Corps still jammed the bridges in a panicked retreat.

At least Lebrun tried to help with Twelfth Corps. He set up some of his artillery on the heights along the other side of the Meuse to provide harassing fire, though when he prepared to send a division back across it MacMahon specifically prevented him. Fifth Corps would have to fight the rear guard action largely on its own.

By 5:00PM de Failly's new positions were crumbling in the face of a formal attack by the Saxon Fourth Corps. An hour later and the only organized resistance to lay between the Germans and the river were Fifth Corps' last reserve: a regiment of Cuirassiers. They mounted a cavalry charge uphill, over broken ground, and against an established defence line.

The few survivors joined the stream of other remnants from Fifth Corps on the Mouzon bridges. In their fright some troops tried to swim, or ford the river with their horses. Men and animals drowned, guns, wagons, lorries and supplies were lost, as was everything abandoned on the western bank of the Meuse. This included thousands of stragglers, 51 cannons, 33 ammunition caissons and part of the corps' treasury.

With nightfall the Battle of Beaumont ended and MacMahon ordered his army to fall back on the fortress of Sedan. And at his headquarters Moltke took an account of the casualties, around 3,500 for his armies and 7,500 for the French, including all those stragglers who were now prisoners. He also took account of the strategic situation, and the growing possibilities of that rarest of military operations: the perfect investment of a field army. It had almost happened at Woerth, but perhaps with additional corps from Metz it could succeed at Sedan.

Closing the Trap

One of the last arrivals to the "Army of Châlons" was General Emmanuel Felix de Wimpffen. The former Governor of Oran in Algeria, he had only arrived in France a few days earlier, and had met with de Palikao during his brief stay in Paris. The Premier gave him sealed orders for MacMahon, then de Wimpffen went by train to Rethel – Reims had already been occupied – and by horseback with a cavalry escort into Sedan itself.

There he found the Army streaming into the city with a tiny 17th Century fortress to be an unregimented mess on the morning of August 31st. The birthplace of the legendary French Marshal Henri d'Auvergne de Turenne, the city sat in the meandering valley of the Meuse, with steep-sided hills that could provide excellent defensive positions and marshes all along the river's course, which could restrict the movement of armies.

MacMahon thought he could use the area as a place to regroup then launch an attack on the German army that surprised him. Fatally, he still greatly underestimated the forces that opposed him. Almost as fatal were the orders de Wimpffen carried with him: that he was to replace de Failly as commander of Fifth Corps, what remained of it, and further, Paris designated him to replace MacMahon as army commander should any accident befall him.

Later in the day, when he met with his corps commanders, they all had complaints about his assumptions and his orders to them. De Failly objected to being relieved of command, Douay did not like the positions his corps had been given northeast of Sedan, Ducrot felt hemmed in after being placed in the narrow Givonne Valley, also to the northeast, and Lebrun warned his garrison force at Bazeilles was being shelled. And on top of all this, they reported clouds of dust to the south and southwest, indicating German troop movements.

MacMahon answered them by first telling de Failly orders were orders and, in any event, his Fifth Corps would be held in Sedan as a reserve. Second, to Douay and Ducrot he replied they would not be there long enough to worry about the poor defences of their encampments. And last, he told them all he did not intend to shelter under the guns of a fortress like Bazaine, and especially one so inadequate as Sedan.

MacMahon advised he would either attack to the southeast, down a tributary of the Meuse called the Chiers River, toward the town of Carignan, or retreat up the Meuse to Mézières where General Joseph Vinoy brought the newly-formed Thirteenth Corps from Paris. Later in the day, with the arrival of the last train from Mézières with Seventh Corps' artillery reserve, MacMahon reconsidered his options yet again.

He thought seriously about making a stand at Sedan and drawing the enemy into battle. He gave orders for the bridges at either end of his perimeter, at Donchéry in the west and Bazeilles to the southeast, to be destroyed. But the demolition party at Donchéry just got off their train when the locomotive engineer panicked and sped down the tracks to Mézières, taking all their equipment and explosives with him.

At Bazeilles First Bavarian Corps spotted the demolition party laying their powder casks and its commander, General von der Tann, ordered a battalion attack which took the bridge for a time and captured the explosives. Back at Donchéry a second party arrived, only to find the bridge and nearby heights held by the Nassau-Hessian Eleventh Corps, who were carrying out a demolition raid of their own – on the railroad line to Mézières.

At Moltke's headquarters there was no wavering or indecision. Only the hope his envelopment plans could be completed before MacMahon decided to move, and then came the worrying news that Bazaine might be trying another breakout. This time in the area of Noisseville, on the eastern side of Metz and close to the battlefield of Colombey-Nouilly. The French had started artillery fire at 8:00AM, then drove the Germans from their observation posts at Colombey.

Manteuffel brought up his corps, though it looked as if Bazaine were assembling a far larger force, and the recall of the two corps still enroute to Sedan was considered. And then...nothing happened, not until 4:00PM did the French finally make an advance. By then Manteuffel had established an effective gun-line, and while Leboeuf's Third Corps took back ground all the way to Noisseville it was no breakout and their operations ceased by 11:00PM.

Around that time Moltke was conducting Wilhelm I on a tour of his son's Third Army headquarters. They were joined by the crown prince at a map table where Moltke showed them the most up-to-date positions of both the German armies and the French. After ordering the Eleventh Corps, weary though they were, to finish crossing the Meuse at Donchéry and block the French line of retreat to the west, he announced to father and son, "now, we have them in a mousetrap."

The investment was not exactly complete, particularly in the mountains north of Sedan, but MacMahon and his corps commanders had little idea just how dangerous of a situation they were in. Before he retired, Moltke gave his staff one more duty: to find a suitable vantage point for the royal entourage to view the coming battle.

The Battle of the Future

The morning of September 1st found a cold mist hanging in the valley, for the moment it obscured everything as the cream of German royalty and their guests encamped on the perfect location to view the coming battle, a clearing on the hills above the village of Frénois, on the southern slopes of the valley and about a mile southwest of Sedan.

It was a glittering array of uniformed nobles more befitting a palace reception or royal hunt than the battle that would decide the course of history. In addition to Wilhelm I and the other kings, princes, dukes, archdukes and grand dukes there was Moltke, Roon, Bismarck, their staffs, foreign correspondents and military attachés from a host of countries.

The most prominent, and highest-ranking, of the attachés was Lieutenant-General Philip Sheridan of the United States Army. Prominent because, almost from the moment they entered France, either Moltke, Roon, Bismarck or their staffs continuously consulted with him, and he was a frequent dinner guest of King Wilhelm. According to legend one of them, either Moltke, Roon or Bismarck – it depends upon which version you believe – came up to Sheridan on this morning and asked, "what do you think of our positions?"

He replied, "if I were down there, I could break through." Whoever asked the question went silent for a moment, then said, "Well I hope the French don't have a Philip Sheridan among them."

And unfortunately for the army now trapped in Sedan, it had many pretenders to the status of a commander who spent four years innovating and executing new strategies and tactics, but none who really understood them. And already, in the still shrouded valley area to the southeast, the muffled booms of cannonades and the crackle of rifle fire could be heard. The battle of the future had begun.

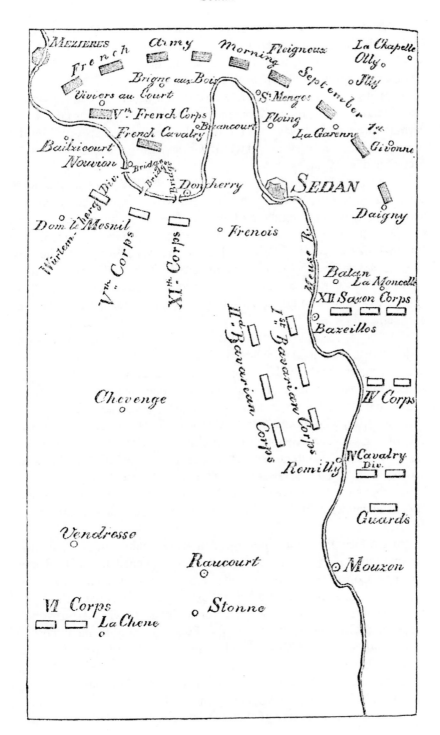

In reality it was underway since 4:00ᴀᴍ when General von der Tann decided the hour had come to use an advantage or lose it. After being driven off the permanent bridge at Bazeilles the previous day, his First Bavarian Corps brought up its Field Pioneer units and they built two pontoon bridges across the Meuse. Von der Tann sent a brigade across and, moving quietly and without commencing the assault with the usual artillery barrage, they got halfway into the town before being discovered by the Marines of General Lebrun's Twelfth Corps, easily the finest troops the French had at Sedan.

A wild and bitter fight ensued, with the civilians in the town contributing to the fight, refusing to evacuate homes after being ordered and probably committing the first atrocities which would make Bazeilles so notorious in its day. The rest of the Corps, joined by the Second Bavarian Corps' gun-line between Frénois and Wadelincourt to the west and the Saxon Fourth Corps' guns at Remilly to the southeast, began a heavy artillery barrage by dawn. Not at Bazeilles itself – the fighting there had become too close-quartered – but at the towns behind it: Balan and Moncelle.

And near Moncelle at 6:00ᴀᴍ the "Army of Châlons" suffered its first major setback when MacMahon, riding in to appraise the situation for himself, suffered a severe leg wound from shellfire. As medical attendants carried him back to Sedan, he transferred his command to the general he considered his best corps commander, August Alexandre Ducrot.

The officer who succeeded MacMahon as First Corps commander after Woerth, he was capable enough and intelligent. However, he had only seen the army chief intermittently since their departure from Reims, and scarcely discussed any plans or strategies with him. Worse than this, neither MacMahon nor Ducrot knew of de Wimpffen's orders from Paris. But de Wimpffen knew, and this would set in motion a farce that exacerbated the disaster.

In the meantime, the chief agent of the French Army's destruction became active as the gun-lines across the region opened up. To the Second Bavarian Corps and Fourth Saxon Corps were soon added the Krupp breechloaders of the Bavarian First just opposite Bazeilles, the Saxon Twelfth overlooking Daigny in the Givonne Valley, the Guard Corps above the town of Givonne itself, the Silesian Fifth Corps at Fléigneux north of Sedan, and the Hessian Eleventh at Floing just northwest of it. By noon all would be in action.

In the hours before then the French would fight a hard, bitter and increasingly desperate series of engagements. The Marines and civilians of Bazeilles fought the hardest of all, many being incinerated when the town's buildings were set ablaze by artillery fire, and by some accounts Bavarian troops.

On the western side of the battle the Fifth and Eleventh Corps' had crossed the Meuse at Donchéry on virtually the same hour the Bavarians entered Bazeilles. At first neither corps encountered so much as a cavalry patrol as they marched into the dawn and toward the sound of the distant guns. It would not be until 9:00AM, when the two corps spread out with the Eleventh in the valley and reaching the outskirts of Floing while the Fifth spread into the hills north of the town did they encounter any resistance.

General Margueritte's reserve cavalry division, nominally attached to Douay's Seventh Corps, attacked with Lancers and three regiments of mounted Chasseurs d'Afrique. Heavy rifle fire broke the initial charge. As the horsemen wheeled left and right the newly-deployed batteries opened up, adding to the confusion and making any regroup impossible. Some managed to return to French lines while hundreds of others fled north, either into the Belgian Ardennes or eventually west to Mézièries.

An hour before this General Ducrot, making his only decision as Army commander, ordered a pullback from Bazeilles and the Givonne Valley in preparation for a retreat to the west. This would have taken the entire "Army of Châlons" straight into the gun-lines of Fifth and Eleventh Corps. The order had only started to be carried out by Lebrun's Twelfth Corps when de Wimpffen appeared at its headquarters, furious and full of fight.

He announced to Lebrun that *he* was the true commander of the Army, and produced the orders from Paris. Lebrun acquiesced, then countermanded the withdraw while de Wimpffen made plans to mount a breakout attack to the southeast, through the Bavarian First and Saxon Fourth Corps' toward Carignan and the eventual linkup with Bazaine's army coming out of Metz.

When Ducrot found out about this he protested all of it. When he met de Wimpffen, just as the sound of German cannonades became continuous, he still urged a retreat to Mézières and Vinoy's Thirteenth Corps. But de Wimpffen would have none of it. "We need a victory!" he demanded, to which Ducrot replied. "You will be very lucky, *mon général*, if this evening you even have a retreat..."

They sent word for the Emperor to break the impasse, but Napoleon III was no longer in the Sedan fortress. By some accounts, when he saw MacMahon being carried by on a litter he realized the end of his reign was at hand. That morning he rode off, even though a chronic gallstone problem made it painful to sit in the saddle for any length of time, to find death in battle rather than live to face surrender.

By 10:00AM, with no imperial decision forthcoming, Ducrot acquiesced to de Wimpffen as well and reversed all orders for a retreat to Mézières. Though by now too late, the Army would try for a breakout to Carignan. At 10:00ᴀᴍ the Bavarian First Corps started to emerge from Bazeilles, on its left flank the Bavarian Second had crossed the Meuse, heading for Balan, the only town between it and Sedan. On the right flank the Saxon Twelfth had taken Daigny and the Guard Corps had reached the head of the Givonne Valley.

As the battle approached midday it became hard to tell which corps of the "Army of Châlons" was getting hammered the most...Lebrun's Twelfth from the Bavarians and Saxons, Ducrot's First by the Guards, Douay's Seventh from the Hessians and Silesians, and even de Wimpffen's under-employed Fifth received fire from the Bavarian Second Corps' gun-line across the river.

Unit cohesion, not just at the corps or division-level but down to regiment and squadron-level, had begun to unravel. Messengers were not getting orders and reports through. Commanders did not know where they were supposed to be, or the nature of the enemy forces they faced.

When de Wimpffen rode to Seventh Corps headquarters to see what units could be spared for the coming breakout to Carignan, Douay claimed his position secure, so long as the Calvaire d'Illy Mountain Pass above him could be held by strong forces. He then gave de Wimpffen one of his divisions on the promise it would be replaced with one from Fifth Corps.

Douay based his optimism on fragmentary reports of the Germans he faced and that his own orders had been carried out. After 1:00ᴘᴍ, in the face of growing enemy activity, after sending a division to Lebrun and not receiving its replacement, Douay rode out to inspect his own lines. He discovered the Calvaire d'Illy Pass to be occupied by stragglers from his own corps, not held by any defensive line, and with the Germans fast approaching.

The Fifth Corps' division never arrived, and in spite of the best efforts by both Douay and Ducrot to throw whatever partial units they could put together either into the pass or onto the slopes before Floing, their lines crumbled. In desperation they turned to General Margueritte for another cavalry charge. When he went to reconnoiter the slopes, a bullet hit him in the face and his escorts carried him back gravely wounded. After his cavalrymen saw him, they rode out in vengeance, and into history.

From their encampment on the hills above Frénois, on the opposite side of the valley, King Wilhelm and his entourage watched the entire charge, its repulse and subsequent disintegration. "What brave gentlemen!" he exclaimed, and thought the French division destroyed. However, it was not until nearly 3:00ᴘᴍ that the unit, now commanded by Gaston de Gallifet, would become so depleted it would be forced to retire.

And according to another legend, after its final charge, Gallifet and his survivors rode past a Prussian infantry regiment. Some accounts say its officers ordered the men to stop firing, others claim it halted simultaneously, then the officers saluted Gallifet as the cease fire orders swept the German lines, and they were allowed to leave the field unharmed.

By then all fronts were collapsing for the French. Even where they had momentary success – at Balan de Wimpffen drove out the Bavarian Second Corps with the forces he assembled for the breakout – they were falling back. In fact, as he tried to rally his troops to mount another attack an avalanche of panicked men and horses plus supply wagons, caissons and artillery pieces poured out of the Bois de la Garenne above his position. The Calvaire d'Illy had been taken by Fifth Corps who, with the Eleventh, had poured an almost geometrically-precise artillery barrage into the Garenne woods.

Now, men from every front streamed to the imagined safety of Sedan's 17th Century fortress. Independently Douay, Lebrun and Ducrot made their way back to the fortress to confront Napoleon III, who had since returned unsuccessful from his suicide mission. He did not need to confer with them to know how hopeless the situation had become. As his generals entered the fortress, the Emperor had a white flag raised. Within minutes the German artillery on all sides fell silent; only the sporadic crackle of small arms fire remained.

Sedan, the battle of the future that would end Imperial France and create a united Germany, had ended and what remained now was to forge its surrender. And for the time being, Moltke could turn his attention to another battlefield, approximately 70 miles to the southeast.

Metz Sputters Out

Between the morning of August 31st and the pre-dawn hours of September 1st, Bazaine assembled a force of 120,000 men around the outlying fortress of St. Julien, on the northeast side of Metz. He had concentrated most of the divisions of his army, lead by the corps commanders Leboeuf, de Ladmirault, Canrobert and Bourbaki, in anticipation of a breakout towards Thionville.

He had even wrote Napoleon III a message, to be sent via dispatch rider if the operation proved successful, that he had broken out and MacMahon should meet him at Thionville. And there was a chance, the best he would ever have, that he could succeed for the German positions around

Noisseville were precarious, in danger of being flanked. And if they did fall then Bazaine's army could take Servigny and St. Barbe, collapsing the German front in the northeast sector and leading to a breakout.

The danger did not go unnoticed by Prussian First Corps commander Edwin von Manteuffel. Bypassing his indignant former superior, he telegraphed Prince Friedrich Karl for help and got it. A newly-arrived Landwehr division reinforced his positions, as did the 18th Division from Ninth Corps, who marched through the night from the west bank of the Moselle to the east and deployed to the north in the Bois de Failly Forest.

By the morning of September 1st a heavy mist hung over the region, similar to the one blanketing Sedan and the Meuse valley. Prussian counterattacks started before the mists finished burning off, at Flanville, at the de Failly Forest and especially Noisseville where the German perimeter had been pushed out the farthest. The French division there fought with a grim determination – Bazaine may not have realized its importance but his infantrymen did – this was their best chance for escape.

Manteuffel committed the Landwehr division and backed them up with a gun-line of 114 field pieces. As at the simultaneous battle to the northwest, the lessons of St. Privat had been learned. No more reckless infantry assaults, artillery would do the brutal work, and at Noisseville the French positions soon became untenable. Their own artillery support would have helped, but no cannons were brought up. They and the other divisions in Leboeuf's corps were busily engaged on either side of Noisseville. To its north Comte de Ladmirault had the entire Fourth Corps involved in the fighting around Servigny.

However, Canrobert had two divisions from his corps standing idle and Bourbaki's entire Guards Corps, plus the Army's artillery reserve and cavalry reserve, were far to the rear, trying to move forward on clogged roads. By 11:00ᴀᴍ the division at Noisseville fell back rather than be encircled. To the north repeated assaults on the de Failly Forest were driven back by the 18th Division. And to the east, lookouts at Fort St. Julien reported a cloud of dust rising into the air; Grand Duke Friedrich Franz II was entering the war with his Thirteenth Corps.

At Metz, Bazaine took these reverses and ominous signs to mean a breakout would now be impossible. He signaled for all his corps to disengage and fall back. The move took Manteuffel by surprise, throughout the afternoon the divisions under his command waited for the fighting to resume. By 6:00ᴘᴍ it finally became obvious that the battle had ended, with most of the French troops filing dejectedly into the Metz fortress.

The Final Ride of Napoleon III

Not until the appearance of General Reille, at the hilltop encampment above Frénois, in his distinctive uniform as an officer of the Imperial Suite, did anyone in the German High Command realize the possibility that the Emperor of France could be in Sedan.

Escorts took the General to Wilhelm I, who stood in front of a semi-circle of assembled German nobility. He saluted, then presented the future Kaiser with a personal letter: "Not having been able to die at the head of my troops, I lay down my sword to your Majesty. I am, on your Majesty's account, your good brother. Napoleon."

As Bismarck studied the letter with Wilhelm, the rest of the entourage stood in stunned silence. The magnitude of not just defeating an army but capturing it was stunning enough, but this? Bismarck quickly dictated a reply and, after Reille rode back to Sedan with it, the entourage broke for an evening meal and a few hours rest.

Few people celebrated or cheered, for most it was too solemn or stunning an occasion, and from the bivouac fires of the troops around them came the words of Lutheran hymns thanking God for his providence this day. In the Sedan fortress, upon Reille's return, the mood would neither be so quiet or so solemn.

On de Wimpffen's initial arrival at the fortress, shortly before Reille departed, he objected strenuously to the white flag being raised. He felt the army still held defensible positions but Napoleon more realistically realized the end had come and sent off his emissary. When Reille brought back the formal reply for surrender negotiations, de Wimpffen again protested, for all eyes turned to him to lead the delegation.

"You assumed the command when you thought there was some honor and profit in exercising it," Ducrot reminded him. "Now you cannot refuse." In the end he did not and rode off to Donchéry with the Emperor's personal representative. They were escorted to a house where Bismarck and Moltke awaited them, and they haggled into the early hours of the following morning over just the preliminaries.

Moltke and Bismarck demanded the surrender of the entire French Army. De Wimpffen proposed an "honorable capitulation" where the army would keep its arms and march out with its colors, on the promise it would not engage Prussia or any of its allies for the duration of the war. Bismarck responded this was an honored tradition for a garrison, not an entire army and pressed for its surrender.

De Wimpffen then threatened to defend Sedan to the last man, and Moltke laid out the facts starkly: the French Army had been reduced to

80,000 men and a few dozen cannon. The German Armies had over three times as many men (250,000), over 500 guns and all the high ground.

Bismarck and Moltke also stated what Prussia and her coalition partners wanted as their conditions to end the war: land, fortresses and frontiers they felt were defensible. Again de Wimpffen, as well as Napoleon's personal envoy, protested that these were too outrageous. They tried to claim the French population was peaceful; Moltke noted the evidence of the last six weeks proved the contrary while Bismarck stated a position which would take on greater importance in the months ahead: that the French people themselves could not be trusted and needed to be punished.

Tensions increased when the envoy stated the sword Napoleon offered in surrender was his own personal sword and not that of France. Moltke, who had been weakening, jumped on this and stated the German conditions to be unchanged. The meeting ended with the truce being continued until the morning when the surrender would be signed.

At 5:00AM on September 2nd, Napoleon III carried out his last act as the last monarch of France. Bypassing de Wimpffen and the rest of his command staff, he rode out of Sedan in his imperial carriage and with three generals from his personal suite. General Reille had ridden ahead to announce his arrival to the German entourage, but got intercepted by Bismarck.

Around 7:00AM he met the Emperor on the road near Frénois. Beyond the generals and a few personal aides there were no bodyguards, no escorting squadrons of cavalry. On both sides most soldiers had only just started to stir, and few took notice of the elderly men dismounted from horses or alighted from the carriage and entered a nearby cottage.

When Moltke arrived Napoleon tried one last negotiating gambit and offered to move the army trapped in Sedan a few miles north to Belgium, where it would be disarmed and interned for the duration of the war. This time Bismarck softened – a weak imperial regime in post-war France suited him nicely – but Moltke held firm.

The Emperor was a prisoner and had no power to negotiate, so while Bismarck escorted him to Castle Bellevue in Frénois, Moltke went to a château overlooking the Meuse River. At 11:00AM he co-signed the surrender terms with General de Wimpffen, ending the last major battle with Imperial France.

At a cost of just over 9,000 killed and wounded, around 1,000 more than what the Guard Corps alone suffered at St. Privat, the German coalition had destroyed an entire French Army. Some 13,000 French troops had been killed during the battle and 21,000 taken prisoner. With the surrender of the "Army of Châlons" came an additional 80,000 enlisted men, 2,866 officers, 40 generals, over 1,000 wagons and lorries, some 6,000 horses, 419 field guns, 139 fortress guns and 66,000 Chassepot rifles.

Only 13,000 troops managed to escape the investment, with 3,000 stragglers crossing the Belgian frontier and the rest making their way to Mézières where they joined General Vinoy's Thirteenth Corps.

To add to his misery, it would not be until after the surrender had been signed that Bismarck allowed Napoleon III to meet Wilhelm I. By all accounts it was an awkward event with the Emperor gaining the minor concession, an aptly Napoleonic one, that officers promising "not to take up arms against Germany, nor to act in any way prejudicial to her interests" would be paroled; some 550 took advantage of it.

Only then did Napoleon learn of Bazaine's failed sortie from Metz and where Bismarck planned to intern him – at the Wilhelmshöhe Palace in Cassal. The battle with Imperial France was over. The less costly, but more trying, battle with the French people was about to begin.

Chapter XVII: The Government of National Defence

> *"All victories breed hate, and that over your superior is foolish or fatal."*
> -Baltasar Gracián (1601 - 1658)

Sedan's Aftermath: Problems and Unity

IT HAS BEEN said by many historians, and one foreign military observer whose name and nationality have been lost to time, that the regiments from New York, Minnesota, Ohio, Vermont, Pennsylvania and the legendary one from Maine who marched into Gettysburg in the summer of 1863 came out of the Herculean battle a united, national army. The same has been said of the corps and divisions from Prussia, Bavaria, Saxony, Würtemberg, Hesse, Baden and Nassau that came to Sedan in the waning summer seven years later.

The truth is the unification process had been underway in both cases for a long time. Four score and seven years for the United States, roughly three score and five for Germany. But something profound had happened, had been forged, in both battles. It was just a little more obvious in Sedan.

Perhaps it was because of all those titled heads of the Germanies watching, from their magnificent vantage point, the success of their Prussian-lead coalition armies. Seemingly, with each cannonade from their gun-lines, and infantry advance or cavalry charge, with each coordinated operation between the various corps and divisions, their independence was melting away. They were watching a national army being welded together, one worthy of Friedrich Barbarossa himself. In the heat of battle, 36 states were being forged into a new version of the ancient dream.

Though, in the immediate aftermath it did not exactly feel that way. This is due to all the problems the victors faced in the following days. The most paramount was dealing with an army of prisoners almost half as large as their own. At the conclusion of battle the French only had enough food and medical supplies to last two days. By September 3rd they had run out, and it had started to rain.

German doctors and medical staffs immediately went to work treating the French wounded, while Field Pioneer companies began constructing a temporary camp for the prisoners on the Iges Peninsula west of Sedan. Surrounded by a loop of the Meuse, the only ways off it would be to either swim the river or climb the barricades erected along its base.

On the afternoon of September 3rd the remnants of his last imperial army grumbled sullen abuses at Napoleon III as his convoy of gilded carriages, heavily-laden wagons and their ornately-clad postilion riders left by a rather different route than what they would take. Bismarck could only pause for a moment and note, "there is a dynasty on its way out." Moltke did not really have much time to spare except, and his comments have been interpreted several ways, to wonder enviously on how Napoleon was taking an untroubled retreat from all his responsibilities.

For Moltke and his staff theirs were only increasing. The two corps arriving from Metz would be detailed to supervise the massive army of prisoners, for whom food and other supplies were already being brought up, lines-of-march established, marching tables for their journey into captivity laid out and orders back to the border regions of the Saar and the Bavarian Palatinate for prison camp construction to greatly expand.

And then there came the local problem of maintaining contact with French forces. Who would they fight and where were they? Already, Moltke had reports of new French units re-occupying Reims, and was forced to detach several cavalry squadrons to investigate. General Vinoy's Thirteenth Corps had sent out a division from Mézières to ascertain what had happened in Sedan.

The Prussian Sixth Corps, the one uncommitted corps from Sedan, was deployed between the evening of September 1st and the morning of the 2nd. It took Rethel, cutting the main northern road to Paris, and used the Fifth and Sixth Cavalry Divisions from the "Army of the Meuse" to reconnoiter the area from Reims to Mézières.

Between the morning of the 2nd and the evening of September 3rd the French division and elements of the Prussian Corps' infantry and cavalry divisions blundered around and into each other in the pelting rain. There were a few skirmishes, and at one point main columns of the opposing forces passed within four miles of themselves. Vinoy learned enough from the stragglers he swept up and his own reconnaissance activities to understand the disaster's magnitude and decided to withdraw his forces. Picking up his other two divisions, at Laon and Soissons, he retreated to Paris. By then, the news of Sedan had finally reached the capital.

Paris: The Raft of the Medusa

In the age before wireless communications, international press organizations and 24-hour news cycles, it took time for information to travel even a short distance. When the telegraph lines to Sedan and its surrounding towns went dead, a nervous silence fell over Paris. The stockpiling of food reserves and other supplies by the military and city authorities continued. Herds of cattle, sheep and oxen from surrounding farms were brought in, as well as whatever grain and vegetables could be harvested.

And there was also a harvest of wild, unfounded rumors. For September 1st they were of French victories, at not only Sedan and Metz but also on the North Sea where German merchant ships were being seized by Admiral Bouet-Willaumez's frigate squadron. All were cheered and believed, while de Palikao worked intently with Eugénie's Council of Regency to raise new armies, and Trochu on Paris defences. By the following day, the victory rumors were competing with the new ones of defeat, but nobody believed them.

On September 3rd Paris returned to its nervous silence. The reports of defeat had increased, and people stopped discounting them. Then, shortly before noon, a Havas Press Agency telegram from Brussels reported the defeat of the French Army at Sedan. It coincided with articles in British newspapers and messages to the War Ministry and Interior Ministry from town officials just outside the battle area of stragglers reporting the army had surrendered. Finally in the afternoon a telegram arrived at the Council of Regency from Napoleon III announcing that the "Army of Châlons" had capitulated and he was now a prisoner of the German coalition.

The news stunned Paris. It was truly beyond the worst case anyone had thought would happen. Not de Palikao or Eugénie, who never considered for a moment that MacMahon's army could be defeated. Not Trochu, who feared a defeat but never thought the entire army would be trapped and surrendered. Nor even Favre, Thiers or Gambetta, who believed it would take a long, grinding war to achieve the results they had just learned about. Uniquely, there were few who considered the capitulation to be a national defeat. Instead, most viewed it as a defeat of the Second Empire and a chance to overthrow it.

By noon on September 4th the Leftists in the Corps Legislatif were ready to strike. While the Imperial Ministers and their conservative allies proposed a slightly modified form of the current structure, the Council of Regency and National Defence, Favre and Thiers wanted it brought down. Their proposals for dissolving the empire barely made it to the floor when a crowd shouting "Vive la Republique!" and "La Decheance" (the Downfall) surged past the few guards around the Legislatif Palace and filled the chamber.

They are more curious then confrontational, even to the conservative deputies, though de Palikao quickly leaves the hall. However, they manage to accomplish what all Paris mobs are so good at: paralyzing the French Government. Soon Favre and his allies learn from this mob where a far larger gathering is taking place and they must somehow stop it. They take to the streets, to the Pont de la Concorde, and head for the Hôtel de Ville.

At virtually the same moment another mob is negotiating their way into Tuileries Palace, the official imperial residence. Unlike the mobs from 1792, 1830 or 1848 they did not storm the palace. They convince the small detail of Imperial Guards to hand over their command to a *Garde Mobile* unit, who then allowed the mob in. They did not sack the palace, though the imperial flag and eagles were torn down and graffiti scrawled on some walls. They also did not find what they had come for; they did not find the "L'Espagnole," the Spaniard, the Empress Eugénie de Guzman Bonaparte.

In truth they had just missed her. At the first gathering of the mob her American dentist led her out one of the palace's side gates. They slipped into the next building over, the Louvre, which by now had been mostly emptied of its treasures and was closed.

However, the heaviest sculptures and largest paintings, the monumental works, remained. And according to legend... the Empress held up her flight into exile by stopping in front of two of the paintings. The first was Jacques Louis David's famous propaganda work, *Napoleon at St. Bernard's Pass*. It showed perfectly the image of dramatic, decisive leadership she had goaded her husband to emulate.

But David knowingly created a fantasy image. Napoleon III's uncle had indeed climbed the pass, he just did it on a mule and not a white stallion with a flowing mane and tail. It was an image no living leader could live up to, especially one of limited military abilities and who suffered from gallstones. And then came the painting by one of David's students: Theodore Géricault.

The most ambitious and controversial of his works, it was also truly monumental in size, over 16 feet by 23, and depicted one of the most notorious sea disasters of the 19th Century: *The Raft of the Medusa.* The frigate *Medusa* foundered off Senegal on the west African coast in 1816. Around 150 of her passengers and crew made it onto a makeshift raft. And 13 days later only a tenth of that number remained alive when they were finally rescued.

The painting shows a contorted pyramid of humanity – intertwined figures set against a chaotic sea and dramatically illuminated, their pleading hands reaching up and out for a distant set of sails, a passing ship oblivious to their plight. From its first showing it had been regarded as political allegory, and so controversial that Géricault soon went into exile in England.

Before following the same route, Eugénie paused in front of his masterwork, dumbstruck by how, after some 50 years, it had never been more aptly allegorical to the state of France than at this moment. Its hour had come; unfortunately, it would only have an audience of one to realize it on this day. But its effect over France would endure for decades to come.

And over at the Hôtel de Ville the drama of the ongoing shipwreck was reaching its latest climax when Favre, Thiers and the crowd they lead arrived to find their true enemies celebrating in its great hall, the Extreme Leftists. Newly freed from prison, the radical journalist Henri Rochefort had been joined by Felix Pyat, a neo-Jacobin orator, Gustave Flourens, an old comrade in Rochefort's conspiracies, Louis Blanqui and Charles Delescluze. Nearly the full roster of Celebrity Leftists.

All were members of the sinister Paris Clubs, radical organizations filled with anarchists and Communists who knew they could run the government better than any politician and fight the war better than any general. For a few tense moments it looked as if another war might break out in France, this time among the survivors on the raft. But the two groups came together to destroy the common enemy: the Second Napoleonic Empire.

By nightfall they declare their Provisional Government constituted and by popular acclamation elected their cabinet. For the moment this consisted of: General Trochu, commander of the Paris defences; Louise Thiers, President of the Third Republic; Jules Favre, Foreign Minister; Leon Gambetta, Interior Minister, as well as Minister for War; Emmanuel Arago, the new Mayor of Paris; Emile Kératry, the Prefect of Police; Louis Ernest Picard, Finance Minister; Henri Rochefort, President of the Barricades Commission; Issac Crémieux, Minister for Justice, and Jules Ferry, the all-important Minister of Supply.

They and a dozen other lesser ministers and presidents of commissions announced their first victories over the enemy: the choice of the Tricolor as the national flag and the official name of their republic, The Government of National Defence. Unfortunately none of this had much to do with the military reality, for on the same night of September 4th Moltke issued orders for the German armies around Sedan to continue their advance – toward Paris.

The Final End of an Era

When Steinmetz had been demoted in command, though not in rank, Moltke gave Prince Friedrich Karl a free hand in dealing with him. He did not have long to wait to exercise that power for on September 7th, after roughly three weeks of behaving himself, the Prince forwarded an official complaint to King Wilhelm that the General had deliberately and repeatedly denied to him the customary military courtesies and civilities due to a superior officer.

The King had at long last had enough. Furious, he declared the actions to be an insult to a Prince of the Royal House and demanded Steinmetz resign his command of the First Army. Baron Edwin Hans von Manteuffel, who had so ably handled the attempted French breakout at Noisseville a week earlier, was promoted to head First Army while Steinmetz returned to Prussia where he became the Governor General of Posen, a city so far to the east that it is now the Polish city of Poznan.

Of all the ends to the Napoleonic Era this one is the saddest. The retirement of the last active-serving officer from that era should have been poignant, not shameful. But the "Lion of Skalitz" had repeatedly disgraced himself – any commander without his special status would have been relieved after Spicheren, and intentionally pushing his army across the line-of-march of another.

Unfortunately, Steinmetz could never accept that his age and special status did not make him the King's General, Wilhelm's senior military adviser while Moltke played with his trains and telegraphs. But even Roon acknowledged Moltke's position and special talents for understanding modern warfare. And there was only room for one at the top.

There were no special ceremonies when Steinmetz left. He merely boarded a train at the nearest operating station to Metz and departed east, into history, while farther to the west history was being made.

The Road to Paris: Resistance Begins

Even though orders were given on the 4th, disentangling and replenishing their units meant Third Army and the "Army of the Meuse" were not ready to advance until September 7th. Ahead of them their Uhlan patrols reconnoitered extensively, and encountered the first serious acts of sabotage.

Roles were now reversing; up until Sedan behind-the-lines sabotage had been one of the primary missions of the Uhlans. But the French civil population, and those units of the Army, the National Guard and the *Garde Mobile* not in headlong retreat, began trying to hinder their enemy's movements. Mostly this took the form of sabotaging roads and rail lines, even down to tearing up paving stones. Some bridges were blown, though these actually provided little hindrance. This would begin to change two days later.

On September 9th the city of Laon, some 30 miles northwest of Reims, formally capitulated to the Sixth Cavalry Division. Its commander, Duke Wilhelm of Mecklenburg-Schwerin and the brother of Grand Duke Friedrich Franz, offered the fortress garrison lenient terms. Its active-duty personnel would have to go into captivity, but the 2,000 *Garde Mobiles* would be dismissed on parole that they would take no further part in the war.

Large numbers of both French and German personnel were still in the fortress, still in its citadel's main courtyard, when its powder magazine was intentionally blown. It did great damage to the fortress, killed its commandant and nearly 300 other troops, while 115 Prussian officers and men were killed and wounded. This included Duke Wilhelm and his executive officer, both of whom would be in the hospital until after the war ended. Though it caused more casualties to the French, the first act of what the war threatened to become had occurred: *Guerre à Outrancé*.

As the professional French Army completed its collapse, this would increasingly be the style of warfare Moltke would encounter – A Nation At Arms. It recalled the tumultuous, and by now thoroughly idealized, days of the French Revolution. Back when the First Republic was at war with virtually every other country in Europe. When *levée en masse* meant something, and when, by 1794, France had become a vast, organized war machine and would eventually field 14 armies.

It was also fired, especially in Paris, by the popular culture of its day. A few years earlier, one of the major sensations in the city that claimed to be the artistic and cultural center of Europe, had been the first-ever showing of Francisco José de Goya's legendary portfolio of sketches of the

Peninsular War. They remain some of the most famous, and brutal, anti-war art works of all time. But few had been seen until nearly 60 years after they were created, and by then times had changed.

Like the heady days of the original revolution, the searing anti-war images became idealized. The phrase "making a Saragossa" came into popular usage. And especially in the Paris Clubs, they were romanticized. Instead of making people horrified of war, de Goya's original intent, it fired the imaginations of a new generation of extremists to welcome it. Soon, they would get their chances.

And while they stoked their fires, the Germans kept moving. By September 16th the "Army of the Meuse" had crossed the Marne River northeast of Paris, between Nanteuil and Dammartin, and the Third Army stood ready to cross it due east of the city, between Meaux and Brie-Cômte-Robert. On the 17th its Fifth Corps had reached the Upper Seine River and was pushing down its right bank to secure the drawbridges at Villeneuve St. Georges. There it encountered a division from Vinoy's Thirteenth Corps foraging for more supplies. A sharp fight ensued, the first major engagement since Sedan, and ended with the French retreating under the guns of Fort Charenton.

By the next day the Second Bavarian Corps from Third Army also reached the Seine and crossed it at Corbeil, southeast of Paris. The initial investment of the city was but two days away. In order to keep pace with the armies the royal headquarters had to move from Reims, to Château-Thierry and then to the Rothschild Palace at Ferrières, due east of Paris. It would be here, while Moltke supervised cutting off the city from the outside world, that Bismarck got the first chance to end the war.

The Opening Duel

Two days after taking the job of Foreign Minister, September 6th, Jules Favre dispatched a circular letter to the other foreign chancelleries of Europe stating that the new French government was ready to seek peace, though only so long as it did not have to yield "an inch of her soil or a stone of her fortresses." A week later, on September 13th, he attended a massive military parade with most of the other members of the Government of National Defence.

Between the men of Trochu's and Vinoy's corps, some 8,000 sailors, 3,000 Marines, a few thousand survivors from the "Army of Châlons" and the National Guard and *Garde Mobile* battalions that had flocked to the city, a parade of over 100,000 men was organized. It stretched from Place de la Bastille to the Arc de Triomphe. Trochu, with an escort of staff officers, led them down the broad avenue.

For the moment, he was the "Man on Horseback" and while the force behind him looked impressive enough, he harbored no illusions about its combat abilities. Trochu did not believe any sortie out of Paris should be attempted. Rather, the garrison should wait for the armies being raised in the provinces, such as the "Army of the Loire," to come and relieve them. However, one man was beginning to think a sortie of another kind might just end the war.

Five days later, as the last mail trains left Paris for the west, Jules Favre departed to the east. Without telling anyone else in the government, he was heading to the spectacular steel and glass Rothschild Palace in Ferrières for a meeting with Bismarck that the British Ambassador had arranged. Unlike the earlier negotiations with de Wimpffen and Napoleon III, this time it would be just Bismarck who would meet with Favre, who was a civilian official, not a military man.

The meeting proved to be doomed from the start. Favre went with the hope he could convince Bismarck that the French were a peace-loving people, temporarily misled by an ambitious, craven Bonaparte, and a peace without annexations would be the best way to end the conflict for both sides.

To his shock and dismay he found Bismarck regarding him as the representative of a people with a 200-year record of aggression against the German states, whose leaders coveted them and constantly tried to conquer and annex them. To the notion that the French would be grateful for a just peace, Bismarck already had an answer, one he previously honed on de Wimpffen's hide.

"One should not," he said, "in general rely on gratitude, and especially not on that of a people." And in particular of a people who are "irritable, envious, jealous and proud to excess. It seems to you that victory is a property reserved for you alone, that the glory of arms is your monopoly..." In summation, Bismarck concluded, "one can rely on nothing in your country." He then went on to outline what Prussia and its partners wanted: land, fortresses and frontiers they alone felt were defensible. This meant all of the Alsace province and the northern half of the Lorraine with all their fortresses.

Favre's response, exaggerated by the bitter arguments, was to burst into tears and cry, "you want to destroy France!" A more experienced diplomat might have held back the tears and taken these extreme demands as the opening gambit in a high-stakes chess game, and begin to make counter moves. Instead he collapsed and withdrew from the board. "I made a mistake in coming here," Favre admitted. "This is to be an endless struggle between two peoples who ought to stretch out their hands to each other. I had hoped for another solution."

In the end he did not even get the most basic concession he had gone to Ferrières for: a temporary armistice so the new government could at least elect a proper national assembly. Bismarck might have granted it, and gained a major negotiating move, but he would have none of it if there were no concessions, such as the fortresses at Toul and Strasbourg. Favre proved he was equally intractable by refusing to consider these and returned to Paris in despair.

He found a city preparing as best it could for the imminent siege. Most of the diplomatic missions had left or were packing. Only the Papal Nuncio, a skeleton staff at the British embassy and the American embassy, with its notable military attaché, General Ambrose Everett Burnside, remained. The following day the last above ground telegraph lines were cut, and on September 20th the infantry vanguards of Crown Prince Friedrich Wilhelm's army and Crown Prince Friedrich August's army linked up at St. Germain-on-Laye. The Siege of Paris had begun.

The Hardening Lines

By the summer of 1870 it was probably too late for an amicable, equable settlement of a conflict between the French and German people. Bismarck had been right, so far as he went; for the German nations there were two centuries of old scores to get some payback. And especially as he was forging a single, united empire out of them, it would have been impossible for him to achieve his primary goal without a victory that included at least some annexation of the Germanic lands of eastern France.

Even if he had wanted to, the highly nationalistic German press would not have let him. The success of Woerth, Spicheren, the battles around Metz and stunning outcome of Sedan had awakened a desire in the German people and its soldiers for unity, security and a lasting peace which only a humiliated and defeated France could achieve. Even Karl Marx, in exile in London, felt it and initially supported the united German response. Only now, as the coalition switched from fighting an imperial regime to a leftist republic did he change his tone.

The French, and Favre and his associates are as good a representative group of this as any other, were blind to it all. Before the war they cared little for the events in the Germanies. When they voted against the declaration of war they worried more about what Napoleon III as the newest Charlemagne would mean for their country and not so much for the German lands he would conquer.

They refused to understand, and could not be made to accept, that the utter crushing of an imperial regime they hated was a defeat for France, especially as they still had the will to fight and believed they possessed the resources to carry on. And in many ways they did, if this had been 1794 and the technologies and tactics of war were far more primitive. But that age had been ebbing out of existence since Napoleon's defeat at Waterloo.

Personal courage, ferocity in the attack and the ability to endure hardships did not mean what they once did. Not in the face of well-educated, trained and disciplined armies equipped with modern weapons and the all-important knowledge of how best to use them.

But the French, for the most part, boisterously refused to even consider this. Leon Gambetta, who initially feared their "September Revolution" might fail in the Provinces the same way the 1848 Revolution did, was pleasantly surprised to hear the news had been greeted with at worst calm resignation, and mostly riotous delight.

In fact, in Lyon and Marseilles local republican elements had preceded Paris in seizing power and, once the news arrived from the capital, successful uprisings began in Nice, Nîmes, Mâcon, St. Étienne, Bordeaux and dozens of smaller cities. From the remaining Imperial Prefects, and the republican candidates who replaced the rest, came the near-universal response that the change had been accepted with "calm and order everywhere." And almost as universal was the determination to continue the war and defend the soil of France.

This response grew to incendiary intensity when Favre reported the terms Bismarck laid out for an end to the war, when the shelling of Strasbourg, actually begun on August 23rd, was widely reported and then came the news of Bazeilles. In Paris, a statue to the city of Strasbourg had become a place of almost religious veneration since its investment. Flowers were laid around it, poets wrote poems to its bravery and suffering. There were no statues to Bazeilles, but the much-exaggerated news of its destruction would serve the Government of National Defence as both a rallying point and a war cry.

The war was changing its character. From now on it would increasingly be a fight between fanatical amateurs and increasingly vexed professional soldiers.

Chapter XVIII: The Disasters Continue

*"In despair there are the most intense enjoyments,
especially when one is very acutely conscious
of the hopelessness of one's situation."*
-Fyodor Mikhailovich Dostoevsky (1821 - 1881)

The State of Siege

WITH THE INVESTMENT of Paris, virtually the entire coalition Moltke commanded became a static force. Two armies, with a total of six corps plus several cavalry divisions, were deployed in an irregular circle some 50 miles in circumference around the capital. A third army, originally six under-strength corps, but with various additions and subtractions now five corps, was encamped on a perimeter 25 miles in circumference around Metz.

Two corps, originally part of Friedrich Karl's army, had been detailed to the massive logistics operation of feeding, housing and transporting the over 100,000 prisoners from the "Army of Châlons" to camps across the border. An additional corps, composed of a Baden division and two Prussian Landwehr divisions, had invested Strasbourg. Another Landwehr division took over the siege of Toul, originally conducted by Field-Pioneer units from Friedrich Wilhelm's Third Army, on September 12th. Additional fortresses, such as Verdun, Thionville, Soissons and those along France's northeastern frontier tied down observation forces up to brigade-size and containing field batteries and cavalry squadrons.

Additional units were detailed across northeastern France for occupation duties, to repair roadways, bridges of all kinds, rail lines and railroad tunnels. In particular the rail tunnel at Nanteuil, to the west of Toul, had been almost completely demolished and re-engineering it would require several weeks. Divisional Field-Pioneer battalions, corps command train battalions and civilian work crews from the Germanies were employed, protected by infantry companies and cavalry squadrons.

Under these conditions, if another French army had appeared in the field, competently trained and commanded, properly equipped with modern weapons and given knowledge of the invaders' weak points, it could have wrecked havoc on the thinly-spread and nearly-static German armies. Repair and siege operations would have been cut back or ended entirely, breakouts from Metz and Paris could have imperiled the forces surrounding them. Supply and communication lines could have been cut, and the German armies might just have been forced to fight their way out of France in order to survive.

Under this scenario the war would have ended in an exhausted stalemate, with the dream of a united Germany just as dead as Napoleon's Imperial France. The problem was such an army barely existed at the start of the war and certainly did not at this point. No matter how much Leon Gambetta and de Freycinet thought they could command one into existence by the force of their personalities. But this does not mean they would not try, repeatedly.

The Curious Case of Edouard Regnier

It could have come straight out of a spy novel or, if the man in question had a couple of siblings, then a Marx Brothers movie. For over a decade after the war the French treated Edouard Regnier as a mysterious, sinister figure. No doubt an agent of Bismarck and the Prussian government, or perhaps even the British government, sent to cause discord and division. They would have done his case more justice to have thought of him a moron and considered what he did a vainglorious attempt at comic relief.

As near as can be ascertained, or perhaps there is a forgotten old file in the Wilhelmstrasse or Whitehall records. Regnier was a French businessman living in Great Britain when the war started. His involvement in it begins shortly after Empress Eugénie and the Prince Imperial, Eugene Louis Joseph Napoleon, arrived at Hastings on the Channel Coast to begin their exile.

He writes to Eugénie about a fantastic scheme: for her to denounce the new republic, place herself under the protection of the fleet, summon the remaining units of the Imperial armies, royalist politicians and civil population to her side. The Empress finds the scheme too outrageous to be plausible and refuses. Though, when he actually visits Hastings he does take away something of value: a photo of the town's sea front with a few words from the Prince Imperial written on its back.

Armed with no other documentation than this, Regnier arrives at the Rothschild Palace in Ferrières just ahead of Jules Favre. In marked contrast to the tenor of his later meeting, Otto von Bismarck gives him a courtly welcome and discusses at some length the diplomatic troubles he's been having.

Journalists of the day, and some historians since then, have wondered why he would devote any time to a man with such flimsy credentials. But other historians have explained it this way: giving some accreditation to Regnier gave Bismarck another card in his own deck to play. And why not deal with the dubious representative of a legitimate imperial government anymore than the legitimate representative of a dubious revolutionary one?

To Bismarck and his foreign ministry, as well as those of his coalition partners, Favre and company were only the winners of a political street brawl in Paris. Did they really speak for the rest of the country? Could not a weak imperial regime do just as well? Bismarck saw to it that Regnier became a Red Cross official and, given a good conduct pass, sent him off to Prince Friedrich Karl's headquarters.

Three days later, Regnier presented his documents to the French sentries at the main checkpoint into Metz. Inside he received an enthusiastic welcome from Bazaine, who wanted to use him for his own ends. Official praise for the new government to the contrary, he did not trust and openly despised the leftists now in power. He wanted to get his army out of Metz and keep it intact for use as a "free agent" in post-war France, where this latest republic would be crushed like the first two and a new imperial regime installed.

The choices here ran from the Empress herself to the Prince Imperial – at the time he was only a few years younger than Franz Josef when he took power – and Prince Louis Napoleon, sitting in exile in Florence. To sound the parties out, Bazaine decided to send Regnier to visit Napoleon III, and from there to Florence, and Canrobert to Britain.

But Canrobert was a practical hand at saying "no" to bad ideas. So the assignment fell to General Charles Bourbaki, who departed Metz on September 25th in mufti and accompanied by Regnier. In Belgium they went their separate ways, Regnier naively thinking he could yet save Imperial France and Bourbaki convinced it was all a fool's errand.

Bourbaki only needed a few hours with Eugénie to realize he had been correct, Regnier would need rather longer to convince. Making his way back to Metz in a remarkably short time, by September 29th, a final bizarre irony befell the general. Bourbaki should have been recognizable to any of the German sentries or officials he encountered; they all bought his cover as yet another Red Cross official.

What they did not accept were his papers; the date on his conduct pass would not allow him back into Metz. So Bourbaki made his way to Tours, where he would be welcomed into the Government of National Defence by Leon Gambetta himself, and his participation in the war would continue. Though by then, in fact before Bourbaki had even left on his fool's errand, the precarious situation for the German armies had started to change.

The First Domino

The full Landwehr Division did not stay long at Toul after it arrived. One of its brigades was sent up north to Châlons, where an increasingly angry population had made life difficult for its occupation detachment. Fortunately, it did not remain under strength for more than a few days when, on September 18th, a train arrived via Nancy with 26 heavy-caliber siege guns.

An earlier attempt to reduce the Toul fortress with field artillery alone had failed. Now those guns, some three dozen in all, were redeployed along with the siege guns. They were located on the heights above the Moselle River, both left and right banks, and on Mont St. Michel. The morning after the emplacements were finished, the 23rd, all guns began a sustained bombardment of Toul.

At 3:30 that afternoon the white flag is run up the spire of its cathedral. The capitulation is handled swiftly, the same conditions granted to MacMahon's army at Sedan are offered here. In the end 109 officers accept the conditions of parole while the remaining garrison, 2,240 officers and men, are taken as prisoners. A large provision of stores, 21 fortress guns and 3,000 Chassepot rifles were taken as prizes.

The first domino had fallen. Though it only freed up half a division's worth of men, it accomplished something far more important – it opened a second rail line across the Moselle for the Germans. While it did not eliminate their supply problems, they were about to be considerably eased.

The Last of its Kind

The German victory at Woerth meant the immediate isolation of the most important fortress in the Alsace province: Strasbourg. At first the Crown Prince's army could only afford an observation force; no matter since the commandant of the fortress, General Jean Uhrich, only had three infantry battalions and his gun crews for a garrison.

Over the first two weeks in August enough stragglers from the First, Fifth and Seventh Corps allowed Uhrich to form two more battalions. And with the call up of the city's *Garde Mobile* units, he soon had a force of 23,000 men. Though by then the Baden Division had arrived and the Prussian divisions, under General von Werder, were en route, as were siege guns and mortars from Coblentz, Magdeburg and Wesel.

While his engineering and artillery commanders made preparations for a formal, *en règle*, siege, Werder decided to try something new. Something terrible, but which also promised to end the operation quickly – the area bombardment of the city.

As a target, Strasbourg offered the possibility that such a tactic might work. The great Vauban himself had modernized the imposing medieval fortress, but he had not given it outlying forts with overlapping fields of fire, as he had at Metz, and more importantly it had been nearly 200 years since he improved it. And since then not only had the science of artillery improved, Strasbourg had sprawled beyond its protective walls.

On August 24th, once the battery emplacements were built, the shelling of Strasbourg began. Most of the districts outside the walls were heavily damaged, especially its new Protestant cathedral, the city's famous library and art museum, and many of its wealthiest mansions were reduced to rubble. There were so many dead they had to be buried in the grounds of the botanical gardens and yet, the operation did not work.

It was partly because of General Uhrich's obstinacy, which soon earned him hero status in Paris, and mostly because High Command had severely underestimated the store of shells and mortar bombs such a bombardment would need. So while new, much larger, orders were put into Gusstahlfabrik and other armaments manufacturers, the siege en *règle* commenced.

On the eve of the Battle of Sedan, the first parallel trenches were dug, as close to the fortress's original *glacis* as possible and eventually extending to the Rhine and Marne canal. Artillery fire from the fort's main citadel and nearest bastions forced a temporary abandonment of the siege works. Eventually the Prussian heavy guns silenced the fortress batteries, though not before two sorties by its garrison had damaged the first parallel and reached as far as the second before being repulsed.

Heavy rains caused a suspension in offensive operations; they even permitted a short truce to be negotiated by Werder and Uhrich so the dead could be gathered and buried on both sides. During the truce, news of MacMahon's defeat at Sedan and the Empire's collapse reached Strasbourg, but neither event compelled Uhrich to surrender.

The siege resumed on September 9th with the parallel trenches repaired and five batteries of specialist siege guns brought up to the first one. They opened fire on the nearest lunette, an arrowhead-shaped fieldwork projecting from the fortress's outer wall, and soon forced its abandonment by the garrison.

Next the Finkmatt Barracks, one of the largest billets in the fortress, was destroyed by artillery fire. By September 14th two more lunettes had been reached by sap trenches, and the two nearest bastions were shelled by siege guns. Mortar batteries were brought in even closer, and their combined weight of fire prevented the garrison from moving in daylight.

Still, the French managed to bring mortars up to the lunettes for counter-battery fire and for a week and a half the last classic siege raged on, until the bastions were breached by shell fire. The first bastion fell on the 24th, after its eastern face had been hit by 600 rounds. The second fell two days later when its western face was breached by 467 rounds, opening a major gap in the inner wall some 36 feet across.

On September 27th General Jean Uhrich finally relented and ordered a white flag run up the cathedral's spire. Negotiations were quickly opened and by 2:00AM the capitulation on Sedan conditions was signed. The siege ended when 500 officers and 17,000 enlisted men, virtually the entire active-duty force, marched into captivity. After they pledged not to take any further part in the war, the *Garde Mobile* contingents were paroled to return home.

In addition to the prisoners, the Germans netted 1,200 artillery pieces, some 200,000 Chassepot rifles and all the money still in the central bank. More importantly, the surrender opened an additional rail line to move supplies and freed up the investing corps to be used elsewhere. And while the fall of Toul had been an annoyance to the Government of National Defence, Strasbourg would be a serious blow.

Paris: The Siege Intensifies

On September 19th, the day before the city's investment began, General Trochu lead the Paris garrison in its attempted sortie. They attacked Crown

Prince Friedrich Wilhelm's army at Châtillon, just south of the Vanves fortress, and were it not for the fortress' guns then the rout they suffered could have easily turned into the destruction and surrender of the entire column.

Nothing went right, and the greatest problem was the nearly total absence of discipline among the newest *Garde Mobile* recruits. A British observer, a lowly coachman who ran a local stable, noted: "Why, sir, giving them fellows Chassepots is much like giving watches to naked savages." And it so proved, with many of the rifles being thrown away without even being fired.

Of course the defeated, along with their allies and sympathizers in the Paris Clubs, had a ready explanation for what happened. They had been incompetently lead by none other than Trochu himself. By September 21st this accusation had grown into a rumor that the Paris Government would capitulate and the next day a massive demonstration closed in on the Hôtel de Ville to angrily demand an answer.

On the 23rd, the same day as the surrender of Toul, Mayor Emmanuel Arago issued a public proclamation repudiating the rumors and restating Jules Favre's famous dispatch that not "an inch of her soil or a stone of her fortresses" would be yielded to the enemy. This kept the extremists and the mobs at bay, though not for long. Trochu planned a new sortie, and this time he would be smart enough to allow another general to lead it.

General Joseph Vinoy's Thirteenth Corps began operations early on the morning of September 30th, at several points along the southern investment line. With supporting fire from the nearby forts and a few field batteries, infantry brigades actually broke through the investment line to L'Hay and Choisy le Roi, both to the east of Châtillon. They got as far south as Chevilly and Thiais, where they were beyond the range of the fortress guns and driven back by strong counterattacks.

Casualties were heavy, including General Pierre-Victor Guilhem, who died leading a charge at Chevilly. The National Government tried to cover over the disaster by claiming they had inflicted at least as many casualties on the Germans as they received. Then everyone forgot about it as far worse news reached Paris on October 1st: Toul and Strasbourg had fallen. In the midst of the funeral mourning at the Statue of Strasbourg, the Government of National Defence realized it had to do something dramatic to raise the hopes of its citizens. What it ended up staging was a stunt which would only prolong the war.

Le Grand Escapade

The siege had not even lasted a week when, on the morning of September 23rd, Paris launched its first balloon. The *Neptune* was the handiwork of Félix Tournachon, the celebrity showman-turned-aeronaut with the stage name of Nadar. As commander of the brand new Balloon Corps, he attended the launch ceremony at Montmartre, the tallest hill in the Paris environs (432 feet). He did so with the elderly Adelaide de Montgolfier, the last surviving child of the Montgolfier brothers (Joseph and Jacques), who launched the first balloon some 87 years earlier, and she sent out the first air-mail letter from the city.

The *Neptune* carried a total of 200 pounds of mail, all on the thin paper that will become an enduring tradition for air-mail letters. Later balloons would quickly double the payload to 450 pounds, roughly 200 kilograms, plus the aeronaut/pilot. A total of 54 balloons would be released from Paris during the siege, and by far the most famous would be the *Armand Barbès* – not because of the mail it carried, but its passengers: Leon Michel Gambetta and his secretary Eugène Spuller.

Approximately seven years earlier Jules Verne published his first science-fiction novella, *Five Weeks in a Balloon*. It is not known if it served as the inspiration for the stunt, or if Verne even attended the launch, but Victor Hugo did and described the October 7th event as a light-hearted, magnificent morale booster for the beleaguered city. Even if Verne had not been involved, it still felt like a Vernian adventure which offered a chance to change the fortunes of the war.

Launched with the *George Sand*, the *Barbès* eventually landed near Tours, about 120 miles southwest of Paris and well beyond any German-occupied territory. The *Sand*, carrying two American diplomats who would negotiate arms purchases for the new French republic in the United States, drifted to the north and came down near the Channel Coast.

But it was Gambetta's escape that would gain the most notoriety and be treated as a major victory over the Germans. He now became one of only two major figures in the Government of National Defence working outside of Paris, the other being Louise Adolphe Thiers, still on his tour of other European capitals with the bizarrely surreal hope of gaining allies for France.

Proclaimed Dictator shortly after his arrival, Gambetta launched himself energetically at the task of raising the new armies his government needed to win the war. While many of his cohorts treated General Bourbaki rather coolly – after all he had been an imperial favorite – Gambetta welcomed him enthusiastically. As did the former engineer he soon appointed War Minister, Charles Louis de Freycinet.

Though 20 years older than the new Dictator of France, de Freycinet would prove equally as energetic to the task of raising those new armies, the first of which they designated the "Army of the Loire" and assigned Bourbaki to command. And this new army could not possibly take to the field soon enough.

Two days after Gambetta's Vernian arrival, on October 9th, Moltke sends the First Bavarian Corps under Baron von der Tann due south from Paris. Its position on the investment line replaced by the Prussian Landwehr divisions from Strasbourg, the Corps is accompanied by the 2nd and 4th Cavalry Divisions on its flanks. The force meets little opposition until just short of Artenay, on the road to Orléans.

There it encounters the Fifteenth Corps from the new-formed Army, along with a sizeable unit of Francs-Tireur irregulars. On October 10th, and in spite of sharp attacks by the irregulars, the French retreat from Artenay. They lose almost 1,000 prisoners and suffer nearly that number killed and wounded. On the following day the Bavarians advance on the one-time medieval capital of France, Orléans, and capture it after bitter fighting. The German armies are no longer a static force.

The Rise of the Francs-Tireurs

With the near-complete disappearance of the regular French armies from the field, a new form of combatants tried to take their place: the Francs-Tireurs. Roughly translated as the French Marksmen or Fencers – not as the French Terrors as they were more popularly defined – they were France's version of the Spanish guerrillas they encountered some 62 years earlier in the Peninsular War.

They made their first appearances shortly after the surrender of the "Army of Châlons" at Sedan. Initially, the Germans treated them as a nuisance and the French population as heroes. The remaining French military officers wished they did not have to deal with them at all, for they were truly irregular in every sense of the word.

Some were retired French soldiers and sailors who answered the call of their country, but chose not to re-enlist in the regular army. Others were foreigners who answered the call to adventure. Among them was the future British Field Marshal Horatio Herbert Kitchener, who took leave from the Royal Military Academy but never saw combat.

Still other foreigners were stimulated by vengeance, and revolutionary fervor. Among the former was the commander of the Francs-Tireurs at

Artenay, a Polish exile known only as Lipowski. And in the latter was the most famous celebrity revolutionary of the day: Giuseppe Garibaldi and his son, Ricciotti. Now 63 and suffering from gout, he came to aid the very country which had tried to kill him only a few years earlier.

If anything, the French Tireur units were even more varied than the foreign ones. The force commanded by Colonel de Cathelineau were Royalist Bretons, Colonel de Charette lead Papal Zouaves from the Rome garrison and even the staff of the former Imperial stables formed a cavalry squadron.

At the extreme other end of the spectrum were the Communist bands operating along the Seine River. Mikhail Bakunin's scratch force fought not the Germans, who would have gladly executed him, but the Government of National Defence. And then there were all the units in between, some of whom fought for their country but most took it as an excuse for an adventurous romp, or banditry.

There were Francs-Tireur units who dressed in the plumed hats, capes and fancy riding boots of Alexandre Dumas' *The Three Musketeers*, taking the "fencing" translation literally. Others dressed as Argentine gauchos, American cowboys and Algerian tribesmen. The quality of their efforts ranged from comic opera buffoonery to irritating interdiction, and occasionally reached the level of nasty surprise. Unfortunately, most of their efforts resulted in a painful increase in lawlessness across the country.

Painful to the civilians they pillaged, painful to the local authorities who often turned to the occupying German forces for assistance, and eventually painful to Gambetta and the other members of the new republic who once advocated the wholesale arming of the civil population.

It had been hoped the Francs-Tireurs would be the answer to the Uhlans. The problem was most did not have the skills, the discipline, the command structure or understanding of then-modern cavalry tactics to be anywhere as effective as the German horsemen. Part of the problem lay in the near-total lack of organization as most of the units were being formed. Trying to fit them later into the structures of the new armies mostly resulted in failure. Another part of the problem lay in pre-war Imperial France where guns were tightly controlled. Under Napoleon III only the military, police and aristocracy were allowed to possess or have knowledge of firearms. For many Francs-Tireurs the "marksmen" part of their title was just as fanciful as those who dressed as musketeers and thought of themselves as "fencers."

Had they been able to carry out reconnaissance sorties, behind-the-lines interdiction and provide some of the roles of cavalry or mounted infantry, *then* the Francs-Tireurs might have become a serious problem for Moltke and his armies. Instead, they remained an irritation which only infrequently rose to the level of shock.

Strangers in a Strange Land

On the same day as Gambetta's balloon escapade, October 7th, Bazaine made his final major attempt at breaking the Metz investment. Starting back on October 1st, daily skirmishes on both banks of the Moselle pushed back the outposts of Prince Friedrich Karl's army and new pontoon bridges were built behind Fort St. Julien and extended to Chambière Island in the Moselle.

When it finally started, the breakout quickly became a corps-level operation with three French corps moving north on an attempted drive to Thionville. They were opposed by four German corps, most of Friedrich Karl's command, which could have developed into a serious situation had Bazaine committed the rest of his army to an attack somewhere else on the investment line.

However, no other operations materialized and by the end of the day most of the territory gained by the advance had been won back by the Germans. All except the Landonchamps Château, where many of the casualties on both sides were suffered. The following morning began with heavy artillery bombardments, and the strong indication the French would renew the operation – until the rains came.

By the end of October 8th, the final breakout attempt had devolved to a gunners' duel which would continue for several more days. On October 10th Bazaine held a council of war with his senior officers to decide the future of their army. The France that existed now was not the France which sent them to war. The Government of National Defence had made repeated statements supporting the besieged army, but had so far done nothing to relieve it.

With the largest French Army still in existence under his command, Bazaine was determined to play a major role in post-war France, one that did not include the present republican government. Virtually all the officers at the council wanted a monarchy. In spite of Empress Eugénie's rejection of Regnier's scheme there was still the Prince Imperial, and Prince Louis Napoleon still sat in exile in Florence.

The council decided that if a post-war monarchy was to be established, whether Napoleonic, Bourbonist or even Orléanist, then their army had to both remain intact and remain neutral until the war ended. Without bothering to inform the current government, Bazaine sent an emissary to

Versailles, where the Germans had recently moved their headquarters, to negotiate a free exit for the army from Metz. But Moltke and Bismarck refused; they did not feel they could trust a French Army to remain neutral and, anyway, they were too busy winning to accept anything less than complete surrender.

The Mounting Toll

With the capitulation of Toul and Strasbourg, more than just infantry divisions were freed up for duties elsewhere. On October 11th the siege guns from Toul, along with ten French mortars taken in the early battles as war prizes, arrived by railroad at Soissons. About 30 miles northwest of Reims, the fortress had initially been bypassed by the German armies as they raced to invest Paris.

Until October 6th only a small observation force had been left to watch it. Then reinforcements arrived, and with the appearance of the siege guns and several Field-Pioneer companies, the formal bombardment started on the morning of October 12th and lasted three days.

The heavy fire opened a break in the fortress' south wall and by 8:00PM on October 15th its commander opened surrender negotiations. While Bazaine, for the time being refused them, Soissons accepted the Sedan terms of surrender. The following day the garrison of 3,800 marched into captivity while 1,000 *Garde Mobiles* were paroled back to their homes. War prizes included 128 fortress guns, an armory of 8,000 small arms and large stores of provisions which the Germans quickly distributed to their forces.

More importantly, the capitulation of Soissons opened rail lines from Reims to Paris. Considerably easing the supply problems for the investing armies around it, whose situation would improve even more two days later with the seizure of Châteaudun, this time some 30 miles northwest of Orléans. This victory finished the opening of the Loire Valley to the German armies. The principal granary of France, its harvests of food grains and fruits were largely completed and quickly seized by the Bavarian Corps holding the area.

At the same time the Saxon cavalry division, supported by other units from Crown Prince Friedrich August's army, took on the *Garde Mobiles* and Francs-Tireurs operating north of Paris. They pushed them all the way back to Amiens on the Somme River though, for the moment, no farther. They took hundreds of prisoners, but harassment activity hardly diminished as the principal Tireur company the Saxons faced were Colonel de

Cathelineau's Bretons.

In Paris the besieged forces were hardly inactive, though until the 21st they would not again be taking the offensive. A week before that, on October 13th, they placated extremist demands for action with the first wanton act of revolutionary destruction, the shelling of Napoleon III's Saint Cloud palace.

Originally a large château purchased by Louis XIV, the "Sun King" who built Versailles, he greatly added to it and gave it to his younger brother as a home. For some 200 years it had been an intimate part of French history. It survived repeated wars and revolutions, but not this time. At 1:00PM the garrison at Fort Valérien, some 2½ miles north of Saint Cloud, began firing mortar grenades at the palace.

After these repeatedly fell short they resorted to cannons, and one of the first shells set fire to the right wing. Prussian officers, realizing they had little in the way of fire fighting gear, ordered their men to rescue what they could in the way of historic artifacts and furnishings. Unfortunately the bombardment continued and little could be saved apart from some paintings and, ironically, the ornate table on which Napoleon III signed the declaration of war barely three months earlier.

What the artillery did not destroy the fires did, fanned as they were by high winds. By nightfall the palace had become a red glow on the horizon, with a black pall of smoke extending over the city. At first the Paris newspapers accused the Germans of the destruction. Later, many congratulated themselves for destroying a famous landmark of the hated Napoleonic Empire. And Trochu, who should have punished those at Fort Valérien for the wanton act, had a bigger problem to deal with: how to turn a disastrous sortie southwest of Paris, once again in the Châtillon region, into a success.

He and General Vinoy, the corps commander responsible for the attempt, decided to call it a "reconnaissance on a grand scale" and for a time they held Bagneux, the village next to Châtillon. They even managed to take a hundred Bavarian prisoners but again, they lost the senior field commander, Comte Picot de Dampierre, in the village assault.

Trochu barely had time to bury the Count before he planned and launched a much larger offensive. This time with Ducrot's Corps against the Prussian divisions encamped between St. Germain-on-Laye and Versailles. The attack started on the morning of October 21st with a bombardment from Fort Valérien and 14 batteries of field guns.

The initially outnumbered Prussians, who possessed only two batteries of field guns, fell back while the French celebrated the capture of the historic Malmaison and pushed as far as the village of Bougival, the farthest point west any breakout attempt would reach. The counter thrust came with two veteran divisions, the 9th and 10th Prussian from Crown Prince Friedrich Wilhelm's Third Army, attacking Ducrot's Corps all along its line of advance.

By nightfall the French had retired, or been driven out of, almost all their gains. They left approximately 500 dead, the Prussians suffered 400, and lost another 120 as prisoners. The response from the Paris government was to declare another victory, place orders with the foundries inside the city for hundreds more Mitrailleuse guns and field artillery pieces, and to plan another sortie.

On the night of October 27th several battalions of National Guard and *Garde Mobiles* were assembled on the northeast side of Paris. Their objective, laying just within artillery range of Forts Aubervilliers and De l'Est, was town of Le Bourget. The government planned it as, hopefully, another victory. Though by then a far greater disaster was coming to its inevitable conclusion, to the east.

The Last Imperial Surrender

Marshal Francois Achille Bazaine held what would be his last council of war on October 24th. Once again he refused to accept a surrender on Sedan conditions and insisted that his army be allowed a free exit from Metz. He did add the offer to embark the army to Algeria for the duration of the war. But questions over whether the French Navy, as a member of the Government of National Defence, would carry out the transfer were left unanswered.

The Navy itself was still in service on the North Sea; by October its frigate squadron had captured over 20 German merchantmen. And in that month Admiral Bouet-Willaumez had used a flotilla of shallow-draft ironclads to carry out the bombardment of Kolberg and other Baltic Sea ports. And his flagship had been none other than the U.S.-built *Dunderberg*, now renamed *Rochambeau*.

Because of these operations and the unanswered questions, the Germans found it easy to reject the offer. They also knew, through the willing surrender of soldiers from Metz, that the distribution of food stores had ended four days earlier. To subsist the army resorted to slaughtering a thousand horses a day and shortages of bread and salt were severe. They now knew it would only be a matter of time.

It would take just another three days before conditions compelled Bazaine to accept the Sedan Terms of surrender. He reasoned that, if he were going to play a significant role in post-war France then his army could not be ravaged by famine and disease. And then there were his corps commanders, like Canrobert, who had demanded for some time that he put an end to the sufferings of the troops and civilians.

On the same night Trochu prepared for the assault on Le Bourget, Bazaine signed the surrender protocol, which would take effect on 10:00ᴀᴍ, October 29th. After 72 days of siege operations, and suffering some 5,750 casualties, Prince Friedrich Karl finally had the victory Moltke promised him, and would immortalize him: the largest surrender of a field army in military history.

In all five corps, containing 21 divisions, not all of which were at full-strength but nonetheless had a total of 173,000 officers and men. Of these nearly 20,000 were so ill they would have to remain in the temporary hospitals around Metz until well enough to make the journey to the camps in the Saar and the Bavarian Palatinate.

In addition to the notorious, and soon to be infamous, Marshal Bazaine, there came an illustrious roll call of other French generals. Marshal Canrobert, Marshal Leboeuf, Comte de Ladmirault, Comte de Lorencez, General Frossard and over 90 other flag-ranked officers marched into captivity. And one who did not was General Georges Ernest Boulanger, who escaped the initial investment.

Among the war prizes were 56 imperial eagles (ceremonial unit standards), 876 fortress guns, 622 field guns, 72 Mitrailleuse guns and over 260,000 small arms. Not until the 20th Century, not until its second global conflict, would the surrender of a field army surpass the scope of this one.

With the capitulation of Metz the professional French Army ceased to exist. Even with the *levées* forced on the civil population and the Francs-Tireur volunteers there would not be enough men to replace those who had been killed or were now in German prison camps. And the capitulation unleashed something far worse for France.

The protocol had scarcely been signed when Moltke issued orders redistributing the investing army. Its First, Seventh and Eighth Corps, together with the 3rd Cavalry Division, were reconstituted as the First Army under Edwin von Manteuffel. The Second, Third, Ninth and Tenth Corps, with the 1st Cavalry Division were returned to Friedrich Karl as the Second Army.

Minus one division left to garrison Metz, the First Army would move north to begin siege operations against Thionville and Montmédy. Once these were finished, Manteuffel would move against the new army being assembled in northern France. Friedrich Karl would take the Second Army to the southwest, into the middle Loire valley where it would take on

Gambetta's "Army of the Loire."

The vulnerable period of the German armies as a largely static force had ended. From now on they would be far more mobile. They would return to the offensive, and eventually start hunting down the citizen armies the Government of National Defence feverishly threw into the field.

The Shockwaves

As with the news of previous disasters, at first the fall of Metz was not believed. Though this time the bearers of the bad news were attacked with particular vehemence. In Paris the rabble-rousing extremist Felix Pyat had his offices attacked by a mob when his journal *Combat* published the first reports of the fall. The Paris government responded by arresting him.

At Tours Gambetta reportedly demanded the heads of those spreading the rumors then, after the disaster had been confirmed, de Freycinet wanted to put a price on Bazaine's head for his treachery. Slowly realizing this would serve no purpose, they instead pushed the new commander of the "Army of the Loire," Crimean War-veteran Claude d'Aurelle de Paladines, to attack the Bavarian Corps at Orléans before Friedrich Karl's army could arrive in the area.

Back in Paris, the local government and civil population still did not believe Metz had surrendered until October 30th, when they were hit with a triple disaster. On that day Louise Thiers arrived in the city on a safe-conduct pass from Bismarck after finishing his tour of neutral European countries. He verified and brought detailed reports on Bazaine's surrender. On the same day the government's *Journal Officiel* admitted that Le Bourget, a town of actually little tactical value to the Paris garrison, had been retaken by the Germans.

And the third disaster to befall the French that day were the results of Thiers' original mission. While he had been courteously greeted by the foreign governments, he received rather thin sympathy for France's plight, and no hope for help, other than assistance in negotiating an armistice.

France was on its own, it had lost its last professional army, and the German armies were increasingly free to operate wherever they wanted. Despair and insurrection were on the wind. And the bitterest phase of the war was about to begin.

Chapter XIX: War to the Knife

"To lead an uninstructed people to war is
to throw them away."
-Confucius (c.551 - c.479B.C.)

Fanaticism and Amateurs

GUERRE À OUTRANCÉ. Guerra y Cuchillo. The phrases were first coined back in the Napoleonic Era, and whether French or Spanish they meant the same thing: "war to the extreme," "war to the death," "war to the knife..." And with disappearance of the professional armies from the order of battle, the war effort would now be conducted by amateurs and fanatics of all kinds.

There were still some professional officers and skilled enlisted men. But generals like Trochu, Ducrot, Bourbaki and Boulanger were few and far between. Increasingly Gambetta and de Freycinet had to turn to elderly veterans from Crimea and the decades-long colonial wars in China and North Africa.

Generals d'Aurelle de Paladines and Charles des Pallières both fought in the Crimean War. General Antoine Chanzy fought in Algeria and would soon take command of the Loire Army's Sixteenth Corps. And General Louis Léon Faidherbe had been the Military Governor of Tunisia and now commanded the "Army of the North," a force being assembled from *Garde Mobiles* units in Picardy, Champagne and Normandy and other provinces to the west and north of Paris.

And while these generals would on occasion produce some interesting results, they knew the impossible was being asked of them by the new republican government. Trying to mold partly-trained reservists and raw recruits into a disciplined fighting force in a matter of weeks, later just days, spoke of desperation and foreshadowed disaster. And most were not shy about arguing this with their civilian leaders.

Initially given command of the "Army of the Loire," Bourbaki fought so strenuously with Gambetta over its premature deployment that he was eventually demoted to corps command and des Paladines advanced to replace him. At least this gave the army a chance for some extra training.

Trochu, as with most of the Paris government leaders, found himself constantly being second-guessed by "experts" from every quarter. Like most of the other commanders he also had to deal with insubordination and insurrection. Both the shelling of Saint Cloud and the storming of Le Bourget were done without his knowledge. However, to punish the officers responsible would have invited an uprising – which he had to deal with soon after the triple defeats had been announced.

Paris in Revolt

In addition to confirming the fall of Metz and the sad results of his own diplomatic efforts, Thiers also brought with him something the radicals found disturbing: the hint of a negotiated armistice. Their suspicions aroused, and the bitterness of the defeats still fresh on their minds, it only took the radicals and agitators a day to organize a mob that stormed the Hôtel de Ville while the government sat in session.

For most of October 31st Trochu, Mayor Arago, Louis Picard, Jules Favre and Jules Ferry were imprisoned in city hall as the mob leaders demanded a city-wide vote to establish a commune, which they firmly felt could better govern and defend Paris. Not until nearly midnight, when Ferry arrived with the new Prefect of Police, Edmond Adam, and Ducrot was reported on his way with 10,000 *Mobiles*, did the mob leaders decide to negotiate.

The most radical leaders, Flourens, Blanqui and Delescluze, wanted a vote the next day on establishing a Commune. Only at 3:00AM, when Ducrot did indeed arrive with several battalions for Trochu to review, did the mob disperse – with the promise that the insurrection was not over.

The next day, November 1st, the city awoke to find itself plastered with notices and proclamations. From the Mayor, the Minister of Public Works and other officials came the announcement of a municipal vote, at first acceding to the extremist demands for the election of Communard-style leaders. Then, later in the day Favre replaces these with notices of a much simpler vote to be held on November 3rd on whether the population wanted immediate elections for all government and municipal posts.

The extremists, many of whom are arrested or flee, smell the old Napoleonic trick of a plebiscite. Which, according to the joke of the day, was a Latin word meaning "yes" to whatever the government wanted. They hang counter proclamations demanding elections to establish their commune and an end to anymore negotiations with the Germans.

Ironically enough, all this takes place on the same day Louise Thiers is spirited out of Paris to conduct negotiations with Bismarck. Thiers is as ignorant of the events taking place inside Paris as the radicals are of his activities at Versailles. The one person who does know about everything is Bismarck. And like any good poker player, he keeps his opponent in the dark.

The German coalition headquarters knows what is going on in Paris, not just through its chain of outposts and observation balloons, which are flown whenever the weather permits, but by their tiny contingent of spies. Far smaller than the number of innocents accused of being German spies, they scarcely have to practice the subtle arts of espionage to gain the wealth of information they send to the Prussian and other German governments. All they have to do is read the plentiful newspapers, which openly report on military secrets, or just read what is hanging on the walls. In a city of growing shortages there would be no lack of paper, ink or paste to hang notices.

And Bismarck has still one further source of information unavailable to Thiers, and continually discounted by Gambetta: reports from the rest of France of the breakdown in government authority. A week earlier, on October 24th, the siege of Schlettstadt ended. One of the last towns in Alsace Province to be held by the French, its commander begged the Germans to take immediate possession of the town as both the garrison, mostly *Garde Mobiles*, and the civilians were rioting and had even set fire to the fortress' powder magazine.

Bismarck also knew of the problems the Government of National Defence was having with many Francs-Tireur units, especially with those commanded by Garibaldi and Bakunin, and its singular lack of success in gaining any allies in the rest of Europe. Still, during the opening negotiations he had been prepared to be more generous, allowing the resupply of Paris during the armistice and perhaps allowing elections in the Alsace and Lorraine.

Then came the news from Paris and the confusing elections over who and what kind of government would be in charge. For Moltke and Bismarck, who were in agreement this time, and Wilhelm I this was too much. To them if a government could not control it citizens then it could not be stable enough to continue negotiations, and the talks with Thiers ended on November 3rd with an ultimatum from Bismarck. At the same time the current Paris government was approved by voters with a ratio of nine to one.

The ultimatum, agreed to by all members of the German coalition, demanded a reparation of three billion francs and the Alsace for the war to end immediately. If it were to continue until the fall of Paris then the reparation would be five billion francs and both the Alsace and the northern half of Lorraine. For there to be a cease-fire and a resupply of Paris than at least one of its main forts would have to be surrendered.

Thiers discussed the ultimatum with Favre and General Ducrot in a ruined no-man's land between the German and French lines. Before returning to Versailles – it was now too dangerous for Thiers to enter Paris – he urged acceptance of the terms for an immediate end. But, on November 5th another envoy came to Versailles to report the ultimatum had been rejected. The revolt, for the moment, was suppressed and the war would continue.

Old Armies on New Maneuvers

Grateful at being freed from siege duty around Metz for nearly two and a half months, the armies of Friedrich Karl and Manteuffel quickly moved out on their new assignments. The Second Army advanced as quickly as it could toward the Loire Valley to reinforce von der Tann's Bavarian Corps in Orléans. Using his cavalry divisions on extensive reconnaissance sorties revealed at least two French Corps concentrating against his rather thinly-held positions. Friedrich Karl promised to get there with all possible speed, but the roads he used grew poor as the activities of local Francs-Tireurs increased.

Manteuffel's First Army changed its duties from one large siege to several smaller ones. Divisions were assigned to the investments of Thionville and Mézières, smaller units were detached to Verdun, Breisach and La Fère. All had been at least under observation since the fall of Sedan. Now, formal sieges either began or were heavily reinforced. And the first to capitulate had proven the most troublesome.

Before the disasters of Metz and Sedan, Verdun had only a small garrison of roughly 2,000 men. However, with stragglers and escapees from the two imperial armies that had grown to over 6,000 by the time its formal investment commenced at the end of September. A duel between the fortress' guns and field artillery proved completely ineffective, despite the advantageous positions of Prussian batteries on the surrounding heights.

On October 9th siege guns via Toul were brought in, though not until the morning of the 13th did the duel begin between the fortress and the new batteries on the Hayvaux Slope to the west and Mont St. Michel to the northeast. A three-day engagement followed in which the fortress knocked out 15 German guns and received little appreciable damage. Then, on the night of October 19th and again on the 28th, the Verdun garrison conducted sorties against both locations. They not only spiked still more guns but, on the later date, they destroyed breastworks and gun shelters at Mont St. Michel.

With the end of the Metz investment Manteuffel substantially increased the forces around Verdun. Five infantry battalions, extra artillery and field-pioneer companies to construct a siege gun park arrived by the beginning of November. As they prepared for a heavier, sustained, bombardment negotiations were opened and, as the garrison had no hope for relief, they surrendered on November 8th. The Germans took possession the next day with the promise that the war matériel in the fortress would be returned at the end of hostilities.

The following day, November 10th, the Breisach Fortress surrendered on Sedan Terms to the newly reinforced investing forces. Located on the Rhine some 35 miles due south of Strasbourg, it had been the last major point of resistance in the Alsace, and the very last impedance to traffic crossing the Rhine. With its capitulation and Verdun's, the problem of supplying its increasingly active armies had considerably eased for the German coalition.

The War Goes Global, Sort Of...

Apart from the blockade and bombardment operations on the Baltic and North Seas, there had been no other naval operations since the start of the war. Prussia, the only German state with any sizable navy, kept most of its fleet safely inside its ports, protected by newly-designed Krupp shore batteries.

Most, but not all. Several gunboats were on far-flung patrols across the world in July. At their next ports-of-call, they received news that hostilities had started, and orders to get all German merchantmen in their areas to the nearest safe ports. In the Caribbean the Prussian gunboat *Meteor* saw to it that local German shipping made it to either U.S. ports, or Havana Harbor in Spain's Cuba colony.

On November 8th the French colonial gunboat *Bouvet* arrived at the harbor entrance to challenge the *Meteor* to combat – after taking several hours to steam up, and for a crowd to gather on the Morro Heights and the Punta just outside of the city to watch the coming spectacle. Following then-international law the two ships proceeded beyond the three-mile limit before turning to engage each other.

By all accounts a spirited battle followed in which the ships continually circled each other, firing repeatedly but to little effect. Until, more than a hour later, the *Meteor* finishes the duel with a shot through the *Bouvet*'s boiler. The French ship immediately went dead in the water, and perhaps in a later age would have been finished off with torpedoes.

But such weapons were then still under development, the spar torpedoes of the American Civil War had proven too dangerous for continued use, and the Prussians decided honor had been served by the crippling shot. By at least one account they offered help to the drifting vessel, until the *Bouvet* made sail and headed for another Spanish port farther down the coast while the *Meteor* returned in triumph to Havana.

Later in the month, and much farther afield, the French gunboat *Dupleix* challenged the German ship *Hertha*, which had sought sanctuary in the port of Nagasaki, on the western coast of Kyushu Island. However, this time there would be no battle as the Japanese government decided to forbid it.

This would prove to be the conclusion of active naval operations for the Franco-Prussian War. The coming winter made continuing the blockade on the Baltic and North Seas extremely trying. And dispatch boats soon came with orders from the new Minister of the Marine (Navy), Admiral Fourichon, for the French ships to return to port so their sailors and marines could be used to create new regiments for Gambetta's armies.

Some ships continued with the unglamorous but vital task of protecting French ports and sea lanes – not that the Prussians ever threatened then, though it did mean French credit did not suffer unduly during the war, and supplies of weapons and other matérial flowed in without hindrance.

The Second Battle of Orléans

While his army had been defeated in the initial battles for Orléans, General d'Aurelle de Paladines soon realized if he was to accomplish anything, it would have to be before Friedrich Karl arrived with his army. Gambetta and de Freycinet had managed to create a miracle, marshaling nearly 600,000 men under arms. Of that number nearly 250,000 were locked up in Paris and the rest were scattered across southern and western France. The roughly 70,000 troops in the Fifteenth and Sixteenth Corps of de Paladines' "Army of the Loire" marked the largest concentration of French forces outside of Paris, and among the best trained.

For the moment it outnumbered the German forces in the area by over three to one, and that moment would soon pass. Already, the vanguard formations of Friedrich Karl's Second Army had reached Troyes, under good conditions just a three-days' march to the east. De Paladines immediately ordered the Fifteenth Corps to advance from Meung, while the Sixteenth moved from Ouzouer, toward Orléans.

Both towns were west of the city which, during the night of November 8th, von der Tann withdrew all his forces from, except for a small detachment of volunteers who stayed to tend the wounded in the field hospital. A month earlier the principal bridges across the Loire and Loiret Rivers were mined by von der Tann, who wisely foresaw he might have to evacuate the city. After they had been blown French movements were considerably restricted, and the Bavarians had fallen back to the forest between Château Montpipeau and Rosières, with the village of Coulmiers in front of the forest's borders.

Von der Tann again chose wisely, this was the one area of clear ground in a heavily forested region. He had hoped it would allow him to use his strong artillery and cavalry forces, but then the unexpected happened. The near-constant rains had made the ground so soft that the Krupp-designed percussion-fused shells did not always detonate, and the French possessed rather more cavalry than expected.

A continual series of sharp, day-long fights ensued as the Bavarian Corps retreated from its positions around Coulmiers, from Baccon to La Rivière, from Préfort to Renardière to Montpipeau and finally to Artenay on their left wing. The fall backs were usually covered by artillery and cavalry screens, usually done in good order by battalion or brigade formation.

Apart from an ammunition supply column overtaken by French cavalry, and the patients and staff in the Orléans hospital, von der Tann had carried off an almost textbook-perfect example of a fighting retreat. The French would claim they had routed the Germans and inflicted heavy losses. From the Mediterranean coast to Normandy, and especially in Paris, they were almost delirious with joy, and technically it was a victory.

More than three months after Saarbrücken the French had their second victory, and this would be the only success they would enjoy in a corps-level engagement. Ironically it also mirrored the German victories around Metz in mid-August; they took the contested territory but suffered almost twice as many killed and wounded: approximately 1,600 versus 800 casualties.

And the fighting retreat continued the next day, November 10th, with the Bavarians striking camp and falling back to Toury, about a dozen miles due north. There it finally got reinforced when the 22nd Division from Friedrich Wilhelm's Third Army out of Chartres deployed to nearby Janville. Here they prepared for the French to arrive. But, already de Paladines had broken off the pursuit and started concentrating his troops around Orléans for the expected attack by the approaching Second Army.

Paris Separates from Reality

News of the Orléans victory did not reach the capital until November 14th when, according to the apocryphal legend, a carrier pigeon covered in blood arrived with the message from Gambetta announcing it. The news marked a watershed in the behavior of the city's civil population as they became fervently, fanatically, convinced of their coming triumph.

From this point on they, and the Paris Press, treated every defeat as a victory, or at worst a blessing in disguise. And every real victory, no matter how small, was the harbinger of the final defeat of the Prussians. Anyone who had earlier advocated an armistice or peace negotiations was lucky to get away with just ridicule and insults. Many were accused of being a traitor, a charge now being used heavily though not frivolously, for it always carried with it the threat of arrest, or summary street justice.

The later news of Artenay's recapture, won in a "pitched battle" after the Bavarians withdrew from it, served only to fuel the city-wide delirium to new heights. Much-delayed reports of Verdun's spirited defence meant the fortress city was unassailable; in fact it had already fallen. General Bourbaki's new command, the "Army of the North," had lifted the siege of Amiens, a city about 70 miles due north of Paris. In reality it would fall less than three days later after a series of hard battles and heavy artillery fire broke the resolve of the defending National Guard and *Garde Mobiles*. No one would report many threw down their weapons and fled, forcing the rest of Bourbaki's army to retire from the city.

What the press did report were stories of how King Wilhelm, then Bismarck, had gone insane and went back to Berlin in that newly-invented restraint system, the straightjacket. After Queen Victoria declined to send aid she was accused of being a German sympathizer, deposed in a popular uprising and soon an army of British chartists and socialists would be arriving to lift the siege.

When not conjuring up imaginary foreign armies to aid them, and Garibaldi's activities in southeastern France provided yet another source for them, the press created new French armies. A private letter, arriving via another pigeon, mentioned "an army in the south." In days this became the "Army of the South" and got added to the surreal list of actual and imagined armies: the "Army of the Loire," "Army of Lyons," "Army of Brittany" and the "Army of Normandy."

Even more surreal were the prophecies that began appearing in several papers following the recapture of Orléans. For them all the general line went: did not Joan of Arc win her first victory against the British in Orléans some four and a half centuries earlier? Did that not lead to the downfall of British domination of France during the Hundred Years War? Should we now not expect the same and soon be delivered from Prussian/German oppression?

Of course the prophetic articles failed to mention that it took another 24 years after the Maid of Orléans' first victory for the war to end with the British driven back to the tiny enclave of Pas de Calais. Yet they no more ignored reality than the legions of "experts" and "inventors" who seemingly flooded every government office in Paris from the Barricades Commission, Henri Rochefort's office, to the Ministry of War, where one staffer wondered if they were not all doctors at Charenton, then a famous insane asylum near the fortress (technically the French called it a "booby hatch").

There were enough lunatic schemes to write a book about them on their own. And among the Mitrailleuse guns hidden in a calliope – it would play Schubert or Wagner to lure the Germans out to their deaths – and steam-powered rams to run down their infantry, the most impossible serves the best example as to how far from reality the population had moved.

Basically a 19th Century version of a Doomsday Weapon, though it is very likely neither its "inventor" nor anyone else who studied the outrageous idea understood the physics that would make it so dangerous. The idea was to fabricate an iron disc 15 miles in diameter and float it over to Versailles Palace by balloons. Then, it would be released from an altitude of one mile and its ten million ton deadweight – at least this part had been accurately calculated – would crush the German headquarters and army underneath it.

The problems with this were...carrying an average payload of around 500 pounds, plus an aeronaut/pilot, it would have required around 40 *million* balloons to lift the disc. The entire population of France, including children, would not have provided enough aeronauts, or built all those balloons, or mined all the iron ore. *If* it had been constructed and lifted then the Doomsday Physics would have set in.

Once airborne the Germans would have easily spotted it, though it would be impossible to outrun the annihilating effects. If dropped from a one mile height it would quickly reach a terminal velocity of 60 miles per hour. From here on the disc would have acted as a giant air piston; the atmosphere under it could not possibly move out of the way fast enough not to be compressed and "squeezed" out.

At the altitude of a quarter of a mile the area of the disc would be 15 times the size of the gap; the compression effects would generate a horizontal wind around its perimeter of 900 miles per hour. At the altitude of a few hundred feet the laws of thermodynamics would come into play. The air would become so compressed and move so fast it would not just heat but superheat, flashing into a white hot plasma shockwave spreading out in a great circle at nearly the speed of sound.

In a matter of seconds not only would Versailles be destroyed but so would Paris and the landscape for dozens of miles in any direction. The forests, those not already burned by the French, would spontaneously combust, creating a region-wide firestorm which could have become a self-feeding monster – with the potential to incinerate most of northwestern Europe, devastate the continent's civilization, disrupt global climate patterns and lower the earth's temperature because of so much ash and other particulate matter in the atmosphere.

Fortunately this flight of fancy never got off the ground, never got beyond its inventor charging those who rejected it as traitors to France, but there were other flights that did.

The True Birth of Aerial Warfare

The first military use of balloons did not occur, as many people think, during the American Civil War but 67 years earlier, at the Battle of Fleurus, 25 miles southeast of Brussels. In 1794 General Jean Baptiste Jourdan employed a civilian balloonist to observe the movements of the Austrian Army opposing him. Writing about it later, Antoine de Jomini doubted the efficacy of using such an invention. But, he never did consider its propaganda value to a besieged population.

Of the 54 balloons launched from Paris most did reach safety, though a few had unusual adventures along the way. Most were fired at, until the French learned to launch them at night, and few came down anywhere near their intended landing spots. The *Niepce*, *Daguerre* and *Galilée* came down in German-heldterritory, though not all their passengers and aeronauts were captured. The ironically named *Vauban* initially landed near the Verdun fortress. After it had fallen to the Germans and three of its four occupants were captured the fourth escaped when the others released the car and it shot into the air.

The *Archimède* landed near Castelze in Holland, the *Ville d'Orléans* came down near Lidfjild, Norway and the *Jacquard* was never seen again after drifting into the North Atlantic. But the most unusual adventure happened in October – several different dates have been given – when none other than Felix Tournachon himself made a rare attempt to return to Paris after being launched from Tours.

Aboard the aptly-named *Intrépide* he carried government dispatches and, luckily catching favorable winds, eventually found himself approaching Fort Charenton on the southeastern side of Paris. Then, another balloon appeared and Tournachon thought it was an outbound compatriot – until he hauled in the French tricolor it had been flying and displayed a Prussian flag.

The German aeronaut fired first, and damaged the *Intrépide* enough to force Tournachon to climb its outer webbing and plug the holes. When he returned to the car he jettisoned enough ballast to shoot into the air, giving him the perfect firing position over the Prussian balloon. Before it could duplicate the maneuver, Tournachon put enough holes in its envelope to cause it to drop into no-man's land between French and German outposts. An Uhlan patrol rescued the German aeronaut, ending the first air combat in military history.

This attempted interception was only the most spectacular German effort to interdict French air operations. They ranged from Saxon princes and other German nobility deploying their falcons to pick off suspected carrier pigeons, which proved occasionally successful, to cross-country chases by light cavalry units and organized rifle fire barrages that were rarely effective. And the efforts ended with a more serious endeavor, one that pointed the way to future warfare.

Only a few are still thought to exist – at least one is on display in a German museum – and the design effort was hurriedly initiated after the first balloon launches in late September. Alfred Krupp put his best weapons technicians, lead by Wilhelm Gross, on the program to create the world's first anti-aircraft gun. And in the remarkably short time of less than three months they had it designed, manufactured, tested and delivered to the investment line around Paris.

The *Preussisches Ballongeschütz* looked, to the observers of the day, like a large telescope with a steel stock mounted on a tripod. To military historians and artillery experts from contemporary times the weapon would have a futuristic look. With a six-foot long barrel and a mounting 15 feet high, it resembled a miniature version of the 88mm. flak gun, also made by Krupp, from the coming century's second global conflict.

It fired a three-pound grenade over 2,000 feet, which could have made it a formidable weapon against low-altitude balloons. Alas, by the time it arrived on the investment line most daylight launches had ended and the winter weather soon curtailed all such operations.

The *Ballongeschütz* never got a chance to prove itself. But the mere fact that German high command felt compelled to order its top arms maker to develop and manufacture the first dedicated weapon for counter-air operations meant they took aerial activity seriously. And this, more so than Tournachon's remarkable feat, marked the real beginning of aerial warfare.

The Relentless Advance

Following the capture of Amiens, Manteuffel's First Army moved in coordination with part of Crown Prince Friedrich August's "Army of the Meuse" to consolidate their gains and continue pressure on Bourbaki's "Army of the North." Far to the southeast, in fact only about 30 miles from the Swiss border, the major fortress-city of Belfort had been formally invested by the German Fourteenth Corps, commanded by the Strasbourg-veteran General von Werder.

It is only in the center where Prince Friedrich Karl is forced to slow and change the direction of his advance. What had been thought of, by both the Germans and the French, as only a three-day march from Troyes to Orléans had grown much longer due to poor roads, bad weather and repeated harassments by Francs-Tireurs.

Then there were the truly impressive deployments of French troops around Orléans. The "Army of the Loire" had now grown to four Corps (the Fifteenth, Sixteenth, Seventeenth and Twentieth) with a division from the Eighteenth Corps and a sizable Francs-Tireur force including de Cathelineau's royalist Bretons and Lipowski's radicals. In total over 200,000 men had been assembled by Gambetta and placed under d'Aurelle de Paladines' cautious command.

The numbers alone dictated Friedrich Karl change his plans and ask for reinforcements, which he promptly received by the assignment of the semi-independent Corps commanded by Grand Duke Friedrich Franz II of Mecklenburg. Originally deployed as a counter to any moves by the "Army of the Loire" to relieve Paris, it had absorbed von der Tann's much-reduced

Bavarian Corps, along with the 4th and 6th Cavalry Divisions and the 17th and 22nd Prussian Infantry Divisions.

As with the assignment of the "Army of the Meuse" to the Crown Prince of Saxony, it had been an astute political move on Moltke's part to assign command of this new corps to the monarch from one of the smaller German states. And Friedrich Franz soon proved his abilities by pulling his troops out of operations around Nogent-le-Rotrou, a regional collection point for French levées, and joining up on Friedrich Karl's right wing.

Before them lay an irregular line of French entrenchments some 37 miles long, built as much for the protection of the "Army of the Loire" as Orléans – though at the time neither the Germans nor Gambetta knew this, and when they found out their reactions would be rather different.

To the north First Army's siege operations ended against the major fortress of Thionville after the two divisions surrounding it brought in 85 heavy guns. The bombardment lasted less than two days and the first parallels were barely dug when the fort's commandant opened negotiations. On November 25th the garrison of 4,000 officers and men became prisoners, its *Garde Mobiles* were released on parole and 199 fortress guns, along with all its stores of supplies, munitions and small arms became war prizes.

Of the two divisions involved one, the 14th, moved farther north to lay siege to smaller border fortresses which had formerly been only under observation. The other, the 13th, would be sent south via railroad to further reinforce operations of Friedrich Karl's Second Army. And two days later, on February 27th, the smaller fortress at La Fère surrendered on Sedan Terms, with 2,300 prisoners taken and the most serviceable of its 113 guns were removed to arm the citadel at Amiens.

And more important than the prisoners, war prizes or release of investing forces were the opening up of additional rail lines these two successes allowed. In particular the capitulation of La Fère meant not only rail service to the Paris armies materially improved, it was opened to Amiens and other points in northern France.

For the French the elation of the victory at Orléans proved short-lived. The Germans had suffered a major retreat more than a defeat and, despite what the newspapers proclaimed, their armies had not fled back across the border. If anything they had redeployed and grown stronger. And the French armies, in particular the triumphant "Army of the Loire," had remained frustratingly inactive. Frustrating for Gambetta, who would soon take matters into his own hands, and more so for the Paris residents. Now they were demanding, and demonstrating for, a war-ending breakout to begin. They would not have long to wait.

Le Grand Sortie

Twice already, on September 19th and October 21st, General August Ducrot lead sorties from Paris. Both failed as breakout attempts – it has been argued that was not their objective – but this time it would be different. It promised to be bigger, to be bloodier, to be the supreme effort. The follow-up to Orléans that would have the Prussians, the only kind of Germans who really mattered, reeling in disarray and fear.

On the same day as the fall of La Fère, the guns on all the Paris forts started firing at sunset. It lasted long enough to convince the city's population that the much-discussed breakout had begun. But the following morning, November 28th, came without the by-now familiar sounds of battle. Instead, troop columns and batteries of new-cast heavy artillery were on the move throughout the city and its suburbs. And everywhere proclamations had been plastered on every available vertical surface.

One came from Trochu and called upon the population to prepare for the supreme effort, and blaming the Germans for all the blood about to be spilled. A second was signed by Favre and the other members of the government still in Paris, imploring the population to remain calm during the coming battle. And the third, most incendiary, came from General Ducrot.

In it he urged his men to be contemptuous of danger, to thirst for vengeance, to avenge him should he fall, and that he swore he would only re-enter Paris "dead or victorious." The last phrase was especially electrifying, in hours it seemed to be on everyone's lips, but would prove to be an unfortunate choice as the grand sortie went awry.

And this happened almost from the start. To alert the government in Tours of the planned breakout, and to coordinate an offensive by the "Army of the Loire" to linkup with it, a balloon was launched with a courier. This turned out to be the *Ville d'Orléans* which, after a harrowing 15-hour flight, had flown 840 miles and landed in Norway. Its message only just got to Gambetta in time to order the Eighteenth Corps, still arriving on the Orléans line, to launch an attack on Friedrich Karl's Second Army around Beaune-la-Rolande.

The town was almost equidistant between the two cities: 30 miles northeast of Orléans and 36 miles due south of Paris. The attack caught the Germans by surprise; by early afternoon Beaune-la-Rolande would be surrounded on three sides by French infantry. However, within hours General Constantin von Alvensleben counterattacked with his entire Third Corps, especially his corps artillery batteries, and the French were driven back to defensive positions at Mont Barrois, Vernouille and Juranville.

At least this attack got underway as planned and very nearly succeeded. To the north Ducrot's breakout ran into one of the problems that hampered Bazaine at Metz. The main attack was planned due east of Paris, across the Marne River near Joinville-le-Pont. But in the night the river had risen and Ducrot's pontoniers had not brought enough pontoon sections to compensate.

Trochu gave orders for all operations to be held up for 24 hours. Unfortunately, the preliminary bombardment by all the Paris forts had been underway since midnight. The French Navy flotilla of river gunboats, led by the famous *Farcy*, were busy since daybreak on the Seine and Marne Rivers, doing what the *Farcy* had become famous for: engaging in duels with German field guns.

More disastrously, General Joseph Vinoy's Thirteenth Corps had already initiated a major diversionary attack south of Paris in the L'Hay and Choisy-le-Roi area, with supporting fire from gunboats and the local forts Ivry and Bicetre. Though he had received news of the delay, Vinoy could not break off the attack until 10:00ᴀᴍ – by which time he had lost 1,000 killed and wounded with a further 300 captured by the Germans, who suffered only 140 casualties.

The 24-hour delay meant the grand sortie did not restart until the morning of November 30th. By then Friedrich Karl's Second Army had become involved in a major battle with the "Army of the Loire" in the Artenay-Pithiviers area north of Orléans, and the armies around Paris were fully alerted to any possible contingency.

On the 30th all the forts and the gunboats again opened fire at the German investment line. Once again diversionary attacks were mounted in several directions: in the north against the village of Epinay on the right bank of the Seine, in the west around Fort Valérien and again in the south against Choisy-le-Roi and nearby Thiais. But the main attack, as before, came in the east as the obstinate Ducrot attacked the same peninsula of land formed by a loop in the Marne River.

According to Trochu's plan he attacked with a force of 150,000 men and 400 field guns – roughly ten divisions – plus the supporting fire from Forts Charenton, Nogent and Rosny. Initially they took ground, capturing the villages of Brie and Champigny just outside the established investment line and at the base of the peninsula formed by the Marne. To go farther meant moving beyond the effective covering fire of the fortress guns, onto a broad plateau ranged-in by Saxon and Würtemberg field batteries.

The artillery Ducrot brought with him were supposed to counter this, but the congestion of so many men, horses and wagons on such a short and narrow peninsula resulted in few getting through. Even the elimination of the slow-moving corps baggage-trains and field kitchens did not reduce this. German troops counterattacked all along the new line and at several points the National Guard and *Garde Mobiles* wavered and broke.

Only the most strenuous efforts by their officers and sergeants kept them from fleeing and by nightfall Ducrot's army had advanced no farther than its initial successes. Now the lack of tents and hot food from the baggage-trains and kitchens began to tell. And Ducrot's further order, for his men to discard their blankets and carry only ammunition and three days of rations, made conditions on the French lines that much more miserable. By comparison, the Würtemberg, Saxon and Prussian troops could look forward to hot food and billeting in either villages and farm buildings or shell-proof earthworks.

A truce was called the next day so both sides could gather up their wounded and dead. Ducrot also used the time to call for supplies of blankets to be brought up, and to receive news from Trochu that the "Army of the Loire" had launched an offensive and hoped to be in the forests of Fontainebleau, some two dozen miles away, by December 6th.

This held out the tantalizing possibility that the breakout might just succeed. In reality the Battle of Loigny-Poupry, as the advance would come to be called, would see the French Fifteenth Corps retreat to Artenay while the rest of de Paladines' army tried to stabilize the lines south of it. However, to a desperate population, and their even more desperate leaders, the possibility meant a supreme effort would have to be made.

That began the following morning with an opening artillery barrage both sides kept up all day. Accounts describe it as so loud shouted orders could not be heard a few feet away, and the ground continually shaking from the cannonades and impacts of the shells. And it went on for eight hours without a letup in the fury. Between the field guns, the fortress guns, the Mitrailleuses and the repeated German attempts to seize the pontoon bridges from the balance of Ducrot's army, the *Garde Mobiles* became completely demoralized.

By nightfall on December 2nd Trochu and Ducrot realized their supreme effort had failed utterly. Their troops were exhausted, broken and most of their supplies and munitions had run out. The only thing they could do was order a retreat, which their army managed to skillfully carry out starting at midnight.

By the morning of December 3rd, aided by diversionary attacks on German outposts and a heavy mist, most of the army made it across the bridges and into Paris. There, on the Avenue du Trone and the Pont d'Austerlitz, most of the city seemed to have turned out to greet the returning army. And to witness Ducrot re-enter neither dead nor victorious but alive and defeated.

The Grand Sortie had cost over 12,000 killed and wounded with thousands more taken prisoner, a classic decimation of an army. The Germans lost approximately half that number, around 6,000, and their investment line remained intact. Paris was no freer than before the attempt, and soon the prospects would grow even dimmer.

The Last Battle of Orléans

The fighting around the villages of Loigny and Poupry had produced roughly 4,000 killed and wounded on both sides, with the French losing another 2,500 men as prisoners. The attempt had brought the "Army of the Loire" to within a scant 40 miles of Paris, the closest any relieving army would achieve. In spite of this weak showing Moltke, and the rest of the coalition high command, had decided enough was enough and telegraphed orders to Prince Friedrich Karl to expedite the attack on Orléans, even before the Battle of Loigny-Poupry had reached its conclusion.

The advance to Pithiviers and beyond had been done against General de Paladines' advice and on Gambetta's personal orders. Now, his army would suffer the consequences of being overextended. The Sixteenth and Seventeenth Corps, both under the command of General Antoine Eugène Chanzy, were too far north to rejoin the Orléans defences before three corps from Friedrich Karl's Second Army had effectively cut them off from the city.

With their removal, de Paladines had lost two of the most combat-effective corps in his army. This was not due to their experience or professionalism but to the basics. They were among the last corps to be universally equipped with the Chassepot rifle and other standardized gear of the old Imperial Army. After them, outfitting the new levées would have to be done with the myriad of weapons and other supplies either manufactured by the Government of National Defence or bought by them on the international market.

And there was one other critical difference. Alone among the French army and corps commanders, General Chanzy had done away with the tradition of billeting his troops in tents. The practice had originated in Algeria more than a generation earlier, and the French Army had stubbornly held onto it. If tents appropriate to the climate had been procured by the old Imperial War Ministry this would not have been a problem. But no one there, not even Marshal Niel, had been that farsighted.

To defend Orléans de Paladines could only rely on the Fifteenth,

Eighteenth and Twentieth Corps. The best of these was the Fifteenth and, stationed between Orléans and Artenay, managed to fend off attacks by all three of the corps which had severed Chanzy's command from the rest of the Army. Alas, it had greater difficulty with the inclement weather; heavy snow storms made rapid movements and communications almost impossible. While the cold had added to the misery of Ducrot's breakout attempt, the snow imperiled the "Army of the Loire" almost as much as German artillery.

This became especially true for the beleaguered Fifteenth Corps which, throughout December 3rd, received scarcely any support from the formations on either side of it. In fact, only Chanzy's severed command made an effort and a united Prussian-Bavarian artillery barrage drove it off. The Fifteenth Corps had to abandon the villages of Chevilly, Le Croix Briquet, Douzy and Huêtre, some of them without a fight.

At the end of the day General de Paladines witnessed the rout of the Corps' 2nd Division, and was forced to order what Moltke himself later called an "eccentric retreat." Only the Fifteenth Corps was allowed to fall back to Orléans, the Eighteenth and Twentieth were to hold their entrenched positions and orders even went out to Chanzy's two corps. Friedrich Karl also gave orders, to exploit the advantages he had gained, and early on the morning of December 4th his Third and Ninth Corps began to move to retake Orléans.

North of the city Third Corps columns entered the towns of Boigny, Neuville and Chézy, finding only stragglers, abandoned field guns and rifles. On the St. Loup Heights overlooking the Orléans suburbs the columns encountered real resistance from French Marines. But by 2:00PM they secured the heights and were setting up their artillery to shell the city.

To the east Twenty Corps had received orders direct from Gambetta in Tours to fall back on Orléans. These were exactly opposite to the orders from de Paladines but the Corps commander, General Crouzat, decided to at least send his cumbersome baggage-train through Jargeau to the city. By 2:00PM his Corps was in combat with a single division from the German Third Corps. Despite his advantage in numbers, he was soon forced to retreat across the Loire River at Jargeau.

Ninth Corps, moving out of La Croix Briquet, also attacked Orléans from the north and was soon battling Fifteenth Corps units for possession of the city's railroad station. Later in the day Grand Duke Friedrich Franz's Corps, advancing beside Ninth Corps, found the entrenched positions at Gidy abandoned, complete with field guns.

Further to the west of Orléans von der Tann's Bavarian Corps, the original occupiers of the city, came upon one village after another with abandoned positions. The cavalry divisions accompanying the corps surprised a dismounted field battery at Montaigu and seized all its guns. On the road to Châteaudun they ran down a column of retreating supply wagons and captured it entirely.

His command crumbling, de Paladines had originally decided to make a final stand in the city while Gambetta, convinced it could be saved, was speeding to it by train to take personal command of the situation. However, with the capture of the Orléans rail station, Gambetta's train got routed back to Tours and de Paladines, by 5:00PM, realized the futility of his situation.

He ordered a general retreat from the city to the south. What remained of the Fifteenth Corps moved south to La Ferté St. Aubin. The Twentieth Corps departed south from Jargeau and the Eighteenth Corps crossed the Loire at Sully. By 6:00PM the first German divisions were entering the gates of Orléans, and negotiations with its remaining authorities were begun for an orderly reoccupation.

At midnight it had largely been completed. The third battle of Orléans had cost the French 20,000 casualties and prisoners while the Germans suffered roughly 17,000 casualties. The "Army of the Loire" had been effectively decimated and split in two. Organized resistance was unraveling all across France and yet, *War To The Knife* continued.

Chapter XX: The Bitter End

> *"An immense river of oblivion is sweeping us away*
> *into a nameless abyss."*
> -Joseph Ernest Renan (1823 - 1892)

State of Denial

SUR.RE´AL.ISM(SU.RE´AL.IZM) n. [F. surréalisme] 1. <u>Art</u>. A modern French movement in art and literature, influenced by Freudianism, purporting to express the subconscious mental activities by presenting images without order or sequence, as in a dream. 2. <u>Humor</u>. Arrested development masquerading as art. 3. <u>Hist</u>. State of mind of the French civilian population and provisional government after the defeat of their two largest armies in December, 1870.

The classic definition of the Latin verb *decimate* is "to take or destroy the 10th part of." And between the killed, wounded and prisoners taken both the "Armies of Paris" and the "Army of the Loire" were not only decisively defeated but decimated by their German opponents, who suffered far fewer casualties by comparison.

And yet none of it seemed to matter. To the Government of National Defence, the full spectrum of the Press and the general public it did not matter that Orléans had been retaken or Paris remained just as besieged as before. Since victories no longer existed – the last engagement of any size the French would win had been on December 1st when Antoine Chanzy's

Sixteenth Corps pushed the Bavarians out of Villépion – defeats now became victories.

They became "blessings in disguise." They pointed out deficiencies in French tactics, training was never mentioned since that had virtually ceased to exist, and a favorite scapegoat for the Press and Paris Clubs: incompetent officers. Soon after the fall of Amiens, on November 17th, General Bourbaki was relieved of command of the "Army of the North." Its original commander, General Louis Faidherbe, got it back and this alone promised to reverse the situation.

Now the latest scapegoat was the one-time "hero of Orléans" himself, General de Paladines and, in the wildest flight of *surréalisme*, the splitting and scattering of his army had actually been a good thing. Now, so the logic went, there were two "Armies of the Loire" where there had been just one and they would soon coordinate an attack to annihilate Friedrich Karl's army.

As the situation grew ever more irredeemably hopeless the rhetoric became more apocalyptic. The Germans were not just to be defeated but hunted down and destroyed. All other foreigners were increasingly looked upon as either their agents of influence – the sincere offers by other governments to negotiate an armistice only fueled this idea – or outright secret agents.

Englishmen, since the heady days of July and the anticipation of a victorious war, were always suspected of working for the Prussians. But now "spy mania" spread to other nationalities. To the Italians, the Spanish and even the Swiss and the Americans, who ironically maintained the two largest foreign field hospitals in Paris. Even more ironic was the fact this paranoia and hatred came to serve the Germans.

In at least one incident four Prussian officers, who were captured during the failed sortie, were given Napoleonic Era paroles, civilian clothes and the freedom to move about Paris. According to some accounts they, for a time, more than doubled the number of spies the various German governments actually had in the city, but it did not last. Within days the threats against them had mounted to such an extent that the War Ministry decided it would be best to trade them for some French officers being held by the Germans. In the end it provided Moltke's command with fresh information about conditions in the city.

And for all the foreigners who were accused of being spies, especially the various newspaper correspondents, the one who actually proved the most useful to the Germans, and even to French authorities, in taking information in and out of the city had been the celebrity foreigner treated by the Press as a hero: U.S. Military Attaché General Ambrose Burnside.

His first use came shortly after Paris had been invested, while the Germans were still relocating their headquarters to Versailles.

Bismarck used Burnside to deliver a list of negotiating requirements to the provisional government. Trochu decided to use him to send a message back that Paris defences were ready, and had his senior aide take the general on a tour of the main forts. Which Burnside, with the help of Philip Sheridan, wrote up in a detailed report on for Moltke.

And like a tennis ball or a shuttlecock he had bounced between the two courts for the last two and a half months, with the French increasingly using him to sell a ruse while the Germans wanted him to convey the truth. All the while passing the kind of detailed, sensitive information which seemingly every other foreigner in Paris was accused of either possessing or trying to glean. Surrealism indeed, but the final set in this match would soon begin, with Moltke showing Burnside the growing siege gun park his armies were assembling outside the investment line at Villacoublay.

The Full Tide of Retreat

With the return of Faidherbe to his old command it had been hoped he could either hold the line against Manteuffel's First Army, or perhaps turn south to relieve Paris. In reality, the "Army of the North" could do neither. After consolidating his hold on Amiens, with the help of a number of fortress guns scavenged from La Fére, Manteuffel crossed the Somme River before December 1st.

On the afternoon of December 5th, the advanced formations of his Eighth Corps entered Rouen, the capital city of Normandy. A few days later Uhlan patrols would reach the Channel Coast, a feat the German Army was not destined to repeat until nearly 70 years later, when Heinz Guderian's panzers would take Abbeville at the mouth of the Somme.

And in an ironic twist which, like so much else in the Government of National Defence bordered on the surreal, General Bourbaki also got his old command back. With the dismissal of General de Paladines, Gambetta handed him the Fifteenth, Eighteenth and Twentieth Corps; once again Bourbaki commanded an "Army of the Loire."

Also in a replay of previous events, de Freycinet ordered him to immediately go on the offensive, retake Blois, approximately 45 miles southwest of Orléans on the Loire River, and promised him he only faced a light cavalry force. Bourbaki responded that if he were to do so, not a soldier or a gun of his army would ever be seen again.

However, instead of replaying Gambetta's explosive response to such an adamant refusal, the War Minister actually traveled from Tours to Bourbaki's headquarters at Bourges, which happened to be over 60 miles *southeast* of Orléans and almost as far from its ordained objective in the west. And what he found appalled him.

"I have never seen anything so wretched," remarked an astounded de Freycinet, which even Moltke quoted in his own report on the war. The camps of Bourbaki's command reminded its general of the squalid conditions of the British camps in Crimea. Only here he had to deal with fewer supplies, worse weather and nearly non-existent discipline.

Flying squads had to be sent out daily to round up deserters, upon whom little punishment was levied because there were so many and Bourbaki rightly feared the draftees might mutiny. Foraging parties had become the other main activity, though the three corps were rapidly depleting a nominally fertile farming region.

All this left few personnel with even less inclination to conduct reconnaissance patrols or other military endeavors. Still, Bourbaki hoped he could whip them into some form of disciplined force by the new year, and de Freycinet implored him to at least make an attempt to occupy Vierzon, less than 20 miles by road to the northwest. Unfortunately, a division from Friedrich Karl's veteran Ninth Corps occupied the city before Bourbaki could attempt the move. And, had it not been for Moltke's general order to his armies of December 17th, then this division, in concert with its cavalry escort, could have easily routed the entire army from Bourges.

As for the other "Army of the Loire," Chanzy's command of Sixteenth and Seventeenth Corps, at least he still maintained contact with the Germans. After being cut off from the other three corps, he had moved his troops farther west, and managed to pull off a true miracle. He restored discipline to his defeated men, restored their spirit, obtained supplies from local forts and got them reinforcements, the newly-formed Twenty-first Corps from St. Laurent.

At this point Chanzy possessed the finest fighting force left to France. Powerful enough to defend itself and even go on the offensive – which they did so repeatedly, only to be defeated again and again. They were pursued by Grand Duke Friedrich Franz's super corps, who took a few days to rest and resupply after the recapture of Orléans before setting out on their new task.

On December 7th Franz advanced on a broad front against Chanzy's forward guard at Meung, less than ten miles southwest of Orléans. After a stubborn fight lasting until nightfall the French were forced to withdraw to Beaugency. The following day this town, further down the Loire River, fell despite a hard battle between the French Sixteenth Corps and two Bavarian divisions.

Chanzy now decided the time was opportune for an offensive, and between December 9th and 11th fought to retake Beaugency and the villages around it. Two Prussian and a Thüringian division joined the battle, as did the French Seventeenth Corps. By December 10th the German Tenth Corps had arrived to reinforce the Grand Duke's hard-pressed forces. Eventually even the French Twenty-first Corps joined for its baptism of fire before the weight of massed German artillery decided it.

On the night of December 11th Chanzy realized the effort could no longer be maintained, not without losing his entire command, and he ordered a retreat. This compelled the Government of National Defence to abandon Tours, just 50 miles from the latest battlefield. Gambetta moved the Assembly to Bordeaux, the inland port city at the end of the Gironde Estuary.

On December 12th Chanzy withdrew his army to the west, to the hill town on Vendôme and the villages around it. The terrain offered the possibilities of building formidable defences however, at a council of war, Chanzy's generals convinced him that further operations with their troops in such miserable conditions were impossible. When Tenth Corps arrived on the morning of December 17th, they found the positions in front of Vendôme abandoned and the town ready to surrender.

Reaching the Limits: The Germans Pause

For several weeks many of the reports reaching Moltke's headquarters, by both telegraph and dispatch rider, spoke of increasing exhaustion of troops and wear on their equipment. Finally, on December 17th, he decided the field armies especially were becoming too worn out and spread out for continued effectiveness and sent orders for an "operational pause."

All major offensive operations ceased immediately. This meant pursuit of Chanzy's "Army of the Loire" ended at Vendôme. And Tours, though empty for the moment of any French troops, would not be entered. In the east Bourbaki's other "Army of the Loire" was kept under observation, after the last divisions of its Eighteenth Corps retreated across the Loire at Gien, 30 miles southeast of Orléans, and continued to Bourges.

In the north Manteuffel's First Army had to give up its siege of LeHavre, where there really was an "Army of Normandy" being formed, and pull back to Rouen. It also compelled him to halt his frustrating pursuit of Faidherbe's "Army of the North," located somewhere in the plateaus and flat country of the Picardie region.

For many divisions, and even corps, the orders could not have come at a more opportune time. The First Bavarian Corps, just pulling back to Orléans after the heavy fighting in Beaugency, needed all its four-pounder and six-pounder field guns replaced because of worn barrels and burned-out vent pieces. Many other units also needed their artillery replaced for similar reasons, reports of which Albrecht von Roon silently collected for use after the war.

Thousands of Dreyse rifles also needed replacement, as did boots, uniforms and greatcoats for men, and harnesses, bridles and saddles for horses. Fortunately, the Etappen Corps attached to all the German Armies, in addition to the Train Battalions attached to all their corps, had managed since September to put together an efficient railroad system.

And their trains brought not just new weapons and supplies but fresh horses and new recruits. Casualties, both combat and non-combat, and illness had considerably reduced the size of some front-line units which had been in combat since the beginning of August. There had been resupply efforts since the start of the war, but this took the form of a major operation, necessitating the suspension of all others until it ended.

One Last Hurrah

The French, with far more serious supply and manpower problems, at first did not notice the lull in German activity. When they did they could do little with it, though Faidherbe attempted to threaten Amiens and Chanzy did push one of his divisions toward Vendôme. The man who took the greatest advantage of the lull would not be French but Italian.

At Autun, a town 90 miles north of Lyons and almost on the border between southern and eastern France, Giuseppe Garibaldi had gathered a "corps" numbering between 12,000 and 30,000. Its size varied from one account to another, and what the various reporters considered a "combatant" versus a "follower." Even at the lower figure he had still gathered the largest Francs-Tireur force in the country, and on November 24th he finally took it into the field.

That Gambetta allowed him to at all can be seen as a measure of the desperation the Government of National Defence had fallen to, much less that he expected Garibaldi could achieve his objective. On October 31st the city of Dijon had surrendered to a Baden division after a brief fight. Since then a large part of the division had moved on to other towns, leaving a relatively small garrison.

In cooperation with a new-formed French Army division, it was hoped Garibaldi could retake Dijon and even move to lift the siege of Belfort. In reality the two forces never got closer to the first objective than Sombernon, to the west, and Saint-Seine-l'Abbaye, northwest, before reinforcements from the Belfort Investment drove them back in early-December.

Despite the "operational pause" General von Werder decided to take Autun and sent out several brigades. On December 16th Garibaldi's force surprised a Prussian supply train and captured 50 prisoners, two field guns, two supply lorries and killed or wounded 200 troops before driving off the rest.

It momentarily halted Werder's offensive, until the 18th when a day-long battle south of Dijon cost both Garibaldi's corps and the French division over 1,000 casualties and 600 prisoners. Apart from harassing sorties these would be the last military operations for the man who lead rebel armies on two continents, and had once been offered a command in the Union Army by Abraham Lincoln.

It was an exciting finale to Garibaldi's career, though not the most fitting one. In his desire to see combat one more time, he missed out on the withdrawal of the French garrison from Rome and the capitulation of the Swiss Guards contingent to King Victor Emmanuel's Army. By mid-October the Italian Parliament had voted overwhelmingly to transfer the royal residence and the national capital from Florence to Rome. And Garibaldi would not be there to participate in his longest-held dream.

The Mounting Doom

Two days after the failure of the Grand Sortie, just enough time for the weight of the disaster to sink in on the city's population, there occurred one of those tragedies which could only add to the gloom and despair running just beneath the surface of Paris. On Monday, December 5th, Alexander Dumas died.

There is no evidence that the war caused his death or contributed to it; he was 68 at the time. However, this did not prevent Victor Hugo and some newspapers from suggesting it. The author of *The Count of Monte Cristo*, *The Three Guardsmen* (*The Three Musketeers'* original title) and *Revenge of Milady* received a small funeral attended by a few friends and his son, Alexander Dumas *fils*, and a temporary interment.

He would not receive a permanent burial until well after the war ended. The famous necropolis of Père Lachaise was, for the time being, well within German artillery range. Also, Trochu had used it since the start of the siege as one of many encampments for his army, for which rumors were growing that the Grand Sortie would not be its last.

In part their spread countered the despair few openly talked about though everyone could feel. In that regard they fell in line with the more surrealist claims that two "Armies of the Loire" were better than one. That the two had reunited and thrown Friedrich Karl's army into the river, presumably the Loire. That Faidherbe's "Army of the North" had retaken Amiens, or was marching for Paris. That the army in LeHavre, the real "Army of Normandy," had moved out and would soon relieve Paris.

The later rumors gained credibility when, over the next two weeks, both Ducrot and Vinoy moved troops to the north. In the relatively short time of three weeks, previous attempts had been at least five weeks apart, the *fourth* breakout attempt began early on the morning of December 21st.

Ducrot and Vinoy executed a two-prong attack against Le Bourget, target of the October 30th attack, and Ville-Evrard to the east. It began with a heavy artillery barrage from Forts Aubervilliers, de l'Est, Rosny, Nogent, assembled field batteries and something new – armored trains mounting heavy guns.

With the help of a morning fog the French initially gained ground. However, they could not gain the heavily contested glass factory at Le Bourget while at Ville-Evrard not all the houses in the village had been properly cleared, especially the basements. Vinoy's surprise attack had been too successful, not all the Prussian troops had the time to evacuate and, after nightfall and with most of the occupying French settling down, a distinctly Prussian bugle call sounded in the darkness.

According to most accounts the commanding officer, General Blaise, recognized it as a Prussian call, just before he and most of his officers were cut down by rifle volleys as they stood around a bonfire. The confused fighting went on till midnight, during which the rather small Prussian force made off with nearly 600 prisoners, and among the dead left behind was General Blaise.

The following morning Vinoy abandoned Ville-Evrard and withdrew his forces from the right bank of the Marne, exposed as they now were to the massed artillery fire of Prussian and Saxon batteries on the heights commanding the left bank. Farther to the north Ducrot's men stubbornly held onto their gains at Le Bourget, despite having no rations and exposed to a night of bitter cold.

Several miles behind them, on the Montmartre heights, civilians with telescopes and binoculars thought they saw their troops digging trenches to begin a counter-siege of Le Bourget. The problem was the frozen ground had become as hard as concrete and all entrenching attempts failed. By December 23rd Trochu had to admit failure and ordered a withdrawal.

On Christmas Eve the Paris government substituted beef for the horse meat they had been distributing, added an ounce of butter to everyone's rations and distributed to the city's restaurants some truly exotic delicacies. Courtesy of the *Jardin d'Acclimation*, the city zoo, those who could afford it dined on camel, yak, Bengal stag, wapitis and zebra. Since mid-October most of the zoo's flocks of exotic birds had been eaten, and soon the elephants Castor and Pollux would be shot to provide New Year's Eve meals.

On the German side every base and almost every outpost had decorated Christmas trees and lavish dinners, usually roasted goose, for the troops. The enlisted men got beer with their dinners, the officers had wine and afterwards they toasted the holiday and their good fortune with schnapps and champagne. And for the residents of Paris Moltke finally gave the go-ahead to what Bismarck had been arguing for, and all the German legislatures and press demanding; 76 siege guns were removed from their park at Villacoublay.

Two days after Christmas the bombardment of Paris began with the shelling of Forts Noisy, Rosny and Nogent on the city's eastern side, but most especially on the exposed trenchworks of the Mont Avon plateau. A heavy snow storm that continued all day impeded the accuracy of the fire. Much more so for the forts, whose observation teams could not even see where the German guns had been emplaced: on the heights behind the villages of Gagny and Raincy.

The snow also muffled the sound of the barrage, except for those on the exposed plateau. On December 28th the storm lifted and the accuracy of German fire greatly improved, while the artillery on Mont Avon was silenced and the forts were heavily battered. Trochu, after arriving to view the situation, ordered the trenchworks abandoned, which German reconnaissance parties found empty the next morning.

By then Prince Kraft of Hohenlohe, overall siege artillery commander, and General Kameke, senior engineering officer, were constructing more emplacements. From St. Cloud in the west to Chevilly in the south and Fontenay in the east Paris was not exactly encircled but ranged-in from the most advantageous positions on the investment line. Of the storm to come Mont Avon had only been a prelude.

No More Miracles

Between the 2nd of December and New Year's Day both Chanzy and Bourbaki managed to pull off the last French miracles of the Franco-Prussian War. They took their beaten, exhausted, thoroughly demoralized and poorly-trained armies and managed to forge them back into fighting shape. If they had also been properly equipped, and used purely on defensive positions, they would have been adequate. Unfortunately they were used on offensive operations, in miserable weather and the Germans were far from idle.

In response to Bourbaki's reappearance, and the re-titling of his command to the "Army of the East," Moltke decided to transfer his nemesis Edwin von Manteuffel from First Army command in the north to lead the new "Army of the South." It comprised Third and Seventh Corps from Friedrich Karl's Second Army, while he retained control of the Third, Ninth, Tenth and Thirteenth Corps, and von der Tann's First Bavarian Corps had since been transferred back to the Paris investment force.

Gambetta, in response to all the fragmentary information he had received on enemy dispositions, believed the Bavarian Corps no longer existed while Friedrich Franz's super corps had been decimated and would not return to battle, that Manteuffel got recalled due to ineptitude and everywhere the German Army was beset with exhaustion, even mutiny. Thus, when Chanzy approached him about new operations, Gambetta urged an offensive to relieve Paris.

Moltke and Friedrich Karl had, in the meantime, suspected just such a move might be in the offing. The Prince ordered all of his corps, minus the Hessian Division which remained in Orléans as a rear guard, to advance on Le Mans. Simultaneously, Manteuffel deployed his "Army of the South" to prevent Bourbaki from either linking up with Chanzy or trying to relieve the siege of Belfort. But first the "Army of the East" had to be found.

Discovering the "Army of the Loire" proved to be much easier. The capital of one of France's prime agricultural regions, Le Mans had been Chanzy's headquarters for the last three weeks. The French Press had reported this for nearly as long and, just outside of Vendôme, Friedrich Karl's army made contact with the detachments he left behind.

Combat began on January 5th, 1871, and would continue almost uninterrupted for nine days, covering over 40 miles of difficult terrain in often miserable weather. With the exception of Metz, Strasbourg, Belfort and other siege operations, this would be the longest engagement of the war.

In many ways it resembled the pivotal Seven Days' Battles of the U.S.

Civil War, consisting as it did of a densely interconnected series of running battles between units ranging from regiment-size on up to corps strength. Except, it was not pivotal. The Battles for Le Mans did not change the course of the war, the victories were not split between the two sides, nor did they suffer the same relative number of casualties.

By January 14th Second Army had 3,400 casualties, with over half of these out of Third Corps alone. Chanzy's army lost almost twice as many, 6,200 killed and wounded, with over 20,000 men taken prisoner and immense stores of supplies, arms, wagons, lorries and horses taken as well. While he believed he could, and should, make an attempt to relieve Paris, his corps commanders eventually convinced him their men were too demoralized, exhausted and ill-supplied to make the attempt. Instead, what remained of the "Army of the Loire" withdrew toward Laval, and eventually Rennes at the base of the Brittany peninsula.

North of this disaster Faidherbe received orders from Gambetta to proceed south and linkup with Chanzy. This only produced further confusing maneuvers, withdrawals and counter marches. Since mid-December he had been able to keep First Army, under Manteuffel and later von Goeben, off-balance and confused. Cities and towns were abandoned, then recaptured; at one point the Germans only held Amiens and La Fère north of Paris. And yet, at every battle Faidherbe's "Army of the North" lost more men, and afterwards the Germans were rounding up hundreds of stragglers and distributing captured supplies among their own units.

In this final stage of the war the battles between First Army and the "Army of the North" did not fall upon each other with the rapidity of those taking place to the south. Nor did they take place in quite so confused an arena as a 40-mile stretch of hills laced with bad roads. They occurred across most of the Picardie region, with names redolent of the global conflicts to come: Normandy, Dieppe, St. Quentin, Cambrai, Arras, the Somme River, Abbville, Amiens, Ham and Vimy Ridge.

And, as if foretelling the future, the final battle in the contest between the two armies would be at St. Quentin, on January 19th, 1871. It involved two French corps, the Twenty-second and Twenty-third, and part of a third, against the veteran Seventh and Eighth Corps of the First Army, backed up by several Landwehr divisions.

In a hot, hard fought battle in the bitter cold the neophyte *Garde Mobiles* gave a good account of themselves, but could not withstand the experienced Prussian divisions. By nightfall St. Quentin and the surrounding villages were in German hands. They had lost 2,400 men killed and wounded, Faidherbe suffered 3,000 casualties with a further 9,000 men taken prisoner. And while his army fell back in disorder to Lille, Douai and Valenciennes on the Belgian border, the German units were too exhausted, and too entangled with each other, to mount a serious pursuit.

In the southeast, Bourbaki had managed to enlarge his "Army of the East" to an impressive 150,000 men. De Freycinet had added two more corps to his command, the Twentieth and Twenty-fourth, and nominally Garibaldi's force was part of the overall command structure. Gambetta, now as completely separated from reality as the radicals in the Paris Clubs, tasked this army with raising the siege of Belfort, invading the Alsace and cutting off all German lines of retreat.

Bourbaki knew these were impossible to achieve; just getting his army out of its camps around Bourges should have been considered a minor miracle. Still, he obeyed his orders and in the first week, in fact just after Christmas, he did what many Paris newspapers claimed as a genuine miracle: Bourbaki occupied Dijon.

In reality General Werder had withdrawn from the city several days earlier to concentrate his corps, a total of 50,000 men, around Belfort and the approaches south of it. Bourbaki understood this as he took the city, left Garibaldi's "force" there as a garrison, and pushed farther east – into the Jura Mountains and during the onset of the region's most severe winter in living memory.

Soon thereafter another reality set in for Bourbaki – the moment he fielded his "Army of the East" it began disintegrating. With the sole exception of poor leadership, the avalanche of problems Clausewitz described as "friction" bedeviled his command almost from the start. And he had to deal with two factors neither Jomini nor Clausewitz wrote about: real avalanches and desertion.

Bourbaki still had to detail some of his best troops as flying squads to pickup stragglers and deserters. The difference between the two? Stragglers generally still have their weapons and are glad to be found. Deserters do not and are not. Deeper into the Jura Mountains the threat from avalanches, dangerously severe weather, crossing ice-clogged rivers and getting lost due to poor maps took priority, even over the scattered encounters with German forces, until Villersexel on January 9th and Lisaine, which began on January 15th.

The first battle, Villersexel, occurred in the Ognon Valley some 20 miles east of Belfort and was won by Werder's divisions. They inflicted 650 casualties and took 700 prisoners. Then, over the next few days, they withdrew to more defensible positions on Lisaine Creek. When Bourbaki reached them he started the battle by deploying two corps, the Fifteenth and Twenty-fourth, with the Eighteenth attempting a flanking move and the

Twentieth held in reserve.

In three days of bitter fighting, and even worse weather, Bourbaki used all his available corps in repeated attacks on the defensive line held by Werder's hard-pressed troops. On the morning of January 18th, after taking between 4,000 and 5,000 casualties and losing nearly 1,000 prisoners, he ordered a retreat and broke off the attack. Frostbite and lack of food were reducing combat effectiveness faster than enemy action. And he had a more serious problem in the offing – his nemesis had found him. Manteuffel's "Army of the South" was coming up behind him in a series of grueling forced marches.

And around Paris the endgame began on the morning of January 5th of 1871, after a one-day delay because of heavy fog. At first only the siege guns on the city's south side, 84 arrayed against three of the forts in this sector and some of the new emplacements constructed between them, started the bombardment. At first these forts, Issy, Vanves and Montrouge, responded with a brisk duel. Including the heavy guns in the enceinte wall's armored bastions, they outnumbered the German artillery by nearly four to one. However, the French allowed themselves to get surprised, and German fire proved to be more accurate.

By mid-afternoon Issy and Vanves were all but silenced and Bavarian field guns had joined in, forcing abandonment of the new trenchworks being dug out to the investment line. Before the day ended several shells fell on the Latin Quarter, not far from the targeted forts. Instead of terrorizing the civilian population it came as something of a relief, with children selling shell fragments across the city as souvenirs.

And yet in the coming day, as one fortress after another was silenced and the whistle of incoming shells grew heavier, most of the population began to realize there would be no relief. The "Armies" of the North, the Loire, the East and Normandy would not be lifting the siege any more than the "Armies of Paris" could break it. But there were more than enough who still believed in *Guerre à Outrancé*, in its romance, in its invented history of success, to give it one more supreme effort.

The Birth of Empire

Unity had been in the back of every German's mind since the start of the war. With each success of the Prussian-lead armies it gained more life, more acceptability. With Sedan it became an inevitability. Afterwards only a major disaster could have derailed the process and, try as they did, the French could not succeed.

The course of the war, the tides of history, were on the side of German unity and its final push ironically came from the absentee castle-builder, King Ludwig II of Bavaria. There is much evidence, and depending on the source it ranges from a not-too-subtle nudge to a direct dictate, that Bismarck pressured Ludwig into petitioning the other German monarchs and their Senates or Houses of Nobles to proclaim King Wilhelm I as Emperor of Germany.

Using his Foreign Ministry, Bismarck negotiated a compact of Byzantine complexity which, in its essential points, made Wilhelm the Emperor *outside* of Germany and the first among equals *inside* it. The other monarchs would not have to give up their lands, titles or many of their powers. They would still send ambassadors to Berlin but the Army, the embryonic Navy and all foreign embassies would be controlled from there.

It was this, and not negotiations to end the war, that occupied Bismarck's time through most of November and December. He astutely judged the time to be right to forge a united Germany in the furnace of war, rather than wait until later when the fires had cooled. And since the French, in their national flight from reality, chose to believe they could throw the German armies out of their country, his course of action suited the moment perfectly.

By December 18th Wilhelm had received the delegation from the North German Confederation. Bavaria and the other southern states followed soon thereafter. They also decided to hold the ceremony in Versailles and, as their armies continued to battle across France, prepared for an event that had not happened in over 700 years, the coronation of the King of Germany.

A month later, on January 18th, 1871, in the Hall of Mirrors which Louis XIV created for just such occasions, the nobility of the Germanies gathered for the last time as independent rulers. Except for the barons, counts, dukes, grand dukes and princes actually on combat operations, the Crown Princes of Prussia and Saxony exempted, they were all there.

With black-robed Lutheran clergy presiding over the ceremony, they sang the Protestant hymns, thanked God for giving them this day and proclaimed King Wilhelm to be Kaiser Wilhelm I. Nearly 65 years the death of the Holy Roman Empire, there is a new empire, an entirely German one, and a new Kaiser.

And at the conclusion they sang the popular song of unity, not as an appeal to that end, but as their national anthem. For now it was Germany above Prussia, Germany above Saxony, Germany above Bavaria, Baden and all the other states. They sang "Deutschland, Deutschland über alles." Europe had a new empire and France, at long last, a new *ennemi héréditaire.*

Its birth came on the same day as the French were engaged at St. Quentin, began retreating from Lisaine Creek and watched helplessly as the Germans entered Tours with no opposition, and linked up their First and Second Armies, with Grand Duke Friedrich Franz marching his corps into Normandy's capital of Rouen. And the next day, as Faidherbe lost St. Quentin, Paris tried one last time for a breakout.

The People's Sortie

While Trochu was nominally in command, with Vinoy, Carré de Bellemare and Ducrot leading the three corps, this one would be radically different. This would largely be a "People's Sortie" with not just the National Guard and *Garde Mobiles* in the ranks, though they were the majority of the forces deployed, but average citizens who demanded participation and the denizens of the Paris Clubs. The last group was finally getting its big chance to prove they could succeed where the professional soldiers, whom they detested even more than the Germans, had failed.

After nightfall on January 18th, while the celebration at Versailles continued, the corps started gathering at Gennevilliers. A town located on a broad peninsula formed by a loop in the Seine River before it entered Paris, it was the one large area of ground not covered by German artillery. This dictated the direction the sorties would take, to the southwest, rather than the north, toward St. Quentin.

The plan was for a simultaneous attack by all three corps on the German lines from St. Cloud to La Jonchère. Vinoy would take the Montretout Heights on the left flank, Bellemare the village of Garches in the center and Ducrot the château of Buzanval on the right. Operations were set to begin at 6:00AM on the 19th except...nothing went right with the People's Sortie from the beginning.

Weeks of bitter cold weather evaporated in a mid-January thaw and heavy rains lashed the area. The Seine rose, pontoon bridges were unusable, and barricades across the permanent bridges at Asnières and Neuilly had not been removed, because specific orders were not given. By 6:00AM only Vinoy's divisions were ready to move, the others were up to four hours behind schedule. Even when they did move it proved slow going as the rain turned the fields into quagmires. The roads, which were only in slightly better shape soon became clogged with carts, wagons, lorries and artillery caissons.

And then came the German artillery fire – accurate, heavy and non-stop once it started. Vinoy's troops managed to take their objective, General Bellemare's seized the outer houses at Garches and Ducrot's occupied the park at Château Buzanval. They managed to hold onto most of their positions during the night, when the cold returned and they froze without adequate rations or blankets.

Before then most of the civilians had panicked and fled. By morning some of the *Garde Mobiles* were near mutiny and at 5:00PM Trochu, who had been on the battlefield all-day, ordered a general retreat. A few hours later he would nearly be shot by a squad of *Mobiles*, who mistook his contingent as they rode across the refrozen fields for a squadron of Uhlans.

By the time it ended the sortie had cost nearly 3,600 casualties with another 500 taken prisoner. Among the dead were the elderly Marquis de Cariolis (aged 67), the scientist Gustave Lambert, a promising young painter named Alexandre Henri Regnault and the actor Jules-Didier Seveste, who was taken back to his beloved Théâtre-Francais mortally wounded. By comparison the Germans lost just over 600 killed and wounded with another 50 prisoners.

While hundreds of field guns pounded the hapless troops back to their lines, the heavier siege artillery continued their bombardment of Paris. One of the latest government proclamations requisitioned all absentee homes and apartments to shelter its victims. More took refuge in the uncompleted Opéra Garnier which, some 38 years later, would be the home of Erik in *The Phantom of the Opera.*

Additional proclamations announced the rationing of bread, the commandeering of all food and fuel found in requisitioned buildings, the rationing of firewood and coal, and the latest, a demand for Trochu to resign. At first the government chose to ignore it; they treated this latest defeat the same way they did the others, as if it had been a victory. But this time the reaction would be different.

No one could ignore the fact that the "People's Sortie" results came on top of four previous failures to breakout, that Paris was being shelled with increasing intensity and forts were being pounded into silence, or that carrier pigeons and foreign embassy officials, such as General Burnside and British Ambassador Lord Richard Bickerton Lyons, had brought in reliable reports of defeats on all the other fronts: the "Army of the Loire" driven out of Le Mans, the "Army of the North" defeated at St. Quentin and the "Army of the East" in retreat after Lisaine.

By January 21st the demands could no longer be ignored; General Trochu resigned as commander of the Paris armies, but stayed on as President of the Council. General Vinoy replaced him as overall commander, though by now the momentum toward overthrow could not be stopped. The following morning a crowd at the Hôtel de Ville demanded a revolutionary government be put in place.

By 2:00PM the crowd had grown to 5,000 and a detachment of 100 *Garde Mobiles* arrived on the street. It has never been ascertained who started firing at whom, or for what reason, but when the *Garde Mobiles* inside the Hôtel de Ville responded with volley after volley the crowd panicked and stampeded. When it ended there were only five dead and several dozen wounded, but it would be enough. The end had come.

Paris Capitulates

The next day, the morning of January 23rd, Jules Favre left Paris incognito and arrived at Versailles to resume negotiations. If he had hoped the non-existent disarray and destroyed corps in the German armies would soften their demands, Bismarck immediately dissuaded him of it, and repeated what he said from two months earlier.

Favre returned to Paris dejected, but the Government of National Defence could not reject the German offer. Paris had perhaps a two-week supply of food left, and its mortality rate had climbed to three times the pre-war rate. Even if the German bombardment ended immediately, famine and disease would decimate the city's population in a matter of months.

And Bismarck held one further threat he used to intimidate his hapless opponents: he had opened negotiations with Empress Eugénie to re-install Napoleon III as the recognized ruler of France. Favre, Thiers and the rest of the Paris Council realized this would lead to civil war and pleaded with Bismarck that republican France would be a better neighbor that a reconstituted imperial France. The ploy worked; it got more concessions out of the Council, such as excluding Gambetta, de Freycinet and the others at Bordeaux from the negotiations.

Curiously, Favre was able to wring a few concessions out of Bismarck: Garibaldi would not be executed as a mercenary or paraded through Berlin as a prisoner, but treated as a general in the French Army. The Paris garrison would not have to throw out its remaining fortress guns and could keep its colors. And fatefully, Bismarck allowed the *Garde Mobiles* in Paris to keep their weapons, but he warned, "you are making a blunder. And sooner or later there will be a heavy reckoning for you with the rifles you are rashly leaving in the hands of those fanatics..."

The Armistice began on the morning of January 28th and was initially set to last 21 days. French and German forces were, wherever possible, to withdraw ten kilometers from each other. All German prisoners were to be immediately released, supply trains were allowed to enter Paris, but the sieges of Belfort and other isolated fortresses would continue if they did not surrender.

It was all over but the shouting, and the final battles.

Part III – The World Changed

"It is not a matter of a temporary crisis, but a
completely new situation in the world.
Another race of men has appeared on the stage."

-Edgar Quinet (1803 - 1875)

Chapter XXI: The Troubled Armistice

> *"It is expedient for the victor to wish for peace*
> *restored; for the vanquished it is necessary."*
> -Lucius Annaeus Seneca (c.4 B.C. - 65 A.D.)

Future War

THE ARMISTICE WAS not universally accepted across the battleground France had become. Not every Francs-Tireur unit honored it, though the prospect of being treated as common criminals by both sides soon brought their operations to an end. More serious were the situations in Dijon with Garibaldi's force and Bourbaki's "Army of the East." Gambetta still hoped they could retrieve some honor for France, get a better negotiating position against the Germans and perhaps even convince French voters in the upcoming elections to continue the war.

While the other armies of the massive, and massively successful, war machine stood down from offensive operations Edwin von Manteuffel's "Army of the South," the smallest with just two corps, continued combat in the southeastern corner of France. According to the terms of the armistice, Moltke could not transfer divisions or corps to Manteuffel – though he could, like the French, resupply his forces in the field.

As a consequence both he and de Freycinet sent, or at least tried to send, supplies to both armies. And for both this meant maintaining the rail lines they held, and holding onto those towns with the all-important railroad stations. In the waning days of this war, as the concepts, traditions and tactics of the Napoleonic Era retreated into history, its last battles would be the Battles of Logistics. The thoroughly modern concept of strategic supply, and the interdiction thereof, would decide the fate of the armies.

This final campaign would be the perfect testing ground for the capabilities, the necessity, of modern logistics. Fought in the depths of winter and over inhospitable mountain terrain, neither the "Army of the South" nor the "Army of the East" could possibly forage enough to live off the land. Both needed logistics just to survive, let alone fight, and both faced their own problems with it.

Manteuffel's army had to guard against the remaining Francs-Tireur units sabotaging his rail lines. He detailed several regiments, especially his Hussars and Dragoons, to secure them. And for a time he left behind the Eighth Brigade from his Second Corps to secure the lines and stations from Tonnerre to Châtillion-sur-Seine, as well to protect against any sorties by the fortress garrison at Langres. And some 40 miles southwest of this town lay Dijon, now in Garibaldi's hands.

For Bourbaki his problems began with the army he commanded, nearly twice the size of Manteuffel's, and it had just come off a bitter defeat at Lisaine Creek. He pulled it back to Montbéliard, in the Doubs River valley south of Belfort, and with its supply and equipment situation so critical he decided to retreat further down the valley to the city of Dôle. Here, following a lengthy and circuitous route through southern France, de Freycinet had managed to stockpile the vitally needed supplies at the city's railroad station.

Manteuffel began the legendary forced marches of his Seventh and Second Corps on January 14th, just as Bourbaki made his final deployments for the Battle of Lisaine. Through heavy fog, deep snow, and finally rain when the temperature climbed 14 degrees Celsius, his troops marched without a day of rest until they reached the Sâone River valley on January 18th.

By now telegrams reached Manteuffel that Bourbaki had been defeated and retreating down the Doubs Valley, the next valley south of his position. The following day he advanced on Gray, the nearest town to have bridges crossing the swift-flowing, and by now ice-clogged, Sâone. Instead of combat Manteuffel's vanguard found Gray abandoned and its two bridges, contrary to Bourbaki's orders from a week earlier, were intact.

It was a bit of tactical good fortune Manteuffel now fully exploited. By the 20th his corps had reached Pesmes and Gy, halfway to Dôle, and on the afternoon of the 21st they attacked the city's garrison. In a sharp fight they captured Dôle, its railroad station and over 230 wagons of provisions and military equipment critically needed by Bourbaki's army.

By January 21st he had reached Besancon, halfway down the Doubs Valley to Dôle. Here he received reinforcements but no supplies, and nine battalions of *Garde Mobiles*, who came armed with newly-issued Enfield Snider rifles – for which, in a perfect example of French logistics' breakdown, there were no ammunition stocks and they had to be released from duty.

Bourbaki's original intention was to resupply at Dôle, then move to Dijon where he could unite with Garibaldi. However, not only did Manteuffel's army now block the way but, also on the 21st, Dijon itself was attacked by the Eighth Brigade, the unit originally assigned to guard the rail lines from Tonnerre to Châtillon-sur-Seine.

Even though he held off the German attack, Garibaldi would be convinced he faced the entire "Army of the South" and consequently made no attempt to break out, or even to mount reconnaissance sorties. At least he had adequate supplies; for Bourbaki the loss of Dôle and its enormous supply cache made his situation even more dire.

He needed to retreat south; now the objective would be Lyons, at the confluence of the Sâone and Rhône Rivers and a major rail hub. Alas, there were few roads in anything approaching good condition to take four corps of dispirited, poorly-fed and insubordinate troops on such a march in the middle of winter. Further, by January 22nd Manteuffel had ordered his two corps to move on Besancon and already they were plundering a badly needed convoy of supply wagons at Saint Vit and capturing four intact bridges across the Doubs River.

Incredibly, orders from de Freycinet were for Bourbaki to concentrate his forces and launch a breakout by either Dôle, Mouchard, Gray or Pontarlier. And if he could not do that, he was to embark his men by train from Chagey, where there was not nearly enough rolling stock to accommodate such of large number of men and their equipment.

Even Moltke called such orders "military dilettanteism" and, by the 26th, conditions in the "Army of the East" had deteriorated to the point where Bourbaki decided there could only be one way to save his honor and possibly his army. He resigned his commission and shot himself. But the suicide attempt failed, he ended up in the hospital with a severe head wound, and command fell to his executive, General Clinchant. Somehow he felt duty-bound to carry out the impossible orders from Bordeaux – perhaps like Napoleon Bonaparte he felt the word was not French – and set in motion a plan that would lead to disaster.

The Final Humiliation

If the "Army of the East" had remained in Besancon, site of the legendary siege by Cardinal Richelieu in 1647, it might have survived the war. Under the aegis of its fortress, one of the best built by Vauban, it would have become invested, but could easily have fended off attacks by an enemy force double its size. However, the critically low state of supplies would compel the army to begin its move on January 27th.

Of the four routes dictated by de Freycinet, the only one not threatened or already blocked by Manteuffel's army was the easternmost, Pontarlier. High in the Jura Mountains, the town lay so far east the Swiss border ran perilously close to it. This was not a route a retreating army would normally take. But all the corps and division commanders knew their men were not in any condition to engage in combat.

Consequently, they tried to move as fast as possible to stay out of reach of Manteuffel's veteran troops. Only their evacuation from Besancon had been observed by his reconnaissance forces. And on the morning of January 28th, almost to the hour the armistice began in Paris, he ordered a general advance of his forces, with the Second Corps moving south to Champagnole and possibly St. Laurent-du-Jura, just below Pontarlier, while the Seventh Corps backed it up by taking Mouchard.

The only combat to occur that day happened when Dragoons pushing east of Champagnole captured another badly needed supply convoy of 56 wagons and a divisional pay-chest. By the 29th word of the armistice had reached both armies, though Gambetta said it did not apply to the three easternmost departments of France and Moltke implied Manteuffel could continue offensive operations if he felt he had a good chance for success.

By 4:00PM that day the First Division of the French Fifteenth Corps had been routed with nearly 2,800 officers and men captured, including two generals, along with ten field guns, seven Mitrailleuses and 48 wagons. A little to the north the entire Eighteenth Corps was engaged by a single division of Seventh Corps. After 90 minutes of heavy fighting the French broke off, with some laying down their weapons and claiming an armistice had taken effect.

On January 30th a single German brigade stopped the entire French Twenty-fourth Corps from attempting a move south. In fact General Clinchant suspended most operations of the "Army of the East" for the day, hoping that the armistice would lead to a complete cease-fire across France. Manteuffel, knowing neither government wanted this, took advantage and pushed the Seventh Corps to take the town of Chaffois, which they found unoccupied, and the Second Corps to assault the forest and village of

Frasne. There, they captured a further 1,500 officers and men before the end of the day.

Clinchant sent his personal aide, Colonel Varaigne to Manteuffel's headquarters at Villeneuve on January 31st to arrange a 36-hour truce. The general refused the offer; only then did the French realize this battle would be carried out to the bitter end. The Seventh and Second Corps advanced on parallel fronts, marching up long passes to take Vaux and Granges St. Marie, capturing, in total, around 4,000 prisoners and everywhere finding abandoned weapons and camp equipment, vivid evidence of the "Army of the East's" disintegration.

That night Clinchant held his final council of war among his available commanders and with the understanding no cease-fire or armistice would save them. None of the generals could guarantee their men would fight and more importantly with what? Supplies of everything except misery were critically low and many troops were throwing away their rifles. In light of the collapse he could not stop, Clinchant gave his final orders to his army: to flee by whatever available mountain roads and trails to the east, into Switzerland.

Manteuffel's army "attacked" Pontarlier the next day, February 1st, on three sides and found it largely unoccupied. The last battle of the Franco-Prussian War would not be fought here but just to the south at LaCluse, near the small fortress at Joux. The fortress itself could not be taken by field artillery and the mountain road at LaCluse was too narrow for combat by anything except regiment and battalion-sized units.

And most important, no one in the "Army of the East" wanted to make a final stand and fight. By early-afternoon the Germans could no longer make any headway pushing east, mostly because all the roads leading out of Pontarlier, as well as the one cutting through LaCluse, were fully blocked with abandoned wagons, lorries, artillery pieces and their caissons.

Of the 150,000 man army that embarked to lift the Belfort siege, retake the Alsace and cut off the retreat of all those German armies: 20,000 were immediately lost when Garibaldi's force remained to garrison Dijon. 10,000 were lost through to the Battle of Lisaine Creek. Between January 17th and the 26th another 20,000 were lost through combat and desertion. Nearly 10,000 more were lost from the 27th to the end of the month. And on February 1st, of the 90,000 that remained just under 2,000 were killed or captured by the Germans, less than 8,000 managed to escape south, a much-reduced division of the Twenty-fourth Corps lead by General Cremer, and the remaining 80,000 fled across the border into Switzerland. The Swiss police and border guards arrested, disarmed and interned them all; they would be the last troops returned to France.

The army upon which so much had been expected accomplished less than nothing. Not only did it fail in all its goals, it had been annihilated, with the exception of a pathetic, under-strength division it had "disappeared from the field." And its destruction would spell the final dissolution of the Government of National Defence.

Peace at Any Price

Under the terms of the Paris Armistice there was to be a 21-day cease fire, later extended by several increments to March 6th, an additional 16 days, during which Paris would get re-provisioned and elections for the National Assembly at Bordeaux would take place across France on February 8th.

The Paris Government needed four days to restore postal service, during which time the first train-load of food and other supplies arrived in the city. A gift from the British people, via the London Relief Committee, it quickly built up to 10,000 tons of flour, 450 tons of rice, 900 tons of biscuits, 360 tons of salted fish, 4,000 tons of fuel and nearly 7,000 head of livestock. It was all received with a grateful resentment. The people welcomed the food, but often grumbled why Great Britain could not have sent an expeditionary force to save them. For that, they would have to wait another 43 years.

Across the rest of France the war quickly ran down. Starting back on January 1st, with the capitulation of the Mézières fortress on the northern Meuse River, most of the other siege operations were ended within the month. By February 1st only the siege of Belfort still continued, and would do so until ten days after the national elections to decide the fate of the war.

That had largely been decided before the polling even began. A few days in advance of the elections Leon Gambetta resigned as Dictator of France, though he stayed in the National Assembly to advocate his position of *guerre à outrancé*. He had many supporters in Paris, but the rest of the country had grown tired of the war.

The heavy casualty numbers weighed on them: over 250,000 dead, three times that number wounded with nearly half a million prisoners in Germany, Switzerland and Belgium. The endless string of defeats and the invincibility of the German armies dispirited them. The disruption to the society and economy was bringing ruin to every corner of their country, and in the end that is the way they voted.

On February 8th half a dozen political parties won some percentage of the 700 seats in the new National Assembly, but no party received a majority. The biggest factions were the Orléanists, followed by the

Bonapartists and the Moderate Republicans. The minority parties were the Bourbonists, the Red Republicans and the Constitutional Monarchists in that order. After a preliminary meeting on February 13th, the Assembly had its first formal session two days later, where they elected Jules Grévy, a Moderate Republican with monarchist leanings, as its president.

On February 17th he helped engineer the selection of Adolphe Thiers as the first real president of the Third Republic. Next they selected his Cabinet, largely a repeat of the earlier Government of National Defence: Jules Favre, Foreign Minister; Ernest Picard, Interior Minister; Jules Dufaure, Justice Minister; Jules Simon, Minister of Public Instruction; General Adolphe LeFlô, War Minister; Felix Lambrecht, Commerce Minister, and Louis Buffet, Finance Minister.

This group, plus several party leaders, left for Versailles on February 20th to negotiate the last extension to the Armistice and the final peace treaty. By then the last active combat operation of the war had ended. The Siege of Belfort concluded not exactly with a surrender but a ceremonial exchange. The fort's garrison marched out with all its personal equipment and colors: the Honors of War. The Germans even provided 150 wagons and horse teams for its baggage train. After 103-day investment they had possession of the fortress, though it would not be for long.

At Versailles Thiers and his Cabinet met Bismarck, Moltke and their team of ministers and generals. Negotiating an extension to the Armistice would be the only easy part to the new talks. Over the next five days Bismarck and Moltke granted a few concessions and Thiers realized they were lucky to receive any. It has long been suggested that it was the British government, and in particular Ambassador Lyons, who got the biggest concession out of the Germans: a reduction in the war reparation of six billion francs to five billion.

Apart from this the only other concessions of any note were the return of Belfort, and the tiny section of southern Alsace around it, and a major reduction in the size and duration of the German occupation of Paris. Kaiser Wilhelm insisted on a victory parade through Paris, which Thiers and his Cabinet feared would turn an increasingly restive population rebellious.

Instead of reviewing an entire army, the Kaiser would have to be content with just a corps made up of selected units from the investing armies around Paris. They were also to stay in only the southwestern corner of the city, near the Champs-Élysées route, and could not stay past the ratification of the peace treaty.

Paris had been the one major district in France where a majority of the population had voted in favor of continuing the war. Thiers and Favre were just starting to realize that maybe leaving all those rifles in the hands of the disbanded *Mobiles* might have not been such a good idea. If they were contemplating Bismarck's warning they certainly did not show it as they raced back to Bordeaux and urged the Assembly to ratify the treaty as soon as possible.

In the meantime 30,000 German troops selected from three different corps entered Paris on March 1st. Even though the area they were billeted in was one of the wealthier districts, and some distance from the restive working-class quarters, they were still greeted with shuttered homes, closed shops and cafés and nearly empty streets. It had been arranged for the Kaiser to review the troops on the afternoon of March 3rd. However, Thiers actually got the Assembly to ratify the treaty by the 2nd and, according to its terms, the Germans had to leave the city within 24 hours.

Early the following morning Wilhelm reviewed his men on a forbiddingly silent Champs-Élysées, where French officials had covered the statues with veils so they did not have to view the humiliation. The thin crowds who did gather were sullen and given to spitting on the ground as the troops marched out of the city. On other streets, in other districts, the crowds were described in some accounts as howling savages, outraged at the "invasion" of the barbarians.

On March 4th the Kaiser reviewed 100,000 troops under much happier conditions in the Bois de Boulogne, the major forest just west of Paris. For just a moment it all seemed calm. Measures taken by General d'Aurelle de Paladines, who now commanded all military forces in Paris, had kept the city relatively calm during the brief German occupation. In Bordeaux, Leon Gambetta had fled to self-imposed exile in Spain after the peace treaty's quick ratification.

It is not that no one did not expect trouble. There were anarchists, Communards and radical republicans in Paris and a number of other major cities. But the one man the new government's leaders, and most foreign observers, thought capable of uniting the factions had left the country. Thiers and Picard made plans to move the National Assembly to Versailles, and Favre was busy talking to various ambassadors about setting up foreign legations on the palace grounds.

They all wanted to return the country to normal as soon as possible. In addition to all the major acts of legislation they passed over the next few days there were two relatively small measures the Assembly's majority felt reasonable: one ended the moratorium on the promissory notes, with which much of the day-to-day business of Paris had been managed. The other made rents that had been unpaid during the war immediately payable. They would ruin the middle and working classes of Paris, and provide the perfect fuel for the coming fire.

The War After the War

From March 3rd to March 6th the German Army completed its withdrawal from Paris, to which it would not return for another 69 years. Shortly after the 6th it also pulled its imperial headquarters from Versailles, in anticipation of Theirs establishing his government there, and returned it to the amazing Rothschild palace at Ferrières. The siege gun park at Villacoublay was dismantled, the forts around Paris turned over to de Paladines and troops around Paris withdrew from their forward outposts.

By March 12th Kaiser Wilhelm I had moved to Nancy, just outside Germany's newly acquired territories, and from there went by train to Berlin, making a triumphant arrival on the 18th. Those divisions of the German armies not detailed to occupation duties, mostly reserve and Landwehr units, began returning to Germany. While the repatriation of French prisoners from German internment camps also started.

Everything seemed to be moving so smoothly. There were demonstrations in Paris and a few other cities against the new government's betrayal of France, though no one took them very seriously. After its arrival in Versailles the French Government ordered the suppression of the six most radical newspapers in Paris, a cavalier act similar to the ones that brought about the July Revolution of 1830, while Thiers ordered 50,000 reinforcements to the city. They were no more than what the treaty allowed, and he felt it would be more than adequate.

Then, on March 18th, Theirs knowingly issued a confrontational command: for the cannons held by local National Guard and *Garde Mobile* units at Montmartre to be handed over to government control. This was not a matter of a few batteries but over 400 field guns, forged during the siege by local foundries.

They were not only of great military significance, they were significant locally to the people of Paris. They were symbols of their heroic resistance against the barbaric invader – a resistance almost everyone in the city felt had been dishonored by the new peace treaty. Seizing the guns would be the perfect spark for the conflagration known as The Paris Commune.

Chapter XXII: Communism's First Glorious Failure

> *"A poorly extinguished fire is quickly re-ignited."*
> -Pierre Corneille (1606 - 1684)

A People's Revolution

TWICE BEFORE, ON October 31st of 1870 and January 22nd of 1871, the Communards, anarchists and other revolutionaries had attempted a popular overthrow of the Paris government. But each time they failed to get support of either the local military or civil population, and they were up against Trochu.

Eight weeks later, however, circumstances had changed. Trochu no longer commanded the Paris garrison and its numbers had been greatly reduced through the disbandment of National Guard and *Garde Mobile* battalions, who fatefully were allowed to keep their weapons. More importantly, after 132 days of the siege the Franco-Prussian War had ended with a humiliating surrender approved by the rest of the country.

A reactionary National Assembly whose majority, if you lumped all like-minded political parties together, was vaguely monarchist, had encamped at Versailles. By their legislation they appeared, or could be made to appear, more interested in destroying the middle and working classes of France than in restoring the country.

All of which felt like a monstrous injustice to the embittered, resentful and increasingly rebellious population of the city. And then came Generals

Clément Thomas, the local National Guard commander, and Lecomte, whose detail was to carry out Thiers' order to remove the artillery on the Montmartre Heights.

Instead they were delayed by insubordinate militia guards and arrested by local Communards. They were taken to a garden on the Rue de Rosiers, and executed by firing squad. They would only be the first of a wave of "revolutionary justice," summary executions, that would sweep Paris for the rest of March and until the end of May.

The artillery cache on Montmartre immediately fell into rebel hands as Lecomte's men fled to warn government officials of the insurrection. They were outpaced by the news that the true people's revolution had finally begun. The Hôtel de Ville and Tuileries Palace were seized as a mob hoisted red flags on the dome of the Pantheon, a former church that had since been converted into a temple to the French Revolution.

Other mobs fanned out across the city, forcing the new government to retreat to Versailles and arresting notable people who had not supported the Commune or its Communist ideas. This meant Victor Hugo was safe but his publisher, Lacroix, got thrown in jail until he intervened. Arrest warrants also went out for other editors and publishers: Paul Dupont, Henri Vrignault of *Le Bien Public* and Richardet of *Le National*. Of these the first two managed to escape but Richardet was arrested as he applied for a passport to leave Paris.

Others would not be so lucky, or escape so easily. Generals Antoine Chanzy and de Paladines, who a few months earlier had been the heroes of the battles around Orléans and Le Mans, were captured but not immediately executed. General Surville was killed as he tried to escape. General Vinoy, who had been de Paladines' executive officer and would soon succeed him, had a mob stone him before he made his escape.

Everywhere paving stones and tree stumps were being dug up for barricades. Barrels, doors and furniture, often pillaged from homes of the wealthy, were added to the barricades while carts, wagons, lorries and the horses to pull them were seized for service in the new revolutionary government. The dreams of Gustave Flourens, Felix Pyat and Charles Delescluze looked as if they were about to come true.

By the evening of March 18th Communard forces held virtually all the government offices inside Paris, most of the city gates and the *enceinte* wall surrounding it. Some of the forts were in their hands and there were ominous signs they were preparing to advance on Versailles, whose only reliable defence, Vinoy discovered, were the Papal Zouaves of the Francs-Tireur commander Colonel de Charette.

Only to the north and east were there forces reliable enough and powerful enough to stop any Communard breakout, the German Army of Crown Prince Friedrich August of Saxony. And it would be to the Germans that Thiers turned to get the troops his government needed to squash a revolt which threatened to become a civil war.

The Return of the Imperial Army

On the morning of March 19th it appeared as though the revolt in Paris had spread nationwide. At Lyons, Marseilles, St. Étienne, Toulouse and Prepignan Communes were either proclaimed or riots started in their name. If the Paris Commune had a single leader capable of uniting all the factions and possessing some kind of national standing then the Thiers government might have fallen.

However, Gambetta remained in exile in Spain, de Freycinet was committed to the new Republican Government and Louis Blanqui had just been arrested in southern France on charges from the October 31st coup attempt. In Paris what the Commune did possess was a surplus of aspirants to that position and all the others in a new government – so many the rebels created the "National Guard Committee" and moved their ruling assembly from Rue de Rosiers at Montmartre to the Hôtel de Ville.

Once encamped they did not form that new government so much as become a super-charged debating society; a carryover from their days in the Paris Clubs. The result was an avalanche of new Proclamations issuing from city hall. One announced their mission, in removing the "government of betrayal" from Paris, had succeeded; no mention was made in removing it from the rest of France. Another said the new government had a duty in assassinating all kings and princes. A third ordered all police forces disbanded, the records in police offices were burned and all criminals who had not done insult to the Commune were immediately released.

But the most important proclamation announced new elections for March 26th. While the Thiers government remained inactive, mostly because it had little to act with, the Communards harangued the stunned and cowed populace until the elections. And of the over 500,000 registered voters less than 200,000 actually came out to cast ballots. A farce by any definition but it gave the "National Guard Committee" an excuse to form a governing council.

It rejected all offers of reconciliation from Versailles and repudiated its earlier ultimatum to the government. The council was named the "Committee of Thirty," selected from the 106 newly-elected government members. It called for the creation of 25 infantry battalions, 15 Mitrailleuse batteries, 20 field artillery batteries and finally started planning for an offensive against Versailles.

In the meantime, Thiers had not been complacently waiting for a people's army to appear in front of the palace complex. While Vinoy set about the task of reorganizing the government's local forces, Thiers and Favre met with the one man who could change the situation confronting the Third Republic. They met with Otto von Bismarck.

At first the Chancellor and Moltke thought about putting several corps of their troops at the disposal of the Republic. After all, killing radicals and insurgents had been a specialty of German armies for decades. Then, they reconsidered and decided on a simpler expedient, one requested by Thiers and Favre in their meeting.

They increased the number of troops the French Army could field in the Paris region to 150,000, and expedited the repatriation of French prisoners of war. This involved more than just speeding up paperwork. Germany transported ten of thousands of troops by train directly to the Paris environs and returned weapons and equipment taken as war prizes. And among the first to arrive would be Marshal Marie Patrice Maurice de MacMahon.

Given command of all French land forces, he sided with Thiers and advised that they wait. Paris had come under siege again and as before, every day the situation grew worse inside its walls while conditions improved on the outside. With Vinoy, Ladmirault, Felix Douay, Georges Boulanger and other generals he quickly organized an investment force to completely seal Paris from the south and west while the Germans reinforced their line north and east.

Never before, and never since, had so many former enemies united to defeat a common foe. It was not just monarchists, Bonapartists and Liberal Republicans but, very tacitly, the German and French armies. While they took no active part in the Commune's suppression, the Crown Prince's army provided reconnaissance reports and prevented additional radicals from crossing their lines, later turning their new prisoners over to the tender mercies of the former Imperial French Army.

They were not prepared to be particularly merciful, which they began proving on April 2nd, when a Communard column of several battalions marched into the suburbs northwest of Paris, well within range of the guns at Fort Valérien. Rather than use its heavy firepower on so small a force, MacMahon sent Vinoy with a repatriated division. As it deployed its field batteries, Vinoy tried one last time to negotiate.

He sent out a Paris police captain, who volunteered for the duty, with a white flag to discuss a truce. When the Communards shot him off his horse and killed him, their skirmishers opened up with irregular fire on the division's front lines. The division responded with full volleys instead of scattered shots, and minutes later an artillery barrage.

The revolutionary fervor of the Communard battalions quickly evaporated amid the fusillades and shrapnel of the Imperial French Army's first battle since their defeat at Sedan. The rebels fled back to the city gates from which they marched, and their rout nearly turned into a disaster, until someone remembered to close them. That night the city nervously awaited an attack by government forces, while the "Committee of Thirty" planned to renew their offensive.

"We Are Betrayed"

In the days between the Communard elections and their first battle for Paris, its leaders filled the streets with rallies to their revolutionary cause. If vicious harangues could win wars then they had already annihilated their reactionary enemies who, so they claimed, wanted to install an Orléanist duke on an illegitimate throne. The defeat did not cause them to check their rancor, but to become even more vehement. In its aftermath they decided all they needed to do was send a Peoples' Army to Versailles and execute the National Assembly before spreading their revolution to the rest of the country.

By the evening the "Committee of Thirty" had camps set out in open areas of Paris where, during the night, they assembled 100,000 men, the equivalent of over six divisions. They were arrayed in three corps, and commanded by the most bizarre set of generals to be seen in the war:

"General" Bergeret lead the corps advancing out of Châtillon. He had been a printer before the war, and completely bereft of military knowledge or experience. "General" Duval was the head claqueur at the Theater Beaumarchais, a professional applauder with a similar military background. Nonetheless he was assigned to command the center corps at Pointe du Jour, on the most direct road to Versailles. And "General" Gustave Flourens at least survived a duel with an opponent in 1869 – he had been severely wounded – and was a member of the Government of National Defence before resigning in December. He received command of the corps on the right wing, stationed at Neuilly.

On the morning of April 3rd Duval's and Bergeret's corps began their attack, while Flourens remained in reserve. Because their army lacked any cavalry, they did without any reconnaissance, and without adequate artillery support. The columns passed within range of Fort Valérien, which remained as silent as the day before...until the fort's commandant allowed more than half the columns to pass it before opening fire in conjunction with Vinoy's deployed field batteries.

Confusion, then panic, reigned throughout the deployed columns. Duval died soon after the battle commenced, while Bergeret's command was cut in two and its vanguard isolated. Without waiting for orders Flourens lead his troops out to rescue the other trapped corps – into the very shadow of Valérien, whose guns cut down the lead formations, which included Flourens himself and lead to still more confusion.

Infantry attacks completed the disaster with those men who were able to retreat fleeing back into Paris crying, "we are betrayed!" They referred to the sudden, and pivotal, activity from Fort Valérien. Its artillery fire did not diminish, not even when the rebel-held forts of Issy and Vanves began trading shots with it.

As for those left on the battlefield, any insurgent found wearing an imperial army uniform was executed immediately as a traitor. Any prisoners attempting to harangue their captors were also executed. The wounded were shot, and the rest of the prisoners were cursed and beaten at every opportunity by the imperial army soldiers.

On the second day of the battle Bergeret, who had been isolated with his lead formations, attempted to break the lines surrounding him but got repulsed. Other Communard forces tried taking the bridge in the town of Sèvres, northeast of Versailles, only to be thrown back with heavy losses. The rebel-held forts continued their duel with Valérien, though because the damage they sustained from German siege guns had not been fully repaired their volume of fire soon declined.

Confusion still reigned on the Communard side as no commander had been designated to take control of the operation following the loss of its first three leaders. Not until the end of the second day would this be rectified when a new rebel Minister of War assigned a trusted subordinate to the task. And, if anything, they proved to be even more bizarre than the previous leaders.

Gustave Paul Cluseret brought all the qualifications of a classic mercenary adventurer to the office of War Minister. Initially in the French Army, he won the Legion of Honor for bravery in Crimea, only to be dishonorably discharged for theft. In 1860 he became a Colonel in Garibaldi's "Red Shirt" army during its Sicilian Campaign. A year later he joined the Union Army and fought under John C. Fremont in the American Civil War. Briefly in 1864 he edited a journal in New York City, where he viciously attacked Ulysses S. Grant and supported Fremont in his Presidential bid.

In 1866 he turned up in England, spying on British military bases for the Fenian Brotherhood. Then he returned to France in time for the Franco-Prussian War and became one of many denizens of the Paris Clubs. Once their revolution succeeded, Cluseret joined the military wing of the Communards and stepped into the empty post on April 4th.

Jaroslas Dombrowski, who became one of Cluseret's friends while in the Paris Clubs, was a Polish exile who first served as a junior officer in the Russian Army. After his dishonorable discharge he became a counterfeiter, then a pimp and a spy for Russian security and, after he fled to Prussia, a spy for its military intelligence. And during the Franco-Prussian War he became one of a tiny handful of spies any of the German states had in Paris.

Now beyond the control of his former employers, he managed to rally the Communard troops for the defence of the western and southern suburbs, only to have them defeated and pushed back in all subsequent engagements. Only the supporting artillery fire from the rebel-held forts of Bicetre, Charenton, Issy, Ivry, Montrouge and Vanves managed to check some of the advances by MacMahon's army. However, this would not last, and in the meantime his cohorts were busy...

Descent into Madness

While his friend tried to rally an army getting pounded into oblivion, Cluseret busied himself not with attempts to resupply or reinforce it, but with the creation of the ominous Jury of Accusation and its operating decrees. They were issued on April 6th and under them, after he managed to return to rebel lines, "General" Bergeret was arrested for "military failure and insubordination."

In fact, the mounting toll of defeats being handed to Communard forces caused the collection of leftists, ultra-leftists and anarchists to do what such fringe-types always do best: turn and devour each other. Of the 106 members of the newly-elected city council, 22 were forced to resign and some were thrown into Mazas Prison.

After the Republic refused the Commune's repeated demands for Blanqui's release, perhaps the only man still in France who could unite the rabble, they turned to collecting hostages to secure it. Since the generals and officials they held were not enough, they began arresting prominent civilians. First hundreds, later thousands, were dragged before Cluseret's Jury of Accusation, then off to jail.

After April 6th many of those arrested were Roman Catholic clergy. The Abbés, parish priests, of churches across Paris and the nuns from the Sisters of Charity were sent to prison. It culminated with the arrest of Georges Darboy, the Arch Bishop of Paris. The International Aid Society for the Care of the Wounded, a humanitarian medical corps that oversaw the operation of the American Ambulance and similar field hospitals, was dissolved on Cluseret's orders. Even as they were treating wounded from the latest battles, all their supplies and equipment were seized, and scores of their doctors and nurses were arrested.

Even more outrageous, when news trickled back into Paris of Queen Victoria meeting with the newly-released Napoleon III and Empress Eugénie on March 27th, the Jury of Accusation ordered the arrest of all British subjects. Throughout the siege British residents of Paris were treated with suspicion, especially the correspondents. For some logic-defying reason the French believed the citizens of the most powerful nation on earth were Prussian spies.

Before the order could be fully carried out the "National Guard Committee," which had not disbanded, intervened. They canceled the order and released the British prisoners. Later, they had to do the same for the representative of the First Communist International, who had been jailed for not being radical enough. At about the same time the Jury of Accusation began attacking the "Committee" for being counter-revolutionary.

Meanwhile, the fighting outside of Paris had been vicious and inconclusive. None of the forts were silenced, and the suburbs were still contested. The difference was, Cluseret kept announcing one glorious victory after another while MacMahon claimed none. Then, on April 18th, the heavy siege guns he moved to the northwestern side of Paris opened fire in conjunction with Fort Valérien on the suburbs of Neuilly and Colombes. By the 20th the latter town had been abandoned and the Maillot Gate in the former had come under artillery fire.

The barricades erected by Dombrowski in the area, and by other commanders throughout Paris, had slowed but did not stop the Republican troops. After he tried, and failed, to retake the one in front of the Maillot Gate he would be removed from his position. His friend would last as War Minister for another ten days, by which time even the "Committee of Thirty" had grown tired of Cluseret's empty victory claims. Not to mention fearful of the demolition-by-artillery taking place against Forts Issy, Vanves and Montrouge on the southern line.

At least they were not thrown in Mazas, like "General" Bergeret, but allowed to serve elsewhere. Cluseret's replacement, another French adventurer named Louis Rossel, lasted just long enough as War Minister to get blamed for the fall of Fort Issy, on May 9th. In turn his replacement, Raoul Rigault from the "Committee for Public Safety," believed if the

Commune was to fall then it must take Paris with it.

Plans for the destruction of public buildings and the execution of hostages were put in motion, while other Communard leaders had convinced themselves that their victory over the Republic was near and gave orders to soldiers manning their crumbling positions to take no prisoners and shoot the enemy wounded.

The final act of madness began on May 15th, the day after Fort Vanves fell and MacMahon's army isolated Fort Montrouge. On that day the esteemed "realist" painter Gustave Courbet, for whom all contact with reality had ended, convinced the Commune authorities to undertake a surreal act of revolutionary justice: the toppling of the Vendôme Column.

One of the first monuments Napoleon Bonaparte erected to himself, the bronze, 142 foot tall column had been cast from 1,200 captured enemy cannons over 60 years earlier. With its base weakened and ropes attached just below Napoleon's statue, it came down with a deafening thud, temporarily drowning out the bands brought in to play for the crowd.

At least the monument had not been a residence or a landmark building. Those, however, were already being filled with barrels of kerosene and gunpowder. Similar incendiary devices were also being planted in the city's new sewer system. If all went according to the insane plan being hatched by the Commune's committees, Paris would be consumed by an inferno not seen since the great fire that nearly destroyed London some 200 years earlier.

No Quarter Given

The problem was the bodies who ran the Commune – the "Committee of Thirty," the "Council of 106," the "National Guard Committee" and the "Committee of Public Safety" – detested each other. They arrested each other's members and released some of the prisoners the others had jailed. They conspired against one another and there is much evidence some members were willing to sell out the Commune to the Republic. As the pace of events quickened, neither Thiers nor MacMahon took up any of the offers, though they came to realize they were in a race to save Paris.

The day after the Vendôme Column came down, May 17th, a munitions factory in the Champ de Mars, a park on the Seine River, blew up with a thunderous explosion. Hundreds were killed or wounded, and thousands of Chassepot rounds detonated throughout the day as fire consumed the building.

On the 18th the last two rebel positions outside the defensive wall, near

Fort Montrouge in the south, were taken by infantry assaults. Now, only the isolated forts remained in their hands and over the next two days they were battered into submission. The next day one of the first churches to be destroyed by the Communards, the Chapell Expiatoire, was set ablaze by the roving bands of women arsonists called "Vengeresses."

Literally "female avengers," they were supposedly widows who had lost their husbands, sons and at times entire families to the previous war and siege. As news of their activities got back to Versailles, it would cause MacMahon and his commanders to issue orders than *any* man, woman or child seen carrying gunpowder, petroleum of any kind or weapons would be shot on sight.

Fort Vanves burst into flames on May 20th after heavy government shelling, forcing temporary abandonment by its garrison. Though they re-entered it and extinguished the fire, the damage rendered the fortress incapable of stopping any further advances by the Republic's army.

On the 21st, in the midst of a disorderly rout of Communards flooding into the city, General Felix Douay found the St. Cloud gate open and almost completely abandoned while de Ladmirault's division easily broke through the gate near Fort Montrouge. Republican troops were now inside Paris itself, leading to the final acts of madness.

Dombrowski, released from jail by one committee after being imprisoned by another, took command of a barricade detachment and held up Comte de Ladmirault's attack – until being mortally wounded and, as some of his men carried him to the Hôtel de Ville where he died, the rest fled in panic. Street by street fighting slowed the government's advance, even though MacMahon now deployed the *Farcy* and other gunboats on the Seine as mobile fire support. By the evening of the 22nd the skyline of Paris, so long obscured by the smoke of battle, began to glow with the fires of the "Vengeresses."

One of the first major city landmarks to be destroyed was the Rue de Royale, where many homes of the wealthy were torched. They would still be burning when Tuileries Palace, the Louvre, the Palais' Royal, Quai d'Orsay and Justice were targeted next. Generals Douay and de Ladmirault tried to push their way into the center of Paris, but the barricades here were taller, better built, better armed and more desperately defended than the ones previously encountered.

They had to be flanked and shelled with field artillery. The gunboats tried to assist, but they also had to help Vinoy's corps in their assault on Montmartre in the northwest corner of Paris. Douay managed to break through first and saved the Louvre, though not its library wing and the adjacent Tuileries Palace, which by then were fully involved.

Close by the Mazarine Library was about to suffer the same fate when Douay's men surprised the women and shot most of them. Unfortunately by then the Hôtel de Ville, the Ministry of Finance, the Prefecture of Police and a half-dozen other major landmark buildings on the nearby streets were ablaze. And while some would be saved, none would escape damage.

A day after the arson teams had begun their work in earnest, the center of Paris resembled a scene from Danté's *The Divine Comedy*, or one of Pieter Breugel's landscape paintings. Along the Seine, Tuileries and the library of the Louvre on the northern bank were still blazing away, the Legion of Honor Palace and Council of State building on the southern bank were in flames, and the Palais du Justice on the Isle de la Cité in the center was also burning.

Incredibly, a few landmarks did escape almost unscathed. The Arc de Triomphe and Hôtel des Invalides were captured by Republican forces soon after they entered the city. The École Militaire and Ministry of War were seized by Vinoy on the same day his corps took the Montmartre Heights. Notre Dame, on the opposite end of the Isle de la Cité, survived because parishioners and clergy, who were doctors at an adjoining temporary hospital and had not been arrested, put out the early fires then guarded the cathedral until Republican troops arrived.

By the morning of May 24th the fires were at last dying and the last bastions of the Communards were falling. Among them were La Roquette prison, where Arch Bishop Darboy and many of the Abbés arrested with him were executed by one of the last rebel military formations, a militia firing squad. In all 64 prisoners were killed over the next 24 hours, until a revolt among the others put an end to the executions until the arrival of Republican troops.

Generals de Paladines and Chanzy were freed from their prison, as were thousands of others. With the liberation of Mazas, La Roquette, St. Pelagie and other prisons in the city all organized resistance ended by around May 28th. But this did not mean the killing ended.

As Paris is a city riddled with catacombs and subterranean quarries – to this day almost no skyscrapers exist within its environs because of them – the hunt for the remaining Communards had to go underground. And as many of them had worked on the decade-long Haussmann rebuilding projects – Paris is a city built atop its own limestone quarries – they knew where to hide.

In some cases the rebels were burned out in much the same way they tried to incinerate Paris, by having kerosene poured down ventilation grates and matches or torches tossed in afterwards. The killing would not end until early June, when hundreds of rebels were discovered in the chalk mines of the Montmartre Heights and deliberately entombed there.

Epilogue and Consequences

It is sometimes difficult to say when and where a war ends. Is it when the armistice takes effect? After the last battle ends? When the treaty is signed? Or the last angry shot is fired? Or when the dead switch from being combat casualties to the result of summary executions?

The Franco-Prussian War offers a number of different terminating dates. Anywhere from January 28th, when the Armistice took effect, to four months later on May 28th, when MacMahon announced the liberation of Paris and the end of the Commune.

The later date is just as good as any of the rest history offers, for its does mark the conclusion of all organized hostilities initiated on July 15th of the previous year. It also neatly expands the scope of the war to include the final revolution in warfare it sparked.

In addition to the universal use of modern communications and transportation systems, the large-scale introduction of rapid-fire weapons and breech-loading artillery, the origins of armored, aerial and maneuver warfare, it also brought about a revolution in revolutionary warfare. From now on this would be seen as pure class warfare, with the inclusion more and more of "celebrity" radical types like Gustave Courbet and the Marquis Henri de Rochefort, the increasing sophistication of political ideology, the "internationalizing" of what had previously been mostly national or sub-national struggles and the most effective response to them. Namely the unification, however temporary, of everyone else against the radical extremists.

Some historians have tried to claim that the Paris Commune was not really a Communist revolution. Certainly it had not been as sophisticated as later versions, no more so than the *Ballongeschütz* versus radar-directed flak guns, but the essentials were all there.

And let us not forget that the Communists of the day, such as Karl Marx and Friedrich Engels, openly championed the Paris Commune and supported it while other members of the First International vacillated, thinking it grotesquely ill-timed and just a little too Jacobin for their taste. But Marx swept all such opposition aside and deliberately united International Communism with the Commune.

Then, after it fell, after the reports and testimonies of its horrific excesses had made it into the newspapers, the First Communist International suffered the consequences of such an association. After 20 years of toiling away in poverty and relative obscurity, overnight Marx became the notorious "Red Terrorist Doctor" to the British press and public. British trade unions quickly disassociated themselves with the International and switched support to the nascent Fabian Society, forerunner to the Labour Party.

It marked the beginning of a decline which, after five years of still more bad press, confrontations with the British government and internal strife, ended with the International dissolved by 1876. It would not be re-established in Karl Marx's lifetime and, when it did, it would reappear rather ironically in Paris.

Back in France the consequences of the revolt were being tallied up by the Third Republic. All the protests and charges of barbarism over the German shelling of Paris fell mute in the stark reality of what the Communards and the government had done to the city. Fully one-third of it had been destroyed, and not just forts, munitions factories, government buildings and palaces. Churches, theaters, train stations, restaurants and private homes by the hundreds were either blown to pieces, consumed by fire or ransacked by mobs.

The most cited casualty figure from the Commune is 20,000 of its members were killed by the French Army. Just how many were combat deaths or summary executions has never been stated, nor have the figures for the wounded and those the Commune killed been released. But it's safe to estimate at least 10,000 died between their own executions and battlefield operations.

It would take more than a decade of fits and starts for Paris to be rebuilt. And this was far from the only problem France had to face. There were all those other cities, towns and villages that had to be rebuilt from the ravages of war. There was the war debt to be paid, the coming flood of refugees from the Alsace and Lorraine, the rebuilding of the army but most of all there now existed a new reality that France, and the folly of its last imperial ruler, had created.

There was a new power in the east and its name was an ancient one. Not heard for over 700 years as the title of a country. Not since the days of Friedrich Barbarossa had Germany been anything but a philosophical argument, a fondly remembered dream. Now, as the Imperial German Empire, it had become reality and the world would never be the same.

Chapter XXIII: Paranoia, Imperial Ambitions and Krupp Steel – Germany Deals With Victory

"Every people has its day in history,
but the day of the German is the harvest of all time."
-Johann Christoph Friedrich von Schiller (1759-1805)

The Cost of a Dream

TO REALIZE THE centuries-long dream of a united German Empire took, compared to its devastated adversary, comparatively light casualties. The total in officers and men were 129,700 with roughly 26,000 killed. In addition to this tens of thousands of horses were killed either in combat or by the miserable weather later in the year. Thousands of wagons, lorries, ambulances and caissons had been lost, along with thousands of weapons. However, only six Krupp cannons were lost to the French and what had been gained in exchange for all these loses was nothing short of astonishing.

Except for the tiny parcel of land around the Belfort Fortress, the new empire gained all of Alsace and the northern third of the Lorraine province. With them came the fortresses of Metz, Strasbourg and Thionville, soon to be renamed Diedenhofen, and millions of inhabitants who now had to chose between being French or German.

And with the exception of the damages inflicted on these new territories, German lands suffered little from the ravages of war. Saarbrücken had been the only town of any size to take any damage during the conflict, and it had been occupied so briefly not much was done to it. The Saar region and the neighboring Bavarian Palatinate suffered more general damage from the "friction" of war. The wear on roads and railroads, the internment camps and other temporary installations had all caused some damage, but nothing compared to what had been inflicted on France.

The new German Empire emerged from the war with all its major cities and industries intact. The disruptions to its economy were more transient than crippling, and certainly the infusion of five billion francs worth of war reparations would improve the situation. And while its international reputation suffered somewhat during the war, especially over the shelling of Paris, the subsequent destruction visited upon the city by the Commune virtually erased it.

Germany emerged largely unscathed and respected by the rest of the world. But now Bismarck and its other architects had to build it into a national entity based on the framework they had forged in the crucible of war. This would prove to be a longer and more difficult struggle than the recently concluded conflict.

Germany Above All

The Second Reich proclaimed in Versailles on January 18th, and finalized by the formal treaty signed in Frankfurt au Main on May 10th, was initially still a confederation, much like the two it had replaced. It was an amalgamation of four kingdoms, five grand duchies, six duchies, seven principalities, over a dozen free cities and even smaller states, plus the long-desired territories of Alsace and northern Lorraine.

Taken together they were the realization of a long-held dream, the recreation of the ancient First Reich, but its newness made it fragile. Bismarck proceeded rather more slowly than the characteristic "störrigkeit," pigheadedness, of his Junkers class would indicate. Inter-state conferences were organized, to be held in Berlin, to create all the necessary structures for the new, modern Reich.

As if they were not already nationalized, the Prussian State Railways and the Prussian Postal and Telegraph Union were formally made so. The thaler, for generations the casually accepted unit of currency among the Germanies, was replaced by the new deutchmark. The parliaments of the old North and South German Confederations were dissolved. The parliaments and other legislative bodies of the individual states were turned into regional entities and subordinated to the new trans-national Reichstag which, of course, Bismarck would lead, and often with an iron hand.

The foreign ministries and war ministries of all the states, at least those who could afford them, were dissolved. The foreign embassies in Dresden, Munich and all the other former national capitals were either turned into consulates or closed. Except, of course, in Berlin where their Foreign and War Ministries became empire-controlling organizations.

Bismarck, at least, saw to it that the "new" German Foreign Ministry made an attempt to employ the best, the most experienced, diplomats and ministry personnel from across the empire. However, Albrecht von Roon at the War Ministry would be a rather different story. He became even more obstinate and reactionary, often in some startling ways and exasperating to his officers, and no one more so than Helmuth von Moltke. "Ruffian" Roon had decided to reassert himself, which would lead to his downfall.

Still, piece by piece and in spite of repeated examples of Prussian arrogance, the new empire came together. In the years following the Franco-Prussian War it proved more stable than many observers, especially those from other countries, had anticipated. In particular it would be more stable than France's Third Republic, which would lurch from crisis to crisis throughout the rest of the 1870s and until the end of the 19th Century.

Ironically enough, and with great mastery, Bismarck would use these events, these repeated examples of instability in a neighboring power, to stabilize his own nation. Not to mention pushing through increases in military spending that often lead to rancorous debates, until France appeared ready to descend into anarchy yet again.

This suited the plans of Moltke quite well. No more willing to rest on his laurels than Bismarck, he constantly sought ways to modernize and improve his new, multi-national army and shape it into a more homogeneous force – to make it both a pillar of national unity and a bulwark against conflict.

For nearly 20 years these two men would serve Europe's newest empire with dedication, and mostly successful policies. Moltke would not retire from his position as chief of the general staff and the Kaiser's first general until 1888. Bismarck remained in his office as First Chancellor of the German Empire until his clash in March, 1890 with the new Kaiser caused his dismissal. However, the third member of their winning triumvirate would not last nearly so long in office.

Roon's Folly

The obstinate and reactionary War Minister could not let himself be satisfied with success. As early as April of 1871, with the victorious armies still returning from the battlefields in France, he openly suggested to the

Kaiser that the war-winning cast-steel artillery be scrapped and bronze guns reintroduced.

At first no one took him seriously except for Alfred Krupp, who saw this as a continuation of their pre-war feud. He fought back with letters to Moltke, Bismarck, Crown Prince Friedrich Wilhelm and Prince Friedrich Karl. He even offered to finance new trials at a gun range to be built near his Gusstahlfabrik works in Essen.

Roon's answer to Krupp, on April 22nd, easily proved infuriating. While he refrained from making direct comment on the offer, he did state there were officers who thought the "increase in velocity" to be a matter of small importance and were advocating the re-introduction of a bronze four-pounder field piece.

In reality the combat reports Moltke was now studying showed that, if anything, the four-pounder had become obsolescent. It was too light, lacking the range and hitting power for modern warfare in any use except in cavalry division batteries. Armed with this and other information "der Kanonenkönig" sent a letter to the Kaiser.

As the letter came from the one other monarch who really counted in modern Germany, Wilhelm I could not ignore it and it stated very starkly: "using bronze for guns is a squandering of men, horses and material." He ended the letter by noting Europeans in 1871 knew they were living in the Steel Age. That the railroads, "the greatness of Germany, the fall of France" – a strategically astute observation – belonged to that Age while the Bronze Age belonged in the past.

Monarch to monarch, Wilhelm agreed with Krupp however, imperial politics being what they were, they had to bide their time. For Krupp, what should have been days of triumph became months of misery. In the aftermath of Sedan he had telegraphed his English friends, "now see what has done our Army!" By the end of 1871 he would be wintering in the English Channel resort town of Torquay. His Villa Hügel castle at Essen lay unfinished – Krupp had the bad luck of ordering limestone for it from French quarries in early-1870 – and his usual winter resort, Nice, would not be a welcoming place for Germans to vacation.

In the meantime his allies went to work against Roon, who was not without allies of his own. Chief among them was the Army's Quartermaster General Eugen Theophil von Podbielski, who sifted through the countless battlefield reports for the ones about the cast-steel cannon either burning out their barrels, or wearing down their breeches so much they had to be replaced altogether.

Reports from the First Bavarian Corps at Orléans, and the armies besieging Paris were especially used to make the case for the return to bronze. But the Kaiser, advised by Moltke, would have none of it. Wilhelm told Roon, Podbielski and like-minded officers they were talking nonsense, and authorized a new series of trials at the Tegel Range.

By the beginning of March, 1872 the trials were underway and Krupp had returned to Essen to settle an argument between his technical department and the Prokura, his managing board of directors. He also came to await the results from Tegel, he did not have long to wait.

A glowing report from his allies was soon in his hands. Large-scale, exhaustive trials with weapons of a variety of calibers had proven the complete supremacy of cast-steel over bronze. The Test Commission ordained that the Krupp weapons would be the only armament for the Artillery Corps. This finally allowed Bismarck to join the fray and he authorized funds to purchase one thousand new cannons for 1872, later augmented by orders for a thousand more by the end of 1873.

At least temporarily Alfred Krupp could not be happier. With the four-pounder obsolete, all new orders were for six- and eight-pounders and up, and they would be of a new, improved design in light of battlefield reports from the war. Jubilant, Krupp soon embarked upon a spending spree to increase the holdings of his firm. Coal and iron mines, and the factories of his competitors, were bought. And within a year Krupp would be facing insolvency as the Financial Panic of 1873 would sweep Europe and North America.

By then in his more accustomed misery, he could at least take solace from the retirement of his enemies. General Podbielski retired from the Army soon after the trials were completed, while Roon got promoted out of his post. The Kaiser made him a Field Marshal and President of the Prussian Cabinet. This took him out of national politics and away from most military matters. Roon was effectively sidelined, and by November of 1873 he retired even from these positions.

Krupp had won. And as the Panic of 1873 receded, and financial solvency returned with huge orders for equipment from virtually every railroad company in the United States and Canada, he became Europe's largest industrial concern. For the moment armaments were only a part of his huge operation. But already he had over a dozen countries across the globe for customers, in addition to the German Empire.

Bismarck Finally Loses a War

Shortly after enacting Universal Suffrage, as voting rights were then called, for men over the age of 25, Bismarck embarked upon his longest war.

Uniquely, it would not be fought by the Empire's Army, or its growing Navy, and his foreign adversary would only have a few regiments of Swiss Guards as a military force. This war would come to be called "Kulturkampf," the Culture War, and the enemy was the Catholic Church.

For most of his adult life Otto von Bismarck harbored a deep resentment of the Catholic Church. He first saw it as an intruder in his righteously Protestant, and mostly Lutheran, realm. Now, he viewed it as a virtual separatist movement within a country he had so recently united. It was paranoia, but not without some justification.

Pius IX, the longest-serving Pope in the modern age, had grown even more reactionary to that age in the final years of his reign. In 1870, while France and Germany went to war, he presided over the First Vatican Council which saw the triumph of Ultramontanism, a movement to strengthen Papal Authority and that of the Curia Romana. The Council restated the orthodox dogmas against materialism, rationalism and liberalism. It declared the Pope's jurisdiction to be immediate and universal, and proclaimed the doctrine of Papal Infallibility.

Those who rejected these declarations were called Old Catholics and predominated in the churches of Switzerland, Austria-Hungary and the new Germany. By 1872 Pius had started to reassert his authority over these churches, and published a reactionary tract called a *Syllabus of Errors*. It contained, among other things, an attack on Protestantism in all its forms.

By 1873 Bismarck had retaliated by severing diplomatic relations with the Vatican, making civil marriage compulsory across Germany and suppressing parochial schools. He became one of the first modern leaders to advocate universal secular education for his country. In contemporary times this is not a controversial position, but in the late 19th Century he had gone too far. His drive for secular education also affected the schools run by the Lutherans and other Protestant denominations, and it quickly produced a strong political reaction.

Unlike what many foreign observers, particularly French observers, stated, the Second Reich was not a dictatorship. It had both the Reichstag, the true national assembly, and the Bundesrat, which functioned like the U.S. House of Representatives in portioning out its members in delegations to the member states. These two bodies inherited from the pre-war, pre-unity, legislatures three main political parties: the Conservatives, the Progressives and the National Liberals.

Now, in reaction to Bismarck's "Kulturkampf," two more political parties quickly formed. The Catholic Party, composed entirely of angry Catholics, attracted a number of defectors/converts from the first three political parties. The fifth party, the Sozieldemokratische Partei

Deutschlands, the Social Democrats or SPD was a wild collection of disaffected members of the National Liberal Party, radical trade unionists, Communists and anarchists.

Not too many years earlier the French were busy shooting such people or, after giving them fair trials, shipping them out to Devil's Island. At least these radicals, in Germany during the late 1870s, were not trying to burn down Berlin and execute royalty, though in 1874 there was a failed assassination attempt on Bismarck.

They did push a radical agenda, while the Catholic Party tried to reverse the Chancellor's secular agenda. It made for rancorous, at times bitter, sessions in the Reichstag where "Kulturkampf" would occasionally threaten other government programs such as the army's modernization, naval expansion and social welfare legislation. In fact, were it not for the heaven-sent crises of the French government then increased military spending would have been almost impossible to achieve.

In fact, were it not for those recurring crises, the new war between Russia and Turkey, the ongoing campaigns in Britain's empire and yet another civil war in Spain, then observers and other governments would have been commenting on German instability. Compared to them, Bismarck's "war" with the Catholic Church was a truly bloodless affair. But in the end it threatened too much, went on too long and the conditions that caused it eventually changed.

On February 7th of 1878, a month after the death of his principal antagonist, King Victor Emmanuel II, Pope Pius IX died at the Vatican. His 32 year reign over, within days the Curia signalled the German government that it would be willing to moderate its positions. And Bismarck replied he was willing to change his, depending on who the conclave chose as Pope.

In the remarkably short time of less than *two weeks* the cardinals chose the moderate and non-confrontational Cardinal Pecci as Pope Leo XIII. Soon after his installation, on March 3rd, Bismarck restored diplomatic relations, and by the beginning of 1879 the "Kulturkampf" was over.

Truth be told, they still did not like each other, but they had fought each other to a standstill and now they needed each other. An enemy that first appeared 30 years earlier had finally started to make a political impact: Communism. Though still not a major force, it had grown enough to be viewed by others as a threat. This would be how Bismarck's last, and longest-running war ended. A stalemate, with an abiding bitterness among some parties that would even carry on past the Chancellor's days in office.

The Empire Gains an Empire

Prussia's imperial ambitions did not end with the unification of Germany. It wanted what most of the other European powers had, an overseas empire. Britain, France and Spain traditionally had the largest. Smaller states like Holland, Denmark and Portugal also had territories. Even new states like Belgium and Italy were gaining them and neither Bismarck nor Kaiser Wilhelm wanted their empire to be left out.

As early as 1872 Germany had become an active member in the international community. Shortly after British Columbia was ceded to Canada by Great Britain in 1871, the question of who owned San Juan Island at the entrance to Puget Sound arose. Canada, the United States and Britain approached the Kaiser to act as the arbiter. After consulting with the ambassadors from all three states, he awarded the island to America.

Six years later, a far more serious problem came to Berlin looking for an honest broker. The latest Russian-Turkish war had just ended with a treaty that left too many questions unresolved. The war had been a bloody one with several costly battles, both sides were extensively armed with Krupp artillery, and Turkey was about to lose all of its Balkan territories and other possessions.

The problem was Turkey and the European Powers did not want Russia to get anything on the continent. In two months of hard negotiations the Congress of Berlin ceded back to Russia the Bessarabia region, which it had lost after the Crimean War, and part of Armenia. The territories of Romania, Bulgaria, Serbia and Montenegro became fully independent while Cyprus was turned over to Britain and Bosnia-Herzegovina to Austria-Hungary.

Russia did not like the results but the other Powers found them fair and forced her to accept them. They also found, as if the French could not have told them, that Bismarck was a tough but fair negotiator. In the following years they would come to Berlin to have other, more minor, matters resolved. All the while Germany financed expeditions to Africa and the Pacific. And another six years later her ambitions for an overseas empire were about to be realized.

Between 1884 and 1885 Berlin hosted a conference, which eventually included 14 countries, to decide the future of colonizing Africa. Large tracts were already held by Britain, France, Spain and Portugal, with Belgium claiming part of the interior. There were disputed territories, unclaimed areas and a great possibility for colonial incidents to boil into global conflict.

It was primarily for this reason, not to "civilize" Africa to European standards or to exploit resources, most of which nobody knew existed, that Bismarck played host to one of the most important international conferences in the last decades of the 19th Century. And by its end Wilhelm I possessed what no previous German king or kaiser ever dreamed of having: overseas colonies.

The Berlin Conference granted to Germany the colonies of Tanganyika and Zanzibar, to be called German East Africa, on the East African coast, and Namibia/German South-West Africa on the west coast. Nor were these the only foreign territories Germany would gain. At around this time German explorers properly mapped and researched the island chains northeast of New Guinea. They christened them the Bismarck Archipelago and they included the previously named Admiralty Islands, Solomon Islands and Trobriand Islands. And the ocean area they enclosed would come to be called the Bismarck Sea.

By the beginning of the 20th Century more territories would be added to Germany's colonial empire, such as Truk and Yap in the Caroline Islands and the port of Tsing-tao on China's Yellow Sea Coast. All of which required the construction of a fleet that would one day rival the size of the Royal Navy.

The Evolution of Paranoia

For a people who waited so long, so many centuries, to see their country reborn it is only natural that some wondered why. The answer to this lay in the last seven centuries of European history: Barbarossa's death during the Third Crusade, the breakup of the First Reich, the Holy Roman Empire, Martin Luther and the Protestant Reformation, the rivalry between the Hapsburg and Bourbon royal families, the Thirty Years' War, the War of Spanish Succession, the War of Austrian Succession, the Seven Years' War and finally, the wars of the French Revolution and Napoleonic Era.

But this is a complex set of answers that requires a thorough understanding of history. A much simpler answer was Sonderweg: the special path of national development unique to the German people. Sonderweg appealed to the philosophers and academics who had spent decades advocating their "Rechsstaat" and "Ständestaat" concepts, perhaps because it allowed them to ignore the reality that the German Empire was neither.

It certainly appealed to the highly nationalistic press, the finally united people and most politicians. It implied the Germans were unique in the world, had undergone special trials of storm and stress, "Sturm und Drang," to achieve this long-sought dream of unity and perfection as Europe's newest empire. Still, it did not explain *why* the German people had been selected for this treatment, but that did not mean there were not people willing to try.

Among the first were Friedrich Wilhelm Nietzsche, at the time of German Unification a 27 year-old classical scholar, Christian critic and author of the long-running philosophical essay *Thus Spake Zarathrusta* – a work he would continually add to until near the end of his life, in which he introduced the idea of the perfectibility of Man through rigorous "self-assertion."

This would lead to the creation and glorification of the "Superman," in concept a great-souled hero who transcends the restrictive morality of Christianity and whose supreme passion is the "will to power." It is this passion that enables the "Superman" to rise above inferior men and creativity in all its forms.

This philosophy appeared during a remarkable confluence of events and scientific achievements. Nietzsche promulgated it at the same time as Bismarck started his final push to German Unification, and the theories of British naturalist Charles Robert Darwin were gaining greater academic and scientific acceptance.

It did not take much intermingling and corrupting of the theories, philosophies and events to produce some interesting conclusions. Perhaps it's a fair enough use of events to depict Bismarck as an example of the "will to power" concept. But to state this alone is the reason for the successful reunification of Germany is pushing it. As is the notion that the Chancellor's secular education program is an example of Man shedding his enslavement by Christian morality.

Nor was Nietzsche and Nietzscheism the only movement or philosophy attempting to explain Sonderweg. There was mysticism, especially the cult of Theosophy as presented by Madame Helena Blavatsky. A Russian-born psychic of German ancestry – her maiden name was Hahn – she at least did travel to Tibet and India. Bringing back, among other things, what she claimed to be the secret racial history of the Aryans.

While Blavatsky would not be the only one to push this pseudo-religion, she did found the Theosophical Society in 1875 and authored a number of hugely popular books in both Germany and America, where she founded the society. In these books, such as *The Secret Doctrine* (1888), she claimed something a growing number of Germans dearly wanted to hear: that the Aryans were the last descendants of a race of super beings who ruled the earth in pre-history days. Blavatsky may have been the first to identify the swastika as an Aryan symbol, the "twice-high sun whisk," and may also have been the originator of a phrase that would echo so fatefully through the 20th Century: *Master Race*.

And her books and society had the good fortune to appear at about the same time as the birth of a new scientific discipline. One created by the scientist Sir Francis Galton, who devised the first fingerprint system, coined the term "anti-cyclone," and was a cousin of Charles Darwin. His discipline borrowed some of the language of evolution-through-natural-selection but none of its science, and he called it Eugenics.

It would take a little while for the pseudo-religion and the pseudo-science to meet up with the philosophies of Nietzsche – to intermingle and corrupt them, to feed upon each other and the anxieties of the times and old prejudices, to produce in a newly-united people a unique paranoia, just as they were deciding that Georg Friedrich Hegel, the Schlegel brothers and the other German philosophers were right: that their culture had a world mission to perform.

Chapter XXIV: Reparations, Refugees and Republican Crises – France Deals With Defeat

> *"It may be horrible, but it's no longer war and*
> *one can breathe again."*
> -Amandine Aurore Lucie Dupin,
> AKA George Sand (1804 - 1876)

The Cost of Their Follies

ON MARCH 1st, 1871, when the National Assembly approved the peace treaty, there occurred an incident that could not escape being symbolic. Upon hearing that his city had been ceded to the Germans Émile Krüss, the mayor of Strasbourg, died of a heart attack. One of the first politicians outside of Paris to declare for the Republic, he and General Jean Uhrich were treated as some of its first heroes. Now the legend would grow of the hero who died of a broken heart.

At least the Germans allowed him to be brought to his home and buried as a Frenchman. For the million and a half residents of the 90% of Alsace and 35% of Lorraine ceded to the German Empire they would now have to decide whether to stay French or become German.

In terms of overall population and territory these losses represented just over four percent of the pre-war French population of 36 million and three percent of its land area. In the reality of the crushing defeat delivered upon it they were not too much, but they still represented the largest loss of French territory and population since the end of the Hundred Years War.

They and not the casualties, loss of international prestige or the reparations and other financial costs, were the bitterest pill for the French to swallow. The mourning, the grief and impotent rage began even before the treaty had been ratified, let alone in the final ceremony on May 10th. Impotent because the loss had been a foregone conclusion since the end of January when the Armistice took effect.

From that point on the French realized they would never again be powerful enough to fight a major war in Europe on their own. The Germans, with no allies other than themselves, had defeated them, destroyed their last imperial regime and exacted virtually everything they wanted from their nation.

The reparations would be paid, prestige regained and the battered economy restored, but the Alsace and Lorraine would be an abiding wound that would never heal. After he returned from exile, Leon Gambetta counseled, "never talk about them, think about them always." For the next 48 years they would be objects of mourning, veneration and dreams of *revanche*: technically "revenge," but its literal meaning was "return match" or "to even the score."

If France wanted the lost provinces back she would need allies, but in the immediate aftermath of the Franco-Prussian War this would be unlikely. Her northern neighbors of Holland, Belgium and Luxembourg, still remembering her territorial ambitions toward them, actually felt safer allying themselves with Germany. Italy *still* had not forgiven France for Napoleon III's actions, and the reactionary Franz Josef would not ally Austria-Hungary with anything called a republic. Russia felt pretty much the same way and Spain, in 1872, consumed itself with another civil war.

That only left the former *ennemi héréditaire*, Great Britain, and there were plenty of antagonisms and problems for the two to overcome. True, they had been allies in Crimea and later, briefly, during the Mexico Adventure, and were ongoing allies in the various wars occurring all over China.

However, the French resented Britain's evenhandedness and neutrality during the war while the English resented the accusations they were Prussian spies and the ungrateful attitude the Parisians displayed to all the supplies they rushed them once the Germans lifted the siege. Then there were the courtesies Britain extended to Napoleon III and his family as the traditional home of exiled European monarchs, though the Bonapartists did not seem to mind.

Fortunately, the situation soon began to change. President Thiers knew one of the quickest ways to restore French prestige was to pay off the reparations and remove the occupation troops from his country. Because French commerce and the material wealth of her overseas empire had not been greatly affected by the war, her credit remained good.

By the end of June, 1871 Thiers had negotiated a loan of two and a half billion francs from a consortium of foreign banks. This freed up all but the half-dozen easternmost departments of metropolitan France from German occupation. By spring the following year he negotiated another loan from the same sources for three billion francs. And on September 5th, 1873, the last part of the indemnity due to Germany was paid. The last German troops departed France on the 16th and, with an ironic portend to the future, the last fortress they turned over to the French Army was Verdun.

At the beginning of 1873 another obstacle to British-French cooperation was removed when Napoleon III died on January 9th. And just under three years later the growing alliance took its biggest step forward when the British government bought the Khedive of Egypt's controlling interest in the Suez Canal. For four million pounds they acquired 90% ownership of the canal. A number of other European states were upset with this turn of events. They had wanted to purchase some control in its operations so their shipping would not be denied use. But France was happy to get a stable partner and, what had been seen from Whitehall as a strategic threat to British naval supremacy would now be an asset. French prestige had started to rebound.

Solving One Problem, Creating Future Ones

Of the million and a half residents in the ceded Alsace and Lorraine territories, approximately 25% left for France. In total 378,000 by government estimates, though the German estimates are for less than half the amount, became refugees. And for some curious reason, they were not especially welcomed in the rest of France.

For all the mourning over their loss, and hatred towards Germany for taking the lands, the flood of its refugees would not be greeted with much compassion or empathy. Perhaps the numbers were too much for a war-battered nation to absorb. Perhaps the other departments and provinces were just too parochial to allow for the settlement of so many outsiders, even if they were French.

Whatever the reasons, the refugees became yet another problem for the Third Republic to resolve. Its priority fell below that of rebuilding the economy, reforming the French Army, rebuilding Paris, repaying the reparation loans, rebuilding the other cities and fortresses damaged in the war and restoring France's international relations. The solution to the refugee problem came almost as an afterthought, readily agreed to, and would echo through the intervening years to the present age.

Since no one, no department or province inside France, proved willing to accept any sizable percentage of the refugees, President Thiers' government initially decided to settle them outside of France, in its overseas colonial empire. But the refugee leaders, and the newspapers who championed their cause, would have nothing to do with such a diaspora. The solution they all readily came to was to make one of the colonies a part of metropolitan France.

The island of Corsica was close enough but far too small in both land area and population to accept over 300,000 refugees. They settled on Algeria, whose vast land area could, in theory, easily absorb them. The legislation was quickly passed transferring Algeria from the Ministry of Marine and Colonies to the Ministry of the Interior. For all intents and purposes Algeria had become part of metropolitan France.

With some grumbling, tens of thousands of Alsace and Lorraine refugees boarded ships for the newest and largest department of their country. In land area, over 900,000 square miles, it could easily absorb them. The problem was the only habitable region was the comparatively small and narrow coastal zone. Already heavily populated with Arabs and Berbers, whose families and tribes had lived there for generations, the local military governor responded with decrees for forcible relocation.

In a matter of months the best lands in the colony, the most fertile and with a pleasant, Mediterranean climate were turned over to the arriving flood of refugees. As for the original Arab and Berber owners, most were moved farther into the interior, to the marginal scrub lands of the steppe where many rivers are intermittent and useless for irrigation.

And to add a far graver insult to injury, because Algeria was now part of France its population received voting rights and representation in the new chambers which superseded the wartime National Assembly – but only if you were of French ancestry. As the Haitians had discovered at the end of the previous century, *Liberté*, *Egalité* and *Fraternité* only applied if you were white, male and European.

As the loss of the Alsace and Lorraine became an abiding wound that would not heal, so too would this grievance. The big difference between the two would be that while the French took Gambetta's counsel and did not talk about it, the Arabs, once they found their voice, would speak often of this injustice and eventually find traction with it.

By the middle of the coming century it became one of the sparks to Arab nationalist movements across North Africa and the rest of the Middle East. In particular it laid the groundwork for the bloody and bitter Algerian Civil War of 1954 to 1962, which would end with independence for Algeria and a near-revolt by the French Army against a national hero who grew up and joined that army in the shadow of France's most humiliating defeat.

And the hatred did not end with Algerian statehood, or the independence of the other European colonies in the Islamic world. The faint echoes of this consequence from the Franco-Prussian War has become one of the fuels for the current wave of Islamic fanaticism. After all, the first attempt to fly a hijacked airliner into a building was made by Algerian fundamentalists trying to destroy the Eiffel Tower, and aborted by a French anti-terrorist squad.

The State of Crises

If the Third Republic wanted to prove to the rest of Europe it was a stable member of the community, it certainly did not begin with good foundations. Though constituted as a republic, the majorities in both its Chamber of Deputies and Senate were nominally held by the royalist parties. Had they really, *really* wanted to, the Bourbonists, Bonapartists, Orléanists and Constitutional Monarchists could have united behind a single candidate and turned France back into a monarchy.

The main problem for them lay in that they hated each other, though that did not mean a continual string of candidates, the famous "men on horseback," would not try. The remaining political parties, the Moderate Republicans and the Red Republicans, detested each other even more so than the royalist factions. At times the Red Republicans took this a step further and despised themselves, occasionally splitting into separate parties or "voting factions," usually over the question of who they would ally with, or if they would stay unified at all.

All this left the largest political party in France with an often disagreeable task. The Moderate Republicans always held the largest number of seats in both assemblies, and yet it almost never had enough to form a majority government. Inevitably this meant either a minority government or a coalition government, until some scandal or defection brought it down.

This would not take long to start happening. Even though he had guided the shipwreck of France through one of its most turbulent periods, Louise Adolphe Thiers had one bill after another defeated by the Monarchist coalition until they forced his resignation on May 24th, 1873. Within hours he would be replaced by the first of the post-war "men on horseback."

Marshal Marie Patrice de MacMahon lead a coalition of Monarchist parties and became the longest-serving of the post-war presidents. He made the Republic's ambassador to Great Britain his Premier and Minister of

Foreign Affairs, Duke Jacques Victor Albert de Broglie. He also had several allies in the Senate, among them the former generals Canrobert, Chanzy and d'Aurelle de Paladines.

Together, they and the rest of MacMahon's ministers laid the groundwork for restoring the Monarchy to France. And yet, they never took the final steps to institute it. MacMahon hesitated, and a new round of crises started. The impatient Duke de Broglie resigned his posts and a succession of hapless appointees replaced him as Premier. The crises continued, finally culminating in the Year of Crises: 1877.

It began with one of those "Theater of the Absurd" incidents which no one would accept as fiction, but always seems to occur in history. At the funeral of the composer Félician David, the military honor guard snubbed him and refused to participate when they learned he would be buried without religious ceremonies.

The insult caused Premier Dufaure's Ministry to resign and MacMahon allowed the Republican coalition to form one under the former Government of National Defence Minister Jules Simon. His premiership lasted just long enough for him to insult the venerable Pope Pius IX, which forced his downfall and the return of de Broglie.

When Dufaure's Ministry was declared unconstitutional by the Chamber of Deputies the Senate, at MacMahon's request, dissolved it and new elections were ordered. In the meantime de Broglie continued with his program to restore the Monarchy. All of it not only threatened to destabilize France, it threatened civil war. Leon Gambetta warned of it, and was threatened with three months in prison. For Bismarck, it was a heaven-sent opportunity to reign in his own rancorous legislature and pass his ambitious military program.

MacMahon, again, hesitated. This time his country teetered in front of the abyss it last visited just six years earlier. He refused to arrest Gambetta and instead worked with him to see the elections carried out safely. The resulting majority, just barely Republican between the Moderates and the Reds, nonetheless forced the resignation of de Broglie as well as the next ministry MacMahon tried to engineer.

By the end of the year the reconstituted Chamber and a timid Senate forced MacMahon to bring back Dufaure as Premier and a Republican Ministry which enacted sweeping changes. Among them, the President would no longer be elected directly by the voters but appointed by both the Chamber of Deputies and the Senate. And, statues could no longer be erected to the living; MacMahon's would be among the last.

As for MacMahon himself, he would not stay past the next scheduled elections. In 1879 he knew his time had come and resigned to allow another "man of horseback" to have a chance, in this case Senator and former General Antoine Chanzy. However, for the moment France was tired of such men. Jules Grévy became President. Charles Louis de Freycinet, the former Government of National Defence War Minister, became Premier. And Gambetta, President of the Chamber of Deputies.

For a few years the Republicans, the Moderates and Reds, were in charge, until they started unraveling. In 1881 Gambetta replaced de Freycinet as Premier but his radical programs were even rejected by the Republican Chamber. In 1882 he resigns and, while attempting to commit suicide, wounds himself in the hand with a revolver, and later dies of blood poisoning.

Four years after this another "man of horseback" appears just when France thinks it needs one. General Georges Ernest Boulanger is recalled from occupation duty in Tunis by new Premier Georges Clemenceau and is appointed Minister of War. He introduces long-contemplated, long-needed, reforms to improve the soldiers' lives and becomes a popular figure.

By the end of 1887 he initiates France's next crisis by igniting the long-simmering desires for *revanche*. Boulanger is removed from command and exiled to Clermont-Ferrand in central France, because he demanded an apology from Germany over the Schnaebelé Affair. The German government admits the overzealous Police Commissioner of Metz had lured Schnaebelé, a French border command official, into its territory and arrested him for spying.

When the response was not to his liking, Boulanger openly pushed for the recall of the French ambassador from Berlin and mobilizing 50,000 troops to the border. This brings down the first Clemenceau Ministry, gives Bismarck another of those heaven-sent opportunities to increase military spending and gets Boulanger dismissed from the Army by the beginning of 1888.

This, coming after the resignation of President Grévy due to a scandal, not only makes the ex-general popular but the head of the Boulangist Movement. In national elections he, with distinct echoes of Napoleon III, is elected Deputy from several departments. In the Chamber of Deputies he launches a bitter duel with its radical President.

By July of 1888 this escalates into a real duel in which both are wounded. Coincidental to it, a national strike by Anarchists and Communists erupts across France the following month. Velvet weavers in Amiens, glass-blowers in Lyons, textile workers in Lille, stone masons and waiters in Paris went into the streets. Those not arrested by the police or the Army eventually exhausted their labor unions' funds and were forced back to work.

Though it ended before August did, the temporary anarchy only served to advance the Boulangist cause. Paul Déroulède, a young nationalist, founded the right-wing "Ligue des Patriotes", and joined a conspiracy that saw Boulanger as the Napoleonic "man on horseback" France needed to straighten out its chaotic democracy. And yet, the conspiracy to make the ex-general the next dictator fell into chaos itself, and charges of misappropriating public funds.

For all the drama it produced, both nationally and internationally, the coup fizzled out pathetically by the first months of 1889. Appropriately enough the joke ended on April 1ˢᵗ when Boulanger fled to Brussels to avoid arrest. The Senate charged him and the rest of his movement's senior leaders with treason and later, sitting as the Court of High Justice, found him, Count Dillon and most of the other leaders guilty.

Boulanger brought the "man on horseback" syndrome full circle and to a close for the 19ᵗʰ Century. To a close because he would be the last serious contender for the role until Marshal Henri Philippe Pétain emerged from the First World War. And full circle because his commander at Metz had once envisioned this would be his role in post-war France. But fate had a different one in store for Marshal Francois Achille Bazaine: national scapegoat.

In 1873 he stood trial for incompetence and treason. Not even with MacMahon as President could Bazaine escape the verdict of guilty. Given a death sentence, MacMahon would at least commute it to 20 years at the Ile Ste Marguerite fortress near Cannes. Allowed to escape, Bazaine would live in exile and near-poverty in Spain. He died in 1888, just as Boulanger started his moment in the sun. He too would die in exile, committing suicide next to his mistress' grave in Brussels in 1891.

The Religion of Defeat

While some in France turned to extremist politics and dreams of *revanche*, many more turned to the traditional refuge of a defeated people: religion. It is no small coincidence that, in the aftermath of the Franco-Prussian War religious cults gained major followings. In particular three Catholic ones, the largest of which actually received a huge boost while the war still raged.

When the "Army of the Loire" forced von der Tann's First Bavarian Corps out of Orléans, many in the French press, and not a few politicians, claimed it as a triumph of France's patron saint, the "Maid of Orléans" –

that it was a divinely-ordained omen of their coming victory over the Germans. Four months later the delusions finally ended, but the veneration of Joan of Arc would continue, as the "Maid of Lorraine."

In the four centuries since her execution by the British, she had been associated with Orléans, the site of her first victory and where she met the Dauphin, later Charles VII. But her home had been the village of Domrémy in southwestern Lorraine, and now her identity switched back to the province. If anything, it made her story even more poignant to France.

A commoner who heard the voices of God and the saints, especially Saint Michael, who rallied her nation in its time of need and defeated a brutal invader, who would be betrayed by her king, put on trial by her church, executed by the invaders and yet remained loyal to her country. If Friedrich Nietzsche, that notorious critic of Christianity, had bothered to examine her life he would have found it to be yet another example of his "will to power" – perhaps even a great-souled being, but not a "superman."

Though she would not be canonized until 1920, the Franco-Prussian War and the annexation of part of her homeland assured her ascension to Patron Saint of France. Unlike the other two cult figures she offered something to nearly everyone. The devout saw the traditional Catholic heroine, republicans saw her as a real-life version of Marianne, the nickname given to the First Republic back in 1792 and the official personification of the country ever since then. The more nationalistic could see in her the lonely patriot, betrayed to her enemies and abandoned by her king, yet still loyal to France. Even radicals admired the heretic in Joan of Arc and her stand against the Catholic Church. She was as universal a figure as one could ask for, a true symbol of national unity.

The next most popular cult figure could not quite approach this level, though she did have the unique advantage of being a living saint: Marie-Bernarde Soubirous. Born in 1844 to an impoverished family in the Pyrenees Mountains of southern France Saint Bernadette, as she would be known, began having Marian (Saint Mary) visions at the age of 14 in the Massabielle Cave near Lourdes.

At first she was not believed, and even threatened with an inquisition, but the news of her visions spread and Lourdes quickly became a pilgrimage site. Bernadette's following grew into a cult before the Franco-Prussian War, and her tireless work tending to the wounded from the conflict only increased it. That work, and her increased post-war activities, may well have contributed to her death in 1879, at the age of just 35.

After this Lourdes became an internationally popular shrine where the stories of miracles began to multiply. Compared to Joan of Arc, Bernadette's ascension to sainthood proceeded rather swiftly. She would be beatified in 1925, and canonized by 1933, less than 90 years after her birth. Her popularity has proved just as enduring as Saint Joan, though she quickly became more of a universal figure of piety and service to the ill and infirm.

The third cult figure combined elements of both Saint Bernadette and Saint Joan: a lifetime's service to small acts of penitence and atonement with visions from the saints and a nationalistic appeal. Saint Marguerite-Marie Alacoque lived in the 17th Century in the Burgundy town of Paray-le-Monial. She founded the Order of the Sacré-Coeur, the Sacred Heart, which urged piety on an increasingly sinful world.

A Catholic version of the more fundamental Protestant sects, its following grew rather slowly in the 18th and 19th Centuries. In fact, right up to the end of the Franco-Prussian War when the more religious among the right-wing discovered it and claimed its tenants could save a nation which had lost its traditional virtues and was now being punished for its sins.

The basilica at Paray-le-Monial, long a site of pilgrimage to venerate Saint Marguerite's relics, became the center for annual festivals of monarchist parties and other right-wing groups. While its appeal was more limited than the other two religious movements, it certainly did not lack for rich benefactors. Sacré-Coeur churches were built all over France, culminating in the massive basilica constructed on the Montmartre Heights.

It took 43 years to build, between 1876 and 1919, and many critics claim it mars the Paris skyline. Others say it was intentionally built over the entombed bodies of the last Communard fighters. Whatever the criticism it has an imposing presence over the City of Light, almost as if God were watching, noting its lack of piety and endemic sinfulness – which the city returned to much faster than it would be rebuilt.

The Slow Climb Back

Had it just been the damage from the German siege operations and shelling, Paris could have been rebuilt in a matter of a year or two. But the Communards had destroyed nearly a third of the city, and repairing its infrastructure took priority. This meant streets and bridges torn up for use as barricades as well as train stations and rail lines. Damage to the all-important water system and sewer system had to be fixed before the authorities could allow the city to repopulate.

Paris soon enough glittered again, but even the new invention of electric illumination could not hide the scars. The Hôtel de Ville, Quai d'Orsay Palace, the Ministry of Finance, the Palace of Justice and other essential buildings to the governance of the city and the country were re-built. The Vendôme Column would be re-raised in a very novel and appropriate way.

At his trial the celebrity artist/anarchist Gustave Courbet was sentenced to restore the column, using his own money. He even had to pay for the casting of a new statue of Napoleon Bonaparte, the original having been beheaded. The project ruined him financially, but he did get to stay out of jail.

However, there were other landmarks that would not be so lucky. Tuileries Palace remained a solemn ruin of blackened walls and other debris in the city's center until 1883, when the land was finally cleared and turned into a park with playgrounds. The Louvre's library would not be restored, neither would the Chapell Expiatoire or scores of other major buildings and hundreds of private homes. Even after their remains had been cleared the empty plots of land still remained as scars, only slowly filled in by new construction.

Finally, in the mid-1880s, the last large tract of unused land remaining in Paris was the Champ de Mars, the site of the former munitions plant. In 1886 the municipal and national governments decided the time had come for the reborn city to have a coming-out party: the Universal Exhibition of 1889.

A world's fair of industrial arts and scientific advances, it would be the latest version of the 1851 Great Exhibition in London. Its centerpiece had been the Crystal Palace, the architecture wonder of its day. The Universal Exhibition needed its own, and out of 700 proposals the exhibition committee chose the tower design of Gustave Eiffel. And without a single change to the finalized plans the French took just over 16 months to build the world's tallest free-standing structure.

It soared over a thousand feet into the air, forever changing the Paris skyline and proving France to be just as capable of producing technological wonders as any other nation. It was properly acclaimed as one of the marvels of its age and yet, when the Exhibition the Eiffel Tower presided over opened on May 6th, 1889, the centenary of the French Revolution's start, the British and American ambassadors lead official delegations to it. However, not a single continental European monarchy sent a representative. The climb back to respectability would indeed be long and slow.

Chapter XXV: Britain Casts a Wary Eye

"An Englishman is never so natural as when he's holding his tongue."
-Henry James (1843 - 1916)

Dealing With the Unexpected

GIVEN HIS UNDERSTANDING and experience that not everything happens the way you expect them, Britain should have had Benjamin Disraeli as Prime Minister in the aftermath of the Franco-Prussian War. Instead it got William Ewart Gladstone, at least until 1874, and a bad case of paranoid jitters.

For once, all the military experts were unanimous in their forecasts about a war's outcome. From celebrity military "analysts" like Friedrich Engels on up to a true British celebrity, and professional soldier, Garnet Joseph Wolseley: they all got it wrong. *No one* expected a German victory to be the result, much less one so complete and crushing.

Additionally, no one in the British government or outside it expected the two biggest consequences of the war to be the creation of a unified German Empire and another French Republic. The world indeed had turned upside down and they wondered what would happen next. Would they become an object of German expansionism?

Would this new French Republic lead to a replay of the Jacobin terror of the previous century and a continent-wide war? Certainly, the events in Paris between March 18ᵗʰ and May 28ᵗʰ did not bode well to those who thought they had just been handed the worst of all possible worlds.

For the moment the British press, government and general public forgot about whatever threat the new German Empire might present and concentrated on the threat they had at home: Communism and the First International. Karl Marx did not help matters by openly paying the Communards homage and endorsing their goals. What he wanted was the creation of a heroic legend of fearless socialists. Instead he got the nickname the "Red Terrorist Doctor" and the International popularly identified as a revolutionary conspiracy cabal.

The British trade unions abandoned the Communists and switched their association to the Fabians, a more respectable band of home grown socialists that included George Bernard Shaw and Herbert George (H.G.) Wells. Marx, for some inexplicable reason, rather enjoyed his notorious fame. This after despising for over 20 years such celebrity anarchist and revolutionary types as Mikhail Bakunin and Guiseppe Garibaldi.

All of it, plus the press and government attacks, hastened the First International's dissolution by 1876. In fact its final meetings were held outside of Great Britain, and its final executive acts were to make sure Bakunin and his associates could not get hold of its remnants. This proved to be an ironically useless gesture as Bakunin himself would be dead before the end of the year while Marx had already begun his descent into obscurity. He would die almost unheralded in 1883, and long before then the British Government and press had turned to fretting over the outside threats.

Militaire Fantasques

The guns had scarcely fallen silent on the battlefields of France, and were still being used with great enthusiasm in Paris, when Military Science Fiction was born with the publication of the *Battle of Dorking* by Lieutenant-Colonel Sir George Tomkyns Chesney. Published in serial form by *Blackwood's Magazine*, in style it differed from every military fantasy published before it and would set the pattern for such tales straight through to contemporary times.

All earlier efforts were either small pamphlets or short stories aimed at raising political awareness of a threat perceived by the author, which he wrote about in general terms. Chesney's novella changed the formula to what we now recognize: it presented a first-person account of a surprise German invasion of southern England and Britain's subsequent collapse.

Dorking is a real location – in its day the last town before London, on the most direct route from the South Downs beaches on the Channel Coast. Sir Chesney, a Royal Engineer with distinguished service in India, where he set up the Royal Indian Civil Engineering College, not only used real locations but came up with a halfway plausible scenario as to how the most powerful military force in the world could not stop the invasion of its homeland.

The Royal Navy, as well as a large portion of the Royal Army, is dispersed to other crises near and far: the "crisis" between America and Britain over the islands in Puget Sound, an uprising in India, a threatened Fenian revolt in Ireland, increased pirate activities in the China Seas and rioting in the West Indies islands. The fact that some of these events were actually happening at the time added a stark immediacy to the story, and then there was the secret weapon.

The appearance of the Mitrailleuse and breech-loading Krupp cannons had been treated in a very sensational way by the British Press. When it came to military matters everyone talked about "secret weapons" and Chesney provided one: floating sea mines. They sink most of the remaining British warships in home waters, leaving the German invasion force to land unhindered, and face what land forces the home government could scrape together.

Here Chesney mixed information about the disasters experienced by the French Army with his own insights of the British. While the Regular Army prepares to refight Waterloo with outmoded weapons and tactics, the Volunteer regiments are even more poorly-equipped, poorly-lead and all suffer from breakdowns in logistics and communications. It all leads to an unmitigated disaster from which there is no happy ending, yet another then-unique feature.

By the summer of 1871, with the Communist threat receding, the *Battle of Dorking* had not only become a sensation in Britain, translated versions were creating a sensation across Europe. The French particularly enjoyed it, as it depicted the British getting the same drubbing they had just received. And the British government had to wonder exactly what Berlin thought of it. After all, the Kaiser himself was arbitrating the San Juan Island dispute at the time.

Prime Minister Gladstone worried so much about the story's effects that, by September 2nd, he gave a speech attacking it, Chesney and all those who trumpeted it. He did so partly out of fear all the extra military spending its readers advocated could ruin the Treasury, and partly to negate any effect it might have on the arbitration. In the end the island went to America, but there is no evidence Wilhelm I had been influenced by the *Battle of Dorking*.

What the story did influence, due to its immense popularity, was the host of other writers across England and Europe who either sought to imitate it, or criticize it. The latter would be especially true of other British writers, just to sample from the titles of their works: *After the Battle of Dorking or, What Became of the Invaders?*; *What Happened After the Battle of Dorking*; *The Other Side at the Battle of Dorking*; *The Battle of Dorking: A Myth*.

The furor and tone of the anti-Chesney stories became rancorous; you would have thought they were arguing over a real battle in a real war, instead of a piece of fiction. In fact, Britain had not seen its like since the post-war debates and official inquiries over the army and government's conduct during the Crimean War. On the continent the reaction was rather different.

Apparently taking Gambetta's advice seriously, most French writers did not turn the dreams of *revanche* into fictional fantasies. Edouard Dangin did produce *La Bataille de Berlin en 1875* but the rest found an old enemy to be more appropriate. *Plus d'Angleterre* told of a future war between France and Britain where the old *ennemi héréditaire* is swiftly and humiliatingly defeated. Since it title had no direct translation into English it was printed in Britain as *Down with England*. It proved so popular in France that a sequel soon appeared, *Plus Encore d'Angleterre*.

These were followed in 1884 by *Les Malheurs de John Bull/The Misfortunes of John Bull*, which is reported as being aggressively anglophobic. An Italian writer wrote a purely naval version of *Dorking* which advocated Italy increase the size of her fleet, especially in light of increased naval activity in the Mediterranean by France and Great Britain. And not to be outdone, an Austro-Hungarian naval officer wrote *Der Grosse Seekrieg Im Jahre 1888*, an overly detailed account of a battle in the English Channel between the two previously mentioned powers.

Partly, all these were written to advocate changes in national policy, much like the pamphlets from earlier in the century. These took advantage of the increased appetite for fiction and the post-war paranoia over a war that turned out quite unlike virtually everyone's expectations. However, it would take more than just raising the levels of national anxiety to get military reforms funded and implemented.

Military Reality, British-Style

At least Sir Chesney was willing to put his mouth where his pen had traveled. He campaigned for and eventually won a seat in the House of

Commons, where he pushed for military reforms and increased spending he knew would be needed to make the Royal Army a modern force and maintaining the world dominance of the Royal Navy. But reform-minded politicians would not be enough to transform so hidebound an institution as Britain's army. It needed Generals and Secretaries for War willing to put reform into practice.

Fortunately Britain had such men – it had Wolseley, Frederick Sleigh Roberts and later, Horatio Herbert Kitchener. Even before the Franco-Prussian War turned the world upside down, Wolseley had taken up the reform banner. In 1869 he published the *Soldier's Pocket-Book for Field Service*, based upon his experiences in the Empire's colonial wars, garrison duty in Canada and observer to the Confederate Army in the U.S. Civil War.

The book won him renown among civilians, the enlisted ranks and like-minded officers, but its criticisms of the army and its administration angered his superiors, and they thought they had the perfect way to deal with him. They kept him in Canada, far away from the usual colonial hot spots where an officer could build a reputation.

But in the beginning of 1870 the Métis leader Louis David Riel organized a rebellion of the local tribes in the Red River area, part of present-day Manitoba, to prevent its annexation by the new Dominion of Canada. While John Alexander MacDonald, Canada's first Prime Minister, negotiated, Wolseley organized the Red River Expedition of British troops and Canadian reservists.

While the rest of Europe watched the Hohenzollern Candidature ignite the Franco-Prussian War, England was initially transfixed by the Red River Rebellion and Wolseley's performance in it, which made him a national hero. During it he became the first British commander to use the railroad to transport his force directly to a theater of operations. His countrymen treated it as if it were the world's first such operation. Wolseley knew better, and when he returned to England to receive his general's commission he used his fame to continue to push for reforms.

They were not long in coming. As Assistant Adjutant General, Wolseley pushed through shorter enlistment periods to garner more recruits, worked on the creation of a reserve force to supplement the Volunteers and ended the centuries-old practice of officer's commissions being purchased rather than earned. The last two ideas had come from reforms first instituted in Prussia, by Scharnhorst and Gneisenau, as did another he advocated to Secretary for War Cardwell: large-scale annual maneuvers. In September of 1871 the first of these were conducted, with both Regular and Volunteer units. And again it was acclaimed by the

British Press as a first-ever innovation.

However, the reforms would not be nearly so easy to carry out in the Royal Army as they had been in the Prussian and other German armies. The British, and especially the officer corps of both the Army and the Navy, clung rather tenaciously to its traditions, even if reality showed them to be antiquated. And then there were the continuing series of colonial wars which often hamstrung both reform efforts and reformers.

The careers of both Wolseley and Frederick Roberts illustrate this. In 1873 Wolseley was sent to the West African Gold Coast, present-day Ghana, to end the slave-trading operations of the Ashanti. After a two-year campaign he succeeded and returned to England, only to be sent back to Africa in 1879. This time he relieved the incompetent Lord Chelmsford after the disaster of Isandhlwana at the start of the Zulu War. This campaign produced an ironic footnote: the death of Napoleon III's son.

Prince Eugene Louis Joseph Bonaparte had obtained permission from the British Government to join its army. Bonapartists in France thought if he were to be a serious contender for a restored French monarchy he needed military experience, even if it came from service with the hated English. And on June 2nd of 1879, while on a reconnaissance sortie, Zulu warriors managed to do what the modern armies of Europe failed to accomplish: they killed a Napoleon in combat.

A year earlier Frederick Roberts commanded one of the divisions ordered into Afghanistan from India at the start of the Second Afghan War. For over two years he fought a series of brutal battles in the harsh terrain, culminating in a battle outside of Kandahar on August 31st of 1880 where he surrounded and destroyed the entire Afghan Army, effectively ending the war.

Now famous across the British Empire, he had barely returned to England when the Army sent Roberts back to India in 1885 as commander-in-chief of all forces on the sub-continent. Three years earlier Wolseley commanded an expedition to Egypt where, in May of 1882, the nominal Egyptian government revolted after having British rule forced on them. Hundreds of Europeans were killed in Alexandria alone, until a fleet of half a dozen Royal Navy battleships, plus cruisers and gunboats, showed up. After they bombarded the city's fortifications, Wolseley landed his troops and by the end of the year had crushed the uprising, securing the safety of the Suez Canal.

Less than two years later, at about the same time Roberts went back to India, Wolseley returned to Egypt. This time he led the rescue of his friend, General Charles "Chinese" Gordon, whose army lay besieged in Khartoum by Islamic fanatics under the command of the mysterious Mahdi. Despite the use of a British version of the Mitrailleuse, the city's defences were overwhelmed and Gordon died. Just two days before Wolseley's army arrived and took back Khartoum from the fanatics, whose prophet-leader died within the year.

Neither Roberts nor Wolseley, nor even Horatio Kitchener, would see England for any length of time again until nearly the end of the 19th Century, when Wolseley finally received his promotion to field marshal and was made commander-in-chief of the British Army. Only then could the much-needed and long-discussed reforms proceed at a better pace than the fits and starts of the last 20 years. To ensure they would continue, Wolseley engineered his own replacement with Lord Frederick Roberts upon retirement in 1900.

In turn Roberts worked closely with the incoming Secretary for War at the very end of his term in office. Sir Richard Burdon Haldane would oversee the founding of the Territorial Army and the establishment of the National and Imperial General Staffs – most of which were first proposed by Sir George Chesney more than 30 years earlier.

Hubris Britannicus

Part of the problem, and some historians say most of the problem, with the way Great Britain treated the new German Empire lay in its own exaggerated view of its position and ability, and the beating they took when the least expected outcomes of the Franco-Prussian War became reality.

Just before it began, most Britons in any position to predict the result shared the conviction of Matthew Arnold, Professor of Poetry at Oxford: "as to the French always beating any number of Germans who come into the field against them. They will never be beaten by any nation but the English, for to every other nation they are, in efficiency and intelligence, decidedly superior."

This feeling that the British alone had the God-given right to defeat the French was compounded by a troubling fact known, for the most part, by only members of the government: that for over a dozen years the British Army had modeled itself on the French Army. The Crimean War had been an undeniable dose of reality to the British military.

The Royal Navy, which prided itself on being the world's most powerful fighting force, had not developed and fielded the era-changing naval technology. France had built the first ironclad warships and used them in battle. On land, France also had the superior technology, from the new ammunition developed by Captain Claude Minié to medical equipment which Florence Nightingale herself borrowed for use in British hospitals.

French tactics, in particular *furia francese* and *charge à l'outrance* were respected. French commanders, derogatory nicknames aside, were thought of as being more competent, especially in light of Lord Fitzroy Raglan and Lord James Thomas Cardigan. Marshal MacMahon was fondly remembered for his bravery at Malakoff Tower. Who could possibly be a better commander for the most powerful army in Europe?

And then came Spicheren Heights and Woerth, but they were treated as flukes. At the grinding battles around Metz and the investment of Bazaine's army there, the British held their breath. Sedan and the collapse of Imperial France opened the full tide of disaster, and the tangible fear that the natural order of the world had just been upended.

If the state of France became the *Raft of the Medusa*, then Britain's felt like a rudderless ship on a storm-tossed sea. It took no direction, which angered both the French and the Germans, though its industries appeared willing to make some profit off the calamity. And to some in England, who had a more knowledgeable view of the conflict, their ship-of-state seemed more like Joseph Mallord Turner's *The Fighting Téméraire*...gallant but obsolete, and perhaps heading for the scrapyard of history.

It is no small wonder that Sir Chesney's *Battle of Dorking* found such a massive and nervous audience. However, there were a few who saw the situation in a calmer, more realistic light, especially after the guns had stopped firing and the peace treaty ratified. Among them was Benjamin Disraeli.

Out of power at the time of the Franco-Prussian War, though still a major figure in the Tory Party, he was one of the few British politicians to have any significant contact with Bismarck during his brief tenure as ambassador to Napoleon III's court in 1862. He came away from his meeting impressed with Bismarck's courtly manner, his love of English authors Byron and Shakespeare, his absolute determination to see the German people united but nothing beyond that.

When he returned from the war, *The Times* correspondent William Russell quickly grew appalled at the anti-German hysteria among his countrymen. He too noted that Bismarck, Moltke and other members of Germany's civilian and military commands were Anglophile, not Anglophobic. And he understood something not readily apparent to most British politicians and the general public: Germany was exhausted from its hard fought and decisive war.

Moltke's "operational pause" in mid-December of 1870 came not a moment too soon. Men and equipment were worn, loses needed to be replaced, transport systems repaired and supplies distributed. The victory parades in the war's immediate aftermath effectively hid the state of exhaustion to the casual observer. But to perceptive men like Russell, Philip Sheridan and others the impression was obvious. Germany could not physically or politically undertake another major war any time soon.

By 1874 the hysteria had moderated and Disraeli began his second, and longest, term as Britain's Prime Minister. His ministry would prove, over the remaining decades of the 19th Century, to have the best relations with the new German Empire. There were no major crises, or "war scares," with Germany or any other major power, though there were plenty of accusations that Russia instigated the crisis in Afghanistan in 1878.

More importantly, when he dealt with Germany Disraeli dealt with Bismarck and Kaiser Wilhelm I: a conservative, cautious monarch and his highly experienced, widely respected First Chancellor. He did not have to deal with the Kaiser's grandson, a man who would prove, according to a none-too-subtle joke, to be to foreign affairs what a guillotine is to a sore throat.

However, even before Wilhelm II's reign the atmosphere of anxiety had been created, the seeds of fear and mistrust already planted. And while Germany had not done anything directly or intently to sow these, and for the moment they mostly lay dormant, it would take great pleasure in the future in cultivating them.

Chapter XXVI: Italy, The United States and Canada – The Unexpected Beneficiaries

> *"God favors fools, drunks and the*
> *United States of America. I cannot fathom*
> *the reason why."*
> -Prince Otto Edward Leopold
> von Bismarck (1815 - 1898)

United at Last

OUTSIDE OF IMPERIAL Germany and, in a perverse and brutally ironic way, Republican France, the country to benefit the most from the Franco-Prussian War would be Italy. In fact it was the first country to benefit directly from the war, for neither of the other two states really existed in September of 1870.

By the middle of the month, as the First Vatican Council was reaching its end, the last units of the French garrison were departing Rome. Among the last to go were Colonel de Charette's Papal Zouaves, who would soon become one of the best Francs-Tireur groups, and what remained were the Swiss Guards under the Papal Commandant General Kanzler.

Already, word had come that the Italian Parliament had sanctioned the transfer of both their national capital and King Victor Emmanuel's royal residence from Florence to Rome. Further, Italian Army troops under General Cadorna were marching on the city. Under the circumstances Kanzler exercised the only viable option – he capitulated the city on September 20th.

This did not go well with Pius IX, whose decades-long campaign to establish the tenet of Papal Infallibility had at last been made dogma by the Vatican Council. Now his domain on Earth had been reduced to a fraction of its size, to the Vatican City complex and of the basilica of St. John Lateran, barely a quarter-square-mile in area. By comparison, the tiny and ancient Republic of San Marino is over one hundred times its size.

Within a month the "occupation" of Rome – liberation to Italian nationalists – had been completed without any major incidents. There would, however, be an abiding resentment within the Curia Romana against the new Italian state. One that would not be resolved until 1929 when Pope Pius XI signed the Lateran Treaty with the government of Benito Mussolini, establishing Catholicism as the state religion of Italy and the Vatican State territories as a sovereign country.

For the rest of Italy, and the overwhelming majority of its population, this final act of unification was greeted with universal rejoicing. The dream had at long last been realized. From the Swiss frontier to Sicily, Italy had accomplished its centuries long journey to being a united country. No longer the playground of foreign emperors, like Napoleon Bonaparte or Franz Josef, or even its own kings and princes, it had become a modern nation. A constitutional monarchy with a single, popular monarch.

Italy would be that rare example of a country which not only reaped the benefits of a conflict without actually having engaged in it, but before the war was even close to ending. She emerged with a reasonably stable economy and on friendly terms with all the other major European Powers. Italy especially enjoyed good relations with the newest, Germany, and the most dominant, Great Britain.

Perhaps the one thing to spoil the celebration for some Italians, and could have spoiled relations with Germany, was Giuseppe Garibaldi. Rather than see the obvious, that the collapse of Imperial France would likely mean the withdrawal of its Rome garrison, he saw one last opportunity to be a guerrilla leader. Not only would he fail to be present at the achievement of his lifelong dream, he nearly became the object of a rift between the German Empire and Italy.

Harboring a hitherto unproclaimed hatred of the Germans, Garibaldi's military activities, rather too serious to be dismissed as "antics," had Moltke and his generals demanding he be declared a bandit and common criminal and treated as such. Fortunately for the infant empire the more astute Bismarck used Garibaldi's fate as a bargaining chip in negotiations with French authorities, most of whom hated the celebrity rebel.

When he finally returned home Garibaldi received a belated hero's welcome, but had to withdraw from public life almost immediately. The rigors of his final war had made a man already in poor health quite ill. Garibaldi would not make his return until 1874 when the population of Caprera elected him to the Italian Parliament. For two years he got to live his dream of governing Italy from Rome, then retired for the last time in 1876. Garibaldi died in 1882, barely a year before the death of his bitterest enemy, Karl Marx.

For Italy the post-war years were spent performing a slow dance into Germany's influence and awakening its own dreams of empire. By 1886 it formally became a member of the Central Powers by joining the alliance of Germany and Austria-Hungary. Four years later it would gain its first colony, Eritrea, on Africa's Red Sea coast. The construction of its empire had begun.

The Beckoning Lands of Freedom

In the midst of all their victory parades and celebrations of unity an annoying fact remained, not every German was happy living in a Prussian-dominated empire. For those who could not, who were unable to accept the terms of what the former Radical-turned-Moderate Ludwig von Rochau called "realpolitik," there were basically three options.

First, become a Radical and join either an extremist political party or some underground revolutionary movement, where you could endlessly discuss, and occasionally plot, the overthrow of the Hohenzollern regime. Curiously, in the post-war years there was no major movement or conspiracy to split Germany back into its separate states.

Second, move to one of the nearby countries. While France would be out of the question, unless you were a Radical on the run, Holland, Switzerland, Belgium, Sweden, Austria-Hungary and even Russia would see modest increases in immigration from Germany. Among those who emigrated locally, and later became a naturalized citizen, was Albert Einstein, who moved to Switzerland before the end of the century.

And third, buy a steamship ticket and emigrate to the Americas. While the United States and Canada were far and away the major destinations, sizable populations of Germans would also settle in Mexico, Brazil, Peru, Bolivia and of course Chile and Argentina. While some went for the adventure and others because they sensed better business opportunities overseas, most left for the New World for the freedom it offered.

And it was not just the freedom of individual rights that beckoned, but the freedom from monarchs, from "war scares" and political turmoil. Tens of thousands of German Mennonites left due to government persecution over their strictly pacifist beliefs. While some went to Holland, where their sect originated, most left Europe for America and Canada.

German, Polish and Austrian Jews by their tens of thousands also came fleeing from religious persecution. Among them would be Felix Frankfurter, from Austria, a young Irving Berlin and his family, originally from Russia, and Samuel Goldwyn from Germany's Polish territory. And, while not fleeing due to religious harassment, a young Hessian cavalry officer chose not to continue service in a Prussian-dominated army but took his family to America instead.

While Friedrich Krueger would not enter U.S. Army service, his son did in 1898 as an enlisted man in the Spanish-American War. Quickly promoted to 2nd Lieutenant, Walter Krueger became a career officer and went on to command the Sixth Army in the South Pacific in World War II.

Joining the Wave

Ironically, the unification of Italy and Germany made it much easier for immigrants in Central and Eastern Europe to depart for the Americas. Travel plans and related documents became simplified as some ethnic groups, such as Poles, realized their nationhood dreams would likely never be realized and a new start in a new land was their only viable alternative.

As trans-Atlantic immigration increased, steamship companies and governments responded to service them. In Germany this meant legislation to ease exit visa procedures for both residents and non-residents, as well as requirements that companies had to care for their passengers once they arrived at the port cities. In America it meant immigration, formerly handled by the coastal states, would now be administered by the federal government. In particular, at the port of New York City the original arrival processing center in the Battery on the foot of Manhattan Island had to be replaced.

Castle Garden was simply too small, too decrepit, too corrupt and dangerous for continued use. Tammany Hall ran too many of the services and concessions, especially under boss William Marcy Tweed, and local criminals preyed upon the immigrants almost from the moment they stepped onto the street. From 1875 on this changed, with the U.S. Government taking over operations and looking for a new location where they could build proper facilities and at least isolate the arrivals from the criminals.

On the other side of the Atlantic, in Germany at least, model facilities were built just outside the North Sea ports of Hamburg and Bremerhaven by the principal German steamship company, the Hamburg-Amerika Line. They were clean, efficient and exclusively handled resident and non-resident immigrants to the Americas.

Eventually, in New York City the U.S. Government repurchased an island in Upper New York Harbor that had once been a location where the British colonial authorities hung pirates, and was appropriately called Gibbet Island. Then it became Fort Gibson, from the 1790s until the end of the Civil War, when the U.S. Army downgraded it to an ammunition dump and finally sold the island to a developer, Samuel Ellis. Though the facilities would not be finished until June 13th, 1897, and destroyed by fire the day after, they began operations on New Year's Day of 1892 and were soon handling up to 10,000 people a day.

As the facilities improved so did the ships that serviced them. Pure-sail ships, such as the clipper ships, were relegated either to cargo work or operating in the Pacific, which steam-powered ships could not cross without mid-ocean coaling stations. Paddle-wheel steamers were either retired or relegated to secondary routes such as the Baltic or Black Seas. For the North Atlantic, and later South Atlantic, routes speed and load-carrying capacity meant large, steel, screw-propelled ships.

The age of the modern ocean liner was born and Great Britain lead the way. In particular, Canadian-born Sir Samuel Cunard pioneered trans-Atlantic steamship travel starting in 1840 with a contract to carry mail. Though he died in 1865, the age he worked for had arrived and his name lived on in his company, the Cunard Line.

To this were added the White Star Line, Cunard's principal competitor, and over a dozen smaller companies in Britain, America, France, Holland and Italy. At the time, in the pre-war, pre-unification days any German competition barely registered. Before the Franco-Prussian War the main immigration route from northern Europe to North America ran through the British Isles.

Plymouth, Portsmouth, Southampton, Bristol, Liverpool and Belfast were the main embarkation ports, and this would continue in the war's immediate aftermath. However, a decade later the situation had changed. The British ports and shipping lanes had competition and it was not just the German ports but Piraievs in Greece, Trieste on the Adriatic, and then part of Austria-Hungary, Naples in Italy, Marseilles and Bordeaux in France and Rotterdam in Holland.

Most of the other ports were served by smaller lines while Hamburg-Amerika exclusively served the German ports, and by the end of the 1880s had an impressive fleet of large, modern ocean liners. And by then it would not just be Germany's civilian ships that America and the other European powers would have to contend with, for the world had at last grown more confrontational.

Incident in Paradise

Back in 1878, the United States concluded negotiations for a coaling station in Pago-Pago Harbor, on the Samoan island of Tutuila. The chain, comprising ten major islands and numerous smaller ones, lay roughly in the middle of the vast constellation of islands and atolls between the eastern side of Australia and the Hawaiian Islands.

The treaty was similar to the one signed three years earlier with the Hawaiian royal family that gave the U.S. exclusive rights to maintain a coaling station at Pearl Harbor. Both chains were strategically located and lay near major sea lanes. While the Hawaiian chain had been U.S.-dominated since the 1820s, by the 1870s the area around the Samoan chain had become something rather different.

Western Polynesia, with its thousands of islands, both grouped and isolated, was one of the last great unexplored regions of the world in the 19th Century. British, French, Dutch, American and, after 1871, German explorers roamed the ocean, laying claim to what western eyes had not yet seen. And after them came the missionaries, businessmen, bureaucrats and military forces.

A decade after the United States established the first military base in the Samoan chain, a German flotilla arrived at Upolu in December of 1888. The next major island over from Tutuila, it contained an excellent deep water harbor at Apia. In accordance with the new Kaiser's temperament on foreign policy, the German warships arrived not to negotiate for a coaling station but to demand one be set up. When Upolu's rulers refused the trio of ships shelled the island.

Appeals for help went to nearby British and American authorities, and in early-March the U.S. Navy cruisers *Trenton* and *Nipsic*, together with the gunboat *Vandalia*, faced the rather smaller Reichsmarine gunboats *Adler*, *Eber* and *Olga*. By then the incoming Secretary of State for the new Benjamin Harrison Administration, the hard-headed and confrontational James Gillespie Blaine, had heightened the crisis with some incendiary rhetoric.

The British warship *Calliope* arrived to try to calm the situation, and found Apia Harbor rather crowded with 15 merchant ships in addition to the American and German flotillas. She also arrived in time to notice the clouds darkening on the eastern horizon.

It would not be until the second half of the 20th Century that tropical storms would be tracked and receive names. The typhoon which hit Upolu, from the night of March 15th until the afternoon of the 17th, came on suddenly and was the most powerful in living memory. Of the 22 ships in

Apia Harbor only the last one survived. And according to legend, as the *Calliope* succeeded in reaching the harbor entrance, the band on the doomed *Trenton* played "Rule Britannia."

Of the remaining warships the *Eber* was thrown broadside onto a reef, and 72 of her 77-man crew perished. The *Adler*, the German flotilla's flagship, turned over and took 20 of her crew with her. The *Olga* was beached after fouling the *Nipsic*'s anchor lines, though none of her crew perished, she was declared a constructive total loss. The *Nipsic* also beached and seven of her crew died. The *Vandalia* slammed into the *Trenton* before sinking and most of her crew jumped to the larger ship, then she went down with 44 hands. The *Trenton* would end up pushed ashore and wrecked, though most of her crew did survive.

In the disaster's aftermath all three Powers quickly agreed to a conference in Berlin. On June 14th, 1889, in what would prove to be one of Bismarck's final foreign policy exercises, the Samoan chain was formerly divided between the Powers, with the United States getting the lion's share to administer.

Germany would only gain control of the two westernmost islands, Savai'i and Upolu. Though by then she would also possess the Admiralty Islands, part of the Solomons, Yap and the Palau Islands, most of the Carolines and especially the massive Truk Atoll, whose lagoon is so large it almost qualifies as a sea surrounded by the Pacific Ocean.

Canada's Quiet Success

Unlike Italy, whose final acquisitions of Venice and Rome were tied directly to German military successes, and who joined the German-dominated Central Powers Alliance, and even unlike the United States, whose initially cordial relations would eventually darken with suspicions and confrontations, Canada would enjoy reasonably good relations with the German Empire. Of course they were almost non-existent.

When Canada confederated on July 1st, 1867, it did not exactly become a truly independent state. The British North America Act, approved by Great Britain's Parliament in March of the same year, combined the territories of Upper and Lower Canada, also called Ontario and Quebec, with Nova Scotia and New Brunswick to form the Dominion of Canada. And while they had autonomy, their own currency, parliament and Prime Minister, the Act still tied them to England.

Among its clauses, it required the Canadian government to secure the British Parliament's approval for any amendments to the Act, which served as Canada's constitution. It also tied Canada diplomatically to the British Imperial Government and internationally it became a solid member of the British Commonwealth. Which meant it had virtually no independent foreign policy and almost no foreign ministry. Its relations with other countries, initially even with the United States, were handled through the British Foreign Office.

This meant that if Great Britain had good relations with the German Empire, as it did for the rest of the 19th Century, then so did Canada. Outside of the British High Commissioner's Office, which the sarcastic noted was the real seat of power in the country, there were few other foreign legations in Ottawa. The interests of other countries were usually served in a low-key manner, by local businessmen who had commercial ties to the country they represented.

Immigration was similarly handled in a low-key manner, much more so than in the United States, and this suited a good many Germans. Certainly the Mennonites and Hutterites, who eschewed most government contact, welcomed it as did many German and Polish Jews. Uniquely, they often settled in Montreal while those of the two Protestant sects decided on western provinces, and nearly everyone else chose Ontario.

They altered the character of many established cities, like Hamilton, or set up their own. Outside of Waterloo, in the center of the fertile Great Lakes Lowland, they founded New Berlin, New Hamburg and other towns. The great influx of German immigrants continued until the very eve of the First World War and then, the world changed.

As with the United States, the global conflict reduced immigration to a trickle for nearly five years. And again like the U.S., increased government control and restrictions kept the flow in the post-war years much lower than it had been at the turn-of-the-century and before. And for Canada there would be a further reason – the bloom had come off the rose.

The bitter, grim fighting of the Great War produced a massive wave of anti-German sentiment throughout the British Commonwealth. The Royal Family no longer recognized its German heritage. Prince Albert and the earlier Hanoverian Kings were forgotten, or at least fiercely ignored, while in Canada the sentiment took on just a slightly more muted tone.

Nobody wanted to be German, much less known to be living in a German community. Out west the Mennonites and Hutterites mostly escaped the wrath because their communities were so isolated. Towns like New Hamburg escaped because they were relatively small. But New Berlin had grown to the size of a small city, and before the conflict had ended it had been renamed Kitchener.

But all this was in a future decades away from the Franco-Prussian

War. In its immediate aftermath both the United States and Canada benefitted from the surge of skilled, industrious and in many cases prosperous immigrants who had had enough of war and wanted little to do with empire.

Chapter XXVII: Pax Germanica

"Give me where to stand, and I will move the earth."
-Archimedes (c.287 - 212B.C.)

The First Cold War

BY THE SUCCESS of her armies and the statecraft of her First Chancellor, Germany had changed the world. Before the battles had even ended Rome was made the seat of power for a united Italy and the temporal domain of the Pope, fixed at the borders of the city since the final collapse of the Roman Empire, had been reduced to just the Vatican and the Basilica of St. John Lateran.

And by the time the guns did fall silent Berlin had transformed itself from the leading city among the Germanies to the capital of the dominant power on continental Europe. A seismic shift had taken place in the structure of empires and most did not like it. For obvious reasons France and Great Britain did not, and each in their own way would never be resigned to it. Austria-Hungary, and in particular Franz Josef, did not like what happened either.

The ceremony in the Hall of Mirrors at Versailles had robbed him of a title which had been a family tradition. Now, "Kaiser" belonged to the Hohenzollerns and the Hapsburgs, who once dominated the Germanies, the rest of central Europe and even Spain, would forever be in eclipse. He did not like it, but Franz Josef was the first major leader to resign himself to the "realpolitik" of the new world.

He had to, for in the aftermath of the Franco-Prussian War his empire became the most isolated power in Europe. Republican France at least got some sympathy; Austria-Hungary did not even get that. As the most autocratic of rulers, the one country Josef might have counted on as an ally, Imperial France, was gone forever.

In the post-war world Republican France wanted nothing to do with him. Britain was cool toward him, Italy even more so, and the Romanov Czars of Russia could never forgive Josef for shattering the Holy Alliance during the Crimean War. The Ottoman Empire remained friendly to Austria-Hungary, but as Europe's habitual sick man this meant very little. So a rapprochement with Prussia-dominated Germany was inevitable, but it still took until the end of the decade for Bismarck to engineer it.

Ironically, the two Powers who had the friendliest relations with the new empire were the bitter antagonists Russia and Turkey. Orders to Krupp alone for its cannons were proof enough of that, and they would be eagerly using them on each other some five years later in the Balkans and Armenia.

This lead to the Berlin Congress of 1878 to settle the problems the war did not, and the resulting Berlin Treaty, signed on August 24th, would be the first rift in relations between Russian and Germany. Their formerly cordial relations began to cool, while the formerly cold relations with Austria-Hungary warmed up. It helped that she got some territory out of the negotiations, though no one at the time foresaw that the acquisition of Bosnia-Hercegovina would bring about a future global war and the doom of almost all the empires involved in the Congress.

This slowly emerging cold war did not have the levels of tensions, anxiety, confrontations and the threat of utter annihilation hanging over it as the 20th Century-version would have. Still, a bipolar set of alliances was gradually being formed, and out of mutual interests rather than a genuine feeling of cordiality.

In spite of their alliance's name, it could be said that for the remaining decades of the 19th Century, Britain respected Germany more than it did France and feared it less than it did Russia. The Entente Cordiale, later the Triple Entente, would not become as formal an alliance as the Central Powers until the very eve of World War I.

It is not that the British did not think they had reasons to hold its partners at arm's length. In January of 1878 there occurred an event just as era-changing, and just a forgotten, as the Battle of Sinope in the Crimean War. At Batum Harbor on Turkey's Black Sea coast an Ottoman Navy guard ship was sunk by a self-propelled torpedo launched from an Imperial Russian Navy patrol boat.

This marked the first time such a weapon had been successfully used in combat, an attempt the year before during the war between Peru and Chile having failed, and the weapon was not British. Though it did have an English connection; the expatriate engineer Robert Whitehead worked in Fiume, Italy on a design from a former Austrian naval officer, Giovanni de Luppis.

Truly an example of international cooperation, the harbinger of future multi-national weapons projects – but it had been used by a Russian warship at a time when no Royal Navy vessel was equipped to use them. It also occurred as British expeditions were launching the Second Afghan War, and London had convinced itself Russia lay behind it.

Similarly, four years later the British government suspected the Russians were behind the 1882 insurrection in Egypt. And further, the brief war gave them serious concerns about the alliance with France when their naval squadron, part of a multi-national armada responding to the crisis, departed soon after its arrival at Alexandria.

The Quai d'Orsay claimed a "war scare" by Germany. London did not see one, Berlin denied one, though that did not mean the French were not honestly fearful of such a prospect. It did mean the Royal Navy squadron of six modern battleships, plus smaller units, had only a few Italian and Greek ships to work with, though they did eventually pound Alexandria into submission.

For the longer term it meant a formal alliance with France was out of the question. It also lead to the classic British military joke: re.treat *noun* 1: an act of withdrawing, especially from something dangerous. 2: standard fleet maneuver of the French Navy.

The Birth of the Arms Race

The success of Krupp's cast-steel breechloaders technically made all other artillery pieces obsolete and yet, there was not a worldwide rush to scrap the old and rearm with the new. Partly, this had to do with Albrecht von Roon's lengthy folly to dump the war-winning weapon for the war-losing bronze muzzleloaders. Partly, with the great cost that would ensue if tens of thousands of field, fortress and naval guns across the world were in fact replaced. Partly because the only proven breechloading design belonged to the very proprietary Alfred Krupp. But mostly this was due to the military reality that von Roon was not the only obstinate, reactionary government official who tried to hold back the future.

Still, as the French disaster proved, holding back the future presented very real perils of its own, and the advance of science and technology could not be denied, even by the foolish. Within months of the conflict's end, the war ministries of both France and Germany decided they needed new service rifles.

The success of the Chassepot, one of the few things the French could be proud of, meant they chose an evolutionary change. They adapted the rifle to use a metallic cartridge and a firing pin, and called it the Gras. The Germans realized the Dreyse had seen its last battle and opted for a revolutionary change.

After years in the wilderness of German bureaucracies, a rather similar ordeal suffered by "der Kanonenkönig" himself, Wilhelm and Peter Paul Mauser finally got official interest in their rifle. It also incorporated the shorter, more rugged firing pin in place of the firing needle, and theirs retracted as the bolt handle was lifted. They substituted a metal cartridge for the cardboard one as well, and produced a breech design machined to such fine tolerances that the danger of escaping gases had been eliminated.

Both the Gras and the Mauser still used the heavy, 11mm. bullet and remained single-shot weapons. By the end of the decade the Germans decided they really needed a repeater and produced a modified Mauser, the Model 71/84: so designated after the years the designs were originally approved.

The new model had an eight-round tubular magazine – a short-lived feature as the nose-to-tail storage of very pointed rounds could, and on occasion did, cause the detonation of primer caps, resulting in a catastrophic chain-fire explosion. Nonetheless the Reich War Ministry proceeded with their plans and by 1887 had completely re-equipped the army with the new Mauser...by which time it had become obsolescent.

In 1884 the expatriate American designer James Paris Lee created the "short" box magazine for rifles while employed at the Enfield works in Middlesex, England. It stacked the ammunition vertically and made loading much easier. A year later Ferdinand Ritter von Mannlicher improved upon this with the invention of a metal clip that held five cartridges and could be dropped out the bottom of the magazine when emptied. And the year after this the French introduced a weapon everyone noticed, the Lebel rifle.

It utilized the smaller 8mm. round and the revolutionary propellant, *Poudre B*, the first successful product to use a stabilized form of nitrocellulose, also called gun cotton. It generated higher velocities, flatter trajectories and even longer ranges – up to 2,000 yards. And suddenly every nation wanted a small-caliber, high-velocity rifle. The modern arms race was underway.

The Lost Kaiser, and the Path Not Taken

In 1888, the year the Boulanger Crisis started in France and three on-going colonial wars preoccupied the British Empire, saw Germany go through its first leadership crisis with the death of Kaiser Wilhelm I on March 9th. He had been in poor health and the transfer of power to his only son occurred smoothly enough, but Crown Prince Friedrich Wilhelm promised to be a very different Kaiser.

In a letter to Bismarck on March 12th, and in his first address to the German people, he openly talked about conducting a more liberal administration. This heartened members of the National Liberal and Progressive parties, and even some in the SPD. The hero of Königgrätz, Woerth, Sedan and the Siege of Paris was about to become their sovereign – the very model of a modern, humane ruler as Kaiser Friedrich III.

In fact his role-models were less his venerable father than Queen Victoria's consort, Prince Albert and his uncle, Leopold I of Belgium. Both were known for initiating reforms and a decidedly less autocratic rule. None of this suited Bismarck particularly well. He wanted Friedrich III to be a younger, handsomer version of his father, and the March 12th letter put the First Chancellor in an especially ill-humor.

Friedrich, in the years since the war, had become a known quantity and personality to the other courts of Europe. State visits, official greeting duties and other such functions allowed most of the other current and future rulers to meet and they were impressed. They respected his war record, even envied it, and he certainly did not match the growing caricature of the German character: strident, bellicose, arrogant and not particularly cultured. Barely 57 – his father had passed away at 91 – Friedrich III looked set to steer the German Empire into the 20th Century.

The problem was that soon after his coronation doctors discovered a tumor, the new Kaiser had throat cancer. These were the days before the German physicist Wilhelm Conrad Roentgen had started his experiments in radiant energy at the University of Würzburg, which lead to the discovery of X-rays. And chemotherapy for cancer would not be developed for at least another seven decades. By March 21st Friedrich's son was given the powers to settle governmental matters while he went to a health clinic on the Italian Riviera.

The best medical specialists in Italy, Germany and Britain were brought to his bedside, and in the end nothing could be done. After a reign of just 99 days, instead of decades, Friedrich III died on June 15th. His time on the throne would be a footnote in history; most historians of the period would scarcely know there had been three Kaisers in the German Empire, not two.

And Bismarck got the kind of sovereign he thought he wanted.

Kaiser Wilhelm II was 29 years old at the time of his coronation. Handsome, mustachioed, and he hid his deformed left arm rather well. His first public speech, to the German Army and not the German people, fairly bristled with the language of an autocrat. He reaffirmed the divine right of kings to be the supreme law of the land and mentioned nothing of the liberal policies his father intentioned.

The new era Friedrich III had promised for Germany was literally over before it began. Now, the new era would be a lot like the old, only with a belligerent attitude. Friedrich considered his son vain, pompous and mercurial. The rest of Europe was about to find this out, and Bismarck would soon discover that maybe he should have been careful with what he wished for.

The Merchants of Death

According to the apocryphal tale, which may just be true, in 1882 the chief engineer for the U.S. Electrical Lighting Company happened upon another American at a Vienna industrial exposition. They had been friends in the States and he advised the engineer, "hang your electricity and chemistry! If you want to make a pile of money, invent something that will enable these Europeans to cut each others' throats with greater facility."

A curious statement given that, at the time, the Europeans were not actually fighting each other – not unless one counts the Boers' recent defeat of British forces in the Cape Colonies. Mostly, they fought their other colonial subjects. The French battled the Algerians, Chinese and Vietnamese. The British fought the Afghans, Egyptians and Indians. The Dutch fought the Indonesians and the Spanish fought the Cubans and Filipinos, when they were not trying to kill themselves. Pax Germanica was in full bloom and the modern arms race had not yet been born.

Nonetheless, the engineer took the advice to heart. After inventing an automatic sprinkler system, vacuum pumps, engine governors and even a better mousetrap, Hiram Maxim turned his skills to weapons design. Two years later, he constructed the prototype to the world's first fully-automatic, recoil-operated machinegun. Unlike the Mitrailleuse and Gatling guns it utilized a single barrel, a belt feed system, was more compact, lighter and cost a fraction of the earlier designs. Just over 20 years after its first introduction on the battlefields of the U.S. Civil War, the rapid-fire weapon had come of age.

Similarly, other crude but innovative weapon concepts were maturing, becoming more practical. The sciences of ballistics, metallurgy, thermodynamics, chemistry and electricity were better understood. And greater knowledge in these areas provided their own impetus to further development.

Perhaps the greatest of these were wrought by the advances in propellants and explosives by the Swedish chemist Alfred Bernhard Nobel. Best known for the creation of a dry, stabilized version of nitroglycerin called dynamite, he also came out with ballistite in 1888. A nitroglycerin-based propellant, it was a significant improvement over *Poudre B*. Almost smokeless, because it burned more evenly and completely, it could be chemically customized to suit different types of weapons and purposes.

And from this basic innovation came the spur to improve artillery design and the shells they used. To exploit the increased muzzle velocities, and handle the increased pressures generated, barrels were lengthened and new metals used. Cast steel, the metal so instrumental in winning the Franco-Prussian War, was no longer good enough for the instruments of war. Now it would be high-carbon steel, case-hardened steel and steel alloys, particularly the nickel and chrome steels from Krupp's Gusstahlfabrik.

Customized propellants and new steels not only improved existing types of weapons, it allowed for the development of an entirely new class of artillery. For decades the European armies had desired a weapon that combined the best features of both a mortar and a field gun. Mortars were ideal for bringing plunging fire down on trenchworks and fortresses. However, traditional cannons easily out-ranged them, while their plunging fire abilities were quite limited.

Development work on such a weapon had been started at the famous Skoda works outside of Prague shortly after the Brüderkrieg had ended. The rapprochement between Austria-Hungary and the German Empire meant German assistance in the breech design, barrel design and propellant research. Eventually they took over the project, and even the Czech and Bohemian words *houfnice* and *haubitze* for the weapon. They corrupted them into a new word: *howitzer*.

Advances in metallurgy not only meant improved gun barrels and shells, but stronger hulls and armor plate. Though navies played little part in the Franco-Prussian War, the technological revolutions it had wrought and the empire it helped create spurred naval construction from the mid-1870s onward. So much so that, by 1889, the British government had passed the Naval Defence Act, which ordained the Royal Navy had to be equal in strength to the next two most powerful navies combined. And at the time the Act became law this meant the rather unlikely alliance of

Germany and Russia.

Technically, France still had the second largest fleet in the world during the 1880s. However, many of its capital ships were old and few had been built in the immediate post-war years. Instead, she concentrated on building smaller ships: coast defence monitors, torpedo boats and, ironically enough, submarines. Inspired by Jules Verne, and advocated by the French Navy's *Jeune École* naval war college, development began as early as the late-1860s with the experimental, compressed air-powered boat *Le Plongeur*.

Notable designers, including Gustave Zédé, who would die in an accident with one of his craft, and even Dupuy de Lome himself worked on a succession of designs. These would culminate in the 1890s with the *Gymnote*, the *Gustave Zédé* and, in 1899, the *Narval*, the world's first commissioned submarine.

Even more ironic, the next nation to commission a submarine would be the United States. Doubly so because the U.S. Navy, after the Civil War, went into retrograde development and America's submarine program was at first privately financed. Willfully taking itself out of the modern age, the service did away with steam power, armor plate and turret-mounted guns until, by the early 1880s, it ranked 20th among the world's navies.

Like Hiram Maxim, the other American "merchants of death" would have to look overseas for customers and financiers. Richard Gatling would sell his guns to European navies as a defence against torpedo boats. Hudson Maxim created a smokeless powder to go along with his older brother's machineguns. Then, he moved to torpedo development, creating a stable high-explosive called Maximite, the propellant Motorite and a delayed-action fuse that made Whitehead's design a truly effective stand-off weapon.

And then there was John Philip Holland, an Irishman who emigrated to America in 1873 through Castle Garden to Paterson, New Jersey. Here he began his life's dream, of building submarines to topple the Royal Navy from its command of the seas and drive the British from Ireland. Initially he found few backers for his dream, until the Fenian Brotherhood stepped in.

They financed his first craft, which grew in size from just over two tons to 19 tons, and went from pedal-power to a primitive gasoline engine. But they also stole the best of his *Fenian Rams* and sailed it as far as New Haven, Connecticut before sinking it. This ended Holland's relations with the Irish terrorists though by then, the late-1880s, his successes brought official interest. The U.S. Government started funding his experiments, just as it later did with Samuel Pierpont Langley and his "aerodromes," and within a decade would launch the *Holland*, the most advanced submarine in the world.

But these were individual inventors and entrepreneurs, their efforts were at best an adjunct to the true merchants of death: Armstrong and Vickers in Great Britain, Schnieder and Creusot in France, Skoda in Austria-Hungary and of course the biggest industrial concern in Europe throughout the last decades of the 19th Century: Krupp of Essen. They not only sold thousands of artillery pieces and several million tons of munitions and armor plate to their own countries' armed forces, but to other nations in Europe and around the world.

Their sales agents competed against each other for clients and by far the most successful were those who worked for the German firms. Though Mauser rifles had not been used in the Franco-Prussian War, the mere fact they now equipped the German Army meant worldwide sales, and not just of their end product. Argentina, Austria-Hungary, Sweden and Turkey obtained manufacturing licenses for Mauser weapons, with most producing them until the latter half of the 20th Century.

Krupp, however, exceeded even that with 24 client states by the end of the century, and by then under the leadership of Alfred's son, Friedrich Alfred "Fritz" Krupp. And in a bizarre, and what pacifists would call monstrous, way he made his father's company armorer of the world. In 1897, and again in 1902, Fritz negotiated secret agreements with most of the world's steel and heavy weapons manufacturers. The 1897 agreement concerned the various processes for hardening armor plate, the 1902 one was for licensed manufacture of Krupp-designed time fuses. And for every ton of armor plate, and every artillery fuse produced the largest arms company received a royalty payment. No matter which nation moved ahead in the pre-World War One arms race, "der Kanonenkönig" would be the winner.

Getting What You Want, and Regretting It

For about a year, from April of 1888 to the middle of 1889, Bismarck thought he had exactly the kind of Kaiser he wanted and Germany needed to enter the 20th Century. More autocratic than his father, Wilhelm II soon proved to be even more so than his grandfather and was approaching his apparent role-model: the very autocratic Franz Josef I.

In fact it was the effort to improve relations with the Hapsburg court that started the rift between Wilhelm and Chancellor Bismarck. For 18 years Germany had managed to pull off the rather remarkable trick of maintaining good relations with three often bitter rivals: Russia, Austria-Hungary and the Ottoman Empire. This had been largely due to the diplomatic efforts of Bismarck himself and later his son, Herbert, who joined him as Foreign Secretary by the mid-1880s.

For that brief "honeymoon" period after Wilhelm II first ascended the throne, Bismarck thought he was shaping the long-term future of Germany. He now had a young, healthy monarch much more to his liking. He made his own son head of the Foreign Ministry and the then-40-year-old Helmuth Johann von Moltke, nephew of the recently retired Chief of the General Staff, had become the new Kaiser's friend and most trusted advisor.

And then, it all began falling apart. The Samoan Crisis had scarcely been resolved when, in the middle of 1889, Wilhelm II initiated a new crisis by refusing to renew a treaty with Russia. In St. Petersburg Czar Alexander III, every bit as autocratic as Franz Josef, reacted not with anger but a diplomatic initiative to woo Berlin back.

Prussia, and most of the other German states such as Saxony, had been faithful allies of Russia since the Napoleonic Era and especially the War of Liberation (1812 - 1814). And more recently Russia had sided with Prussia in both the *Brüderkrieg* and the Franco-Prussian War. The Bismarcks, both father and son, sided with many of the other German monarchs in maintaining friendly relations with Russia.

But the Kaiser was not called the "All-Highest" for nothing, and Wilhelm II took that title to heart more so than either his father or his grandfather. He would bend Germany to his will and he had the very nationalistic press to help him. Vienna, after all, lay closer to Berlin than St. Petersburg and the Hapsburgs were German whereas the Romanovs were not. And in an age where the pseudo-scientific concepts of "race" and "blood" were gaining greater credence a closer alliance with the largest German population outside of Germany made increasing sense.

And as if this crisis were not enough there came a domestic one where Wilhelm decided, rather bizarrely, to be more socialist than the Socialists. In a hugely mistaken notion that he could lure away voters from the SPD, he undid most of Bismarck's anti-social legislation and advocated restricting child labor, making Sunday a legal day of rest and giving workers' committees some participation in business management. The press also picked up on this and by the end of 1889 were calling Wilhelm II the "Labor Emperor."

In many ways these proposals were much like his late father's forgotten liberal policies. They would be the final breaking point between Bismarck and the Kaiser he thought he wanted. They were the harbinger of the future erratic policy swings from a ruler who would prove to be a very mercurial autocrat, and an often ill-timed guillotine.

For Bismarck it was all too much. He confided to Fritz Krupp that he felt "like an old circus horse" who was being whipped to go through his routines and had grown tired of the circus. At the beginning of January, 1890 he privately submitted his resignations from the offices of the Prime Minister of Prussia and First Chancellor of the German Empire.

Then began a strange pantomime dance between Bismarck, who had second thoughts about leaving public service, and Wilhelm II, who did not really want to accept. Intermediaries negotiated, and by February Bismarck had been persuaded to rescind his resignations. Unfortunately, the contentions that caused the rift were brought back up and neither the Chancellor nor the Kaiser had changed their positions on anything.

By early-March "störrigkeit" had set back in and on the 18th both Bismarck and his son Herbert publicly submitted their resignations. This time Wilhelm II accepted, though he tried to put the best facade on the train wreck by bestowing the rank of Field Marshal and the title of Duke of Lauenburg on the older Bismarck, who in turn declined both honors.

Within days the Kaiser appointed his replacement as Chancellor, setting the precedent for the further militarization of his government: General Leon von de Caprera de Montecuculi. By the end of the decade, this would only increase as approximately 90% of the Second Reich's annual budget would be devoted to its army and navy. Pax Germanica would have as its price constant expansion and rearmament. Moving the earth would prove very expensive.

Chapter XXVIII: Europe in 1901

"War makes rattling good history, but peace is poor reading."
-Thomas Hardy (1840 - 1928)

The Franco-Prussian War at 30

IN 1901 THERE were few ceremonies in either France or Germany marking the 30-year anniversary of the end of Franco-Prussian War. Not that the war had been forgotten, far from it, it was just that back then most ceremonies commemorating a war were either done at its start date, or the date of one of its major battles.

Thus the official ceremonies for the war's 30th anniversary happened the year before, on either July 15th or September 1st, but its concluding date is a more appropriate time to remember what it had wrought. America had learned this with its Civil War. The Europeans would not learn it until the grim aftermath of the Great War some two decades later.

By the 30-year mark the world it created had become accepted as normal, though in all quarters there remained varying degrees of resentment. Certainly this was true in France, where the dreams of *revanche* still abided, and echoed in the continuing devotion to the "Maid of Lorraine/Orléans" cult and the rise of proto-fascist groups like AISE. It had supplanted the Boulangists, the Croix de Fue and Paul Déroulède's Ligue des Patriotes as France's leading nationalist group.

In Great Britain the resentment had become formalized in government circles with the official recognition that the German Empire, not France or Russia, had become their principal competitor in the world. In popular culture it had grown into paranoia over her ever-growing military power, especially the size of her navy. This would spark the appearance, just two years later, of Erskine Childer's *Riddle of the Sands*, a story of pre-World War I intrigue that marked the birth of the modern spy novel.

In Germany the resentment took the form of "success was just not good enough" and *Einkreisung*, a mirror-image paranoia to what the English were feeling. The unity hymn which had become the country's first national anthem – Wilhelm II had since replaced it with one of his favorites – had grown into something else. At its creation, "Deutschland, Deutschland über Alles" meant Germany above Prussia, above Saxony, Bavaria, Baden and all the other Germanic states. An ideal of one people, one country. Now, it meant Germany above France, Germany above England, above Russia and the all the other countries who would stand in its path to greatness.

Sonderweg, that special path Germany took toward its unity, was changing into *Einkreisung*, a sense of being hemmed in, encircled by antagonistic powers. From the Kaiser on down many Germans felt they were not being allowed to have their fair share of the world. The problems were there was no more undiscovered territory to split up among the Powers and just how much did the new empire want? A decade earlier the Alldeutsche Verband, the Pan-German League, distributed signs to merchants across the country. It read: "The World Belongs to Germans."

The Franco-Prussian War had not just created an empire, it unleashed a Teutonic power that seemingly could not be stopped. In 30 years its population had soared by almost 40%, from 41 million to just under 57 million, and this in spite of the constant flow of emigration. It had become the industrial powerhouse of Europe. In almost every category of manufacture and development only the United States or Great Britain surpassed it, and then not by much.

The war itself had become the most studied in human history. By 1901 there are over 7,000 books published on it: histories, biographies, autobiographies and diaries from generals and politicians to the common soldier. In military academies around the world its battles and the exploits of its legends were studied. And in some cases, the wrong lessons were being learned.

General von Bredow's "Death Run" at the Metz battle of Vionville-Mars-le-Tour got widely studied as the way to conduct a cavalry operation on the modern battlefield. But its success lay in the way Bredow used the local terrain features to mask the approach of his brigade. Not every cavalry operation would have the advantage of favorable terrain to work with, as the French generals Michel, Margueritte and de Gallifet would attest.

But the complete annihilation of Michel's brigade at Woerth, and the destruction of Margueritte's and de Gallifet's division at Sedan were ignored in the classrooms. Although, the French did erect a monument at Frénois where Kaiser Wilhelm I made his remark about the division's bravery in the face of what should have been another annihilation.

Also not studied at the academies, because no one at the time thought of it as a real subject, was the pace of change in weapons. For a comparison, 30 years after Waterloo and the end of the Napoleonic Wars, the primary weapons of the European armies were substantially the same: muzzleloading muskets and cannons. While some small arms had rifled barrels and used percussion caps, neither technology was in widespread use, and it would be years before anyone thought of applying such innovations to artillery.

By the 30th anniversary of the Franco-Prussian War all the weapons used in it were hopelessly obsolete and no longer in use. The Dreyse and Chassepot Needle Guns had not been replaced not once, but several times. The Krupp breechloaders had also been replaced several times, in some cases by an entirely new class of field gun, the howitzer.

The Mitrailleuse had given way to the Maxim machinegun, black power to smokeless powders and nitroglycerin-based explosives. Artillery shells, armor plate and land mines had all been improved, and projectile weapons in all categories could boast of greater ranges – in some cases, like naval guns, beyond the distances they could be accurately aimed. Standoff kill technology had not quite reached the intercontinental range, but it was well on its way.

For 30 years Pax Germanica had kept the peace in western Europe and would continue to do so for another 13 years. But already that peace had started to fray, and it was not entirely Germany's fault. Forces outside its, or any government's, control were shaping the coming age of cataclysm and slaughter.

Beneath the Deceptively Calm Surface

Many historians writing of this period, and especially of this year, depict it as a time of peace and serenity. A time when one age, the Victorian Age, passed to another, the Edwardian Age. Overshadowing the anniversary of any conflict was the death of Queen Victoria on January 22nd.

Her funeral lasted two days and over 40 European monarchs attended it. Nearly all were related by blood to her, including her "hot-headed" and "conceited" grandson, Wilhelm II. That it went off without any major incidents was probably due to the fact that it took place relatively quickly and in Britain. Europe, by the mid-1890s, had become a rather dangerous place for titled nobility and elected leaders.

The overlapping Age of the Anarchist started in earnest on June 24th of 1894 when Cesario Santo got close enough to stab to death Sadi Carnot, the President of France, who was visiting Lyons. Within a month some 3,500 anarchists had been arrested in France, Italy and Germany on similar suspected plots. A Muslim fanatic assassinated the Shah of Persia almost exactly two years later, on May 1st of 1896. The following year saw the assassinations of the Spanish Prime Minister and the President of Uruguay, together with the attempted killings of the Presidents of Mexico and Brazil.

In 1898 the European anarchists succeeded with the rather pointless assassination of the Empress of Austria-Hungary, Franz Josef's wife Elizabeth, while she vacationed in Switzerland. Two years later they went into high-gear for the new century with the murder of Italy's King Umberto I and attempted shootings of the future King Edward VII of Britain as he visited Brussels, and the new Shah of Persia, who had just arrived in Paris to tour its latest International Exhibition.

All these incidents occurred during the summer of 1900, resulting in another wave of arrests and the suppression of radical groups across the continent. In turn this forced many anarchists, Communists and revolutionary types to flee to America. Though, ironically, King Umberto's assassin had recently returned from there.

Apart from the low-intensity war between these radicals and the established order, Europe in the new century remained relatively conflict-free. Though that did not mean they were not busy throughout the rest of the world participating in various campaigns and other mayhem.

The brief Spanish-American War, fought between April 25th and August 16th, 1898, resulted in the United States formally becoming an imperial power with the acquisition of the Philippines, Puerto Rico, a number of smaller islands and the dominance over a technically independent Cuba. The British and French did not mind it too much, as it prevented the rumored sale of one or more of these territories by a cash-strapped Spain to Germany.

At the Wilhelmstrasse they did grumble about it, but the explosion of the *Maine*, America's first modern battleship, in Havana Harbor had cast a pall over any attempt to aid Spain. Still, they did try to intimidate America by briefly sending the flagship of their Pacific Station Squadron, the battleship *Kaiser,* into Manila Bay just before the arrival of Admiral Dewey's cruiser squadron.

What they were more enthusiastic about, especially Wilhelm II, was a reported clash in September of 1898 between British and French troops in Africa. The Fashoda Crisis came at the end of a multi-year fiasco over the "race" to claim sovereignty of the Upper Nile Valley. The British, French, Italians and even the Belgians sent in expeditions from various points of the compass, starting back in 1896.

The Italians went in first, from Eritrea on the Red Sea, but were defeated by the Ethiopians at Adowa in March of that year. The Belgians dispatched a sizable column of local troops from Stanleyville on the Upper Congo River, nearly 1,000 miles south of Fashoda. But they only got halfway there, to Lake Albert on the White Nile, before the Congolese troops mutinied. They killed many of their Belgian officers, ate some, and scattered the others into the jungle.

This left the French, coming in from West Africa and lead by Captain Jean-Baptiste Marchand, and the British lead by Horatio Kitchener, ostensibly sailing up the White Nile to rescue the Italian survivors of the Adowa defeat. Marchand reached the Sudanese town of Fashoda first, where he found the Egyptian Army fort and European-run outpost lying in ruins.

Kitchener, the one-time volunteer to the French Army back in 1870, arrived next with orders to remove Marchand's expedition. Since he arrived with a far larger force than 12 officers and 150 enlisted men he eventually won the confrontation. He even subjected Marchand to the further humiliation of giving him a boat ride to Cairo to file his report.

Then, by the middle of the following year, a far worse crisis erupted in the South African territories. The British Colonial Secretary Joseph Chamberlain, and the High Commissioner for South Africa Sir Alfred Miner, intentionally pushed the Boer republics of Transvaal and the Orange Free State to confrontation over voting rights for their British residents. On October 12th, 1899, fighting broke out between British and Afrikaner forces, the Second Boer War had begun.

This time, unlike the short war of 1880-1881, it would be long, viciously bloody and both sides had been preparing for some time. Unlike December 1880, when the British only had 1,800 regular troops in the Transvaal and not a single cavalry unit anywhere in the Territories, they now had 20,000 men on the ground and 50,000 more arriving by troop ships.

But the Boers had also been preparing. In a rare example of Franco-German cooperation, both Krupp and Creusot shipped artillery to the Transvaal and the Orange Free State, from 75mm. howitzers to 94-pounder "Long Tom" heavy cannons. These plus large quantities of Mauser's latest

'98 model rifle were shipped through the Portuguese settlements in Mozambique and Germany's own Namibia colony.

The final months of 1899 were anything but calm and serene for the British Empire. The shock of the war beginning much faster than anticipated was quickly followed by Afrikaner invasions of Natal and the Cape Colony. The towns of Utrecht and Newcastle were occupied, while the critical railroad junction at Ladysmith would shortly be invested. The troops already in the Territories held off further expansion while the additional 50,000 disembarked from their ships. By early December they had been formed into three commands for a coordinated counterattack and then, everything got worse.

"Black Week" began on December 10th, and by the 17th all three commands had been defeated with heavy casualties. The British public, press and government were stunned; as stunned as the French had been after Sedan though their monarch was not captured and their government did not fall. Those who did were the British commanders in South Africa, starting with the brave but incompetent General Redvers Buller, commander-in-chief of British Forces in South Africa.

Lord Frederick Sleight Roberts and Horatio Kitchener replaced him, though not before the even more disastrous Battle of Spion Kop, where the British Army not only learned the hard lessons about smokeless powder and how easy it made concealed firing but encountered a new reality, one they had been working hard at to ignore. As the only major army not to adopt the howitzer, they discovered just how deadly and accurate its indirect fire could be. In greatest secrecy they contacted the small armaments firm Ehrhardt in Germany to purchase 108 of their 15-pounder howitzers for immediate shipment.

The Farce of 1898 had been replaced with the Disaster of the New Century, and 1900 arrived with a storm of Anglophobia across the European continent. The French got some payback for Fashoda, press attacks on Queen Victoria and her army grew so insulting that the British Government recalled their ambassador. Boer envoys were received with honor in Paris, Berlin, Amsterdam, Brussels and other European capitals. Many of these governments rushed to send military attachés and observers to the Boer headquarters to report on the success of the weapons and tactics the British Army had so arrogantly ignored.

Britain's own highly nationalistic press saw these developments as attacks and responded in kind. When reports came in of volunteer forces being raised in some countries to aid the Afrikaner republics, including an Irish brigade in Chicago, the overstretched British Army did an about-face and accepted the formerly dismissed offers of volunteer contingents from

Canada, the Australian colonies and New Zealand. On the continent French-German relations suddenly became better than they had been since 1870, and to many observers it all looked like the prelude to war between the British Empire and the rest of Europe. And then came China.

Since 1839 the Chinese government had been repeatedly defeated in a series of wars with the Western Powers, principally Britain and France. By the 1890s Russia, Germany, Japan and even Portugal and Italy had joined them, all demanding "concessions" – control of territories they would administer on behalf of the government. It had lead to corruption, resentment of foreign influence and the creation of secret societies to counter the presence of foreign officials and military forces.

By the middle of 1900 the situation in China had grown so confrontational that government troops killed the Chancellor of the Japanese legation in Beijing. On June 20th Baron von Ketteler, German ambassador to the Chinese court, was murdered by a civilian mob. Soon thereafter the Dowager Empress Tze-Hsi pushed her government to aid the secret societies "Fist of Righteous Harmony" and the "Great Sword Society" in purging China of foreign influences. Before the end of June China had declared war on Britain, France, Germany, Russia, Japan, the United States, Austria-Hungary and Italy. The Boxer Rebellion had beaten out the Boer War to become a global conflict.

Suddenly Europe forgot about its growing tensions with Britain, and forgot about the Boers; it helped that Lord Roberts had since defeated the Afrikaners at Paardeberg and broke the sieges at Ladysmith, Kimberley and Mafeking. In China the foreign legation compound in Beijing was invested, just as reinforcements of U.S. and British Royal Marines had arrived in response to the mounting tensions.

On the Chinese coast a multi-national task force of mostly British, Russian and Japanese warships assembled. They captured Tientsin, a port city only 80 miles southeast of Beijing, in early July. With the rail lines to the capital destroyed, the relief expedition began an overland march, which soon bogged down with repeated attacks by Chinese troops and boxers.

The Chinese also counterattacked at Tientsin, and were defeated by a force of Russian soldiers, and U.S. and British Marines. They in turn rescued the relief expedition, which fell back to the port. There it received considerable reinforcement: 12,000 newly-arrived Japanese troops, 3,000 more Russians, 3,000 Americans and 1,000 French Marines.

By now enough small gunboats had arrived to escort the expedition up the Hai River to Beijing. And it would be the German *Iltis* that captured the lion's share of the glory when it took on the ancient forts guarding the river single-handedly. Though their guns pounded the boat into a blazing wreck and wounded its captain, it helped land Marines who flanked and took the forts.

After approximately two months of siege by a hostile city, the foreign legation compound and other holdout areas in Beijing were rescued by the expedition. The Imperial Chinese government capitulated soon after this, and entered into lengthy negotiations that extended to the end of the year. Before then additional Russian and German troops arrived to carry out punitive operations in other Chinese regions.

Europe, Russia and America had triumphed. Europe was at peace, Britain was respected and no longer a pariah, the deceptive calm had returned. So much so that, when Paul Kruger arrived on a Dutch steamer in the closing months of the 19th Century, he found the governments of Europe too busy with China, and too happy with the restored calm to unsettle it again over the Boer Republics.

The Children of War

The dashing young men who were lieutenants and captains in the Franco-Prussian War were, by 1901, in their 50s and 60s. They were fewer in number, and not all were in military service. In the German Army the senior ranks of its officer corps were almost entirely veterans of the conflict. It made for a very close-knit community, as true a "Brotherhood of War" as there ever would be in the modern age.

Both Paul von Beneckendorff und von Hindenburg and Alfred von Schlieffen were, in fact, veterans of the Brüderkrieg as well as the later conflict. By 1901 both were in the top echelon of the German Army. Hindenburg had just been promoted to Lieutenant-General and would soon be given a corps command. Schlieffen was the long-serving Chief of the General Staff, and consumed with perfecting the "Schlieffen Plan," the operation that promised to win the next major war in Europe for Germany by attacking its hereditary enemy, France, through an invasion of Belgium before turning to deal with its new enemy, Russia.

But he would not live to see his plan, or at least a version of it, put into action. Schlieffen would die a year before the Great War started. Moltke the Younger, who had been a staff officer in the Franco-Prussian War, held his uncle's position as Chief of the General Staff when the Guns of August thundered, only to resign after his failure to properly execute Schlieffen's plan and would die in 1916. Hindenburg had actually retired from the Army in 1911, then been recalled that fateful August to defeat the Russians at Tannenberg and eventually become army chief.

And then there was that dashing and bold Würtemberg cavalry officer, who achieved his greatest fame and influence outside of military service. Rising to the rank of Lieutenant-General, Ferdinand von Zeppelin would be appointed Würtemberg's ambassador to the Hohenzollern court. Here he ran afoul in its Byzantine world, by suggesting the German Army was rather too Prussian-dominated.

Forced to resign in 1890, he could well have ended up a broken man like Ludwig August von Benedek and Charles Denis Bourbaki – honorable men who faithfully served their countries, only to have their lives and careers ruined by political machinations. But Zeppelin remembered the startling success the French Army's Balloon Corps had in 1884 with *La France*, the world's first non-rigid, powered airship.

While it proved to have limited utility, it was electrically-powered and barely had the lifting capacity to take up its batteries plus a two-man crew, Zeppelin went to work on something with considerably more capabilities. Financially supported by King Wilhelm II of Würtemberg, he built a construction facility and a wooden floating hangar on Lake Bondensee near the Swiss border.

Here, far from the military establishment that turfed him out, though not too far that he could not keep track of the progress made by Alberto Santos-Dumont in Paris, Zeppelin constructed the world's first rigid airship. And on July 2nd, 1900, the LZ1 slowly rose into the air at dusk for a maiden flight of 18 minutes.

It did not maneuver well, nearly crashed when its balance weight jammed in the forward position, and after just three more flights the LZ1 would have to be dismantled so Zeppelin could sell the scrap to pay off his creditors. Not an auspicious beginning, but the "crazy old count" would persevere, King Wilhelm II would come to his rescue again, and he would live long enough to see his "Jules Verne" contraption carry passengers around Germany, and bombs to its enemies. While later technologies would supersede the zeppelin in both areas, on that summer's eve at the end of the 19th Century the concepts of long-range air travel and strategic bombardment were born.

Circumstances for the Children of War in France were rather different. For one thing, there were less of them. This lay not just in the far higher casualty rates during the Franco-Prussian War, but in all the colonial wars France continued to fight after it. And then there were those political crises at home. The Broglie and Boulangist crises in particular caused a number of veteran officers to either leave the army, or be purged once the crisis ended. And then there was the Dreyfus Affair.

This disaster stretched over most of the 1890s and shook France to its foundations. Army Captain Alfred Dreyfus was an Alsatian Jew, and a true child of the war, convicted of treason with evidence forged by the French Army's Intelligence Department. When it ended in 1899 the true culprit, Colonel Esterhazy, had fled the country. Colonel Henri, head of Intelligence, had committed suicide. Émile Zola, ironically the author of the one great novel on the Franco-Prussian War, *La Debacle*, went into exile after publishing *J'Accuse*, a letter condemning the French Army. And Dreyfus, after spending four years in Devil's Island and being convicted again was finally pardoned by President Emile Loubet, who had just entered the office after his predecessor died of a heart attack brought on by the crisis.

It proved to be the worse crisis the French Army had confronted since the Franco-Prussian War. As well as those nationalist groups like AISE, Ligue des Patriotes and especially the Anti-Semitic League, whose offices were raided after being declared an outlaw organization. A multi-year purge resulted in still more veteran officers of the war being forced into early retirement until very few were left.

In fact, on the eve of the Great War there only seemed to be Marshal Joseph Jacques Joffre, who had been a newly-minted lieutenant in the Engineering Corps back in 1870. It could be said that the true children of the Franco-Prussian War were all the other commanders of the cataclysm that began in 1914. Henri Philippe Omer Pétain, Ferdinand Foch, Erik von Falkenhayn and Erich von Ludendorff had all been pre-teenage children in the fateful summer of 1870. As had Alfred Dreyfus.

They had all grown up in its shadows of legendary success and crushing failure. The French had to prove they were better than their fathers and grandfathers, especially if the dreams of *revanche* were to be achieved. And ironically, so did the Germans, since they now foresaw they would taking on the world.

The French had never forgotten, would not let themselves forget, how much misery their country had endured. The Germans, on the other hand, had lost sight of how closely-fought many of the battles had been. And completely forgot how everyone else in Europe thought Napoleon III would win the Franco-Prussian War. Its lessons were being imperfectly learned, many in the German military were actually looking forward to the next major conflict, and at times their Kaiser seemed eager to start one.

In the immediate future there would be a bloody coup in Serbia, where its pro-Austrian king and queen were murdered, and the family replaced by a pro-Russian dynasty. Then there would be a pair of crises over Morocco, in 1905 and 1911, the Italian invasion of Tripoli and Cyrenaica (present-day Libya) also in 1911 and two wars in the Balkans, in 1912 and

1913. And throughout all this German naval officers had taken up a new tradition. Every night they drank a toast to "Der Tag," to "The Day" when their High Seas Fleet would challenge the Royal Navy to its supremacy of the world's oceans, and win.

Epilogue: Echoes in the Age of Slaughter

> *"...in the interests of humanity, it is to be hoped
> that wars will become the less frequent, as
> they become the more terrible."*
> -Field Marshal Helmuth von Moltke (1800-1891)

ACCORDING TO MOST historians, the War to End All Wars wiped the Franco-Prussian War from peoples' memory. After 43 years of Pax Germanica, and nearly five years of the most horrific war in human history, France had fulfilled its dreams of *revanche*. The Alsace and Lorraine were restored to it, Germany had been humbled and for good measure Poland and many of the states held by the former Austro-Hungarian Empire were freed.

The Hohenzollerns, the Hapsburgs, the Romanovs and the Ottoman Empire were all consigned to the dust bin of history. As was, so everyone thought, the Franco-Prussian War. After all, the empire it created had disappeared, replaced by the Weimar Republic. But not quite; there were still echoes of it to be found, if you knew where to look.

In his masterwork on intolerance and world domination, Adolf Hitler mentions how he read popular histories of the war. And from there he not only became fascinated with military service but the history of the Germans and their strive for unity in the face of all the lesser races trying to prevent them. In *Mein Kampf* he notes the Austrians, which he identifies as the best racial stock of all the Germans, and wonders why they were not included in this, the greatest of all German triumphs.

Apparently those popular histories failed to connect the Franco-

Prussian War to the earlier Austro-Prussian War/*Bruderkrieg*. For if Austria had joined the later conflict it would have done so as an ally of Imperial France to defeat the Prussian-led coalition. Still, Hitler remained cognizant of the war as he set about his dreams of creating the Nazi superstate, spreading racial purity throughout Europe and world domination.

Of course his most famous nod to that earlier era of German triumph was the naming of the Third Reich's first true battleship after the man who forged modern Germany. Hitler even allowed a famous original portrait of Bismarck to be included in its admiral's quarters, which would be lost when the ship went down on May 27th, 1941.

However, 21 months earlier a slightly more subtle homage to the Franco-Prussian War occurred when Hitler deliberately chose September 1st as the date to launch the invasion of Poland. The date on which the Second Reich traditionally celebrated the Franco-Prussian War, the date on which Moltke's armies prevented the First Imperial French Army from breaking its investment and crushing the second one at Sedan, and the day when one empire ended and another began. For an historically-minded German their second global conflict could not have started more auspiciously.

As for the French, they too remembered the Franco-Prussian War, and not just by dredging up the name "Uhlans" to identify the enemy. That name belonged to a different era, a more chivalrous age; the far more harsh-sounding "Nazis" suited what the *ennemi héréditaire* had become. However, when the time came the French resurrected a more appropriate one.

In early-August of 1944, as the allied armies were at last making their breakout from the Normandy beachhead, the resistance groups in Paris became more active. Especially after August 18th when the Paris police force openly revolted against Nazi occupation by raising the flag of the Free French Forces over its prefecture building, the one rebuilt in the wake of the Paris Commune. The most numerous of these were the leftists who called themselves the FTP, the Francs-Tireurs et Partisans.

After the Second World War the echoes became fewer. The rising tide of Communist success meant no one was really interested in reading about its early failures. Not until the cracks and schisms in its monolith did the subject regain popularity, and by then the Commune had become at least partly separated from its major precipitating event.

The Franco-Prussian War was becoming lost, swamped by all the history that came after it. The births of aerial warfare and armored warfare were attributed to the First World War. Since the Mitrailleuse does not look like a machinegun or even a Gatling gun – so the joke goes "it's a French Impressionist version of a Gatling gun" – the age of rapid-fire weapons is attributed to those conflicts where Maxim's products were first used. Krupp's breechloading cannons were revolutionary, but the common conceit of popular culture is that everyone stopped using muzzleloading artillery after the American Civil War.

Though it set the stage for so much that came after it, the Franco-Prussian War is mostly forgotten. But if you listen carefully to history, you can still hear its faint echoes.

Bibliography

"A Few Facts about Artillery." Published in *Artillery Post - Newsletter of the American Civil War Artillery Association*, Vol.4, No.2. Rochester, NY., December 2008.

Askins, Bill, ed. *The NRA Guide to Firearms Assembly: Rifles and Shotguns, Pistols and Revolvers*. The National Rifle Association of America, 1980.

Baldick, Robert. *The Siege of Paris*. New English Library, London, 1964.

Barbey, Adelaide, ed. *The Hachette Guide to France: 1986 - 1987 edition*. Pantheon Books, New York, 1985 & 1986.

Bell, David A. "Total War." Published in *Military History Magazine*, Vol.24, No.2. Weider History Group, Inc., Leesburg, VA. April 2007.

Bercuson, David J., and J.L. Granatstein. *Dictionary of Canadian Military History*. Oxford University Press, Don Mills, Ont., Canada, 1992.

Berlin, Isaiah. *Karl Marx: His Life and Environment*. Oxford University

Press, New York, 1939 & 1963.

Botting, Douglas. *Dr. Eckener's Dream Machine: The Historic Saga of the Round-the-World Zeppelin.* Harper Collins Publishers, London, 2001.

Brockett, L.P. *The Great War of 1870 Between France and Germany, Comprising a History of its Origin and Causes, the Biographies of the King of Prussia, the Ex-Emperor of France, and the Statesmen and Generals of the Two Countries, the Financial, Social and Military.* 1871.

Brownstone, David M., Irene M. Franck and Douglass Brownstone. *Island of Hope, Island of Tears.* Barnes and Noble Books, New York, 1979.

Clarke, I.F. *Voices Prophesying War 1763 - 1984.* Oxford University Press, London, 1966.

Durschmied, Eric. *How Chance and Stupidity Have Changed History: The Hinge Factor.* MJF Books/Fine Communications, New York, 1999.

Emerson, Edwin Jr., and Marion Mills Miller. *The Nineteenth Century and After: A History Year by Year From A.D.1800 to the Present.*, Vol. 1-3. P.F. Collier and Son, Pub., New York, 1906.

Evans, Alun. *Brassey's Guide to War Films.* Brassey, Dulles, VA, 2000.

Flint, Roy K., Peter W. Kozumplik, and Thomas J. Waraksa. *The Arab-Israeli Wars, The Chinese Civil War and the Korean War.* Avery Publishing Group, Wayne, New Jersey, 1987.

Fromkin, David. *Europe's Last Summer: Who Started the Great War of 1914?* Alfred A. Knopf, New York, 2004.

Garraty, John A., and Mark C. Carnes, eds. *American National Biography.* Oxford University Press, New York, 1999.

Gibbons, Tony. *The Complete Encyclopedia of Battleships: A Technical Directory of Capital Ships From 1860 to the Present Day.* Salamander Books Ltd./Crescent Books, New York, 1983.

Gordon, Arthur, and Marvin W. McFarland. *The History of Flight.* Golden Press Inc., New York, 1964.

Griehl, Manfred; and Geoffrey Brooks, trans. *Luftwaffe Over America: The Secret Plans to Bomb the United States in World War II*. Barnes and Noble Books, New York, 2004.

Herold, J. Christopher. *The Age of Napoleon*. American Heritage, div. of Forbes inc., Houghton Mifflin Co., c1963 & 1978.

"History of the Chicago Mercantile Battery." Published in *Artillery Post - Newsletter of the American Civil War Artillery Association*, Vol.5, No.1. Rochester, NY., February 2009.

"History of the Parrott Gun." Published in *Artillery Post - Newsletter of the American Civil War Artillery Association*, Vol.4, No.1. Rochester, NY., February 2008.

Hitler, Adolf. *Mein Kampf*. Adarsh Books, New Delhi, 2002.

Hogg, Ian. *Twentieth-Century Artillery*. Barnes and Noble Books, New York, 2000.

Howard, Michael. *The Franco-Prussian War*. Dorset Press, 1961 & 1990.

Hudson, Roger, ed. *William Russell - Special Correspondent of The Times*. The Folio Society, London, c1995.

Jomini, Antoine Henri de. *The Art of War: Restored Edition*. Legacy Books Press Classics, Kingston, Ontario, 2008.

Judd, Dennis. *Someone Has Blundered: Calamities of the British Army in the Victorian Age*. The Windrush Press, Gloucestershire, UK, 1973 & 1999.

Kunitz, Stanley J., and Vineta Colby, eds. *European Authors 1000-1900: A Biographical Dictionary of European Literature*. H.W. Wilson Co., New York, 1967.

Lanning, Lt. Colonel (Ret.) Michael Lee. *The Military 100: A Ranking of the Most Influential Military Leaders of All Time*. Barnes and Noble Books, New York, 1996.

Liddell Hart, Basil Henry. *Strategy*. Meridian, New York, 1954, 1967 & 1991.

Lyon, Hugh. *The Encyclopedia of the World's Warships: A Technical Directory of Major Fighting Ships From 1900 to the Present Day.* Salamander Books, London, 1978.

McPherson, James M. *Battle Cry of Freedom: The Civil War Era.* Ballantine Books/Oxford University Press, New York, 1988.

Magnusson, Magnus, general ed. *Cambridge Biographical Dictionary.* Cambridge University Press, New York, 1990.

Maltin, Leonard, ed. *Leonard Maltin's Movie and Video Guide 2002 edition.* Signet Books/New American Library, New York, 2001.

Manchester, William. *The Arms of Krupp 1587 - 1968.* Bantam Books, New York, 1964.

Miller, David, and John Jordan. *Modern Submarine Warfare.* Military Press, New York, 1987.

Moltke, Helmuth von. *The Franco-German War of 1870-71.* Greenhill Books, London, 1992.

O'Connell, Robert L. *Soul of the Sword: An Illustrated History of Weaponry and Warfare from Prehistory to the Present.* The Free Press, New York, 2002.

Ousby, Ian. *The Road to Verdun: World War I's Most Momentous Battle and the Folly of Nationalism.* Doubleday, New York, 2002.

Pflanze, Otto. *Bismarck and the Development of Germany: the Period of Unification 1815 - 1871.* Princeton University Press, Princeton, 1963.

Reynolds, E.G.B. *British Enfield Rifles.* The National Rifle Association of America, 1990.

Richardson, Joanna, trans. *Paris Under Siege: A Journal of the Events of 1870 - 1871.* The Folio Society, London, 1982.

"Rifled Artillery Projectiles." Published in *Artillery Post - Newsletter of the American Civil War Artillery Association*, Vol.3, No.2. Rochester, NY., December 2006.

Rogers, Tom. *Insultingly Stupid Movie Physics: Hollywood's Best Mistakes, Goofs and Flat-out Destructions of the Basic Laws of the Universe.* Sourcebooks Hysteria, Naperville, IL., 2007.

"The Artillery Battery." Published in *Artillery Post - Newsletter of the American Civil War Artillery Association*, Vol.3, No.1. Rochester, NY., February 2006.

"The Limber Box." Published in *Artillery Post - Newsletter of the American Civil War Artillery Association*, Vol.3, No.1. Rochester, NY., February 2006.

Webster's Biographical Dictionary. G.&C. Merriam Company, Springfield, MA., 1980.

Index

Vicksburg. 90, 123
Victor, Duke Jacques. 351
Victoria, Queen. . . 72, 73, 130, 280, 329, 388, 391
Victorian Age. 388, 402
Vienna. . . 7, 18, 31, 52, 54, 57, 59, 60, 71, 75, 81, 93, 99, 105, 185, 380, 384
Vietnam War. 1
Vietnamese. 380
Villa Hügel. 338
Villacoublay. 294, 300, 321
Villafranca. 83, 84
Villafranca Treaty. 83, 84
Ville d'Orléans. 283, 286
Ville-Evrard. 299
Villeneuve. 317
Villeneuve St. Georges. 253
Villépion. 293
Villersexel.. 303
Vimereux. 46
Vimy Ridge. 302
Vinoy, General Joseph. . . . 235, 248, 269, 287, 299, 306, 307, 323, 325, 332
Vionville. 212, 214-217
Vionville, Battle of.. . 214, 217, 219, 228, 233, 387
"Vive la Republique". 249
Vrignault. 323
Wallachia. 41, 71, 75-77, 159
wapitis. 300
War Ministry. . 71, 88, 89, 143, 144, 173, 174, 177, 204, 248, 289, 293, 337, 378
War of Austrian Succession. 343
War of Spanish Succession. 343
Warsaw. 20, 62, 66
Washington D.C.. . . . . 89, 123, 125
Washington, President George. 51
Waterloo (city, Canada). 373
Waterloo, Battle of.. . 18, 82, 83, 85, 110, 118, 152, 158, 160, 224, 256, 359, 388
Watts. 115
Weimar Republic. 397
Weissenburg. 152, 191, 193, 200, 203
Wellington, Arthur Wellesley, Duke of. 15-17, 21, 25, 26, 28, 32, 54, 70
Wells, Herbert George (H.G.). 358
Werden, General Karl Wilhelm von. 153
Wesel. 261
West Africa.. . . . . 343, 390
West African Gold Coast 362
Wettin, Crown Prince Friedrich August Albert
. . . . 140, 153, 226
What Happened After the Battle of Dorking
. . . . 360
Wheatstone, Sir Charles. 44
Whig Party. 116

Whitehead, Robert. 377
Wilhelm II of Würtemberg. 394
Wilhelmshöhe Palace. 245
"will to power". 344, 354
Wilson's Creek, Battle of. 117
Wittelsbach, King Ludwig I of Bavaria. . . . 64
Wittelsbach, King Ludwig II of Bavaria.. . . 99, 140, 305
Wittlich.. 184
Woerth. 193-195
Woerth, Battle of. . . . 194-197, 200-203, 206, 234, 238, 255, 261, 364, 379, 388
Wolseley, Garnet Joseph.. . . 95, 357, 361-363
World War I. 1, 20, 376, 387
World War II.. . . . . 1, 178, 369, 402
Wrangel, General Friedrich Heinrich von.. 150
Würtemberg. . 7, 38, 62, 66, 98, 100, 111, 140, 152, 170, 187, 193, 194, 196, 202, 214, 223, 246, 287, 288, 394
Würtembergers. 89, 174
X-rays. 379
yak. 300
Yamamoto, Admiral Isoroku 165
Yap Island. 343, 372
Year of Revolution, the. . . . 49, 59-62, 65, 69, 70, 139, 187
Yellow Sea. 343
Yorck, General Hans Ludwig. 152, 161
zebra. 300
zeppelin. 394
Zeppelin, Lieutenant/General Count Ferdinand
von. 194, 207, 394
Zola, Emile. 4, 188, 395
Zollparlament. 43, 94, 111
Zollverein. 43, 44, 71, 94, 111, 180
Zulu. 362
Zulu War. 362

About the Author

JOHN-ALLEN PRICE is an independent historian from Lewiston, New York. He is the author of several historical fiction novels, each one meticulously researched. He is also the author of the new introduction of *The Art of War: Restored Edition*, marking his debut as a history writer. *The War that Changed the World* is his first non-fiction book.

Also Available from Legacy Books Press

A Funny Thing Happened on the Way to the Agora
Ancient Greek and Roman Humour

By R. Drew Griffith and Robert B. Marks

ISBN: 978-0-9784652-0-9

Ancient Greece and Rome aren't usually remembered for their sense of humour. However, in reality the ancient Greeks and Romans often refused to take themselves seriously. Strange and outlandish activities abounded – including somebody accidentally exposing himself while dancing sideways at his wedding (those wearing bed sheets didn't wear underwear) and a group of drunk young men thinking their house is sinking at sea, and tossing all their furniture out the windows.

R. Drew Griffith and Robert B. Marks take you on a lively and funny journey through the more bizarre activities of the ancient world, ranging everywhere from moochers to quacks to shrews to willing suckers, and even revealing the most terrible thing you can do to anybody involving a radish.

The Secret History of Star Wars
The Art of Storytelling and the Making of a Modern Epic

By Michael Kaminski

ISBN: 978-0-9784652-3-0

Star Wars is one of the most important cultural phenomena of the Western world. The tale of Luke Skywalker, Han Solo, and the fall and redemption of Anakin Skywalker has become modern myth, an epic tragedy of the corruption of a young man in love into darkness, the rise of evil, and the power of good triumphing in the end.

But it didn't start out that way.

In this thorough account of one of cinema's most lasting works, Michael Kaminski presents the true history of how *Star Wars* was written, from its beginnings as a science fiction fairy tale to its development over three decades into the epic we now know, chronicling the methods, techniques, thought processes, and struggles of its creator. For this unauthorized account, he has pored through over four hundred sources, from interviews to original scripts, to track how the most powerful modern epic in the world was created, expanded, and finalized into the tale an entire generation has grown up with.

LaVergne, TN USA
19 February 2011
217155LV00004B/25/P